Sentence Skills
A Workbook for Writers

First Canadian Edition

John Langan
Atlantic Community College

Sharon Winstanley
Seneca College

McGraw-Hill Ryerson Limited
Toronto Montreal New York Auckland Bogotá Caracas
Lisbon London Madrid Mexico Milan New Delhi
San Juan Singapore Sydney Tokyo

McGraw-Hill
Ryerson Limited

A Subsidiary of The **McGraw·Hill** Companies

SENTENCE SKILLS: A Workbook for Writers
First Canadian Edition

ISBN: 0-07-552633-6

2 3 4 5 6 7 8 9 10 BBM 5 4 3 2 1 0 9

Printed and bound in Canada

Care has been taken to trace ownership of copyright material contained in this text. The publisher will gladly take any information that will enable them to rectify any reference or credit in subsequent editions.

Editor-in-Chief: Dave Ward
Supervising Editor: Margaret Henderson
Production Editor: Liba Berry
Developmental Editor: Laurie Graham
Production Co-ordinator: Nicla Dattolico
Designer: Rafael Hernandez
Cover Design: Dianna Little
Typesetter: Bookman Typesetting Co.
Typeface(s): Times Roman
Printer: Best Book Manufacturers

Canadian Cataloguing in Publication Data
Langan, John, 1942–
    Sentence skills: a workbook for writers

1st Canadian ed.
Includes index.
ISBN 0-07-552633-6

1. English language - Sentences - Problems, exercises, etc.   2. English language - Grammar - Problems, exercises, etc.   3. English language - Rhetoric - Problems, exercises, etc.   I. Winstanley, Sharon.   II. Title.
PE1441.L36 1997   428.2   C96-932050-7

CONTENTS

TO THE INSTRUCTOR

Sentence Skills will help students master the essential rules of grammar, mechanics, punctuation, and usage needed for clear writing. The book contains a number of features to aid teachers and their students.

- ■ ***Coverage of basic writing skills is exceptionally thorough.*** The book pays special attention to fragments, run-ons, verbs, and other areas where students often have serious problems. At the same time, a glance at the table of contents shows that the book treats skills (such as dictionary use and spelling improvement) not found in other tests. In addition, entire sections of the book are devoted to editing, proofreading, and sentence variety.

- ■ ***The book has a clear and flexible format.*** Part One presents and gives practice in all the essential basic writing skills. Part Two then reinforces those skills through mastery, editing, and proofreading tests. Part Three uses sentence-combining exercises to help students achieve variety in their writing. Part Four presents writing assignments that enable students to transfer the skills they have learned to realistic writing situations. Since parts, sections, and chapters are self-contained, teachers can move easily from, for instance, a rule in Part One to a mastery test in Part Two to a combining activity in Part Three or a writing assignment in Part Four.

- ■ ***Practice materials are numerous.*** Most skills are reinforced by activities, review tests, and mastery tests, as well as ditto masters and tests in the Instructor's Manual. For most of the skills in the book, there are over one hundred practice exercises.

- ■ ***Practice materials are varied and lively.*** In many basic writing texts, exercises are monotonous and dry, causing students to lose interest in the skills presented. In *Sentence Skills*, exercises involve students in various ways. An inductive opening project allows students to see what they already know about a given skill. Within chapters, students may be asked to underline answers, add words, generate their own sentences, or edit passages. And the lively and engaging practice materials in the book both maintain interest and help students appreciate the value of vigorous details in writing.

- **_Terminology is kept to a minimum._**   In general, rules are explained using words students already know. A clause is a _word group;_ a co-ordinating conjunction is a _joining word;_ a nonrestrictive element is an _interrupter._ At the same time, traditional grammatical terms are mentioned briefly for those students who learned them at an earlier point in school and are comfortable seeing them again.

- **_Self-teaching is encouraged._**   Students may check their answers to the introductory projects and the practice activities in Part One by referring to the answers in Appendix B. In this way, they are given the responsibility for teaching themselves. At the same time, to ensure that the answer key is used as a learning tool only, answers are _not_ given for the review tests in Part One or for any of the reinforcement tests in Part Two. These answers appear in the Instructor's Manual; they can be copied and handed out to students at the discretion of the instructor.

- **_Diagnostic and achievement tests are provided._**   These tests appear in Appendix A of the book. Each test may be given in two parts, the second of which gives teachers a particularly detailed picture of a student's skill level.

- **_Three valuable learning aids accompany the book._**   A set of _thirty ditto masters_, ready to run, enables teachers to check students' progress on most of the skills in the book. A _software disk_ will help students review and practise many of the skills in the text. And the comprehensive _Instructor's Manual_ includes (1) a complete set of additional mastery tests, (2) a model syllabus along with suggestions for both teaching the course and using the software, and (3) an easily copied answer key. The manual is 21.5 cm by 28 cm in size, so that both the answer pages and the added mastery tests can be conveniently reproduced on copying machines.

    The ditto masters, software disk, and Instructor's Manual are available by contacting the local McGraw-Hill representative or by writing to the College English Editor, College Division, McGraw-Hill Ryerson Limited, 300 Water Street, Whitby, Ontario, L1N 9B6.

CHANGES IN THE FIFTH EDITION

The helpful comments of writing instructors who have used previous versions of _Sentence Skills_ have prompted some important changes in the new edition.

1   The book now features a convenient _Annotated Instructor's Edition_ which is identical to the student book except that it includes answers to all of the activities and tests.

2 Additions have been made to key chapters:

■ the chapter on sentence fragments contains added hints on using the comma when correcting fragments;

■ the chapter on run-on sentences has been expanded to show subordination as a method of correcting run-ons;

■ the chapter on the apostrophe has simplified the use of the apostrophe with words ending in *s*; also, it now provides more practice in distinguishing between possessive words and simple plurals;

■ the chapter on commas now offers practice from the very start with the problem of unnecessary commas;

■ the chapter in Part One on paper format has been reinforced by the addition of two combined editing tests in Part Two.

3 A revised set of ditto masters, free to instructors adopting the book, provides more tests and activities than were available previously.

4 Three chapters ("Misplaced Modifiers," "Dangling Modifiers," and "Faulty Parallelism") have been resequenced; changes have been made in the format of certain tests; and practice materials have been updated, corrected where necessary, and in general freshened throughout.

5 Part Four, "Writing Assignments," has been almost completely rewritten. It now provides step-by-step instructions to beginning students on how to write a variety of simple paragraphs.

6 Some brief insertions have been added to assist students using computers at home or in their writing classes. The added passages do not interrupt the flow of the text or its content; they are simply "generic" advice, not specific to any one word processing program, offered so that students may take advantage of the ways in which the use of a computer may facilitate the various stages of the writing and editing processes.

ACKNOWLEDGMENTS

Reviewers who have been of assistance include Esther Chassé, Yukon College; Jim Howard, Selkirk College; Fred Joblin, Georgian College; and Trudy Olsen, Sheridan College. My special thanks go to Fred Joblin for his careful, accurate, and thoughtful help in pinpointing areas due for revision and change. To each reviewer, I am grateful for their help and their sensitivities to the needs of students from various parts of Canada. As with previous Canadian editions of John

Langan's texts, I owe Dave Ward, Editor-In-Chief, thanks for his faith and humour in the pursuit of this project. Again with this third in the Langan/Winstanley series, I am deeply in the debt of Laurie Graham, Developmental Editor, for her patience, good nature, and general acuity.

SHARON WINSTANLEY

PART ONE

SENTENCE
SKILLS

INTRODUCTION

Part One explains the basic skills needed to write clear, error-free sentences. Before you begin working with these skills, however, you will want to read the chapter titled "Why Learn Sentence Skills?," which explains how you will benefit personally from writing standard English. While the skills are presented within four traditional categories (grammar, mechanics, punctuation, and word use), each section is self-contained so that you can go directly to the skills you need to work on. Note, however, that you may find it helpful to cover "Subjects and Verbs" before turning to other skills. Typically, the main features of a skill are presented on the first pages of a section; secondary points are developed later. Numerous activities are provided so that you can practise skills enough to make them habits. The activities are varied and range from underlining answers to writing complete sentences involving the skill in question. One or more review tests at the end of each section offer additional practice activities.

WHY LEARN SENTENCE SKILLS?

THE IMPORTANCE OF SENTENCE SKILLS

Why should someone planning a career as a nurse have to learn sentence skills? Why should an accounting student have to pass a competency test in grammar as part of a college education? Why should a potential physical therapist or graphic artist or computer programmer have to spend hours on the rules of English? Perhaps you have asked questions like these after finding yourself in a class with this book. On the other hand, perhaps you *know* you need to strengthen basic writing skills, even though you may be unclear about the specific ways the skills will be of use to you. Whatever your views, you should understand why sentence skills—all the rules that make up standard English—are so important.

Clear Communication

Standard English, or "language by the book," is needed to communicate your thoughts to others with a minimal amount of distortion and misinterpretation. Knowing the traditional rules of grammar, punctuation, and usage will help you write clear sentences when communicating with others. You may have heard of the party game in which one person whispers a message to the next person; the message is passed, in turn, along a line of several other people. By the time the last person in line is asked to give the message aloud, it is usually so garbled and inaccurate that it barely resembles the original. Written communication in some form of English other than standard English carries the same potential for confusion.

To see how important standard English is to written communication, examine the pairs of sentences below and answer the question in each case.

1. Which sentence indicates that there might be a plot against Theo?
   a. We should leave Theo. These fumes might be poisonous.
   b. We should leave, Theo. These fumes might be poisonous.
2. Which sentence encourages self-mutilation?
   a. Leave your paper and hand in the dissecting kit.
   b. Leave your paper, and hand in the dissecting kit.
3. Which sentence indicates that the writer has a weak grasp of geography?
   a. As a child, I lived in Leduc, which is close to Edmonton and the Gaspé.
   b. As a child, I lived in Leduc, which is close to Edmonton, and the Gaspé.
4. In which sentence does the animal-control officer seem dangerous?
   a. Foaming at the mouth, the animal control officer picked up the stray.
   b. Foaming at the mouth, the stray was picked up by the animal control officer.
5. Which announcer was probably fired from the job?
   a. Outside the Juno Awards theatre, the announcer called the guests names as they arrived.
   b. Outside the Juno Awards theatre, the announcer called the guests' names as they arrived.
6. On the basis of the opening lines below of two student exam essays, which student seems likely to earn a higher grade?
   a. Defence mechanisms is the way people hides their inner feelings and deals with stress. There is several types that we use to be protecting our true feelings.
   b. Defence mechanisms are the methods people use to cope with stress. Using a defence mechanism allows a person to hide his or her real desires and goals.
7. On the basis of the following lines taken from two English papers, which student seems likely to earn a higher grade?
   a. Among the big campus problems are apathy, students' do not participate in college activities'. Such as clubs student government and in the college theatre.
   b. The most pressing problem on campus is the disgraceful state of the student lounge area. The floor is dirty, the chairs are torn, and the ceiling leaks.

8. On the basis of the following sentences taken from two employee reports, which worker is more likely to be promoted?
   a. The spring line failed by 20 per cent in the meeting of projected profit expectations. Which were issued in January of this year.
   b. Profits from our spring line were disappointing. They fell 20 per cent short of January's predictions.
9. On the basis of the following paragraphs taken from two job application letters, which job prospect would you favour?
   a. Let me say in closing that their are an array of personal qualities I have presented in this letter, together, these make me hopeful of being interviewed for this attraktive position.

   sincerly yours'

   Brian Davis

   b. I feel I have the qualifications needed to do an excellent job as assistant manager of the jewelry department at Horton's. I look forward to discussing the position further at a personal interview.

   Sincerely yours,

   Enzo Diamante

The first choice following each of the nine questions contains sentence-skills mistakes—from missing or misplaced commas to misspellings to wordy or pretentious language. As a result of these mistakes, clear communication cannot occur—and misunderstandings, lower grades, and missed job opportunities are probable results. The point, then, is that all the rules that make up standard written English should be a priority if you want your writing to be clear and effective.

Success in College and Postsecondary Education

Standard English is essential if you want to succeed in college. Any report, paper, review, essay exam, or assignment you are responsible for should be written in the best standard English you can produce. If not, it won't matter how fine your ideas are or how hard you worked—most likely, you will receive a lower grade than you would otherwise deserve. In addition, because standard English requires you to express your thoughts in precise, clear sentences, training yourself to follow the rules can help you think more logically. And the basic logic you learn to practise at the sentence level will help as you work to produce well-reasoned papers in all your subjects.

Success at Work

Knowing standard English will also help you achieve job success. Studies have shown repeatedly that skilful communication, more than any other factor, is the key to job satisfaction and steady career progress. A solid understanding of standard English is a basic part of this vital communication ability. Moreover, most experts agree that we are now living in an "age of information"—a time when people who use language skilfully have a great advantage over those who do not. Fewer of us will be working in factories or at other types of manual labour. Many more of us will be working with information in various forms—accumulating it, processing it, analyzing it. No matter what kind of job you are preparing yourself for, technical or not, you will need to know standard English to keep pace with this new age. Otherwise, you are likely to be left behind, limited to low-paying jobs that offer few challenges or financial rewards.

Success in Everyday Life

Standard English will help you succeed not just at school and work but in everyday life as well. It will help you feel more comfortable, for example, in writing letters to friends and relatives. It will enable you to write effective notes to your children's schools. It will help command attention to a letter of complaint that you write to a company about a product. It will allow you to write letters of inquiry about a hospital or credit card or utility or legal bill or about any kind of service. It is a simple fact that in our daily lives, those who can use and write standard English have more power than those who cannot.

HOW THIS BOOK IS ORGANIZED

- A good way to get a quick sense of any book is to turn to the table of contents. By referring to pages vii–xi, you will see that the book is organized into four basic parts. What are they?

  _____

  _____

  _____

  _____

- Part One deals with the sentence skills themselves. How many skills areas are covered in all? (*count them*) _____

■ Part Two reinforces the skills presented in Part One. What are the four kinds of reinforcement activities in Part Two?

_____

_____

_____

_____

■ Turn to the introduction to Part Three to learn the purpose of that part of the book and write the purpose here: _____

_____

■ Turn to the introduction to Part Four to find the purpose of that part of the book and write the purpose here: _____

_____

■ Helpful charts in the book include the (*fill in the missing words*) _____ on the inside front cover, the _____ charts in Appendix C, and the _____ of sentence skills on the inside back cover.

■ Finally, three appendixes at the end of the book contain:

_____

_____

_____

HOW TO USE THIS BOOK

1. Take the Diagnostic Test

The first step in getting the most out of *Sentence Skills* is to take the diagnostic test on pages 457–461. By analyzing which sections of the test gave you trouble, you will discover which skills you need to concentrate on. When you turn to an individual skill, begin by reading and thinking about the introductory project. Often, you will be pleasantly surprised to find that you know more about this area of English than you thought you did. After all, you may have been speaking English with fluency and ease for many years; you have an instinctive knowledge of how the language works. This knowledge gives you a solid base for refining your skills.

2. Work on Specific Skills Where Needed

Your next step is to work on the skill by reading the explanations and completing the practices. You can check your answers to each practice activity by turning to the answer key at the back of the book. Try to figure out *why* you got some answers wrong—you want to uncover any weak spots in your understanding.

3. Use Chapter Review Tests and Tests in Part Two

Finally, use the review tests at the end of a chapter to evaluate your understanding of the skill in its entirety. Your teacher may also ask you to take the mastery tests or other reinforcement tests in Part Two of the book. The answers to these tests are *not* in the answer key in order to help ensure that you take the time needed to learn each skill thoroughly.

4. Work on Sentence Activities in Part Three and Writing Assignments in Part Four

While you are working through individual skills, you should also take time for the sentence-combining activities in Part Three and the writing assignments in Part Four. The writing assignments in Part Four are a brief but important part of the book. To make standard English an everyday part of your writing, you must write not just single sentences but paragraphs and essays. The writing assignments will prove to you that clear, logical writing hinges on error-free sentences. You will see how the sentence skills you are practising "fit in" and contribute to the construction of a sustained piece of writing. In the world of sports, athletes spend many days refining the small moves—serves, backhands, pitches, lay-ups—so that they can reach their larger objective of winning the game. In the same way, you must work intently on writing clear sentences in order to produce effective papers.

The emphasis in this book is, nevertheless, on writing clear, error-free sentences, not on composition. And the heart of the book is the practice material that helps reinforce the sentence skills you learn. A great deal of effort has been taken to make the practices lively and engaging and to avoid the dull, repetitive skills work that has given grammar books such a bad reputation. This text will help you stay interested as you work on the rules you need to learn. The rest is a matter of your personal determination and hard work. If you decide—and only you can decide—that effective writing is important to your school and career goals and that you want to learn the basic skills needed to write clearly and effectively, this book will help you reach those goals.

SUBJECTS AND VERBS

INTRODUCTORY PROJECT

Understanding subjects and verbs is a big step toward mastering many sentence skills. As a speaker of English, you already have an instinctive feel for these basic building blocks of English sentences. Insert an appropriate word into each space below. The answer will be a *subject*.

1. The _____ will soon be over.

2. _____ cannot be trusted.

3. A strange _____ appeared in my backyard.

4. _____ is one of my favourite activities.

Now insert an appropriate word into the following spaces. Each answer will be a *verb*.

5. The prisoner _____ at the judge.

6. My sister _____ much harder than I do.

7. The players _____ in the locker room.

8. Rob and Marilyn _____ with the teacher.

Finally, insert appropriate words into the following spaces. Your answers will be a *subject* and *verb*, respectively.

9. The _____ almost _____ out of the tree.

10. Many _____ today _____ sex and violence.

11. The _____ carefully _____ the patient.

12. A _____ quickly _____ the ball.

The basic building blocks of English sentences are *subjects* and *verbs*. Understanding them is an important first step toward mastering a number of sentence skills.

Every sentence has a subject and a verb. Who or what the sentence speaks about is called the *subject*; what the sentence says about the subject is called the *verb*. In the following sentences, the subject is underlined once and the verb twice:

People gossip.
The truck belched fumes.
He waved at me.
The Canadian Arctic contains the least inhabited area in North America.
That woman is a millionaire.
The pants feel itchy.

A SIMPLE WAY TO FIND A SUBJECT

To find a *subject*, ask *who* or *what* the sentence is about. As shown below, your answer is the subject.

Who is the first sentence about? People
What is the second sentence about? The truck
Who is the third sentence about? He
What is the fourth sentence about? The Canadian Arctic
Who is the fifth sentence about? That woman
What is the sixth sentence about? The pants

It helps to remember that the subject of a sentence is always a *noun* (any person, place, or thing) or a pronoun. Nouns may also name ideas or concepts, such as *truth*, *beauty*, or *honesty*. A *pronoun* is simply a word like *he*, *she*, *it*, *you*, or *they* used in place of a noun. In the preceding sentences, the subjects are persons (*People*, *He*, *woman*), a place (*Canadian Arctic*), and things (*truck*, *pants*). And note that one pronoun (*He*) is used as a subject.

A SIMPLE WAY TO FIND A VERB

One way to find a *verb* is to ask what the sentence *says about* the subject. As shown below, your answer is the verb.

What does the first sentence *say about* people? They <u>gossip</u>.

What does the second sentence *say about* the truck? It <u>belched</u> (fumes).

What does the third sentence *say about* him? He <u>waved</u> (at me).

What does the fourth sentence *say about* the Canadian Arctic? It <u>contains</u> (the least inhabited area in North America).

What does the fifth sentence *say about* that woman? She <u>is</u> (a millionaire).

What does the sixth sentence *say about* the pants? They <u>feel</u> (itchy).

A second way to find the verb is to put *I*, *you*, *he*, *she*, *it*, or *they* in front of the word you think is a verb. If the result makes sense, you have a verb. For example, you could put *they* in front of *gossip* in the first sentence above, with the result, *they gossip*, making sense. Therefore, you know that *gossip* is a verb. You could use the same test with the other verbs as well.

1. **Action Verbs**   Finally, it helps to remember that most verbs show action. In "People gossip," the action is gossiping. In "The truck belched fumes," the action is belching. In "He waved at me," the action is waving. In "The Canadian Arctic contains the least inhabited area in North America," the action is containing.

2. **Linking Verbs**   Certain other verbs, known as *linking verbs*, do not show action. They do, however, give information about the subject of the sentence. In "That woman is a millionaire," the linking verb *is* tells us that the woman is a millionaire. In "The pants feel itchy," the linking verb *feel* gives us the information that the pants are itchy.

Practice 1: Finding Subjects and Verbs

In each of the following sentences, draw one line under the subject and two lines under the verb.

Ask *who* or *what* the sentence is about to find the subject. Then ask what the sentence *says about* the subject to find the verb.

1. I ate an entire pizza by myself.
2. Water snakes swim in that lake.
3. Sally failed the test.
4. The television movie ended suddenly.
5. Kerry borrowed change for the pay telephone.
6. The children stared in wide-eyed wonderment at the Santa Claus Parade floats.

7. An old newspaper tumbled down the dirty street.

8. Crystal starts every morning with a series of yoga exercises.

9. My part-time job limits my study time.

10. The windstorm blew over the storage shed in the backyard.

Practice 2: Finding Linking Verbs and Subjects

Follow the directions given for Practice 1. Note that all of the verbs here are *linking verbs*.

1. My sister is a terrible speller.

2. Potato chips are Devon's favourite snack.

3. The defendant appeared very nervous in the witness box.

4. Art became a father at the age of twenty.

5. The ride going somewhere always seems longer than the ride coming back.

6. That apartment building was an abandoned factory two years ago.

7. My first two weeks on the sales job were the worst ones of my life.

8. The plastic banana split and styrofoam birthday cake in the bakery window look like real desserts.

9. Jane always feels energized after a cup of coffee.

10. Rooms with white walls appear larger than those with dark-coloured walls.

Practice 3: Finding Subjects and Verbs

Follow the directions given for Practice 1.

1. That clock runs about five minutes fast.

2. The new player on the team is much too sure of himself.

3. Late-afternoon shoppers filled the aisles of the supermarket.

4. Garbage trucks rumbled down my street on their way to the dump.

5. The children drew pictures on the steamed window.

6. The picture fell suddenly to the floor.

7. Chipmunks live in the woodpile behind my house.

8. Our loud uncle monopolized the conversation at the dinner table.

9. The tomatoes were soft to the touch.

10. The insurance company cancelled my policy because of a speeding ticket.

MORE ABOUT SUBJECTS AND VERBS

Distinguishing Subjects from Prepositional Phrases

The subject of a sentence never appears within a prepositional phrase. A *prepositional phrase** is simply a group of words beginning with a preposition and ending with the answer to the question *what* or *when*. This "answering word or phrase" is called the *object of the preposition*. Here is a list of common prepositions.

about	before	by	in, into	through
above	behind	down	inside	to
across	below	during	of	toward
among	beneath	except	off	under
around	beside	for	on, onto	up
at	between	from	over	with

Cross out prepositional phrases when looking for the subject of a sentence.

In the middle of the night, we heard footsteps on the roof.

The magazines on the table belong in the garage.

Before the opening face-off, the tenor skated onto the rink.

The hardware store across the street went out of business.

In spite of our advice, Sally quit her job at Burger King.

Practice: Eliminating Prepositional Phrases to Discover Subject and Verbs

Cross out prepositional phrases. Then draw a single line under subjects and a double line under verbs.

1. For that course, you need three different books.
2. The key to the front door slipped from my hand into a puddle.
3. The check-out lines at the supermarket moved very slowly.
4. With his son, Frank walked to the playground.
5. No quarrel between good friends lasts for a very long time.

*Remember the word *position* appears inside the grammatical term *preposition*. This tip may help you to find prepositional phrases.

6. In one weekend, Maria planted a large vegetable garden in her backyard.
7. Either of my brothers is a reliable worker.
8. The drawer of the dresser sticks on rainy days.
9. During the movie, several people walked out in protest.
10. At a single sitting, my brother reads five or more comic books.

Verbs of More Than One Word

Many verbs consist of more than one word. Here, for example, are some of the many forms of the verb *to help*:

helps	should have been helping	will have helped
helped	can help	would have been helped
is helping	would have been helping	has been helped
was helping	will be helping	had been helped
may help	had been helping	must have helped
should help	helped	having helped
will help	have helped	should have been helped
does help	has helped	had helped

Below are sentences that contain verbs of more than one word:

Diane <u>is working</u> overtime this week.
Another book <u>has been written</u> about the Mulroney family.
We <u>should have stopped</u> for gas at the last station.
The game <u>has</u> just <u>been cancelled</u>.

Notes

1 Words like *not*, *just*, *never*, *only*, and *always* are **not** part of the verb although they may appear within the verb.

Diane <u>is</u> not <u>working</u> overtime this week.
The boys <u>should</u> just not <u>have stayed</u> out so late.
The game <u>has</u> always <u>been played</u> regardless of the weather.

2 No verb preceded by *to* is ever the verb of a sentence.*

Sarah <u>wants</u> to go with us.
The newly married couple <u>decided</u> to rent a house for a year.
The store <u>needs</u> extra people to help out at Christmas.

3 No *-ing* word by itself is ever the verb of a sentence. (It may be part of the verb, but it **must have a helping verb** in front of it.)**

We planning the trip for months. (This is not a sentence because the verb is not complete.)
We <u>were planning</u> the trip for months. (This is a complete sentence.)

Practice: Identifying Subjects and Verbs

Draw a single line under subjects and a double line under verbs. Be sure to include all parts of the verb.

1. He has been sleeping all day.
2. The wood foundations of the shed were attacked by termites.
3. I have not washed my car for several months.
4. The teacher had not warned us about the quiz.
5. The bus will be leaving shortly.
6. You should not try to pet that temperamental hamster.
7. They have just been married by a judge.
8. He could make a living with his wood carvings.
9. Carol has decided to ask her boss for a raise.
10. The company should have purchased word processors rather than electronic typewriters.

Compound Subjects and Verbs

A sentence may have more than one verb:

The <u>dancer</u> <u>stumbled</u> and <u>fell</u>.
<u>Crystal</u> <u>washed</u> her hair, <u>blew</u> it dry, and <u>parted</u> it in the middle.

---

* *To go*, *to rent*, and *to help* are *infinitive forms*, or "beginning points" of verbs. These never change. The *main verbs* are called *finite* forms.
** *-ing* forms of verbs are *present participles*. The word *part* appears within *participle*. So these *-ing* forms are only parts of the complete verb.

A sentence may have more than one subject:

Cats and dogs are sometimes the best of friends.

The striking workers and their bosses could not come to an agreement.

A sentence may have several subjects and several verbs:

Holly and I read the book and reported on it to the class.

Pete, Nick, and Linda caught the fish in the morning, cleaned them in the afternoon, and ate them that night.

Practice: Finding Compound Subjects and Verbs

Draw a single line under subjects and a double line under verbs. Be sure to mark *all* the subjects and verbs.

1. The hypnotist locked his assistant in a box and sawed her in half.
2. Connie began her paper at 7:30 p.m. and finished it at midnight.
3. On the shipping pier, the Nissans, Toyotas, and Hondas glittered in the sun.
4. Tony added the column of figures three times and got three different totals.
5. The car sputtered, stalled, and then started again.
6. Whiteflies, mites, and aphids infected my houseplants.
7. Lori found two lost rabbits and kept them at home as pets.
8. We walked over to the corner deli and bought extra cheese for the party.
9. At the new shopping mall, Tony and Crystal looked in windows for two hours and then bought one pair of tube socks.
10. My aunt and uncle married in their twenties, divorced in their thirties, and then remarried in their forties.

■ Review Test 1

Draw one line under the subjects and two lines under the verbs. Cross out prepositional phrases where needed to help find subjects. Underline all the parts of a verb. And remember that you may find more than one subject and verb in a sentence.

1. I had not heard about the cancellation of the class.
2. James should have gotten an estimate from the plumber.
3. The family played badminton and volleyball at the picnic.
4. A solution to the problem popped suddenly into my head.
5. My room-mate and I will have to study all night for the test.
6. Dave has not been eating in the cafeteria this semester.

7. The white moon hung above the castle like a grinning skull.
8. Len and Marie drove all night and arrived at their cottage early Saturday morning.
9. The game has been postponed because of bad weather and will be rescheduled for later in the season.
10. The sun reflected sharply off the lake and forced me to wear sunglasses.

■ Review Test 2

Follow the directions given for Review Test 1.

1. The doctors were speaking gently to the parents of the little girl.
2. A rumour has been spreading about the possible closing of the plant.
3. Diesel trucks with heavy exhaust fumes should be banned from the road.
4. The dental assistant should have warned me about the pain.
5. With their fingers, the children started to draw pictures on the steamed window.
6. Three buildings down the street from my house have been demolished.
7. Rats, squirrels, and bats lived in the attic of the abandoned house.
8. Chan and Bob will be anchoring the long-distance team in the track meet.
9. Reluctantly, I crawled from my bed and stumbled to the bathroom.
10. Tiddlywinks, pick-up sticks, and hearts were our favourite games as children.

SENTENCE FRAGMENTS

INTRODUCTORY PROJECT

Every sentence must have a subject and a verb and must express a complete thought. A word group that lacks a subject or a verb and that does not express a complete thought is a *fragment*.

Listed below is a number of fragments and sentences. Complete the statement that explains each fragment.

1. Children.   *Fragment*
   Children cry.   *Sentence*

   "Children" is a fragment because, while it has a subject (*Children*), it lacks a _Verb_ (*cry*) and so does not express a complete thought.

2. Dances.   *Fragment*
   Crystal dances.   *Sentence*

   "Dances" is a fragment because, while it has a verb (*Dances*), it lacks a _Subject_ (*Crystal*) and so does not express a complete thought.

3. Staring through the window.   *Fragment*
   Bigfoot was staring through the window.   *Sentence*

   "Staring through the window" is a fragment because it lacks a _Subject_ (*Bigfoot*) and also part of the _verb_ (*was*) and because it does not express a complete thought.

4. When the dentist began drilling.   *Fragment*
   When the dentist began drilling, I closed my eyes.   *Sentence*

   "When the dentist began drilling" is a fragment because we want to know *what happened when* the dentist began drilling. The word group does not follow through and _express a Full Thought._

Answers are on page 472.

WHAT SENTENCE FRAGMENTS ARE

Every sentence must have a subject and a verb and must express a complete thought. A word group that lacks a subject or a verb and that does not express a complete thought is a *fragment*. Following are the most common types of fragments that people write:

1 Dependent-word fragments
2 *-ing* and *to* fragments
3 Added-detail fragments
4 Missing-subject fragments

Once you understand the specific kind or kinds of fragments that you may write, you should be able to eliminate them from your writing. The following pages explain all four fragment types.

1 DEPENDENT-WORD FRAGMENTS

Some word groups that begin with a dependent word are fragments. Here is a list of common dependent words:

Dependent Words

after	if, even if	when, whenever
although, though	in order that	where, wherever
as	since	whether
because	that, so that	which, whichever
before	unless	while
even though	until	who
how	what, whatever	whose

Whenever you start a sentence with one of these words, you must be careful that a fragment does not result. The word group beginning with the dependent word *After* in the selection below is a fragment.

After I stopped drinking coffee. I began sleeping better at night.

A *dependent statement*—one starting with a dependent word like *After*—cannot stand alone. It *depends on another statement* to complete the thought. "After I stopped drinking coffee" is a dependent statement. It leaves us hanging. We expect in the same sentence to find out *what happened after* the writer stopped drinking coffee. When a writer does not follow through and complete a thought, a fragment results.

To correct the fragment, simply follow through and complete the thought:

After I stopped drinking coffee, I began sleeping better at night.

Remember, then, that *dependent statements by themselves* are fragments. They must be attached to a statement that makes sense standing alone.*

Here are two other selections with dependent-word fragments.

Brian sat nervously in the dental clinic. While waiting to have his wisdom tooth pulled.

Maria decided to throw away the boxes. That had accumulated for years in the basement.

"While waiting to have his wisdom tooth pulled" is a fragment; it does not make sense standing by itself. We want to know in the same statement *what Brian did* while waiting to have his tooth pulled. The writer must complete the thought. Likewise, "That had accumulated for years in the basement" is not in itself a complete thought. We want to know in the same statement what *that* refers to.

How to Correct Dependent-Word Fragments

1. **Attach the Dependent-Word Fragment to the Appropriate Sentence**
   In most cases, you can correct a dependent-word fragment by attaching it to the sentence that comes after it or the sentence that comes before it:

   After I stopped drinking coffee, I began sleeping better at night.
   (The fragment has been attached to the sentence that comes after it.)
   Brian sat nervously in the dental clinic while waiting to have his wisdom tooth pulled.
   (The fragment has been attached to the sentence that comes before it.)

* Some instructors refer to a dependent-word fragment as a *dependent clause*. A *clause* is simply a group of words having a subject and a verb. A clause may be *independent* (expressing a complete thought and able to stand alone) or *dependent* (*not* expressing a complete thought and not able to stand alone). A dependent clause by itself is a fragment. It can be corrected simply by adding an independent clause.

Maria decided to throw away the boxes that had accumulated for years in the basement.
(The fragment has been attached to the sentence that comes before it.)

2. **Eliminate the Dependent Word to Form a Sentence** Another way of correcting a dependent-word fragment is to eliminate the dependent word and make a new sentence:

I stopped drinking coffee.
He was waiting to have his wisdom tooth pulled.
They had accumulated for years in the basement.

Do not use this second method of correction too frequently, however, for it may cut down on interest and variety in your writing style.

Notes

1 Use a comma if a dependent-word group comes at the *beginning* of a sentence (see also pages 183–184):

After I stopped drinking coffee, I began sleeping better at night.

However, do not generally use a comma if the dependent-word group comes at the end of a sentence:

Brian sat nervously in the dental clinic while waiting to have his wisdom tooth pulled.
Maria decided to throw away the boxes that had accumulated for years in the basement.

2 Sometimes the dependent word *who*, *that*, *which*, or *where* appears not at the very start but *near* the start of a word group. A fragment often results.

Today I visited Hilda Cooper. A friend who is in the hospital. I was frightened by her loss of weight.

"A friend who is in the hospital" is not in itself a complete thought. We want to know in the same statement *who* the friend is. The fragment can be corrected by attaching it to the sentence that comes before it.

Today I visited Hilda Cooper, a friend who is in the hospital.

(Here a comma is used to set off "a friend who is in the hospital," which is extra material placed at the end of the sentence.)

Practice 1: Forming a Sentence based on a Dependent Fragment

Turn each of the dependent-word groups into a sentence by adding a complete thought. Put a comma after the dependent-word group if a dependent word starts the sentence.

Examples   After I got out of high school

After I got out of high school, I spent a year travelling.

The watch which I got fixed

The watch which I got fixed has just stopped working again.

1. After my professor spit out a dental cap

   After my professor spit out a dental cap, we all started laughing.

2. When I woke up in the vampire's embrace

   When I woke up in The vampires embrace, I screamed.

3. When my car stalled in the glaring alien light

   _____

   _____

4. The supermarket that I went to

   _____

   _____

5. Before I left the spaceship

   _____

   _____

Practice 2: Discovering and Correcting Dependent Fragments

Underline the dependent-word fragment (or fragments) in each selection. Then correct each fragment by attaching it to the sentence that comes before or the sentence that comes after—whichever sounds more natural. Put a comma after the dependent-word group if it starts the sentence.

1. Although the air-conditioner was working. I still felt warm in the room. I wondered if I had a fever.

   _____

   _____

   _____

   _____

2. When Tony got into his car this morning. He discovered that he had left the car windows open. The seats and rug were soaked. Since it had rained overnight.

   _____

   _____

   _____

   _____

3. After cutting fish at the restaurant all day. Jenny smelled like a cat-food factory. She couldn't wait to take a hot, perfumed bath.

   _____

   _____

   _____

   _____

4. Frank raked out the soggy leaves. That were at the bottom of the concrete fish pond. When two bullfrogs jumped out at him. He dropped the rake and ran.

   _____

   _____

   _____

   _____

5. Because he had eaten and drunk too much. He had to leave the party early. His stomach was like a volcano. That was ready to erupt.

   _____

   _____

   _____

   _____

2 -*ING* AND *TO* FRAGMENTS (PARTICIPIAL AND INFINITIVE FRAGMENTS)

When an -*ing* word appears at or near the start of a word group, a fragment may result. Such fragments often lack a subject and part of the verb. Underline the word groups in the selections below that contain -*ing* words. Each is a fragment.

Selection 1

I spent all day in the employment office. Trying to find a job that suited me. The prospects looked bleak.

Selection 2

Crystal surprised Tony on the nature hike. Picking blobs of resin off pine trees. Then she chewed them like bubblegum.

Selection 3

Mike took an aisle seat on the bus. His reason being that he had more legroom there.

People sometimes write -*ing* fragments because they think the subject in one sentence will work for the next word group as well. In the first selection above, they might think the subject *I* in the opening sentence will also serve as the subject for "Trying to find a job that suited me." But the subject must actually be *in* the sentence.

How to Correct -*ing* Fragments

1   Attach the fragment to the sentence that comes before or the sentence that comes after it, whichever makes sense. *Selection 1* above could read, "I spent all day in the employment office, trying to find a job that suited me." (Note that here a comma is used to set off "trying to find a job that suited me," which is extra material placed at the end of the sentence.)

2   Add a subject and change the -*ing* verb part to the correct form of the verb. *Selection 2* could read, "She picked blobs of resin off pine trees."

3   Change *being* to the correct form of the verb *be* (*am*, *are*, *is*, *was*, *were*). *Selection 3* could read, "His reason was that he had more legroom there."

4   Combining a present participle (-*ing* form) with an infinitive is simply combining two *non-finite* forms of a verb. Even this combination does not produce a "real," or *finite* verb. Add a *finite form* of the verb "to be" to each of the fragments above, and you will discover each fragment needs a subject as well.

How to Correct *to* Fragments

When *to* appears at or near the start of a word group, a fragment sometimes results.

> To remind people of their selfishness. Leon leaves handwritten notes on cars that take up two parking spaces.

The first word group in the selection above is a fragment. It can be corrected by adding it to the sentence that comes after it:

> To remind people of their selfishness, Leon leaves handwritten notes on cars that take up two parking spaces.

(Note that here a comma is used to set off "To remind people of their selfishness," which is introductory material in the sentence.)

Practice 1: Correcting Participial Fragments

Underline the *-ing* fragment in each of the following selections. Then make the fragment a sentence by rewriting it, using the method described in parentheses.

Example   The dog eyed me with suspicion. <u>Not knowing whether its owner was at home.</u> I hesitated to open the gate.

> *Not knowing whether its owner was at home, I hesitated to open the gate.*

1. Bill lay in bed after the alarm rang. Wishing that he had $100,000. Then he would not have to go to work.
   (Add the fragment to the preceding sentence.)

   _____

   _____

2. Investigating the strange, mournful cries in his neighbour's yard. George found a ferret tangled in its leash.
   (Add the fragment to the sentence that comes after it.)

   _____

   _____

3. I had to drive to the most remote parking lot to get a space. As a result, being late for class.
   (Add the subject *I* and change *being* to the correct form of the verb *was*.)

   _____

   _____

Practice 2: Discovering and Correcting Participial and Infinitive Fragments

Underline the *-ing* or *to* fragment in each selection. Then rewrite each selection correctly, using one of the methods of correction described on pages 24–25.

1. Glistening with dew. The gigantic web hung between the branches of the tree. The spider waited patiently for a visitor.

   _____

   _____

   _____

2. Maria is pleased with the carpet of Astroturf in her kitchen. Claiming that crumbs settle in the grass so she never sees them.

   _____

   _____

   _____

3. Ron picked through the box of chocolates. Removing the kinds he didn't like. He saved these for his wife and ate the rest.

   _____

   _____

   _____

4. The grass I was walking on suddenly became squishy. Having hiked into a marsh of some kind.

   _____

   _____

   _____

5. Steve drove quickly to the bank. To cash his paycheque. Otherwise, he would have no money for the weekend.

   _____

   _____

   _____

3 ADDED-DETAIL FRAGMENTS

Added-detail fragments lack a subject and a verb. They often begin with one of the following words.

also	except	including
especially	for example	such as

Locate and underline the one added-detail fragment in each of the following selections:

Selection 1

Tony has trouble accepting criticism. Except from Crystal. She has a knack for tact.

Selection 2

My apartment has its drawbacks. For example, no hot water in the morning.

Selection 3

I've worked at many jobs while in school. Among them, server, painter, and security guard.

People often write added-detail fragments for much the same reason they write *-ing* fragments. They think the subject and verb in one sentence will serve for the next word group as well. But the subject and verb must be in *each* word group.

How to Correct Added-Detail Fragments

1   Attach the fragment to the complete thought that precedes it. *Selection 1* could read: "Tony has trouble accepting criticism, except from Crystal." (Note that here a comma is used to set off "except from Crystal," which is extra material placed at the end of the sentence.)

2   Add a subject and a verb to the fragment to make it a complete sentence. *Selection 2* could read: "My apartment has its drawbacks. For example, there is no hot water in the morning."

3   Change words as necessary to make the fragment part of the preceding sentence. *Selection 3* could read: "Among the many jobs I've worked at while in school have been server, painter, and security guard."

Practice 1: Finding and Correcting Fragments

Underline the fragment in each selection below. Then make each one a sentence by rewriting it, using the method described in parentheses.

Example   My husband and I share the household chores. <u>Including meals.</u>
I do the cooking and he does the eating.
(Add the fragment to the preceding sentence.)
<u>*My husband and I share the household chores, including meals.*</u>

1. Bill is very accident-prone. For example, managing to cut his hand while crumbling a piece of shredded wheat.
   (Correct the fragment by adding the subject *he* and changing *managing* to *managed*.)

   _____

   _____

2. Tina's job in the customer service department depressed her. All day, people complained. About missing parts, rude salespeople, and errors on bills.
   (Add the fragment to the preceding sentence.)

   _____

   _____

3. My mother is always giving me household hints. For example, using club soda on stains. Unfortunately, I never remember them.
   (Correct the fragment by adding the subject and verb *she suggests*.)

   _____

   _____

Practice 2: Finding and Correcting Added-Detail Fragments

Underline the added-detail fragment in each selection. Then rewrite that part of the selection needed to correct the fragment. Use one of the three methods of correction described on page 27.

1. My little boy is constantly into mischief. Such as tearing the labels off all the cans in the cupboard.

   _____

   _____

2. The old house was filled with expensive woodwork. For example, a hand-carved mantel and a mahogany banister.

_____

_____

3. Andy used to have many bad eating habits. For instance, chewing with his mouth open.

_____

_____

4. I put potatoes in the microwave oven without first punching holes in them. Ten minutes later, there were several explosions. With potatoes splattering all over the walls of the oven.

_____

_____

_____

5. Janet looked forward to seeing former class-mates at the high-school reunion. Including the football player she had had a wild crush on. She wondered if he had grown fat and bald.

_____

_____

_____

4 MISSING-SUBJECT FRAGMENTS

Underline the word group in which the subject is missing in each selection below.

Selection 1

One example of my father's generosity is that he visits sick friends in the hospital. And takes along get-well cards with a few dollars folded in them.

Selection 2

The weightlifter grunted as he heaved the barbells into the air. Then, with a loud groan, dropped them.

People write missing-subject fragments because they think the subject in one sentence will apply to the next word group as well. But the subject, as well as the verb, must be in each word group to make it a sentence.

How to Correct Missing-Subject Fragments

1 Attach the fragment to the preceding sentence. *Selection 1* could read: "One example of my father's generosity is that he visits sick friends in the hospital and takes along get-well cards with a few dollars folded in them."

2 Add a subject (which can often be a pronoun standing for the subject in the preceding sentence). *Selection 2* could read: "Then, with a loud groan, he dropped them."

Practice: Discovering and Correcting Missing Subject Fragments

Underline the missing-subject fragment in each selection. Then rewrite that part of the selection needed to correct the fragment. Use one of the two methods of correction described above.

1. Fred went to the refrigerator to get milk for his breakfast cereal. And discovered a carton of chocolate milk left in the corner.

   _____

   _____

2. At the laundromat, I loaded the dryer with wet clothes. Then noticed the "Out of order" sign taped over the coin slot.

   _____

   _____

3. Our neighbourhood's most eligible bachelor got married this weekend. But did not invite us to the wedding. We all wondered what the bride was like.

   _____

   _____

4. Larry's father could not accept his son's lifestyle. Also, was constantly criticizing his choice of friends.

   _____

   _____

5. Wendy stared at the blank page in desperation. And decided that the first sentence of a paper is always the hardest to write.

   _____

   _____

A REVIEW: HOW TO CHECK
FOR SENTENCE FRAGMENTS

1 Read your paper aloud from the *last* sentence to the *first*. You will be better able to see and hear whether each word group you read is a complete thought.

2 If you suspect a sentence might be a fragment, ask yourself, does this contain a subject and a verb and express a complete thought?

3 More specifically, be on the lookout for the most common fragments:

■ Dependent-word fragments (starting with words like *after*, *because*, *since*, *when*, and *before*)

■ *-ing* and *to* fragments (*-ing* or *to* at or near the start of a word group)

■ Added-detail fragments (starting with words like *for example*, *such as*, *also*, and *especially*)

■ Missing-subject fragments (a verb is present but not the subject)

■ **Review Test 1**

Turn each of the following word groups into a complete sentence. Use the space provided.

Examples Feeling very confident

Feeling very confident, I began my speech.

Until the rain started

We played softball until the rain started.

1. Before you sit down

_____

2. When the noise stopped

_____

3. To get to the game on time

_____

4. During my walk along the trail

_____

5. Because I was short on cash

_____

6. Lucy, whom I know well

_____

7. Up in the attic

_____

8. Through hard work

_____

9. Which I agreed to do

_____

10. Was ready for a change

_____

■ Review Test 2

Underline the fragment in each selection. Then correct the fragment in the space provided.

Example Sam received all kinds of junk mail. <u>Then complained to the post office.</u> Eventually, some of the mail stopped coming.
Then he complained to the post office.
_____

1. After seeing an offensive hygiene spray ad on television. I resolved never to buy that type of product again.

_____

_____

2. People worked together on the assembly line. Moving quickly and efficiently. They wanted to make as much money as possible.

_____

_____

3. Mark was offered several different jobs. And accepted one that featured a four-day work week.

_____

_____

4. Our yard sale was an enormous success. We sold everything. Except for the self-portrait of my grandfather.

   _____

   _____

5. While they were taking a midnight walk. Tony and Crystal saw hundreds of lightning bugs flickering over the lake. They were also attacked by hundreds of bomber-sized mosquitoes.

   _____

   _____

   _____

6. Andy always wins at hide-and-seek. Peeking through his fingers as he counts to one hundred. The other kids will soon catch on.

   _____

   _____

7. Natalie has worked on the crossword puzzle all day. All the while, mumbling each clue out loud. I hope she finishes soon.

   _____

   _____

8. Italian food is mouth-watering. Especially pizza. Fettuccine is delicious, too.

   _____

   _____

9. Crystal looked at the enormous diamond on Holly's finger. And decided it was fake. The diamond was the size of a small headlight.

   _____

   _____

10. I often take pictures in my backyard. For instance, of a neighbour stealing flowers from my new planter.

    _____

    _____

■ Review Test 3

In the space provided, write *C* in front of the four word groups that are complete sentences; write *frag* in front of the six fragments. The first two items are done for you.

frag   1. When Crystal prepares for a day at the beach.

_C_   2. She first selects a colourful bikini with a matching beach coat.

Frag   3. Second, gathering together a pair of large, dark sunglasses, a beach bag and towel, suntan lotion, and a very comfortable lounge chair.

Frag   4. Also, a large-brimmed hat in an unusual bright colour.

_C_   5. In addition, she takes along a radio to listen to her favourite music.

Frag   6. Occasionally bringing along a good book to read as well.

_C_   7. She also tucks in the beach bag some fattening snacks.

_____   8. Such as potato chips and oatmeal cookies.

_C_   9. Before leaving, she checks to make sure her fingernail polish matches her toe-nail polish.

_____   10. Then on her way to a great afternoon at the lake.

Now correct the fragments you have found. Attach each fragment to the sentence that comes before or after it, or make whatever other change is needed to turn the fragment into a sentence. Use the space provided. The first one is corrected for you.

1. _When Crystal prepares for a day at the beach, she first selects a colourful bikini with a matching beach coat._

2. _____

_____

3. _____

_____

4. _____

_____

5. _____

_____

6. _____

_____

■ Review Test 4

Write quickly for five minutes about the high school you attended. Don't worry about spelling, punctuation, finding exact words, or organizing your thoughts. Just focus on writing as many words as you can without stopping.

After you have finished, go back and make whatever changes are needed to correct any fragments in your writing.

■ Grammatical Reminder

The Infinitive Form: The form of a verb beginning with the word *to* is called the *infinitive form*. It is <u>never</u> used as the main verb in a sentence. *Infinitive* stems from the word *infinite*, meaning *having no limits*. The infinitive form: i.e., *to do*, *to make*, *to begin* is the beginning-point for all other forms of any verb. All verb forms used as main verbs in sentences *have limits*; they are altered or *limited* by some change to show time [tense], relation to subject [person and number], and so on. The infinitive form <u>never</u> changes, but is used in combination with other *finite verb forms* as in the examples shown.

> I was *beginning* <u>to understand</u> surveying when the lecture ended.
>
> Maria *swerved* <u>to avoid</u> the vampire's embrace.

Participles and Gerunds ("-ing" forms of verbs):   *Present participles and gerunds* are two uses of the "-ing" form of any verb. *Present <u>participles</u>* are only <u>parts</u> of a verb form; their name should help you remember this fact. A present participle <u>must</u> be used with a "helping" or auxiliary verb: eg., "I *am making* the cat's breakfast."

- *Participles* are sometimes used to describe things in English: eg., "He had a *winning* way about him." In these cases, they act as *adjectives*.
- *Gerunds* are the same "-ing" forms used as nouns (or as subjects or objects) in sentences: eg., "*Winning* was the only thing that mattered to him."

The following examples may help you to see the difference between *participles used as part of a verb form* and *participles <u>mistakenly used as a complete verb</u>*. You will also see an example of a *the gerund verb form* in its use as a noun/subject.

> *Being* part of a huge crowd in the spaceship. (This is *not* a sentence, because a *present <u>participle</u>*, or, only <u>part</u> of a verb has been used.)
>
> *Being* part of a huge crowd in the spaceship *was* a disorienting experience. (Now this is a sentence, because it contains a *finite*, or "real," non-partial verb form: i.e., *was*.)

or

> I *was disoriented*, being part of a huge crowd in the spaceship.

Gerund as Subject of a Sentence:

> *Eating* was my only reasonable choice.
>
> *Cleaning* the cat box is a disgusting chore.

RUN-ONS

INTRODUCTORY PROJECT

A run-on occurs when two sentences are run together with no adequate sign given to mark the break between them. Shown below are four run-on sentences and four correctly marked sentences. Complete the statement that explains how each run-on has been corrected.

1. A man coughed in the movie theatre the result was a chain reaction of copycat coughing. *Run-on*

    A man coughed in the movie theatre. The result was a chain reaction of copycat coughing. *Correct*

    The run-on has been corrected by using a ___Period___ and a capital letter to separate the two complete thoughts.

2. I heard laughter inside the house, no one answered the bell. *Run-on*

    I heard laughter inside the house, but no one answered the bell. *Correct*

    The run-on has been corrected by using a joining word ___But___ to connect the two complete thoughts.

3. A car sped around the corner, it sprayed slush all over the pedestrians. *Run-on*

    A car sped around the corner; it sprayed slush all over the pedestrians. *Correct*

    The run-on has been corrected by using a ___Semi colon___ to connect the two closely related thoughts.

4. I had a campus map, I still could not find my classroom building. *Run-on*

    Although I had a campus map, I still could not find my classroom building. *Correct*

    The run-on has been corrected by using the subordinating word ___Although___ to connect the two closely related thoughts.

    Answers are on page 472.

WHAT ARE RUN-ONS?

A *run-on* is two complete thoughts that are run together with no adequate sign given to mark the break between them.* As a result of the run-on, the reader is confused, unsure of where one thought ends and the next one begins. Some run-ons have no punctuation at all to mark the break between the thoughts. Such run-ons are known as *fused sentences*: they are fused or joined together as if they were only one thought.

Fused Sentence

Rita decided to stop smoking she didn't want to die of lung cancer.

Fused Sentence

The exam was postponed the class was cancelled as well.

In other run-ons, known as *comma splices*, a comma is used to connect or "splice" together the two complete thoughts. However, a comma alone is *not enough* to connect two complete thoughts. Some connection stronger than a comma alone is needed. A comma indicates a pause in a sentence; it *cannot* "glue" together two independent thoughts.

Comma Splice

Rita decided to stop smoking, she didn't want to die of lung cancer.

Comma Splice

The exam was postponed, the class was cancelled as well.

Comma splices are the most common kind of run-on mistake. Students sense that some kind of connection is needed between thoughts, and so they put a comma at the dividing point. But the comma alone is *not sufficient*, and a stronger, clearer mark between the two thoughts is needed.

---

* Some instructors refer to each complete thought in a run-on sentence as an *independent clause*. A *clause* is simply a group of words having a subject and a verb. A clause may be *independent* (expressing a complete thought and able to stand alone) or *dependent* (*not* expressing a complete thought and not able to stand alone). A run-on sentence is two independent clauses that are run together with no adequate sign given to mark the break between them.

A Warning: Words That Can Lead to Run-Ons

People often write run-ons when the second complete thought begins with one of the following words:

I	we	there	now
you	they	this	then
he, she, it		that	next

Remember to be on the alert for run-ons whenever you use one of these words in your writing.

CORRECTING RUN-ONS

Here are four common methods of correcting a run-on:

1   Use a period and a capital letter to separate the two complete thoughts. (In other words, make two separate sentences of the two complete thoughts.)

Rita decided to stop smoking. She didn't want to die of lung cancer.
The exam was postponed. The class was cancelled as well.

2   Use a comma plus a joining word (*and*, *but*, *for*, *or*, *nor*, *so*, *yet*) to connect the two complete thoughts.

Rita decided to stop smoking, for she didn't want to die of lung cancer.
The exam was postponed, and the class was cancelled as well.

3   Use a semi-colon to connect the two complete thoughts.

Rita decided to stop smoking; she didn't want to die of lung cancer.
The exam was postponed; the class was cancelled as well.

4   Use subordination.

Because Rita didn't want to die of lung cancer, she decided to stop smoking.
When the exam was postponed, the class was cancelled as well.

The following pages will give you practice in all four methods of correcting run-ons. The use of subordination will be explained even further on pages 385–386, in a section of the book that deals with sentence variety.

METHOD 1: PERIOD AND A CAPITAL LETTER

One way of correcting a run-on is to use a period and a capital letter at the break between the two complete thoughts. Use this method especially if the thoughts are not closely related or if another method would make the sentence too long.

Practice 1: Correcting Fused Sentences

Locate the split in each of the following run-ons. Each is a *fused sentence*—that is, each consists of two sentences that are fused or joined together with no punctuation at all between them. Reading each sentence aloud will help you "hear" where a major break or split in the thought occurs. At such a point, your voice will probably drop and pause.

Correct the run-on by putting a period at the end of the first thought and a capital letter at the start of the second thought.

Example   Gary was not a success at his job. His mouth moved faster than his hands.

1. Jerry's motorized wheelchair broke down he was unable to go to class.
2. The subway train hurtled through the station a blur of spray paint and graffiti flashed in front of my eyes.
3. Jenny panicked the car had stalled in a treacherous traffic intersection.
4. Half the class flunked the exam the other half of the students were absent.
5. One reason for the high cost of new furniture is the cost of good wood one walnut tree in 1982 sold for $40,000.
6. The wedding reception began to get out of hand guests started to throw cake at each other.
7. Carla's pitchfork turned over the rich earth earthworms poked their heads out of new furrows.
8. There were a lot of unusual people at the party a few of the ladies had shaved heads.
9. Bill talks all the time his tongue is getting calluses.
10. Hundreds of crushed cars were piled in neat stacks the rusted hulks resembled flattened tin cans.

Practice 2: Correcting Fused Sentences, Splices

Locate the split in each of the following run-ons. Some of the run-ons are *fused sentences*, and some of them are *comma splices*—run-ons spliced or joined together only with a comma. Correct each run-on by putting a period at the end of the first thought and a capital letter at the start of the next thought.

1. I wish Carl wouldn't fall asleep in class, his snoring drowns out the lecture.

2. The unemployment rate in Canada is expected to decrease, current drops in interest rates should increase consumer spending and create jobs.

3. Our car radio is not working properly we get whistling noises and static instead of music.

4. That shopping mall has the smell of death about it half the stores are empty.

5. Cats sleep in all sorts of unusual places, our new cat likes to curl up in the bathroom sink.

6. Every day, Canadians use 50 billion litres of water this amount would cover Toronto to a depth of 20 metres.

7. The driver had an unusual excuse for speeding, he said he had just washed his car and was trying to dry it.

8. The telephone rang at least fifteen times nobody felt like getting up to answer it.

9. Some of our foods have misleading names, for example, English muffins were actually invented in North America.

10. The gunslinger lay dead on the bar-room floor his last words were, "You don't have the guts to pull that trigger."

Practice 3: Continuing a Sentence Group

Write a second sentence to go with each sentence below. Start the second sentence with the word given in italics.

Example   **He**   My dog's ears snapped up. <u>He had heard a wolf howling</u>
<u>on television.</u>

They   1. I could not find my car keys. _____

_____

Then   2. The first thing Bill ate for dessert was a peach. _____

_____

She   3. My daughter began screaming. _____

_____

It   4. The toaster oven was acting strangely. _____

_____

There   5. Cars had to stop suddenly at the intersection. _____

_____

METHOD 2: COMMA AND A JOINING WORD

Another way of correcting a run-on is to use a comma plus a joining word to connect the two complete thoughts. Joining words (also called *co-ordinating conjunctions*) include *and*, *but*, *for*, *or*, *nor*, *so*, and *yet*. Here is what the four most common joining words mean:

and   in addition, along with

> Crystal was watching *Hockey Night in Canada*, and she was doing her homework as well.

(*And* means *in addition:* Crystal was watching *Hockey Night in Canada*;* *in addition*, she was doing her homework.)

but   however, except, on the other hand, just the opposite

> I voted for the prime minister two years ago, but I would not vote for him today.

(*But* means *however:* I voted for the prime minister two years ago;* *however*, I would not vote for him today.)

for   because, the reason that, the cause for something

> Saturday is the worst day to shop, for people jam the stores.

(*For* means *because:* Saturday is the worst day to shop *because* people jam the stores.) If you are not comfortable using *for*, you may want to use *because* instead of *for* in the activities that follow. If you do use *because*, omit the comma before it.

so   as a result, therefore

> Our son misbehaved again, so he was sent upstairs without dessert.

(*So* means *as a result:* Our son misbehaved again;* *as a result*, he was sent upstairs without dessert.)

---

* Adverbial conjunctions, used with a semi-colon and a comma, are explained on page 44.

Practice 1: Correcting Run-on Sentences

Insert the comma and the joining word (*and*, *but*, *for*, *so*) that logically connect the two thoughts in each sentence. You will notice that some of the run-ons are *fused sentences* (there is no punctuation between the two complete thoughts) and some are *comma splices* (there is only a comma between the two complete thoughts).

Example   A trip to the zoo always depresses me, _∧ *for* I hate to see animals in cages.

1. The telephone was ringing someone was at the front door as well.

2. Something was obviously wrong with the meat loaf it was glowing in the dark.

3. Nick and Lisa enjoyed the movie, they wished the seats had been more comfortable.

4. Brett moved from Halifax to Vancouver he wanted to get as far away as possible from his ex-wife.

5. I decided to go back to school I felt my brain was turning to slush.

6. Crystal loved the rose cashmere sweater, she had nothing to wear with it.

7. Chan's son has joined the Armed Forces, his daughter is thinking of joining, too.

8. Teresa began working the second shift she is not able to eat supper with her family any more.

9. Fred remembered to get the hamburger he forgot to buy the hamburger rolls.

10. My TV wasn't working I walked over to a friend's house to watch the game.

Practice 2: Continuing Sentences with Commas and Conjunctions

Add a complete and closely related thought to go with each of the following statements. Use a comma plus the italicized joining word when you write the second thought.

Example   **but**   I was sick with the flu, <u>but I still had to study for the test.</u>

so   1.   The night was hot and humid _____

_____

but   2.   Fred wanted to get a pizza _____

_____

and   3. Crystal went shopping in the morning _____

_____

for   4. I'm going to sell my car _____

_____

but   5. I expected the exam to be easy _____

_____

METHOD 3: SEMI-COLON

A third method of correcting a run-on is to use a semi-colon to mark the break between two thoughts. A *semi-colon* (;) is made up of a period and a comma and is sometimes called a *strong comma*. The semi-colon signals more of a pause than a comma alone but not quite the full pause of a period.

Semi-colon Alone

Here are some earlier sentences that were connected with a comma plus a joining word. Notice that a semi-colon, unlike the comma, can be used alone to connect the two **complete thoughts** in each sentence:

Something was obviously wrong with the meat loaf; it was glowing in the dark.

Fred remembered to get the hamburger; he forgot to buy the hamburger rolls.

I decided to go back to school; I felt my brain was turning to slush.

The occasional use of the semi-colon can add variety to sentences. For some people, however, the semi-colon is a confusing mark of punctuation. Keep in mind that if you are not comfortable using it, you can and should use one of the other methods of correcting a run-on sentence.

Practice: Using a Semi-colon Between Complete Thoughts

Insert a semi-colon where the break occurs between the two complete thoughts in each of the following sentences.

Example   She had a wig on; it looked more like a hat than a wig.

1. Our *Maclean's* subscription just ran out nobody remembered to renew it.
2. Sarah wanted to watch a *Star Trek* rerun the rest of the family insisted on turning to the CBC news.

3. Bonnie put a freshly baked batch of chocolate-chip cookies on the counter to cool everyone gathered round for samples.

4. About $25,000,000 worth of pizza is eaten each year an average of 300 new pizza parlours open every week.

5. Ali never heard the third-base coach screaming for him to stop he was out at home plate by 3 metres.

Semi-colon with a Transition

A semi-colon is sometimes used with a transitional word and a comma to join two complete thoughts:

I figured the ball game would cost me about five dollars; however, I didn't consider the high price of food and drinks.

Fred and Maria have a low-interest mortgage on their house; otherwise, they would move to another neighbourhood.

Sharon didn't understand the teacher's point; therefore, she asked him to repeat it.

Note: Sometimes transitional words do not join complete thoughts but are merely interrupters in a sentence (see page 185):

My parents, moreover, plan to go on the trip.

I believe, however, that they'll change their minds.

Common Transitional Words

Here is a list of common transitional words (also known as *adverbial conjunctions*).

however	moreover	therefore
on the other hand	in addition	as a result
nevertheless	also	consequently
instead	furthermore	otherwise

Practice 1: Using Transitional Words with Correct Punctuation

Choose a logical transitional word from the box above and write it in the space provided. In addition, put a semi-colon *before* the transition and a comma *after* it.

Example It was raining harder than ever <u>; however,</u> Bobby was determined
to go to the amusement park.

1. The tree could be sprayed with insecticide _____ the spider
   mites will kill it.

2. I helped the magician set up his props _____ I agreed to let
   him saw me in half.

3. Fred never finished panelling his basement _____ he hired a
   carpenter to complete the job.

4. My house was robbed last week _____ I bought a watchdog.

5. Carla is taking five courses this semester _____ she is working forty hours a week.

Practice 2: Using Semi-colons and Commas Correctly

Punctuate each sentence by using a semi-colon and a comma.

Example A band rehearses in the garage next door; as a result I'm thinking
of moving.

1. I arrived early to get a good seat however there were already a hundred people
   outside the door.
2. Foul language marred the live boxing match as a result next time they will
   probably use a tape delay.
3. The fluorescent lights in the library gave Ming a headache furthermore they
   distracted her by making a loud humming sound.
4. The broken shells on the beach were like tiny razors consequently we walked
   about with extreme caution.
5. Ted carefully combed and recombed his hair nevertheless his bald spot still
   showed.

METHOD 4: SUBORDINATION

A fourth method of joining together related thoughts is to use subordination.
Subordination is a way of showing that one thought in a sentence is *not as important* as another thought. Here are three earlier sentences that have been recast so
that one idea is subordinated to (made less emphatic than) the other idea:

Because Rita didn't want to die of lung cancer, she decided to stop smoking.

The wedding reception began to get out of hand when the guests started to throw food at each other.

Although Sarah wanted to watch a *Star Trek* rerun, the rest of the family insisted on turning to the CBC news.

Common Dependent Words

Notice that when we subordinate, we use dependent words like *because*, *when*, and *although*. Here is a brief list of common dependent words:

after	before	unless
although	even though	until
as	if	when
because	since	while

Subordination is explained in full on pages 385–386.

Practice 1: Practising Subordination

Choose a logical dependent word from the box on the previous page and write it in the space provided.

Example _____Although_____ going up a ladder is easy, looking down can be difficult.

1. The teacher is lowering my grade in the course _____ I was late three times for class.

2. _____ the airplane dropped a few metres, my stomach rose a few centimetres.

3. _____ the football game was being played, we sent out for a pizza.

4. _____ the football game was over, we went out for another pizza.

5. You should talk to a guidance counsellor _____ you decide on
    your courses for next semester.

Practice 2: Writing Sentences Using Subordination

Rewrite the five sentences below, so that one idea is subordinate to the other. Use
one of the dependent words in the box in each case.

Example   My house was burglarized last week; I bought a watchdog.

Because my house was burglarized last week, I bought a

watchdog.

Note: As in the example above, use a comma if a dependent statement starts
a sentence.

1. Sharon didn't understand the teacher's point; she asked him to repeat it.

    _____

    _____

2. Fred remembered to get the hamburger; he forgot to get the hamburger rolls.

    _____

    _____

3. Michael gulped two cups of strong coffee; his heart started to flutter.

    _____

    _____

4. A car sped around the corner; it sprayed slush all over the pedestrians.

    _____

    _____

5. Crystal loved the rose cashmere sweater; she had nothing to wear with it.

    _____

    _____

A REVIEW: HOW TO CHECK FOR RUN-ONS

1 To see if a sentence is a run-on, read it aloud and listen for a break marking two complete thoughts. Your voice will probably drop and pause at the break.

2 To check an entire paper read it aloud from the *last* sentence to the *first*. Doing so will help you hear and see each complete thought.

3 Be on the lookout for words that can lead to run-on sentences:

I	he, she, it	they	this	then
you	we	there	that	next

4 Correct run-on sentences by using one of the following methods:

- A period and a capital letter
- A comma and a joining word (*and*, *but*, *for*, *or*, *nor*, *so*, *yet*)
- A semi-colon
- Subordination (as explained above and on pages 385–386)

■ Review Test 1

Some of the run-ons that follow are *fused sentences*, having no punctuation between the two complete thoughts; others are *comma splices*, having only a comma between the two complete thoughts.

Correct the run-ons by using one of the following three methods:

- A period and a capital letter
- A comma and a joining word (*and*, *but*, *for*, or *so*)
- A semi-colon

Use whichever method seems most appropriate in each case.

Example   Fred pulled the cellophane off the cake, the icing came along with it.
and

1. I found the cat sleeping on the stove the dog was eating the morning mail.

2. Angela has a twenty-kilometre drive to school she sometimes arrives late for class.

3. I lifted the empty Coke bottle above me a few more drops fell out of it and into my thirsty mouth.

4. These pants are guaranteed to wear like iron they also feel like iron.

5. I saw a black-and-white blob on the highway soon the odour of skunk wafted through my car.

6. She gets A's in her math homework by using her pocket calculator she is not allowed to use the calculator at school.

7. Flies were getting into the house the window screen was torn.

8. Maria moans and groans upon getting up in the morning she sounds like a crazy woman.

9. Crystal met Tony at Harvey's they shared a large order of fries.

10. The carpet in their house needs to be replaced the walls should be painted as well.

■ Review Test 2

Correct the run-on in each sentence by using subordination. Choose from among the following dependent words:

after	before	unless
although	even though	until
as	if	when
because	since	while

Example   Tony hated going to a new barber, he was afraid of butchered hair.

Because Tony was afraid of butchered hair, he hated going to a new barber.

1. The meal and conversation were enjoyable, I kept worrying about the cheque.

_____

_____

2. My wet fingers stuck to the frosty ice-cube tray, I had to pry them loose.

_____

_____

3. I take a late-afternoon nap, my mind and body are refreshed and ready for my night course.

   _____

   _____

4. Our daughter jumped up screaming a black spider was on her leg.

   _____

   _____

5. I wanted badly to cry I remained cold and silent.

   _____

   _____

6. Ming does the food shopping every two weeks she first cashes her paycheque at the bank.

   _____

   _____

7. Follow the instructions carefully, you'll have the computer set up and working in no time.

   _____

   _____

8. Every child in the neighbourhood was in the backyard, Frank stepped outside to investigate.

   _____

   _____

9. My first year in college was not a success, I spent most of my time in the video arcade.

   _____

   _____

10. A burglar was in our upstairs bedroom going through our drawers, we were in the den downstairs watching television.

   _____

   _____

■ Review Test 3

On a separate sheet of paper, write six sentences, each of which has two complete thoughts. Use a period and a capital letter between the thoughts in two of the sentences. Use a comma and a joining word (*and*, *but*, *or*, *nor*, *for*, *so*, *yet*) to join the thoughts in another two sentences. Use a semi-colon to join the thoughts in the final two sentences.

In addition, select two of the six sentences and rewrite them so each uses a dependent word and contains a subordinated thought.

■ Review Test 4

Write quickly for five minutes about a frightening experience you had. Don't worry about spelling, punctuation, finding exact words, or organizing your thoughts. Just focus on writing as many words as you can without stopping.

Have another student read your paragraph aloud. Note where you both *hear* and *see* run-on sentences or fragments.

STANDARD
ENGLISH
VERBS

INTRODUCTORY PROJECT

Underline what you think is the correct form of the verb in each of the sentences below.

That radio station once (play, played) rock.

It now (play, plays) classical music.

When Vanessa was a little girl, she (hope, hoped) to become a movie star.

Now she (hope, hopes) to be accepted at law school.

At first, my father (juggle, juggled) with balls of yarn.

Now that he is an expert, he (juggle, juggles) raw eggs.

On the basis of the above examples, complete the following statements.

1. The first sentence in each pair refers to an action in the (past time, present time), and the regular verb has an _____ ending.
2. The second sentence in each pair refers to an action in the (past time, present time), and the regular verb has an _____ ending.

Answers are on page 474.

Many people have grown up in communities where nonstandard verb forms are used in everyday life. Such forms include *they be*, *it done*, *we has*, *you was*, *she don't*, and *it ain't*. Community dialects have richness and power but are a drawback in college and the world at large, where standard English verb forms must be used. Standard English helps ensure clear communication among English-speaking people everywhere, and it is especially important in the world of work.

This chapter compares the community dialect and the standard English forms of a regular verb and three common irregular verbs.

REGULAR VERBS: NONSTANDARD DIALECT AND STANDARD FORMS

The chart below compares community dialect (nonstandard) and standard English forms of the regular verb *to talk*.

TO TALK

Nonstandard Community Dialect		**Standard English**	
(Do *not* use in your writing)		(Use for clear communication)	
Present tense			
I talks	we talks	I talk	we talk
you talks	you talks	you talk	you talk
he, she, it talk	they talks	he, she, it talks	they talk
Past tense			
I talk	we talk	I talked	we talked
you talk	you talk	you talked	you talked
he, she, it talk	they talk	he, she, it talked	they talked

One of the most common nonstandard forms results from dropping the endings of regular verbs. For example, people might say "Rose work until ten o'clock tonight" instead of "Rose works until ten o'clock tonight." Or they'll say "I work overtime yesterday" instead of "I worked overtime yesterday." To avoid such nonstandard usage, memorize the forms shown above for the regular verb *talk*. Then use the activities that follow to help make the inclusion of verb endings a writing habit.

Present Tense Endings

The verb ending -*s* or -*es* is needed with a regular verb in the present tense when the subject is *he*, *she*, *it*, or any one person or thing.

He	He lifts weights.
She	She runs.
It	It amazes me.
One person	Their son Ted swims.
One person	Their daughter Grace dances.
One thing	Their house jumps at night with all the exercise.

Practice 1: Using Correct Present Tense Endings

All but one of the ten sentences that follow need -*s* or -*es* endings. Cross out the nonstandard verb forms and write the standard forms in the spaces provided. Mark the one sentence that needs no change with a *C*.

ends   **Example**   The sale ~~end~~ tomorrow.

_____ 1. Renée hate it when I criticize her singing.

_____ 2. Whenever my sister tries to tell a joke, she always mess it up.

_____ 3. Ice cream feel good going down a sore throat.

_____ 4. Frank cover his ears every time his baby sister cries.

_____ 5. "Dinner sure smell good," said Lisa as she walked into the kitchen.

_____ 6. My brother wants to be an astronaut so he can see stars.

_____ 7. The picture on our television set blur whenever there is a storm.

_____ 8. My mother think women should get equal pay for equal work.

_____ 9. Sometimes Devon pretend that he is living in a penthouse.

_____ 10. It seem as if we are working more and more but getting paid less and less.

Practice 2: Discovering Necessary Verb Endings

Rewrite the short selection below, adding present tense -*s* verb endings wherever needed.

Angela react badly when she get caught in a traffic jam. She open the dashboard compartment and pull out an old pack of Juicy Fruit Gum that she keep for such occasions. She unwrap a dried-up stick of gum and chomp down viciously, trying to revive its flavour. She get out of the car and look down the highway, trying to see where the delay is. Back in the car, she drum her fingers on the steering wheel. If the jam last long enough, she start talking to herself and angrily kick off her shoes.

_____

_____

_____

_____

_____

_____

_____

_____

_____

_____

_____

Past Tense Endings

The verb ending *-d* or *-ed* is needed with a regular verb in the past tense.

Yesterday we finish<u>ed</u> painting the house.
I complet<u>ed</u> the paper an hour before class.
Fred's car stall<u>ed</u> on his way to work this morning.

Practice 1: Using Correct Past Tense Endings

All but one of the ten sentences that follow need *-d* or *-ed* endings. Cross out the nonstandard verb forms and write the standard forms in the spaces provided. Mark the one sentence that needs no change with a *C*.

jumped **Example**   The cat ~~jump~~ on my lap when I sat down.

_____ 1. As the burglar alarm went off, three men race out the door.

_____ 2. Crystal's new lipstick was so red that it glow in the dark.

———————— 3. Devon smelled gas when he walk into the apartment.

———————— 4. As soon as the pilot sight the runway, he turned on his landing lights.

———————— 5. While the bear stare hungrily at him, the tourist reached for his camera.

———————— 6. Cecile studied for three hours and then decide to get some sleep.

———————— 7. Just as Miss Muffet seated herself, a large spider joined her.

———————— 8. Frank hurried to cash his paycheque because he need money for the weekend.

———————— 9. The server dropped the tray with a loud crash; bits of broken glass scatter all over the floor.

———————— 10. A customer who twisted his ankle in the restaurant's parking lot decide to sue.

Practice 2: Discovering Necessary Past Tense Endings

Rewrite this selection, adding past tense -*d* or -*ed* verb endings where needed.

> Bill's boss shout at Bill. Feeling bad, Bill went home and curse his wife. Then his wife scream at their son. Angry himself, the son went out and cruelly tease a little girl who live next door until she wail. Bad feelings were pass on as one person wound the next with ugly words. No one manage to break the vicious cycle.

——

——

——

——

——

——

THREE COMMON IRREGULAR VERBS: NONSTANDARD DIALECT AND STANDARD FORMS

The following charts compare the nonstandard and standard forms of the common irregular verbs *to be*, *to have*, and *to do*. (For more on irregular verbs, see the next chapter, beginning on page 61.)

TO BE

Nonstandard Usage		**Standard English**	
(Do not use in your writing)		(Use for clear communication)	

Present Tense

I be (*or* is)	we be	I am	we are
you be	you be	you are	you are
he, she, it be	they be	he, she, it is	they are

Past Tense

I were	we was	I was	we were
you was	you was	you were	you were
he, she, it were	they was	he, she, it was	they were

TO HAVE

Nonstandard Usage		**Standard English**	
(Do not use in your writing)		(Use for clear communication)	

Present Tense

I has	we has	I have	we have
you has	you has	you have	you have
he, she, it, have	they has	he, she, it has	they have

Past Tense

I has	we has	I had	we had
you has	you as	you had	you had
he, she, it have	they has	he, she, it had	they had

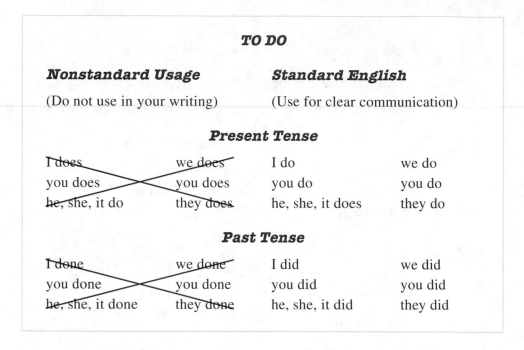

TO DO

Nonstandard Usage		Standard English	
(Do not use in your writing)		(Use for clear communication)	

Present Tense

I does	we does	I do	we do
you does	you does	you do	you do
he, she, it do	they does	he, she, it does	they do

Past Tense

I done	we done	I did	we did
you done	you done	you did	you did
he, she, it done	they done	he, she, it did	they did

Note: Many people have trouble with one negative form of *to do*. They will say, for example, "She don't listen" instead of "She doesn't listen," or they will say "This pen don't work" instead of "This pen doesn't work." Be careful to avoid the common mistake of using *don't* instead of *doesn't*.

Practice 1: Using Standard English Verb Forms

Underline the standard form of the irregular verbs *to be*, *to have*, or *to do*.

1. This week, my Aunt Agatha (have, has) a dentist's appointment.
2. She (does, do) not enjoy going to the dentist.
3. She (is, are) always frightened by the shiny instruments.
4. The drills (is, are) the worst thing in the office.
5. When Aunt Agatha (was, were) a little girl, she (have, had) a bad experience at the dentist's.
6. The dentist told her he (was, were) going to pull out all her teeth.
7. Aunt Agatha (do, did) not realize that he (was, were) only joking.
8. Her parents (was, were) unprepared for her screams of terror.
9. From then on, she (has, had) a bad attitude toward dentists.
10. Even now, she refuses to keep an appointment unless I (am, are) with her in the waiting room.

Practice 2: Using Correct Forms of Irregular Verbs

Cross out the nonstandard verb form in each sentence. Then write the standard form of *to be*, *to have*, or *to do* in the space provided.

_____   1. If it be not raining tomorrow, we're going camping.

_____   2. You is invited to join us.

_____   3. You has to bring your own sleeping bag and flashlight.

_____   4. It don't hurt to bring a raincoat also, in case of a sudden shower.

_____   5. The stars is beautiful on a warm summer night.

_____   6. Last year we have a great time on a family camping trip.

_____   7. We done all the cooking ourselves.

_____   8. The food tasted good even though it have some dead leaves in it.

_____   9. Then we discovered that we has no insect repellent.

_____   10. When we got home, we was covered with mosquito bites.

Practice 3: Practising Use of Standard Verb Forms

Fill in each blank with the standard form of *to be*, *to have*, or *to do*.

My mother sings alto in our community choir. She _____ to go to choir practice every Friday night and _____ expected to know all the music. If she _____ not know her part, the other choir members _____ things like glare at her and _____ likely to make nasty comments, she says. Last weekend, my mother _____ house guests and _____ not have time to learn all the notes. The music _____ very difficult, and she thought the other people _____ going to make fun of her. But they _____ very understanding when she told them that she _____ laryngitis and couldn't make a sound.

■ Review Test 1

Underline the standard verb form.

1. Paul (pound, pounded) the mashed potatoes until they turned into glue.
2. The velvety banana (rest, rests) on the shiny counter.

3. My neighbour's daughter (have, has) a brand-new Toyota.
4. It (is, be) fire-engine red with black leather upholstery.
5. The tree in the backyard (have, had) to be cut down.
6. When Ronald (talk, talks) about his ex-wife, his eyes grow hard and cold.
7. Every time my heart (skip, skips) a beat, I worry about my health.
8. My friend Pat (do, does) everything at the last minute.
9. The pattern on the wallpaper (look, looks) like fuzzy brown spiders marching in rows.
10. My hand (tremble, trembled) when I gave my speech in front of the class.

■ Review Test 2

Cross out the nonstandard verb forms in the sentences that follow. Then write the standard English verb forms in the space above, as shown.

Example She ~~watch~~ *watches* closely while the children ~~plays~~ *play* in the water.

1. The stores was all closed by the time the movie were over.
2. If you does your assignment on time, that teacher are going to like you.
3. The boxer pull his punches; the fight were fixed.
4. The tires is whitewalls; they be very good-looking.
5. He typically start to write a research paper the night before it be due.
6. It don't matter to him whether he have to stay up all night.
7. Helen anchor the relay team since she be the fastest runner.
8. I done Bill a favour that I hope he don't forget.
9. Last night I sneak into the kitchen and remove some Maple Buds from the candy jar.
10. I add the figures again and again, but I still weren't able to understand the bank statement.

IRREGULAR
VERBS

INTRODUCTORY PROJECT

You may already have a sense of which common English verbs are regular and which are not. To test yourself, fill in the past tense and past participle of the verbs below. Five are regular verbs and so take -d or -ed in the past tense and past participle. Five are irregular verbs and will probably not sound right when you try to add -d or -ed. Put I for *irregular* in front of these verbs. Also, see if you can write in their irregular verb forms.

Present Tense	Irregular	Past Tense	Past Participle
fall	I	fell	fallen
1. scream			
2. write			
3. steal			
4. ask			
5. kiss			
6. choose			
7. ride			
8. chew			
9. think			
10. dance			

Answers are on page 475.

A BRIEF REVIEW OF REGULAR VERBS

Every verb has four principal parts: the present tense, the past tense, the past participle, and the present participle. These parts can be used to build all the verb tenses (the times shown by a verb).

The past and past participle of a regular verb are formed by adding *-d* or *-ed* to the present. The *past participle* is the form of the verb used with the helping verb *have*, *has*, or *had* (or some form of *to be* with passive verbs). The *present participle* is formed by adding *-ing* to the present. Here are the principal forms of some regular verbs:

Present Tense	*Past Tense*	*Past Participle*	*Present Participle*
laugh	laughed	laughed	laughing
ask	asked	asked	asking
touch	touched	touched	touching
decide	decided	decided	deciding
explode	exploded	exploded	exploding

Most verbs in English are regular.

LIST OF IRREGULAR VERBS

Irregular verbs have irregular forms in the past tense and past participle. For example, the past tense of the irregular verb *to grow* is *grew;* the past participle is *grown.*

Almost everyone has some degree of trouble with irregular verbs. When you are unsure about the form of a verb, you can check the list of irregular verbs on the following pages. (The present participle is not shown on this list because it is formed simply by adding *-ing* to the base form of the verb.) Or you can check a dictionary, which gives the principal parts of irregular verbs.

Present Tense	*Past Tense*	*Past Participle*
arise	arose	arisen
awake	awoke *or* awaked	awoke
be (am, are, is)	was (were)	been
become	became	become
begin	began	begun
bend	bent	bent
bite	bit	bitten
blow	blew	blown
break	broke	broken
bring	brought	brought
build	built	built
burst	burst	burst
buy	bought	bought
catch	caught	caught
choose	chose	chosen
come	came	come
cost	cost	cost
cut	cut	cut
do (does)	did	done
draw	drew	drawn
drink	drank	drunk
drive	drove	driven
eat	ate	eaten
fall	fell	fallen
feed	fed	fed
feel	felt	felt
fight	fought	fought
find	found	found
fly	flew	flown
freeze	froze	frozen
get	got	got *or* gotten
give	gave	given
go (goes)	went	gone
grow	grew	grown
have (has)	had	had
hear	heard	heard
hide	hid	hidden
hold	held	held
hurt	hurt	hurt
keep	kept	kept
know	knew	known

Present Tense	Past Tense	Past Participle
lay	laid	laid
lead	led	led
leave	left	left
lend	lent	lent
let	let	let
lie	lay	lain
light	lit	lit
lose	lost	lost
make	made	made
meet	met	met
pay	paid	paid
ride	rode	ridden
ring	rang	rung
rise	rose	risen
run	ran	run
say	said	said
see	saw	seen
sell	sold	sold
send	sent	sent
shake	shook	shaken
shrink	shrank	shrunk
shut	shut	shut
sing	sang	sung
sit	sat	sat
sleep	slept	slept
speak	spoke	spoken
spend	spent	spent
stand	stood	stood
steal	stole	stolen
stick	stuck	stuck
sting	stung	stung
swear	swore	sworn
swim	swam	swum
take	took	taken
teach	taught	taught
tear	tore	torn
tell	told	told
think	thought	thought
wake	woke *or* waked	woken *or* waked
wear	wore	worn
win	won	won
write	wrote	written

Practice 1: Using Correct Forms of Verbs

Cross out the incorrect verb form in the following sentences. Then write the correct form of the verb in the space provided.

began **Example** When the mud slide started, the whole neighbourhood ~~begun~~ going downhill.

1. The game-show contestant learned she had chose the box with a penny in it.

2. The mechanic done an expensive valve job on my engine without getting my permission.

3. Angela has wore that ring since the day Demian bought it for her.

4. She has wrote a paper that will make you roar with laughter.

5. The gas-station attendant gived him the wrong change.

6. My sister be at school when a stranger came asking for her at our home.

7. The basketball team has broke the school record for most losses in a year.

8. Because I had lended him the money, I had a natural concern about what he did with it.

9. I seen that stray dog nosing around the yard yesterday.

10. I knowed her face from somewhere, but I couldn't remember just where.

Practice 2

For each of the italicized verbs in the following sentences, fill in the three missing forms in the order shown in the box:

> a. Present tense, which takes an *-s* ending when the subject is *he, she, it*, or any *one person* or *thing* (see page 54)
> b. Past tense
> c. Past participle—the form that goes with the helping verb *have, has,* or *had*

Example My little nephew loves to *break* things. Every Christmas he (a) _____*breaks*_____ his new toys the minute they're unwrapped.

Last year he (b) _____*broke*_____ five toys in seven minutes and then went on to smash his family's new china platter. His mother says he won't be happy until he has (c) _____ broken _____ their hearts.

1. Mary Beth wears contact lenses in order to *see* well. In fact, she (a) _____ so poorly without the lenses that the world is a multi-coloured blur. Once, when she lost one lens, she thought she (b) _____ a frog in the sink. She had really (c) _____ a lump of green soap.

2. When I was younger, I used to hate it when my gym class had to *choose* sides for a baseball game. Each captain, of course, (a) _____ the better players first. Since I was near-sighted and couldn't see a fly ball until it fell on my head, I would often have to wait half the period until one or the other captain (b) _____ me. If I had had my way, I would have (c) _____ to play chess.

3. My father loves to *take* pictures. Whenever we go on vacation, he (a) _____ at least ten rolls of film along. Last year, he (b) _____ over two hundred pictures of the same mountain scenery. Only after he had (c) _____ his last shot were we allowed to climb the mountain.

4. Teachers must love to *speak* to their classes. My English teacher (a) _____ so much that he has to get a drink of water midway through his lecture. Last Wednesday, he (b) _____ for the entire class period. I guess he never heard that old expression "Speak only when you're (c) _____ to."

5. Our next-door neighbour's pet poodle loves to *swim*. When there is no lake or pond handy, she (a) _____ in the family bathtub. Two summers ago, Fifi (b) _____ across the river in which the family was fishing. She won't be satisfied until she has (c) _____ across Lake Erie.

6. Convertibles may be old-fashioned, but they are fun to *drive*. My cousin has a sky-blue Chevrolet convertible which she (a) _____ to work. One day she (b) _____ with the top down and then forgot to

put it back up again. That night it rained, and the seat was so wet the next day that she has (c) _____ with the top up ever since.

7. Annabella loves buying new things to *wear*. She (a) _____ a different outfit every day of the year. Last year, she never (b) _____ the same clothing twice. She often complains that she gets tired of her clothes long before they're (c) _____ out.

8. My eight-year-old nephew likes to *blow* up balloons. Every year he (a) _____ up several dozen for his parents' New Year's Eve party. Last year, he (b) _____ up fifty balloons, including one in the shape of a Canadian flag. When he tiptoed downstairs at midnight, he was thrilled to see all the guests cheering him for the balloon he had (c) _____ up.

9. Every year, I can't wait for summer vacation to *begin*. As soon as it (a) _____, I can get to work on all the things around the house that I had to ignore during school. This past May, the minute my exams were over, I (b) _____ cleaning out the garage, painting the windowsills, and building a bookcase. I must have (c) _____ half a dozen projects. Unfortunately, it's now Labour Day, and I haven't finished any of them.

10. We always have trouble getting our younger son, Teddy, to stop watching television and *go* to sleep. He never (a) _____ to his room until 10 or 11 p.m. In the past, when he finally (b) _____ upstairs, we did not check on him, since there was no TV set in his room. The night we finally did decide to look in on Teddy, we found him reading *TV Guide* with a flashlight under the covers and told him things had (c) _____ too far.

TROUBLESOME IRREGULAR VERBS

Three common irregular verbs that often give people trouble are *to be*, *to have*, and *to do*. See pages 56–58 for a discussion of these verbs. Three sets of other irregular verbs that can lead to difficulties are *to lie-to lay*, *to sit-to set*, and *to rise-to raise*.

To Lie-To Lay

The principal parts of *to lie* and *to lay* are as follows:

Present Tense	Past Tense	Past Participle
lie	lay	lain
lay	laid	laid

To lie means *to rest* or *recline*. *To lay* means *to put something down*.

To Lie

Tony *lies* on the couch.

This morning he *lay* in the tub.

He has *lain* in bed all week with the flu.

To Lay

I *lay* the mail on the table.

Yesterday I *laid* the mail on the counter.

I have *laid* the mail where everyone will see it.

Practice: Correctly Using *To Lie* and *To Lay*

Underline the correct verb. Use a form of *lie* if you can substitute *recline*. Use a form of *lay* if you can substitute *place*.

1. Maria is the sort of person who (lies, lays) her cards on the table.

2. I am going to (lie, lay) another log on the fire.

3. (Lying, Laying) down for an hour after supper helps Fred regain his energy.

4. I have (lain, laid) all the visitors' coats in the largest bedroom.

5. Frankenstein's creature (lay, laid) on the table, waiting for lightning to recharge his batteries.

To Sit-To Set

The principal parts of *to sit* and *to set* are as follows:

Present Tense	Past Tense	Past Participle
sit	sat	sat
set	set	set

To sit means *to take a seat* or *to rest*. *To set* means *to put* or *to place*.

To Sit	To Set
I *sit* down during work breaks.	Tony *sets* out the knives, forks, and spoons.
I *sat* in the doctor's office for three hours.	His sister already *set* out the dishes.
I have always *sat* in the last desk.	They have just *set* out the dinnerware.

Practice: Correctly Using *To Sit* and *To Set*

Underline the correct form of the verb. Use a form of *to sit* if you can substitute *to rest*. Use a form of *to set* if you can substitute *to place*.

1. During family arguments I try to (sit, set) on the fence instead of taking sides.
2. I walked three blocks before (sitting, setting) down the heavy suitcases.
3. Charlie (sat, set) the grapefruit on the teacher's desk.
4. That poor man has not (sat, set) down once today.
5. You can (sit, set) the laundry basket on top of the washer.

To Rise-To Raise

The principal parts of *to rise* and *to raise* are as follows:

Present Tense	Past Tense	Past Participle
rise	rose	risen
raise	raised	raised

To rise means *to get up* or *to move up*. *To raise* (which is a regular verb with simple *-ed* endings) means *to lift up* or *to increase in amount*.

To Rise	To Raise
The soldiers *rise* at dawn.	I'm going to *raise* the stakes in the card game.
The crowd *rose* to applaud the batter.	I *raised* the shades to let in the sun.
Dracula has *risen* from the grave.	I would have quit if the company had not *raised* my salary.

Practice: Correctly Using *To Rise* and *To Raise*

Underline the correct verb. Use a form of *to rise* if you can substitute *to get up* or *to move up*. Use a form of *to raise* if you can substitute *to lift up* or *to increase*.

1. Even though I can sleep late on Sunday if I want to, I usually (rise, raise) early.

2. Some dealers (rise, raise) rather than lower their prices before a sale.

3. After five days of steady rain, the water in the dam had (risen, raised) to a dangerous level.

4. The building owner (rose, raised) the rent in order to force the tenants out of the apartment.

5. The cost of living (rises, raises) steadily from year to year.

■ Review Test 1

Cross out the incorrect verb form. Then write the correct form of the verb in the space provided.

_____   1. While I was kneading the meat loaf, someone rung the doorbell.

_____   2. My grade one teacher, Ms. Rickstein, teached me the meaning of fear.

_____   3. Crystal brang a sweatshirt, for she knew the mountains got cold at night.

_____   4. We done the grocery shopping on Thursday evening.

_____   5. She had went home early from the dance, for she didn't like any of the people she had seen there.

_____   6. The police officer came with me when I drived home to get my ownership card.

_____   7. The boy next door growed ten centimetres in less than a year.

_____   8. We had gave the building owner notice three times that our plumbing system needed repairs, and each time he failed to respond.

_____   9. I had ate so much food at the buffet that I needed to loosen my belt.

_____   10. Last summer I swum the width of that river and back again.

■ Review Test 2

Write short sentences that use the form requested for the following irregular verbs.

Example   Past tense of *to ride*:   The Lone Ranger rode into the sunset.

1. Past tense of *to break*: _____

2. Past participle of *to bring*: _____

3. Past participle of *to grow*: _____

4. Past tense of *to choose*: _____

5. Present tense of *to do*: _____

6. Past tense of *to drink*: _____

7. Past participle of *to write*: _____

8. Present tense of *to give*: _____

9. Past participle of *to begin*: _____

10. Present tense of *to go*: _____

SUBJECT-VERB AGREEMENT

A verb must agree with its subject in number. A *singular subject* (one person or thing) takes a singular verb. A *plural subject* (more than one person or thing) takes a plural verb. Mistakes in subject-verb agreement are sometimes made in the following situations:

1 When words come between the subject and the verb
2 When a verb comes before the subject
3 With indefinite pronouns
4 With compound subjects
5 With *who*, *which*, and *that*

Each situation is explained on the following pages.

WORDS BETWEEN THE SUBJECT AND THE VERB

Words that come between the subject and the verb do not change subject-verb agreement. In the following sentence,

> The breakfast cereals in the pantry are made mostly of sugar.

the subject (*cereals*) is plural and so the verb (*are*) is plural. The words *in the pantry* that come between the subject and the verb do not affect subject-verb agreement. To help find the subject of certain sentences, you should cross out prepositional phrases (explained on page 13):

> One ~~of the crooked politicians~~ was jailed for a month.
> The posters ~~on my little brother's wall~~ included rock singers, monsters, and action-movie stars.

Following is a list of common prepositions:

about	before	by	inside	over
above	behind	during	into	through
across	below	except	of	to
among	beneath	for	off	toward
around	beside	from	on	under
at	between	in	onto	with

Practice: Finding Subjects and Verbs

Underline the subject and lightly cross out any words that come between the subject and the verb. Then double-underline the verb choice in parentheses that you believe is correct.

Example   The price ~~of the stereo speakers~~ (is, are) too high for my wallet.

1. The blue stain ~~on the sheets~~ (comes, come) from the cheap dish towel that I put in the washer with them.

2. The sports jacket, ~~along with the~~ two pairs of pants, (sells, sell) ~~for just~~ fifty dollars.

3. The roots ~~of the apple tree~~ (is, are) very shallow.

4. Nick's sisters, ~~who wanted to be at his surprise party,~~ (was, were) unable to come because of flooded roads.

5. The dust-covered photo albums ~~in the attic~~ (belongs, belong) to my grandmother.

6. The cost of long-distance calls ~~made on office telephones~~ (is, are) deducted from our pay.

7. Two cups of coffee ~~in the morning~~ (does, do) not make up a hearty breakfast.

8. The moon ~~as well as some stars~~ (is, are) shining brightly tonight.

9. The electrical wiring ~~in the apartment~~ (is, are) dangerous and needs replacing.

10. Chapter Four ~~of the psychology book,~~ along with six weeks of class notes, (is, are) to be the basis of the test.

VERB BEFORE THE SUBJECT

A verb agrees with its subject even when the verb comes *before* the subject. Words that may precede the subject include *there*, *here*, and, in questions, *who*, *which*, *what*, and *where*.

Inside the storage shed are the garden tools.
At the street corner were two homeless persons.
There are times I'm ready to quit my job.
Where are the instructions for the microwave oven?

If you are unsure about the subject, ask *who* or *what* of the verb. With the first sentence above, you might ask, "What are inside the storage shed?" The answer, garden *tools*, is the subject.

Practice: Finding Subjects that Follow Verbs

Underline the subject in each sentence. Then double-underline the correct verb in parentheses.

1. There (is, are) long lines at the check-out counter.
2. Scampering to the door to greet Maria Grimaldi (was, were) her two little dogs.
3. Filling the forest floor (was, were) dozens of pine cones.
4. There (is, are) pretzels in the kitchen if you want something to go with the cheese.
5. At the end of the line, hoping to get seats for the movie, (was, were) Janet and Maureen.
6. There (is, are) rats nesting under the backyard woodpile.
7. Swaggering down the street (was, were) several tough-looking boys.
8. On the very top of that mountain (is, are) a house for sale.
9. At the soap opera convention, there (was, were) fans from all over the country.
10. Under a large plastic dome on the side of the counter (lies, lie) a pile of gooey pastries.

INDEFINITE PRONOUNS

The following words, known as *indefinite pronouns,** always take singular verbs:

(-one words)	(-body words)	(-thing words)	
one	nobody	nothing	each
anyone	anybody	anything	either
everyone	everybody	everything	neither
someone	somebody	something	

Note: *Both* always takes a plural verb.

Indefinite pronouns refer to groups of things or people where the writer cannot, or does not, wish to specify the individual objects or people. The words *group* and *number* are *nouns*, but follow the same rule; they take singular verbs.

Practice: Choosing Correct Verb Forms

Write the correct form of the verb in the space provided.

ignores, ignore

1. Everyone in the neighbourhood _____ Charlie Brown.

dances, dance

2. Nobody _____ the way he does.

deserves, deserve

3. Either of our hockey team's forwards _____ to be a Junior "A" player.

was, were

4. Both of the race drivers _____ injured.

appears, appear

5. Everyone who received an invitation _____ to be here.

offers, offer

6. No one ever _____ to work on that committee.

owns, own

7. One of my sisters _____ a VW convertible.

has, have

8. Somebody _____ been taking shopping carts from the supermarket.

thinks, think

9. Everyone that I talked to _____ the curfew is a good idea.

has, have

10. Each of the candidates _____ talked about withdrawing from the race.

COMPOUND SUBJECTS

Subjects joined by *and* generally take a plural verb.

Yoga and biking are Crystal's ways of staying in shape.
Ambition and good luck are the keys to his success.

When subjects are joined by *or, either ... or, neither ... nor, not only ... but also,* the verb agrees with the subject closer to the verb.

Either the restaurant manager or his assistants deserve to be fired for the spoiled meat used in the stew.

The nearer subject, *assistants*, is plural, and so the verb is plural.

Practice: Choosing Verb Forms with Compound Subjects

Write the correct form of the verb in the space provided.

matches,
match
1. This tie and shirt _____ the suit, but the shoes look terrible.

has, have
2. The kitchen and the bathroom _____ to be cleaned.

is, are
3. A good starting salary and a bonus system _____ the most attractive features of my new job.

plan, plans
4. Neither Ellen nor her brothers _____ to work at a temporary job during their holiday break from college.

is, are
5. For better or worse, working on his van and playing video games _____ Pete's main interests in life.

WHO, WHICH, AND THAT

When *who*, *which*, and *that* are used as subjects, they take singular verbs if the word they stand for is singular and plural verbs if the word they stand for is plural. For example, in the sentence

Gary is one of those people <u>who</u> <u>are</u> very private.

the verb is plural because *who* stands for *people*, which is plural. On the other hand, in the sentence

Gary is a person <u>who</u> <u>is</u> very private.

the verb is singular because *who* stands for *person*, which is singular.

Practice: Choosing Correct Verbs with Relative Pronouns

Write the correct form of the verb in the space provided.

was, were
1. I removed the sheets that _____ jamming my washer.

stumbles,
stumble
2. This job isn't for people who _____ over tough decisions.

blares,
blare
3. The radio that _____ all night belongs to my insomniac neighbour.

gives, give
4. The Geo is one of the small North American cars that _____ very high gasoline mileage.

appears,
appear
5. The strange smell that _____ in our neighbourhood on rainy days is being investigated.

■ Review Test 1

In the following sentences, underline the subject. Then complete each sentence using *is*, *are*, *was*, *were*, *have*, or *has*.

Example   The <u>hot dogs</u> in that fast-food spot <u>*are hazardous to your health.*</u>

1. Neither of the songs _____

2. The new provincial tax on alcohol and cigarettes _____

_____

3. The shadowy figure behind the cemetery walls _____

_____

4. The movie actor and her agent _____

5. Larry is one of those people who _____

6. The football coach, along with ten of his assistants, _____

_____

7. Coming up the back alley _____

8. Someone sitting behind the goalie's crease at the rink _____

_____

9. The first several weeks that I spent in college _____

10. Tony's gentle voice and pleasant smile _____

■ Review Test 2

Underline the correct word in the parentheses.

1. Excessive use of alcohol, caffeine, or cigarettes (damages, damage) a mother's unborn child.

2. Neither of the newspaper articles (gives, give) all the facts of the murder case.

3. There (is, are) five formulas that we have to memorize for the test.

4. The rug and the wallpaper in that room (has, have) to be replaced.

5. The old man standing under the park trees (does, do) not look happy.

6. The scratch on the CD (was, were) there when I bought it.

7. Heavy snows and months of subfreezing temperatures in Winnipeg (is, are) two reasons why I moved to Florida.

8. I don't enjoy persons who (likes, like) to play pranks.

9. The price of the set of dishes you like so much (is, are) $345.

10. What time in the morning (does, do) planes leave for Saskatoon?

■ Review Test 3

There are eight mistakes in subject-verb agreement in the following passage. Cross out each incorrect verb and write the correct form above it. In addition, underline the subject of each of the verbs that must be changed. The first sentence has been corrected for you.

There are several <u>things</u> that ~~makes~~ *make* Tracy want to quit her job as a server. First of all, she is never permitted to sit down. Even when there is no customers seated at her tables, she must find something useful to do, such as folding napkins or refilling ketchup bottles. By the end of the night, her feet feel like two chunks of raw hamburger. Secondly, she finds it difficult to be cheerful all of the time, one of the qualities which is expected of her. People who go out to eat in a restaurant wants to enjoy themselves, and they don't like their spirits dampened by a grouchy server. This means that when Tracy feels sick or depressed, she can't let her feelings show. Instead, she has to pretend that the occasion is as pleasant for her as it is for her customers, night after night. Neither of these problems, however, bother her as much as people who are fussy. <u>Both the child who demands</u> ~~extra fudge sauce on her ice cream and the adult who asks for cleaner silverware~~ <u>silverware</u> has to be satisfied. In addition, each night at least one of the customers at her tables insist on being a perfectionist. As Tracy learned her first day on the job, the customer is always right—even if the person complains that the peas have too many wrinkles. Though she may feel like dumping the peas in the customer's lap, Tracy must pretend that each of her customers are royalty and hurry to find some less wrinkled peas. Sometimes she wishes people would just stay home and eat.

CONSISTENT
VERB TENSE

KEEPING TENSES CONSISTENT

Do not shift tenses unnecessarily. If you begin writing a paper in the present tense, don't shift suddenly to the past. If you begin in the past, don't shift without reason to the present. Notice the inconsistent verb tenses in the following selection:

> Smoke <u>spilled</u> from the front of the overheated car. The driver <u>opens</u> up the hood, then <u>jumped</u> back as steam <u>billows</u> out.

The verbs must be consistently in the **present tense**:

> Smoke <u>spills</u> from the front of the overheated car. The driver <u>opens</u> up the hood, then <u>jumps</u> back as steam <u>billows</u> out.

Or the verbs must be consistently in the **past tense**:

> Smoke <u>spilled</u> from the front of the overheated car. The driver <u>opened</u> up the hood, then <u>jumped</u> back as steam <u>billowed</u> out.

Practice: Maintaining Consistent Verb Tense

In each selection one verb must be changed so that it agrees in tense with the other verbs. Cross out the incorrect verb and write the correct form in the space at the left.

looked

Example   I gave away my striped sweater after three people told me I ~~look~~ like a giant bee.

Cause's

1. Mike peels and eats pickled eggs at movies; the smell ~~caused~~ other people to move away from him.

decided

2. The nursing program attracted Lorne, but he weighed the pluses and minuses and then decides to enrol in the X-ray technician course instead.

_____

3. I grabbed for the last bag of pretzels on the supermarket shelf. But when I pick it up, I discovered there was a tear in the cellophane bag.

_____

4. Claire waits eagerly for the mail carrier each day. Part of her hoped to get a letter in which someone declares he is madly in love with her and will cherish her forever.

_____

5. The first thing Jerry does every day is weigh himself. The scale informed him what he can eat that day.

_____

6. My sister sprinkles detergent flakes on my head and then ran around telling everyone that I had dandruff.

_____

7. When André peeled back the old shingles, he discovers the roof was rotted through.

_____ 8. My father knocked on the bedroom door. When he asks me if he could come in, I said, "Not right now."

_____ 9. Fred is so unaggressive that when a clerk overcharged him for an item, he pays the money and makes no comment.

_____ 10. When my doctor told me I needed an operation, I swallow hard and my stomach churned.

■ Review Test 1

Change verbs where needed in the following selection so that they are consistently in the past tense. Cross out each incorrect verb and write the correct form above it, as shown in the example. You will need to make nine corrections.

Last week, I began driving to work, as usual. I drove up the expressway

ramp and ~~merge~~ *merged* into three lanes of speeding cars on the Trans Canada

Highway. I turned on the radio and settle *settled* in for another twenty-five minutes

of tension and pressure. Then, about ten kilometres on, I saw something

5   unusual. Up ahead, stranded on the narrow concrete island that separated

three lanes of eastbound traffic from three lanes of westbound traffic, was

a small brown dog. Streams of zooming cars pass *ed* the animal like two

rushing rivers. Several times, the dog attempt *ed* to cross the road. He move *ed* *d*

gingerly onto the highway, only to jump back at the approach of a car. I

10 realize *d* it was only a matter of time before the panicky dog bolt *ed* into the

traffic and kill *ed* itself. I didn't know what to do. I slow *ed* my car down a little

and wondered if I should pull onto the shoulder. Then, I heard a welcome

sound—a police siren. Someone must have called the Provincial Police about

the dog. In my rearview mirror, I saw the patrol car and a white van

15 labelled "Animal Control." I drove on, confident that the dog would be

rescue and relieve *d* that someone had cared enough to save its small life.

■ Review Test 2

Change verbs where needed in the following selection so that they are consistently in the past tense. Cross out each incorrect verb and then write the correct form in the space provided. You will need to make ten corrections in all. The first example has been done for you.

The first time I tried to parallel park on my own was a memorable experience. My first mistake was trying to move into the parking place hood first. I got the car's front end close to the curb, but the rear end ~~remains~~ out in the street. I then backed out and pull up beside the car in
5 front of the parking place. This is where I make my second mistake. Because I was worried that someone might steal my place, I fail to pull up enough alongside the car. So when I backed in, my rear wheels are against the curb while the car's hood was out in the street blocking traffic. I then had to pull out, and I attempt to park once more. As I backed in the second
10 time, I remember my driving-school instructor's advice. She trained me not to turn the wheels in until the steering wheel of my car is even with the rear bumper of the car in front of the parking place. I did this and the car slips neatly into the space, with only a few centimetres left between the tires and the curb. As I was congratulating myself on my success, the car
15 behind me pulls out, leaving a parking space big enough for a Mack truck.

1. _remained_
2. _Pulled_
3. _Made_
4. _Failed_
5. _attempted_

6. _Were_
7. _Slipped_
8. _pulled_
9. _She'd_
10. _was_

ADDITIONAL INFORMATION ABOUT VERBS

The purpose of this special chapter is to provide additional information about verbs. Some people will find the grammar terms here a helpful reminder of earlier school learning about verbs. For them, the terms will increase their understanding of how verbs function in English. Other people may welcome more detailed information about terms used elsewhere in the text. In either case, remember that the most common mistakes that people make when writing verbs have been treated in earlier sections of the book.

VERB TENSE

Verbs tell us the time of an action. The time that a verb shows is usually called *tense*. The most common tenses are the simple present, past, and future. In addition, there are nine other tenses that enable us to express more specific ideas about time than we could with the simple tenses alone. Shown on the next page are the twelve verb tenses and examples of each tense. Read them over to increase your sense of the many different ways of expressing time in English.

TENSES	*EXAMPLES*
Present	I *work*. Jill *works*.
Past	Simon *worked* on the lawn.
Future	You *will work* overtime this week.
Present perfect	Gail *has worked* hard on the puzzle. They *have worked* well together.
Past perfect	They *had finished* the work before their shift ended.
Future perfect	The volunteers *will have worked* many unpaid hours.

PROGRESSIVE FORMS OF VERB TENSES

Present progressive	I *am* not *working* today. You *are working* the second shift. The clothes dryer *is* not *working* properly.
Past progressive	She *was working* outside. The plumbers *were working* here this morning.
Future progressive	The sound system *will be working* by tonight.
Present perfect progressive	Married life *has* not *been working* out for that couple.
Past perfect progressive	I *had been working* overtime until recently.
Future perfect progressive	My sister *will have been working* at that store for eleven straight months by the time she takes a vacation next week.

The perfect tenses are formed by adding *have*, *has*, or *had* to the past participle (the form of the verb that ends, usually, in *-ed*). The progressive tenses are formed by adding *am*, *is*, *are*, *was*, or *were* to the present participle (the form of the verb that ends in *-ing*). The perfect progressive tenses are formed by adding *have*, *has*, or *had* plus *been* to the present participle.

Certain tenses are explained in more detail on the following pages.

Present Perfect Tense (*have* or *has* + past participle)

The present perfect tense expresses an action that began in the past and has recently been completed or is continuing in the present.

The city has just agreed on a contract with the sanitation workers.
Tony's parents have lived in that house for twenty years.
Crystal has watched *Star Trek* reruns since she was a little girl.

Past Perfect Tense (*had* + past participle)

The past perfect tense expresses a past action that was completed before another past action.

Crystal had learned to dance by the time she was five.
The class had just started when the fire bell rang.
Bad weather had never been a problem on our vacations until last year.

Present Progressive Tense (*am*, *is*, or *are* + the *-ing* form)

The present progressive tense expresses an action still in progress.

I am taking an early train into the city every day this week.
Karl is playing lacrosse over at the field.
The vegetables are growing rapidly.

Past Progressive Tense (*was* or *were* + the *-ing* form)

The past progressive expresses an action that was in progress in the past.

I was spending twenty dollars a week on cigarettes before I quit.
Last week, the store was selling many items at half price.
My friends were driving over to pick me up when the accident occurred.

Practice: Using Verb Tenses Correctly

For the sentences that follow, fill in the present tense or past perfect tense or the present progressive tense or past progressive tense of the verb shown. Use the tense that seems to express the meaning of each sentence best.

Example   **park**   This summer, Mike ___is parking___ cars at a French restaurant.

walk   1. We _____ for three kilometres before we realized we were lost.

feel   2. The new mail carrier _____ good about her job until the first dog bit her.

place   3. After an hour, the server _____ only a basket of stale rolls on our table.

try   4. All last winter, my little brother _____ to get a job carrying groceries at the supermarket.

grow   5. This year, Aunt Agatha _____ tomatoes—she must have about five hundred already.

look   6. I _____ everywhere for the paper; finally I found it under the cat.

study   7. Miriam _____ French for three years so she can talk to her poodle.

see   8. James loves karate; he _____ every Jackie Chan movie in existence.

watch   9. Naheed _____ soap operas for four hours a day in the two months she was unemployed.

throw   10. The pitcher _____ to second; unfortunately, the runner was on third.

VERBALS

Verbals are words formed from verbs. Verbals, like verbs, often express action. They can add variety to your sentences and vigour to your writing style. The three kinds of verbals are *infinitives*, *participles*, and *gerunds*.

Infinitive

An infinitive is *to* plus the base form of the verb.

I started *to practise*.
Don't try *to lift* that table.
I asked Russ *to drive* me home.

Participle

A participle is a verb form used as an adjective (a descriptive word). The present participle ends in *-ing*. The past participle ends in *-ed* or has an irregular ending, such as *n*.

> *Favouring* his *cramped* leg, the *screaming* boy waded out of the pool.
> The *laughing* child held up her *locked* piggy bank.
> *Using* a shovel and a bucket, I scooped water out of the *flooded* basement.

Gerund

A gerund is the *-ing* form of a verb used as a noun.

> *Studying* wears me out.
> *Playing* basketball is my main pleasure during the week.
> Through *jogging*, you can get yourself in shape.

Practice: Identifying Verbals

In the space beside each sentence, identify the italicized word as a participle (*P*), an infinitive (*I*), or a gerund (*G*).

_____   1. The *sobbing* child could not find his parents.

_____   2. *Gossiping* with neighbours is my favourite pastime.

_____   3. *Painting* the front porch is a chore Fred promises to get to every spring.

_____   4. All my brother ever wants *to do* is watch music videos.

_____   5. Crystal always liked *to race* through a pile of dead leaves.

_____   6. My boss's *greying* hair gives him a look of authority.

_____   7. *Glowing* embers were all that remained of the fire.

_____   8. It doesn't matter if you win or lose—just try *to break* even.

_____   9. *Holding* her nose, my mother asked, "What's that awful smell?"

_____   10. People think *smoking* a pipe makes a man look sophisticated.

ACTIVE AND PASSIVE VERBS

When the subject of a sentence *performs the action of a verb*, the verb is in the *active voice*. When the subject of a sentence *receives the action of a verb*, the verb is in the *passive voice*.

The passive form of a verb consists of a form of the verb *to be* plus the past participle of the main verb. Look at the active and passive forms of the verbs below.

Active	*Passive*
Crystal *ate* the vanilla pudding. (The subject, *Crystal*, is the doer of the action.)	The vanilla pudding *was eaten by* Crystal. (The subject, *pudding*, does not act. Instead, something happens to it.)
The plumber *replaced* the hot-water heater. (The subject, *plumber*, is the doer of the action.)	The hot-water heater *was replaced by* the plumber. (The subject, *heater*, does not act. Instead, something happens to it.)

In general, active verbs are more effective than passive ones. Active verbs give your writing a simpler and more vigorous style. The passive form of verbs is appropriate, however, when the performer of the action is unknown or is less important than the receiver of the action. For example:

My house was vandalized last night.
(The performer of the action is unknown.)

Mark was seriously injured as a result of your negligence.
(The receiver of the action, *Mark*, is being emphasized.)

Practice: Using the Passive and Active Voices

Change the following sentences from the passive to the active voice. Note that you may have to add a subject in some cases.

Examples The moped was ridden by Tony.
Tony rode the moped.

The basketball team was given a standing ovation.
The crowd gave the basketball team a standing ovation.
(Here a subject had to be added.)

1. The surprise party was organized by Angela.

2. Many people were offended by the comedian.

3. The old woman's groceries are paid for by the neighbours.

4. The horse chestnuts were knocked off the trees by the boys.

_____

5. The devil was driven out of Regan by the exorcist.

_____

6. The huge moving van was loaded by four perspiring workers.

_____

7. A tray of glasses was dropped by the inexperienced server.

_____

8. Umbrellas are always being lost by my forgetful Aunt Agatha.

_____

9. Gordie Howe's NHL goal-scoring record was finally broken by Wayne Gretzky.

_____

10. A bomb was found in the suitcase by the airport security staff.

_____

■ Review Test

On a separate sheet of paper, write three sentences apiece that use:

1. Present perfect tense
2. Past perfect tense
3. Present progressive tense
4. Past progressive tense
5. Infinitive
6. Participle
7. Gerund
8. Passive voice (when the subject is unknown or is less important than the receiver of an action—see pages 88–89)

PRONOUN REFERENCE, AGREEMENT, AND POINT OF VIEW

Pronouns are words that take the place of nouns (persons, places, ideas, or things). In fact, the word *pronoun* means *for a noun*. Pronouns are short cuts that keep you from unnecessarily repeating words in writing. Here are some examples of pronouns:

> Maria shampooed *her* dog. (*Her* is a pronoun that takes the place of *Maria*.)
>
> As the door swung open, *it* creaked. (*It* replaces *door*.)
>
> When the motorcyclists arrived at Harvey's, *they* removed *their* helmets. (*They* and *their* replace *motorcyclists*.)

This section presents rules that will help you avoid three common mistakes people make with pronouns. The rules are as follows:

1 A pronoun must refer clearly to the word it replaces.

2 A pronoun must agree in number with the word or words it replaces.

3 Pronouns should not shift unnecessarily in point of view.

PRONOUN REFERENCE

A sentence may be confusing and unclear if a pronoun appears to refer to more than one word or if the pronoun does not refer to any specific word. Look at this sentence:

> Our family never buys fresh vegetables at that store because they charge too much.

Who charges too much? There is no specific word that *they* refers to. Be clear:

> Our family never buys fresh vegetables at that store because the owners charge too much.

Here are sentences with other kinds of faulty pronoun reference. Read the explanations of why they are faulty and look carefully at the ways they are corrected.

Faulty	*Clear*
Crystal told Gina that she had gained weight. (*Who* had gained weight: Crystal or Gina? Be clear.)	Crystal told Gina, "You've gained weight." (Quotation marks, which can sometimes be used to correct an unclear reference, are explained on page 173.)

Faulty	***Clear***
My older brother is an electrician, but I'm not interested in it.	My older brother is an electrician, but I'm not interested in becoming one.
(There is no specific word that *it* refers to. It would not make sense to say, "I'm not interested in electrician.")	
Our teacher did not explain the assignment, which made me angry.	I was angry that the teacher did not explain the assignment.
(Does *which* mean that the teacher's failure to explain the assignment made you angry or that the assignment itself made you angry? Be clear.)	

Practice: Clarifying Pronoun References

Rewrite each of the following sentences to make clear the vague pronoun reference. Add, change, or omit words as necessary.

Example   Lana thanked Naheed for the gift, which was very thoughtful of her.

Lana thanked Naheed for the thoughtful gift.

1. Mario insisted to Harry that it was his turn to drive.

_____

_____

2. I failed two of my courses last semester because they graded unfairly.

_____

_____

3. Don was offered an accounting job which pleased his parents very much.

_____

_____

4. When Tony questioned the mechanic, he became very upset.

_____

_____

5. I was very nervous about the biology exam, which was unexpected.

_____

_____

6. Paul told his younger brother that the dog had chewed his new running shoes.

_____

_____

7. My cousin is an astrologer, but I don't believe in it.

_____

_____

8. Liz told Elaine that she had been promoted.

_____

_____

9. Whenever I start enjoying a new television show, they take it off the air.

_____

_____

10. When the centre fielder heard the crack of the bat, he raced toward the fence but was unable to catch it.

_____

_____

PRONOUN AGREEMENT

A pronoun must agree in *number* with the word or words it replaces. If the word a pronoun refers to is *singular*, the pronoun must be *singular*; if the word is *plural*, the pronoun must be *plural*. (Note that the word a pronoun refers to is known as the *antecedent*.)

Crystal agreed to lend me (her) Celine Dion albums.

The gravediggers sipped coffee during (their) break.

In the first example, the pronoun *her* refers to the singular word *Crystal*; in the second example, the pronoun *their* refers to the plural word *gravediggers*.

Practice: Choosing Pronouns in Agreement with Antecedents

Write the appropriate pronoun (*they, their, them, it*) in the blank space in each of the following sentences.

Example   My credit cards got me into debt, so I burned _____*them*_____.

1. After the hikers arrived at the camp, _____ removed _____ heavy packs.

2. That breakfast cereal is delicious, but _____ has almost no nutrients.

3. I never miss my favourite television shows any more, for I use a VCR to tape _____.

4. The heat was so oppressive during the race that _____ caused several runners to pass out.

5. Lisa's parents went to a marriage counsellor, and _____ are getting along better now.

Indefinite Pronouns

The following words, known as *indefinite pronouns*,* are always singular.

(-*one* words)	(-*body* words)	
one	nobody	each
anyone	anybody	either
everyone	everybody	neither
someone	somebody	

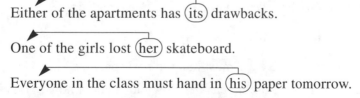

Either of the apartments has (its) drawbacks.

One of the girls lost (her) skateboard.

Everyone in the class must hand in (his) paper tomorrow.

In each example, the pronoun is singular because it refers to one of the indefinite pronouns. There are two important points to remember about indefinite pronouns.

---

* Indefinite pronouns do not name people described by the writer. They identify individuals or groups in a non-specific way.

Point 1:   In the last example above, if the members of the class were all female, the pronoun would be *her*. If the students were a mixed group of men and women, the pronoun form would be *his or her:*

Everyone in the class must hand in *his or her* paper tomorrow.

Some writers follow the traditional practice of using *his* to refer to both men and women. Some use *his or her* to avoid an implied sexual bias. Perhaps the best practice, though, is to avoid using either *his* or the somewhat awkward *his or her*. This can be done by rewriting a sentence **in the plural**:

All students in the class must hand in their papers tomorrow.

Here are some examples of sentences that can be rewritten in the plural.

A young child is seldom willing to share her toys with others.
Young children are seldom willing to share their toys with others.

Anyone who does not wear his seat belt will be fined.
People who do not wear their seat belts will be fined.

A newly elected politician should not forget his or her campaign promises.
Newly elected politicians should not forget their campaign promises.

Point 2:   In informal spoken English, *plural* pronouns are often used with the indefinite pronouns. Instead of saying

Everybody has *his or her* own idea of an ideal vacation.

we are likely to say

Everybody has *their* own idea of an ideal vacation.

Here are other examples:

Everyone in the class must hand in *their* papers.
Everybody in our club has *their* own idea about how to raise money.
No one in our family skips *their* chores.

In such cases, the indefinite pronouns are clearly plural in meaning. Also, the use of such plurals helps people to avoid the awkward *his or her*. In time, the plural pronoun may be accepted in formal speech or writing. Until that happens, however, you should use the grammatically correct singular form in your writing.

Practice: Choosing Correct Pronouns

Underline the correct pronoun.

Example   Neither of those houses has (<u>its</u>, their) own garage.

1. Neither of the boys brought (his, their) homework in today.
2. Each server is responsible for (his or her, their) own section.
3. It seems as though no one in my fraternity wants to pay (his, their) dues these days.
4. None of the boys remembered to bring (his, their) radio.
5. Each of my sisters has (her, their) own room.
6. Any man who purchased one of those ill-made suits probably wasted (his, their) money.
7. Almost every woman on our street leaves for (her, their) job about the same time each morning.
8. Before a discussion in our women's club, each member must decide on one question that (she, they) wants to ask.
9. Either of the travel routes has (their, its) share of places to see.
10. Any player on the men's team who gains weight is in danger of losing (his, their) job.

PRONOUN POINT OF VIEW

Pronouns should not shift their point of view unnecessarily. When writing a paper, be consistent in your use of first-, second-, or third-person pronouns.

Type of Pronoun	*Singular*	*Plural*
First-person pronouns	I (my, mine, me)	we (our, us)
Second-person pronouns	you (your)	you (your)
Third-person pronouns	he (his, him)	they (their, them)
	she (her)	
	it (its)	

Note: Any person, place, or thing, as well as any indefinite pronoun like *one, anyone, someone,* and so on (page 95), is a third-person word.

For instance, if you start writing in the first person *I*, don't jump suddenly to the second person *you*. Or if you are writing in the third person *they*, don't shift unexpectedly to *you*. Look at the examples.

Inconsistent	*Consistent*
One reason that *I* like living in the city is that *you* always have a wide choice of sports events to attend. (The most common mistake people make is to let a *you* slip into their writing after they start with another pronoun.)	One reason that *I* like living in the city is that *I* always have a wide choice of sports events to attend.
Someone dieting should have the help of friends; *you* should also have plenty of willpower.	*Someone* dieting should have the help of friends; *he or she* should also have plenty of willpower.
Students who work while *they* are going to school face special problems. For one thing, *you* seldom have enough study time.	Students who work while *they* are going to school face special problems. For one thing, *they* seldom have enough study time.

Practice: Choosing Consistent Pronouns

Cross out inconsistent pronouns in the following sentences and write the correction above the error.

Example   I work much better when the boss doesn't hover over ~~you~~ *me* with instructions on what to do.

1. What I don't like about eating vegetarian food is that you always feel hungry an hour later.

2. Students may not leave the exam room unless you have finished the exam.

3. These days people never seem to get the recognition they deserve, no matter how hard you work.

4. If our pets could talk, we would find it easier to take care of them. As it is, you can never be sure what a pet means by a bark or a meow.

5. Whenever a woman feels she is being discriminated against, you should register a complaint.

6. If a person plans to make a complaint, you should check all the facts first.

7. I work at a shop where you do not get paid for all the holidays you should.

8. If you think you're coming down with cold symptoms, one should take action right away.

9. Once we were at the campsite, you had only a radio as contact with the outside world.

10. In our office, we can have a long coffee break anytime you want it.

■ Review Test 1

Underline the correct word in the parentheses.

1. When the moon and stars come out, (it, the night) is beautiful.
2. If a person drives defensively, (he, they) will be constantly aware of other drivers' actions on the road.
3. Hitting the wall with her skateboard, she chipped (it, the skateboard).
4. Persons wanting old furniture should check the newspaper classified section; also, (they, you) might stop at yard sales.
5. We drove for hours and (we, you) got scared by the heavy fog.
6. Larry is the kind of player that always gives (his, their) best for the team.
7. Although we had a delightful vacation, (you, we) are always glad to get home.
8. I've always loved butterfly exhibits, so I decided to start collecting (them, butterflies).
9. When Sally asked why she was being given a ticket, (he, the officer) said she ran a stop sign.
10. I buy my clothes at the outlet store because (it has, they have) the best prices.

■ Review Test 2

Cross out the pronoun error in each sentence and write the correction in the space provided at the left. Then circle the letter that correctly describes the type of error that was made.

Examples ___People___ ~~Anyone~~ turning in their papers late will be penalized.

Mistake in: a. pronoun reference (b.) pronoun agreement

___Gabriel___ When Damian takes his son Gabriel to the park, ~~he~~ enjoys himself.

Mistake in: (a.) pronoun reference b. pronoun point of view _____we_____ From where we stood, ~~you~~ could see three Great Lakes.

Mistake in: a. pronoun agreement ⓑ pronoun point of view

_____ 1. After throwing the dog a stick, I took it home.

Mistake in: a. pronoun reference b. pronoun agreement

_____ 2. Everyone on the women's team was in the locker room packing their travel bag.

Mistake in: a. pronoun agreement b. pronoun point of view

_____ 3. Jesse walks the dog so he won't get fat.

Mistake in: a. pronoun reference b. pronoun point of view

_____ 4. One of the children forgot to put on their rubber boots.

Mistake in: a. pronoun agreement b. pronoun point of view

_____ 5. I've been taking allergy pills, and now it doesn't bother me as much.

Mistake in: a. pronoun reference b. pronoun agreement

_____ 6. When people face a common problem, your personal relationship often becomes stronger.

Mistake in: a. pronoun agreement b. pronoun point of view

_____ 7. Everyone who was at the dance has their own memories of the sudden fire.

Mistake in: a. pronoun reference b. pronoun agreement

Hint: You may want to rewrite item *7* in the plural, using the lines below.

_____

_____

_____ 8. Sometimes our teacher has Theo write on the board because chalk dust makes him sneeze.

Mistake in: a. pronoun reference b. pronoun point of view

_____ 9. Even though I closed the bedroom door, you could still hear the television downstairs.

Mistake in: a. pronoun agreement b. pronoun point of view

_____ 10. If a person walks through those woods, you will see at least ten kinds of nesting birds.

Mistake in: a. pronoun agreement   b. pronoun point of view

Hint: Rewrite item *10* in the plural, using the lines below.

_____

_____

PRONOUN TYPES

INTRODUCTORY PROJECT

In each pair, put a check mark beside the sentence that you think uses pronouns correctly.

Andy and *I* enrolled in a computer course. _____

Andy and *me* enrolled in a computer course. _____

The police officer pointed to my sister and *me*. _____

The police officer pointed to my sister and *I*. _____

Crystal prefers men *whom* take pride in their bodies. _____

Crystal prefers men *who* take pride in their bodies. _____

The players are confident that the league championship is *theirs'*.
_____

The players are confident that the league championship is *theirs*.
_____

Them concert tickets are too expensive. _____

Those concert tickets are too expensive. _____

Our parents should spend some money on *themself* for a change.
_____

Our parents should spend some money on *themselves* for a change.
_____

Answers are on page 480.

This section describes some common types of pronouns: subject and object pronouns, possessive pronouns, demonstrative pronouns, and reflexive pronouns.

SUBJECT AND OBJECT PRONOUNS

Pronouns change their form depending upon the place that they occupy in a sentence. Here is a list of subject and object pronouns:

Subject Pronouns	Object Pronouns
I	me
you	you (no change)
he	him
she	her
it	it (no change)
we	us
they	them

Subject Pronouns

The subject pronouns are subjects of verbs.

> *They* are getting tired. (*They* is the subject of the verb *are getting*.)
> *She* will decide tomorrow. (*She* is the subject of the verb *will decide*.)
> *We* women organized the game. (*We* is the subject of the verb *organized*.)

Several rules for using subject pronouns, and mistakes people sometimes make, are explained starting below.

Rule 1: Use a subject pronoun in a sentence with a compound (more than one) subject.

Incorrect	Correct
Ali and *me* went shopping yesterday.	Ali and *I* went shopping yesterday.
Him and *me* spent lots of money.	*He* and *I* spent lots of money.

If you are not sure what pronoun to use, try each pronoun by itself in the sentence. The correct pronoun will be the one that sounds right. For example, "*Me* went shopping yesterday" does not sound right; "*I* went shopping yesterday" does.

Rule 2:   Use a **subject pronoun** after forms of the linking verb *to be*. Forms of *to be* include *am, are, is, was, were, has been, have been*, and others.

> It was *I* who telephoned.
>
> It may be *they* at the door.
>
> It is *she*.

The sentences above may sound strange and stilted to you since they are seldom used in conversation. When we speak with one another, forms such as "It was me," "It may be them," and "It is her" are widely accepted. In formal writing, however, the grammatically correct forms are still preferred. You can avoid having to use the pronoun form after *be* simply by rewording a sentence. Here is how the preceding examples could be reworded:

> *I* was the one who telephoned.
>
> *They* may be at the door.
>
> *She* is here.

Rule 3:   Use **subject pronouns** after *than* or *as* when a verb is understood after the pronoun.

> You read faster than I (read). (The verb *read* is understood after *I*.)
>
> Tom is as stubborn as I (am). (The verb *am* is understood after *I*.)
>
> We don't go out as much as they (do). (The verb *do* is understood after *they*.)

Notes

a   Avoid mistakes by simply adding the "missing" verb at the end of the sentence.

b   Use **object pronouns** after *than* or *as* when a verb is not understood after the pronoun.

> The law applies to you as well as to me.
>
> Our boss paid Monica more than me.

Object Pronouns

The object pronouns* (*me*, *him*, *her*, *us*, *them*) are the objects of verbs or prepositions. (Prepositions are connecting words like *for*, *at*, *about*, *to*, *before*, *by*, *with*, and *of*. See also page 13.)

> Naheed chose *me*. (*Me* is the object of the verb *chose*.)
> We met *them* at the ballpark. (*Them* is the object of the verb *met*.)
> Don't mention UFOs to *us*. (*Us* is the object of the preposition *to*.)
> I live near *her*. (*Her* is the object of the preposition *near*.)

People are sometimes uncertain about what pronoun to use when two objects follow the verb.

Incorrect	*Correct*
I spoke to George and *he*.	I spoke to George and *him*.
She pointed at Linda and *I*.	She pointed at Linda and *me*.

Hint: If you are not sure what pronoun to use, try each pronoun by itself in the sentence. The correct pronoun will be the one that sounds right. For example, "I spoke to he" doesn't sound right; "I spoke to him" does.

Practice 1: Finding Subject and Object Forms of Pronouns

Underline the correct subject or object pronoun in each of the following sentences. Then show whether your answer is a subject or an object pronoun by circling the *S* or *O* in the margin. The first one is done for you as an example.

S (*O*) 1. I left the decision to (her, she).

S *O* 2. My sister and (I, me) decided to combine funds to buy our parents' Christmas present.

S *O* 3. He arrived sooner than (they, them).

S *O* 4. Give more spaghetti to Tranh and (her, she).

S *O* 5. Natalie and (she, her) gave the car an oil change.

S *O* 6. The two people failed for cheating on the test were Mary and (he, him).

S *O* 7. (She, Her) and Barbara are jealous of my success.

* An *object* receives the action of a verb, so long as that verb is not a *linking verb,* or a verb of *appearance* or *becoming* (*to seem, to appear*).

S O 8. (We, Us) fellows decided to organize a football game.

S O 9. I don't feel he is a better volleyball player than (me, I).

S O 10. (Her, She) and (I, me) are not talking to each other.

Practice 2: Choosing Subject or Object Pronouns

Write in a subject or an object pronoun that fits in the space provided. Use as many different pronouns as possible. The first one is done for you as an example.

1. Crystal ran after Sue and _____*me*_____ to return the suntan lotion she had borrowed.

2. Mr. Spud, our football coach, asked Gary and _____ to play on both offence and defence.

3. Pull the map out of the glove compartment and give it to _____.

4. The bowling team presented _____ with a bronze trophy.

5. The teacher caught Theo and _____ whispering together during the exam.

6. No one was dressed up as much as _____ was.

7. My sister and _____ decided to care for the stray puppy.

8. I'm tired of _____ and their polite artificial smiles.

9. The neighbours' party was organized by _____ and our neighbours.

10. My uncle entertained _____ kids with his Leslie Nielsen imitation.

RELATIVE PRONOUNS

Relative pronouns do two things at once. First, they refer to, or *relate to*, someone or something already mentioned in the sentence. Second, they start a short word group that gives additional information about this someone or something. Here is a list of relative pronouns, followed by some example sentences:

who	which
whose	that
whom	

The only friend *who* really understands me is moving away.

The child *whom* Ben and Ayesha adopted is from Somalia.

Chocolate, *which* is my favourite food, upsets my stomach.

I guessed at half the questions *that* were on the test.

In the example sentences, *who* refers to *friend*, *whom* refers to *child*, *which* refers to *chocolate*, and *that* refers to *questions*. In addition, each of these relative pronouns begins a group of words that describes the person or thing being referred to. For example, the words *whom Ben and Ayesha adopted* tell which child the sentence is about, and the words *which is my favourite food* give added information about chocolate.

Points to Remember about Relative Pronouns

Point 1:   *Whose* means *belonging to whom*. Be careful not to confuse *whose* with *who's*, which means *who is*.

Point 2:   *Who*, *whose*, and *whom* all refer to people. *Which* refers to *things*. *That* can refer to either people or things.

I don't know *whose* book this is.

Don't sit on the chair *which* is broken.

Let's elect a captain *that* cares about winning.

Point 3:   *Who*, *whose*, *whom*, and *which* can also be used to ask questions. When they are used in this way, they are called *interrogative* pronouns:

Who murdered the secret agent?

Whose fingerprints were on the bloodstained knife?

To *whom* have the detectives been talking?

Which suspect is going to confess?

Note: In informal usage, *who* is generally used instead of *whom* as an interrogative pronoun. Informally, we can say or write, "*Who* are you rooting for in the game?" or "*Who* did the teacher fail?" More formal usage would use *whom*: "*Whom* are you rooting for in the game?" and "*Whom* did the teacher fail?"

Point 4:   *Who* and *whom* are used differently. *Who* is a **subject pronoun**. Use *who* as the **subject of a verb**:

Let's see *who* will be teaching the course.

Whom is an **object pronoun**. Use *whom* as the **object of a verb or a preposition**:

Dr. Kelsey is the teacher *whom* I like best.

I haven't decided for *whom* I will vote.

You may want to review the material on subject and object pronouns on pages 103–105.

Here is an easy way to decide whether to use *who* or *whom*. Find the first verb after the place where the *who* or *whom* will go. See if it already has a subject. If it does have a subject, use the object pronoun *whom*. If there is no subject, give it one by using the subject pronoun *who*. Notice how *who* and *whom* are used in the sentences that follow:

I don't know *who* sideswiped my car.

The suspect *whom* the police arrested finally confessed.

In the first sentence, *who* is used to give the verb *sideswiped* a subject. In the second sentence, the verb *arrested* already has a subject, *police*. Therefore, *whom* is the correct pronoun.

Practice 1: Choosing Correct Relative Pronouns

Underline the correct pronoun in each of the following sentences.

1. My grandfather, (who, which) is seventy-nine, goes bowling every Friday.
2. The plant (who, which) Sherise got for her birthday finally died.
3. I wish I had a relative (who, whom) would give me a million dollars.
4. I don't know to (who, whom) I should send my complaint letter.
5. Nobody knew (who, whom) was responsible for the mistake.

Practice 2

Write five sentences using *who*, *whose*, *whom*, *which*, and *that*.

POSSESSIVE PRONOUNS

Here is a list of possessive pronouns:

my, mine	our, ours
your, yours	your, yours
his	their, theirs
her, hers	
its	

Possessive pronouns show ownership or possession.

> Damian revved up *his* motorcycle and blasted off.
>
> The keys are *mine*.

Points to Remember about Possessive Pronouns

Point 1: A possessive pronoun *never* uses an apostrophe. (See also page 167.)

Incorrect	**Correct**
That coat is *hers'*.	That coat is *hers*.
The card table is *theirs'*.	The card table is *theirs*.

Point 2: Do not use any of the following nonstandard forms to show possession.

Incorrect	**Correct**
I met a friend of *him*.	I met a friend of *his*.
Can I use *you* car?	Can I use *your* car?
Me sister is in the hospital.	*My* sister is in the hospital.
That magazine is *mines*.	That magazine is *mine*.

Practice: Using Possessive Pronouns Correctly

Cross out the incorrect pronoun form in each of the sentences that follow. Write the correct form in the space at the left.

_____My_____ **Example** ~~Me~~ car has broken down again.

_____ 1. That car won't be safe until you get its' brakes fixed.

_____ 2. If you are a friend of him, you're welcome to stay with us.

_____ 3. The seat you are sitting on is mines.

_____ 4. The neighbours called they dogs to chase the cat off the lawn.

_____ 5. The coffee pot is ours'.

DEMONSTRATIVE PRONOUNS

Demonstrative pronouns point to or single out a person or thing. There are four demonstrative pronouns:

this	these
that	those

Generally speaking, *this* and *these* refer to things close at hand; *that* and *those* refer to things farther away.

Is anyone using *this* spoon?

I am going to throw away *these* magazines.

I just bought *that* white Volvo.

Pick up *those* toys in the corner.

Note: Do not use *them*, *this here*, *that there*, *these here*, or *those there* to point out. Use only *this*, *that*, *these*, or *those*.

Incorrect	*Correct*
Them tires are badly worn.	*Those* tires are badly worn.
This here book looks hard to read.	*This* book looks hard to read.
That there candy is delicious.	*That* candy is delicious.
Those there squirrels are pests.	*Those* squirrels are pests.

Practice 1: Using Demonstrative Pronouns Correctly

Cross out the incorrect form of the demonstrative pronoun and write the correct form in the space provided.

Those   ***Example***   ~~Them~~ clothes need washing.

_____   1.   That there dog will bite you if it gets a chance.

_____   2.   This here fingernail is not growing straight.

_____   3.   Them girls cannot be trusted.

_____   4.   Carry in those there shopping bags if you want to help.

_____   5.   The place where I'd like to live is that there corner house.

Practice 2: Using Demonstrative Pronouns in Sentences

Write four sentences using *this*, *that*, *these*, and *those*.

_____

_____

_____

_____

REFLEXIVE PRONOUNS

Reflexive pronouns are those pronouns that refer back to the subject of a sentence. Here is a list of reflexive pronouns:

myself	ourselves
yourself	yourselves
himsclf	themselves
herself	
itself	

Sometimes the reflexive pronoun is used for emphasis:

You will have to wash the dishes *yourself*.
We *ourselves* are willing to forget the matter.
The prime minister *himself* turns down his living-room thermostat.

Points to Remember about Reflexive Pronouns

Point 1: In the plural *-self* becomes *-selves*.

Crystal washes *herself* in Freeman bath oil.
They treated *themselves* to a Bermuda vacation.

Point 2: Be careful that you do not use any of the following incorrect forms as reflexive pronouns.

Incorrect	*Correct*
He believes in *hisself*.	He believes in *himself*.
We drove the children *ourself*.	We drove the children *ourselves*.
They saw *themself* in the fun-house mirror.	They saw *themselves* in the fun-house mirror.
I'll do it *meself*.	I'll do it *myself*.

Practice: Using Reflective Pronouns Correctly

Cross out the incorrect form of the reflexive pronoun and write the correct form in the space at the left.

themselves   **Example**   She believes that God helps those who help ~~themself~~.

_____   1. Tony considers hisself the strongest wrestler in the class.

_____   2. The striking players are only making theirselves look greedy.

_____   3. You must carry your luggage yourselfs.

_____   4. Many fire fighters themself do not have smoke detectors in their homes.

_____   5. We decided to finish the basement by ourself.

■ Review Test 1

Underline the correct word in the parentheses.

1. I'm going to leave if (that, that there) server doesn't come over here soon.
2. Though secured by a chain, the snarling German shepherd still terrified Lee and (I, me).
3. That FM radio is (mine, mines).
4. Watching Alan and (I, me) dancing made him grit his teeth.
5. My aunts promised (us, we) girls a trip to Banff for graduation.
6. The service manager did not remember (who, whom) worked on my car.
7. I think (those, those there) people should be kicked out of the theatre for talking.
8. The giggling boys only made (themself, themselves) look foolish.
9. If the decision were up to (they, them), my position in the company would be that of full-time pencil sharpener.
10. If (she, her) and Sandy had reported the leak, the cellar would not have flooded.

■ Review Test 2

Cross out the pronoun error in each sentence and write the correct form above it.

Example   Terry and ~~me~~ have already seen the movie.
         I

1. Our friends have gotten theirselves into debt by overusing credit cards.
2. This here heat pump will save on your energy bill.
3. Watching the soccer game, us fans soon realized that our team would lose.
4. If you and her get confused about directions, stop and check at a service station.
5. Tony felt both sorry for and angry at the drug addict whom tried to steal his car.
6. Before he came up to bat, the baseball player crossed hisself for good luck.
7. Jane and me refused to join the union.
8. The parents theirselfs must share the blame for their child's failure in school.
9. Our class painted more colourful posters than them.
10. You and me have got to have a talk.

■ Review Test 3

On separate paper, write sentences that use correctly each of the following words or word groups.

Example   Peter and him   <u>The coach suspended Peter and him.</u>

1. those
2. Sarah and she
3. faster than I
4. ours
5. Crystal and me
6. whom
7. yourselves
8. with Linda and him
9. you and I
10. the neighbours and us

ADJECTIVES AND ADVERBS

INTRODUCTORY PROJECT

Write in an appropriate word to complete each of the sentences below.

1. The teenage years were a _____ time for me.

2. The mechanic listened _____ while I described my car problem.

3. Basketball is a _____ game than football.

4. My brother is the _____ person in our family.

Now complete the following sentences.

The word inserted in the first sentence is an (adjective, adverb); it describes the word *time*.

The word inserted in the second sentence is an (adjective, adverb);

it ends in the two letters _____ and describes the word *listened*.

The word inserted in the third sentence is a comparative adjective; it

is preceded by *more* or ends in the two letters _____.

The word inserted in the fourth sentence is a superlative adjective; it

is preceded by *most* or ends in the three letters _____.

Answers are on page 481.

Adjectives and adverbs are descriptive words. Their purpose is to make the meanings of the words they describe more specific.

ADJECTIVES

What Are Adjectives?

Adjectives describe nouns (names of persons, places, ideas, or things) or pronouns.

Angela is a *kind* woman. (The adjective *kind* describes the noun *woman*.)

He is *tired*. (The adjective *tired* describes the pronoun *he*.)

Adjectives usually come **before** the word they describe (as in *kind woman*). But they also come **after forms of the linking verb** *to be* (*is*, *are*, *was*, *were*, and so on). Less often, they follow verbs such as *to feel*, *to look*, *to smell*, *to sound*, *to taste*, *to appear*, *to become*, and *to seem*.

That dresser is *heavy*. (The adjective *heavy* describes the dresser.)

The children are *restless*. (The adjective *restless* describes the children.)

These pants are *itchy*. (The adjective *itchy* describes the pants.)

Using Adjectives to Compare

For most *short* adjectives, add *-er* when comparing two things and *-est* when comparing three or more things.

I am *taller* than my brother, but my father is the *tallest* person in the house.

The farm market sells *fresher* vegetables than the corner store, but the *freshest* vegetables are the ones grown in my own garden.

For most *longer* adjectives (two or more syllables), add *more* when comparing two things and *most* when comparing three or more things.

Backgammon is *more enjoyable* to me than checkers, but chess is the *most enjoyable* game of all.

My mother is *more talkative* than my father, but my grandfather is the *most talkative* person in the house.

Points to Remember about Adjectives: Comparative and Superlative Forms

Point 1:   Be careful that you do not use both an *-er* ending and *more*, or both an *-est* ending and *most*.

Incorrect	Correct
Football is a *more livelier* game than baseball.	Football is a *livelier* game than baseball.
Tod Traynor was voted the *most likeliest* to succeed in our high school class.	Tod Traynor was voted the *most likely* to succeed in our high school class.

Point 2:   Pay special attention to the following four words, each of which has irregular forms.

	Comparative (Two)	Superlative (Three or More)
bad	worse	worst
good, well	better	best
little	less	least
much, many	more	most

Practice 1: Choosing Comparative and Superlative Forms

Fill in the comparative or superlative forms for the following words. Two are done for you as examples.

	Comparative (Two)	Superlative (Three or More)
fast	faster	fastest
timid	more timid	most timid
kind		
ambitious		
generous		
fine		
likeable		

Practice 2: Choosing Correct Comparative and Superlative Forms

Add to each sentence the correct form of the word in the margin.

> ***Example***   *bad*   The _____*worst*_____ day of my life was the one when my house caught fire.

comfortable   1. My jeans are the _____ pants I own.

difficult   2. My biology exam was the _____ of my five exams.

easy   3. The _____ way to get a good grade in the class is to take effective notes.

little   4. I made _____ money in my job as a delivery person than I did as a golf caddy.

good   5. The _____ pay I ever made was as a drill press operator in a machine shop.

long   6. The ticket lines for the rock concert were the _____ I had ever seen.

memorable   7. The _____ days of my childhood were the ones I spent on trips with my grandfather.

experienced   8. I am a _____ driver than my sister, but my brother is the _____ driver in the family.

bad   9. This year's drought is _____ than last year's; forecasters are saying that next year's drought may be the _____ of this century.

good   10. Sweet Revenge's cheesecake is _____ than its custard pie.

ADVERBS

What Are Adverbs?

Adverbs describe verbs, adjectives, or other adverbs. They usually end in *-ly*.

> Angela spoke *kindly* to the confused man. (The adverb *kindly* describes the verb *spoke*.)
>
> The man said he was *completely* alone in the world. (The adverb *completely* describes the adjective *alone*.)
>
> Angela listened *very* sympathetically to his story. (The adverb *very* describes the adverb *sympathetically*.)

A Common Mistake with Adjectives and Adverbs

Perhaps the most common mistake that people make with adjectives and adverbs is to use an adjective instead of an adverb after a verb.

Incorrect	*Correct*
Tony breathed *heavy*.	Tony breathed *heavily*.
I rest *comfortable* in that chair.	I rest *comfortably* in that chair.
She learned *quick*.	She learned *quickly*.

Practice: Choosing Between Adjectives and Adverbs

Underline the adjective or adverb needed.

1. Her pink top clashed (violent, violently) with her orange skirt.
2. If I had not run (quick, quickly), the werewolf would have caught me.
3. The crowd pushed (angry, angrily) toward the mosh-pit at the concert.
4. Sam peered with (considerable, considerably) effort through the grimy cellar window.
5. The trees swayed (gentle, gently) in the wind.
6. I was (real, really) tired.
7. I exercise (regular, regularly), and my eating habits are also (regular, regularly).
8. Sarah sat very (quiet, quietly) on the stairs, listening to her parents quarrel (angry, angrily) in the kitchen.
9. I listened (careful, carefully) to the hypnotist's (exact, exactly) instructions.
10. (Slow, Slowly) but (sure, surely), I improved my grades in school.

Well and *Good*

Two words often confused are *well* and *good*. *Good* is an **adjective**; it describes **nouns**. *Well* is usually an **adverb**; it describes **verbs**. *Well* (rather than *good*) is also used when referring to a person's health.

I became a *good* swimmer. (*Good* is an adjective describing the noun *swimmer*.)

For a change, two-year-old Tommy was *good* during the church service. (*Good* is an adjective describing Tommy and comes after *was*, a form of the verb *be*.)

Maryann did *well* on that exam. (*Well* is an adverb describing the verb *did*.)

I explained that I wasn't feeling *well*. (*Well* is used in reference to health.)

Practice: Using Adjectives and Adverbs Correctly

Write *well* or *good* in the sentences that follow.

1. He writes _____ enough to pass the course.

2. We always have a _____ time at the county fair.

3. The mayor and city councillor know each other very _____.

4. Jim has not been feeling _____ lately.

5. I did not do _____ when I took the word processing test.

■ Review Test 1

Cross out the adjective or adverb error in each sentence and write the correction in the space at the left.

frequently

harder

Examples My boss ~~frequent~~ tells me to slow down.

For me, the country is a ~~more harder~~ place to live than the city.

_____ 1. Make sure the job is done safe.

_____ 2. He was found innocent of the charges, but the judge lectured him harsh.

_____ 3. I am the taller of the five children in my family.

_____ 4. Tranh swam effortless through the water, not making a single awkward movement.

_____ 5. At this time it is importanter to be in school than to have a full-time job.

_____ 6. His eyes are his most attractivest feature.

_____ 7. I slept light, for the stereo blared noisily upstairs.

_____ 8. Mr. Scott is the helpfulest of my teachers.

_____ 9. Despite reforms, conditions at the prison are more worse than before.

_____ 10. Tony didn't feel good after eating diced eggplant in clam sauce.

■ Review Test 2

Write a sentence that uses correctly each of the following adjectives and adverbs.

1. nervous _____

2. nervously _____

3. good _____

4. well _____

5. carefully _____

6. most honest _____

7. easier _____

8. best _____

9. more useful _____

10. loudest _____

MISPLACED MODIFIERS

INTRODUCTORY PROJECT

Because of misplaced words, each of the sentences below has more than one possible meaning. Explain both the intended meaning and the unintended meaning in each sentence. Also, circle the words that you think create the confusion because they are misplaced.

1. The farmers sprayed the apple trees wearing masks.

   Intended meaning: _____

   Unintended meaning: _____

2. The woman reached out for the faith healer who had a terminal disease.

   Intended meaning: _____

   Unintended meaning: _____

Answers are on page 482.

WHAT MISPLACED MODIFIERS ARE AND HOW TO CORRECT THEM

Misplaced modifiers are words that, because of awkward placement, do not describe the words the writer intended them to describe. Misplaced modifiers often confuse the meaning of a sentence. To avoid them, place words as close as possible to what they describe.

Misplaced Words	*Correctly Placed Words*
They could see the Petrocan blimp *sitting on the front lawn*. (The Petrocan blimp was sitting on the front lawn?)	Sitting on the front lawn, they could see the Petrocan blimp. (The intended meaning—that the Petrocan blimp was visible from the front lawn—is now clear.)
We had a hamburger after the movie, *which was too greasy for my taste*. (The movie was too greasy for your taste?)	After the movie, we had a hamburger, which was too greasy for my taste. (The intended meaning—that the hamburger was greasy—is now clear.)
Our phone *almost* rang fifteen times last night. (The phone almost rang fifteen times, but in fact did not ring at all?)	Our phone rang almost fifteen times last night. (The intended meaning—that the phone rang a little under fifteen times—is now clear.)

Other single-word modifiers to watch out for include *only*, *even*, *hardly*, *nearly*, and *often*. Such words should be placed immediately before the word they modify.

Practice 1: Placing Modifying Phrases Correctly

Underline the misplaced word or words in each sentence. Then rewrite the sentence, placing related words together and thereby making the meaning clear.

Example   Anita returned the hamburger to the supermarket that was spoiled.

Anita returned the hamburger that was spoiled to the supermarket.

1. They finally found a laundromat driving around in their car.

   _____

   _____

2. I read that Marc Garneau was a Canadian pilot who became an astronaut in the library.

   _____

   _____

3. Trisha was thinking about her lost chemistry book taking the elevator.

   _____

   _____

4. Crystal selected a doughnut from the bakery filled with banana cream.

   _____

   _____

5. Simon almost worked twenty hours overtime to pay some overdue bills.

   _____

   _____

6. Tickets have gone on sale for next week's championship game in the college bookstore.

   _____

   _____

7. I returned the orange socks to the department store that my uncle gave me.

   _____

   _____

8. The camper saw the black bear looking through the binoculars.

   _____

9. I nearly earned two hundred dollars last week.

   _____

10. Mushrooms should be stored in the refrigerator enclosed in a paper bag.

   _____

   _____

Practice 2: Placing Modifying Phrases Correctly

Rewrite each sentence, adding the *italicized* words. Make sure that the intended meaning is clear and that two different interpretations are not possible.

Example   I borrowed a pen for the essay test. (Insert *that ran out of ink*.)

For the essay test, I borrowed a pen that ran out of ink.

1. We agreed to go out to dinner tonight. (Insert *in our science class*.)

   _____

   _____

2. Bob and I decided to get married. (Insert *on a rainy day in June* to show when the decision was made.)

   _____

   _____

3. Cecile decided to hail a taxi. (Insert *weighed down with heavy packages*.)

   _____

   _____

4. I've looked everywhere for an instruction book on how to play the guitar. (Insert *without success*.)

   _____

   _____

5. Mother told me to wash the car. (Insert *over the phone*.)

   _____

   _____

■ Review Test 1

Place an *M* for *misplaced* or a *C* for *correct* in front of each sentence.

_____   1. Larry spotted the missing dog on his way to the bank.

_____   2. Larry, while on his way to the bank, spotted the missing dog.

_____   3. Marie brought a casserole right out of the oven to the new neighbours.

_____   4. Marie brought a casserole to the new neighbours right out of the oven.

_____   5. My sister smiled at the usher in the theatre with long sideburns.

_____ 6. My sister smiled at the usher with long sideburns in the theatre.

_____ 7. A cheerful man with one leg hopped onto the bus.

_____ 8. A cheerful man hopped onto the bus with one leg.

_____ 9. The weary hunter shot at the ducks sitting in his car.

_____ 10. Sitting in his car, the weary hunter shot at the ducks.

_____ 11. Bill saw a kangaroo at the window under the influence of whisky.

_____ 12. Bill saw a kangaroo under the influence of whisky at the window.

_____ 13. Under the influence of whisky, Bill saw a kangaroo at the window.

_____ 14. I was attacked by a stray dog working in the yard.

_____ 15. While working in the yard, I was attacked by a stray dog.

_____ 16. He remembered with dismay that he had to wash the windows.

_____ 17. He remembered that he had to wash the windows with dismay.

_____ 18. With dismay, he remembered that he had to wash the windows.

_____ 19. Ann received a sports car for her birthday that has a sun roof.

_____ 20. Ann received a sports car that has a sun roof for her birthday.

■ Review Test 2

Underline the five misplaced modifiers in the following passage. Then correct them in the spaces provided on the next page.

Before heading to work in the morning, joggers almost fill all the streets. They quietly pound the sidewalks wearing brightly coloured sweatsuits and sneakers. Groups of early feeding pigeons and squirrels scatter as the joggers move easily down the streets. The joggers are gazed at by people

5 who are waiting at bus stops wearing expressions of wonder and envy. Occasionally, a jogger stops to tie a shoelace kneeling on the concrete. The joggers pass supermarkets and vegetable trucks parked at loading ramps. On rainy days, the runners watch for slick spots on the sidewalk, but they don't worry about the rain or cold. Pushing on at a steady pace, they count the

10 number of kilometres travelled. Finally, the joggers take quick showers and think about the workday ahead back at their homes. They will return to their special world of running the next morning.

1. _____

2. _____

   _____

3. _____

   _____

4. _____

5. _____

   _____

DANGLING
MODIFIERS

INTRODUCTORY PROJECT

Because of dangling words, each of the sentences below has more than one possible meaning. In each case, explain both the intended meaning and the unintended meaning.

1. Munching leaves from a tall tree, the children were fascinated by the six-metre-high giraffe.

    Intended meaning: _____

    Unintended meaning: _____

2. Arriving home after ten months in Bosnia, the neighbours threw a community party for Michael.

    Intended meaning: _____

    _____

    Unintended meaning: _____

    _____

Answers are on page 483.

WHAT DANGLING MODIFIERS ARE
AND HOW TO CORRECT THEM

A modifier that opens a sentence must be followed **immediately** by the word it is meant to describe. Otherwise, the modifier is said to be *dangling*, and the sentence takes on an unintended meaning. For example, in the sentence

While sleeping in his backyard, a Frisbee hit Bill on the head.

the unintended meaning is that the *Frisbee* was sleeping in his backyard. What the writer meant, of course, was that *Bill* was sleeping in his backyard. The writer should have placed *Bill* right after the modifier:

While sleeping in his backyard, *Bill* was hit on the head by a Frisbee.

The sentence could also be corrected by placing the subject within the opening word group:

While *Bill* was sleeping in his backyard, a Frisbee hit him on the head.

Other sentences with dangling modifiers follow. Read the explanations of why they are dangling and look carefully at the ways they are corrected.

Dangling	*Correct*
Having almost no money, my survival depended on my parents. (*Who* has almost no money? The answer is not *survival* but *I*. The subject *I* must be added.)	Having almost no money, *I* depended on my parents for survival. *Or:* Since *I* had almost no money, I depended on my parents for survival.
Riding his bike, a German shepherd bit Tony's ankle. (*Who* is riding the bike? The answer is not *German shepherd*, as it unintentionally seems to be, but *Tony*. The subject *Tony* must be added.)	Riding his bike, *Tony* was bitten on the ankle by a German shepherd. *Or:* While *Tony* was riding his bike, a German shepherd bit him on the ankle.
When trying to lose weight, all snacks are best avoided. (*Who* is trying to lose weight? The answer is not *snacks* but *you*. The subject *you* must be added.)	When trying to lose weight, *you* should avoid all snacks. *Or:* When *you* are trying to lose weight, avoid all snacks.

These examples make clear two ways of correcting a dangling modifier. Decide on a logical subject and do one of the following:

1   Place the subject *within* the opening word group:

Since *I* had almost no money, I depended on my parents for survival.

Note: In some cases an appropriate **subordinating** word, such as *since*, must be added, and the verb may have to be changed slightly as well.

2   Place the subject right *after* the opening word group:

Having almost no money, *I* depended on my parents for survival.

Sometimes even more rewriting is necessary to correct a dangling modifier. What is important to remember is that a modifier must be placed **as close as possible to the word that it modifies**.

Practice 1: Correcting Dangling Modifiers

Rewrite each sentence to correct the dangling modifier. Mark the one sentence that is correct with a *C*.

1. Folded into a tiny square, I could not read the message.

   _____

   _____

2. Wading into the lake, tadpoles swirled around my ankles.

   _____

   _____

3. Soaked to the skin, Chris was miserable waiting in the unsheltered doorway.

   _____

   _____

4. Hanging on the wall, I saw a photograph of my mother.

   _____

   _____

5. Settling comfortably into the chair, the television captured my attention for the next hour.

   _____

   _____

6. Driving home after a tiring day at work, the white line became blurry.

_____

_____

7. Soaring high over the left-field fence, the batter hit his first home run.

_____

_____

8. Threadbare and dirty, Maria knew it was time to replace the rug.

_____

_____

9. After spending most of the night outdoors in a tent, the sun rose and we went into the house.

_____

_____

10. Hot and sizzling, we bit into the apple tarts.

_____

_____

Practice 2: Correctly Placing Subjects and Subordinate Clauses

Complete the following sentences. In each case, a logical subject should follow the opening words.

Example   Checking the oil gauge, _I saw that my car was a litre low._

1. Since failing the first test, _____

2. Before learning how to dance, _____

3. While flying the kite, _____

4. After taking my coffee break, _____

5. Though very tired, _____

■ Review Test 1

Place a _D_ for _dangling_ or a _C_ for _correct_ in front of each sentence. Remember that the opening words are a dangling modifier if they are not followed immediately by a logical subject.

——————— 1. Hanging in the closet for a year, Crystal forgot she owned an aqua dress.

——————— 2. Crystal forgot she owned an aqua dress that had been hanging in the closet for a year.

——————— 3. Having eaten several spicy tacos, my stomach began a dance of rebellion.

——————— 4. Having eaten several spicy tacos, I began to feel my stomach doing a dance of rebellion.

——————— 5. Hitching a ride, I was picked up by a transport truck.

——————— 6. Hitching a ride, a transport truck picked me up.

——————— 7. While waiting for the bus, rain began to fall.

——————— 8. While waiting for the bus, it began to rain.

——————— 9. While I was waiting for the bus, rain began to fall.

——————— 10. Being tired, my chores were not finished.

——————— 11. Because I was tired, I did not finish my chores.

——————— 12. While I was practising yoga exercises, a postal carrier rang the doorbell.

——————— 13. While practising yoga exercises, a postal carrier rang the doorbell.

——————— 14. Containing dangerous chemicals, people are not swimming in the lake.

——————— 15. Containing dangerous chemicals, the lake is not open for swimming.

——————— 16. Because the lake contains dangerous chemicals, it is not open for swimming.

——————— 17. Falling heavily, Dan broke his arm.

——————— 18. Falling heavily, Dan's arm was broken.

——————— 19. Just before finishing the book, the power failed.

——————— 20. Just before I finished the book, the power failed.

■ Review Test 2

Underline the five dangling modifiers in the following passage. Then correct them in the spaces provided below.

When my brother Rick gets hold of an R.L. Stine book, he forgets the rest of the world exists. Absorbed in his book, dinner is forgotten. He must be reminded to eat even when we have meat loaf, his favourite meal. Rick not only ignores the other people in the family but also forgets his chores.

5 Reading after breakfast, lunch, and dinner, a lot of dishes pile up and

wastebaskets are not emptied. We try to understand; in fact, we think he's lucky. Sitting in the middle of a room, his book seems to drown out the television, radio, and screaming children. Never wanting any sleep, his book still has his attention at 1:00 a.m. We bought a new rocking chair once **10** when Rick was in the middle of the latest R.L. Stine. Rocking away, his eyes never left the pages long enough to notice it. Only after finishing the book did he ask, "When did we get the new chair?"

1. _____
   _____

2. _____
   _____

3. _____
   _____

4. _____
   _____

5. _____
   _____

FAULTY PARALLELISM

Answers are on page 484.

INTRODUCTORY PROJECT

Read aloud each pair of sentences below. Put a check mark beside the sentence that reads more smoothly and clearly and sounds more natural.

Pair 1

I use my TV remote-control to change channels, to adjust the volume, and for turning the set on and off.

I use my TV remote-control to change channels, to adjust the volume, and to turn the set on and off.

Pair 2

One option the employees had was to take a cut in pay; the other was longer hours of work.

One option the employees had was to take a cut in pay; the other was to work longer hours.

Pair 3

The refrigerator has a cracked vegetable drawer, one of the shelves is missing, and a strange freezer smell.

The refrigerator has a cracked vegetable drawer, a missing shelf, and a strange freezer smell.

Answers are on page 484.

PARALLELISM EXPLAINED

Words in a pair or a series should have a parallel structure. By balancing the items in a pair or a series so that they have the same structure, you will make your sentences clearer and easier to read. Notice how the parallel sentences that follow read more smoothly than the nonparallel ones.

Nonparallel (Not Balanced)	*Parallel (Balanced)*
I attended three classes in the morning, studied most of the afternoon, and my sales job was in the evening.	I attended three classes in the morning, studied most of the afternoon, and worked at my sales job in the evening. (A balanced series of **past tense verbs**: *attended, studied, worked*.)
Doug spends his free time reading, listening to music, and he watches TV sports.	Doug spends his free time reading, listening to music, and watching TV sports. (A balanced series of **-ing words**: *reading, listening, watching*.)
After the camping trip I was exhausted, irritable, and wanted to eat.	After the camping trip I was exhausted, irritable, and hungry. (A balanced series of **descriptive words**: *exhausted, irritable, hungry*.)
My hope for retirement is to be healthy, to live in a comfortable house, and having plenty of money.	My hope for retirement is to be healthy, to live in a comfortable house, and to have plenty of money. (A balanced series of **to verbs**: *to be, to live, to have*.)
Nightly, Fred puts out the garbage, checks the locks on the doors, and the burglar alarm is turned on.	Nightly, Fred puts out the garbage, checks the locks on the doors, and turns on the burglar alarm. (Balanced verbs and word order: *puts out the garbage, checks the locks, turns on the burglar alarm*.)

Balancing sentences is not a skill you need worry about when writing first drafts. But when you rewrite, you should try to put matching words and ideas into matching structures. Such parallelism will improve your writing style.

Practice 1: Balancing Sentences

The unbalanced part of each sentence is italicized. Rewrite this part so that it matches the rest of the sentence.

Example In the afternoon, I changed two diapers, ironed several shirts, and was watching soap operas. _watched_

1. After the exercise class, I woke up with stiff knees, throbbing legs, and *arms that ached.* _____

2. Our favourite restaurant specializes in delicious omelettes, *soups that are freshly made*, and inexpensive desserts. _____

3. The man running the check-out counter was tall, thin, and *having a bad temper.* _____

4. Caulking the windows, *to replace weather stripping*, and painting the garage are my chores for the weekend. _____

5. With her pale skin and *her eyes that were green*, she appeared ghostly in the moonlight. _____

6. As a Leonard Cohen fan, I love to see his videos and *hearing him sing.* _____

7. After calling the police, checking the area hospitals, and *we prayed*, we could only wait. _____

8. The stars appeared on talk shows, signed autographs, and *were attending* opening nights in order to promote their latest movie. _____

9. Our teenagers tie up the phone for hours, joking with their friends, deciding what to wear, and *complaints about their strict parents.* _____

10. In Allan's nightmare, he was audited by Revenue Canada, investigated by private detectives, and *bill collectors were chasing him.* _____

Practice 2: Creating Parallel Structure

Complete the following statements. The first two parts of each statement are parallel in form; the part that you add should be parallel in form as well.

Example   Three things I like about myself are my sense of humour, my thoughtfulness, and _my self-discipline._

1. Among the drawbacks of apartment living are noisy neighbours, yearly rent increases, and _____

2. Three bad habits I have resolved to change are losing my temper, showing up late for appointments, and _____

3. The best features of my part-time job are good pay, flexible hours, and

    _____

4. Cigarette smoking is expensive, disgusting, and _____

5. Lessons I had to learn after moving from my parents' home included how to budget my money, how to take care of my own laundry, and

    _____

■ Review Test 1

Cross out the unbalanced part of each sentence. Then rewrite the unbalanced part so that it matches the other item or items in the sentence.

Example   I enjoy watering the grass and ~~to work~~ in the garden.
        working

1. Our production supervisor warned Jonathan to punch in on time, dress appropriately for the job, and he should stop taking extra breaks.

    _____

2. On his ninetieth birthday, the old man mused that his long life was due to hard work, a loving wife, and because he had a sense of humour.

    _____

3. The philosopher's advice is to live for the present, find some joy in each day, and by helping others.

    _____

4. Freshly prepared food, an attractive decor, and having prompt service are signs of a good restaurant.

    _____

5. Maria has tickets for reckless driving, speeding, and she parked illegally.

    _____

6. Washing clothes, cooking meals, and to take care of children used to be called "women's work."

   _____

7. Our compact car provides better mileage; more comfort is provided by our station wagon.

   _____

8. As the first bartender to arrive each day, Jennifer must slice lemons, get ice, and she has to check the inventory.

   _____

9. Last week I finished my term paper, took all my final exams, and an interview for a summer job.

   _____

10. On our ideal vacation, I enjoy lazing in the sun, eating delicious food, and to be with special friends.

   _____

■ Review Test 2

On a separate sheet of paper, write five sentences of your own that use parallel structure. Each sentence should contain three items in a series. Use the same formats provided for the five sentences on page 134: past tense verbs; *-ing* words; descriptive words; *to* verbs; and present tense verbs and word order.

■ Review Test 3

There are six nonparallel parts in the following passage. The first is corrected for you as an example. Underline and correct the other five.

My sister used to drive an old VW "Bug." With its dented body, torn upholstery, and <u>fenders that were rusted</u>, the car was a real eyesore. Worse, though, the car was in terrible shape mechanically. The engine coughed, the tailpipe rattled, and there were squealing brakes. My father spent many
5 hours searching for cures for the car's many ailments. He often spoke about pushing the car off a cliff or to explode it and put it out of its misery. He wasn't serious, of course, but one day the little car saved my father the trouble. As Kathy was driving one afternoon, smoke began pouring through the back seat of the car. My sister parked on the side of the road and began

10 to check the engine. Quickly, another motorist pulled over, jumped out of his car, and pushing my sister away from the VW. The car smouldered a few minutes and then bursting into flames. Firefighters arrived in about ten minutes but were too late. The car's tires had melted, its body was black, the glass popping out of the windows, and the steering wheel was twisted.

15 When Kathy told the family what had happened, everyone was sympathetic. I suspect, however, that my father shed no tears that the Bug was gone from our lives.

1. _rusty fenders_
2. _____
3. _____
4. _____
5. _____
6. _____

PAPER FORMAT

INTRODUCTORY PROJECT

Which of the paper openings below seems clearer and easier to read?

A

	Finding Faces	
	It takes just a little imagination to find faces in the	
	objects around you. For instance, clouds are sometimes	
	shaped like faces. If you lie on the ground on a partly	

B

	"finding faces"
	It takes just a little imagination to find faces in the objects
	around you. For instance, clouds are sometimes shaped like
	faces. If you lie on the ground on a partly cloudy day, cha-
	nces are you will be able to spot many well-known faces

What are three reasons for your choice?

_____

_____

_____

_____

Answers are on page 484.

PAPER FORMATTING GUIDELINES

Here are guidelines to follow in preparing a paper for an instructor.

1 Use full-sized bond or typewriter paper, 21.5 cm by 28 cm ($8\frac{1}{2}$ by 11 inches).

2 Keep wide margins 2.5 cm (1 to $1\frac{1}{2}$ inches) all around the paper. In particular, do not crowd the right-hand and bottom margins. The white space makes your paper more readable; also, the instructor has room for comments.

3 If you write by hand:

Use a blue or black pen (*not* a pencil).

Be careful not to overlap letters or to make decorative loops on letters.

Write on every other line.

Make all your letters distinct. Pay special attention to *a*, *e*, *i*, *o*, and *u*—five letters that people sometimes write illegibly.

Keep your capital letters clearly distinct from your small letters. You may even want to print all capital letters.

4 If you word-process your paper:

Check whether your instructor prefers full justification or "ragged right" line format;

Double space the text of each paragraph;

Use spellcheck to correct any errors in spelling;

Insert two line-spaces between your title and your first paragraph; and

Remove any tear-strips from the edges of your paper.

5 Centre the title of your paper on the first line of page one. Do *not* put quotation marks around the title or underline the title or put a period after the title. Capitalize all the major words in a title, including the first word. Small connecting words within a title, such as *of*, *for*, *the*, *in*, and *to*, are not capitalized.

6 Skip a line between the title and the first line of your text. Indent the first line of each paragraph about five spaces (1.25 cm or half an inch) from the left-hand margin.

7 Make commas, periods, and other punctuation marks firm and clear. Leave a slight space after each period. When you are word-processing, leave a double space after a period.

8 Whenever possible, avoid breaking a word at the end of a line. If you must break a word, break only between syllables (see page 202). Do not break words of one syllable.

9 Put your name, the date, and the course number where your instructor asks for them.

Also keep in mind these important points about the *title* and the *first sentence* of your paper:

10 The title should be several words that tell what the paper is about. It should usually *not* be a complete sentence. For example, if you are writing a paper about your jealous sister, the title could simply be "My Jealous Sister."

11 Do not rely on the title to help explain the first sentence of your paper. The first sentence must exist independently of the title. For instance, if the title of your paper is "My Jealous Sister," the first sentence should *not* be, "She has been this way as long as I can remember." Rather, the first sentence might be, "My sister has always been a jealous person."

Practice 1: Finding Format Errors

Identify the mistakes in format in the following lines from a student paper. Explain the mistakes in the spaces provided. One mistake is described for you as an example.

	"The generation gap in our house"
	When I was a girl, I never argued with my parents about
	differences between their attitude and mine. My father
	would deliver his judgement on an issue and that was alw-
	ays the end of the matter. There was no discussion permit-
	ted, so I gradually began to express my disagreement in other

1. Hyphenate only between syllables (al-ways). _____

2. _____

3. _____

4. _____

5. _____

6. _____

Practice 2: Writing Appropriate Titles

As already stated, a title should tell in several words what a paper is about. Often a title can be based on the sentence that expresses the main idea of a paper.

Following are five main-idea sentences from student papers. Write a suitable and specific title for each paper, basing the title on the main idea.

Example Title: _Ageing Canadians as Outcasts_

Our society treats ageing Canadians as outcasts in many ways.

1. Title: _____

Selfishness is a common trait in young children.

2. Title: _____

Exercising every morning offers a number of benefits.

3. Title: _____

My teenage son is a stubborn person.

4. Title: _____

To survive in college, a person must learn certain essential study skills.

5. Title: _____

Only after I was married did I fully realize the drawbacks and values of single life.

Practice 3: Writing Complete Opening Sentences

In four of the five following sentences, the writer has mistakenly used the title to help explain the first sentence. But as has already been stated, you must *not* rely on the title to help explain your first sentence.

Rewrite the sentences so that they stand independently of the title. Put *Correct* under the one sentence that is independent of the title.

Example Title: Flunking an Exam

First sentence: I managed to do this because of several bad habits.

Rewritten: _I managed to flunk an exam because of several bad habits._

1. Title: The Worst Day of My Life
   First sentence: It began when my supervisor at work gave me a message to call home.

   Rewritten: _____

   _____

2. Title: Catholic Church Services
   First sentence: They have undergone many changes in the last few years.

   Rewritten: _____

   _____

3. Title: An Embarrassing Incident
   First sentence: This happened to me when I was working as a server at the
   Royal York Hotel.

   Rewritten: _____

   _____

4. Title: The Inability to Share
   First sentence: The inability to share can cause great strains in a relationship.

   Rewritten: _____

   _____

5. Title: Offensive Television Commercials
   First sentence: Many that I watch are degrading to human dignity.

   Rewritten: _____

   _____

■ Review Test

Use the space provided below to rewrite the following sentences from a student paper, correcting the mistakes in format.

	"my husband's Grandfather"
	He was seventy-four when I first met him, and yet in many ways
	he was the youngest person I ever knew. I couldn't help being
	impressed with the strength of his handshake, the tightness
	of his jaw, and the firm muscles of his body. When he learned
	that I was a jogger, he invited me to go running.

CAPITAL LETTERS

You probably know a good deal about the uses of capital letters. Answering the questions below will help you check your knowledge.

1. Write the full name of a person you know: _____

2. In what city and province or country were you born? _____

   _____

3. What is your present street address? _____

4. Name a country where you want to travel for a "fling": _____

5. Name a school that you attended: _____

6. Give the name of a store where you buy food: _____

7. Name a company where you or anyone you know works: _____

   _____

8. What day of the week gives you the best chance to relax? _____

9. What holiday is your favourite? _____

10. What brand of toothpaste do you use? _____

11. Give the brand name of a candy or chewing gum you like: _____

    _____

12. Name a song or a television show you enjoy: _____

13. Write the title of a magazine or newspaper you read: _____

    _____

Items 14–16: Three capital letters are needed in the lines below. Underline the words you think should be capitalized. Then write them, capitalized, in the spaces provided.

> on Stanley Cup night, my room-mate said, "let's buy some snacks and invite a few friends over to watch the game." i knew my plans to write a term paper would have to be changed.

14. _____   15. _____   16. _____

Answers are on page 485.

MAIN USES OF CAPITAL LETTERS

Capital letters are used with:

1 The first word in a sentence or direct quotation
2 Names of persons and the word *I*
3 Names of particular places
4 Names of days of the week, months, and holidays
5 Names of commercial products
6 Titles of books, magazines, articles, films, television shows, songs, poems, stories, papers that you write, and the like
7 Names of companies, associations, unions, clubs, religious and political groups, and other organizations

Each use is illustrated on the pages that follow.

First Word in a Sentence or Direct Quotation

Our company has begun laying people off.
The doctor said, "This may hurt a bit."
"My husband," said Maria, "is a light eater. When it's light, he starts to eat."

Note: In the third example, *My* and *When* are capitalized because they start new sentences. But *is* is not capitalized, because it is part of the first sentence.

Names of Persons and the Word *I*

At the picnic, I met Tony Curry and Crystal Marino.

Names of Particular Places

After graduating from Richview Collegiate in Toronto, I worked for a summer at a nearby Holiday Inn on Burnhamthorpe Road and Highway 27.

But: Use small letters if the specific name of a place is not given.

After graduating from high school in my native city, I worked for a summer at a nearby hotel close to a major highway.

Names of Days of the Week, Months, and Holidays

This year Victoria Day falls on the second last Monday in May.

But: Use small letters for the seasons—summer, fall, winter, spring.

In the early summer and fall, my hay fever bothers me.

Names of Commercial Products

The consumer magazine rates highly Cheerios breakfast cereal, Häagen-Dazs ice cream, and President's Choice peanut butter.

But: Use small letters for the *type* of product (breakfast cereal, ice cream, peanut butter, or whatever).

Titles of Books, Magazines, Articles, Films, Television Shows, Songs, Poems, Stories, Papers That You Write, and the Like

My oral report was on *The Diviners* by Margaret Laurence.

While watching *The Young and the Restless* on television, I thumbed through *Flare* magazine and *The Globe and Mail*.

Names of Companies, Associations, Unions, Clubs, Religious and Political Groups, and Other Organizations

A new bill before Parliament is opposed by the National Action Committee for Women.

My wife is Jewish; I am Roman Catholic. We are both members of the Liberal Party.

My parents have life insurance with the Co-operators, auto insurance with Zurich, and medical insurance with Blue Cross.

Practice: Using Capitalization Correctly

Cross out the words that need capitals in the sentences that follow. Then write the capitalized forms of the words in the space provided. The number of spaces tells you how many corrections to make in each case.

Example   Rose said, "~~Why~~ should I bother to *eat* this ~~cadbury's~~ bar? I should just apply it directly to my hips."   _____Why_____   _____Cadbury's_____

1. Vince wanted to go to the halloween party dressed as a thanksgiving turkey, but he was afraid someone might try to carve him.

   _____   _____

2. Laurie called upstairs, "if you're not ready in five minutes, i'm leaving without you."

   _____   _____

3. The old ford rattled its way from quebec to manitoba on four balding goodyear tires.

   _____   _____   _____   _____

4. Among the dusty boxes in the attic lay a stack of old *star weekly* magazines dating back to world war II.

   _____   _____   _____

5. Cheri DaCosta, a member of the northside improvement association, urged the city to clean up the third Street neighbourhood.

   _____   _____   _____   _____

6. At soundworks, a discount store on Laurier boulevard, she purchased a panasonic stereo amplifier.

   _____   _____   _____

7. Tom finished basic training at camp borden and was transferred to a base near Lahr, germany.

   _____   _____   _____

8. On thursday nights Maria goes to the weight watchers' meeting at a nearby high school.

   _____   _____   _____

9. The two films they enjoyed most during the horror film festival held in february were *return of dracula* and *alien.*

   _____   _____   _____   _____

10. My sister bought a pair of club monaco jeans at the burlington mall.

   _____   _____   _____   _____

OTHER USES OF CAPITAL LETTERS

Capital letters are also used with:

1 Names that show family relationships
2 Titles of persons when used with their names
3 Specific school courses
4 Languages

5 Geographic locations
6 Historical periods and events
7 Races, nations, and nationalities
8 Opening and closing of a letter

Each use is illustrated on the pages that follow.

Names That Show Family Relationships

Aunt Fern and Uncle Jack are selling their house.
I asked Grandfather to start the fire.
Is Mother feeling better?

But: Do not capitalize words like *mother*, *father*, *grandmother*, *grandfather*, *uncle*, *aunt*, and so on when they are preceded by *my* or another possessive word.

My aunt and uncle are selling their house.
I asked my grandfather to start the fire.
Is my mother feeling better?

Titles of Persons When Used with Their Names

I wrote an angry letter to Premier Harris.
Can you drive to Dr. Stein's office?
We asked Professor Bushkin about his attendance policy.

But: Use small letters when titles appear by themselves, without specific names.

I wrote an angry letter to my premier.
Can you drive to the doctor's office?
We asked our professor about his attendance policy.

Specific School Courses

My courses this semester include Accounting I, Introduction to Data Processing, Business Law, General Psychology, and Basic Math.

But: Use small letters for general subject areas.

This semester I'm taking mostly business courses, but I have a psychology course and a math course as well.

Languages

Lisette speaks English and French equally well.

Geographic Locations

I lived in the West for many years and then moved to the Maritimes.

But: Use small letters in giving directions.

Go south for about five miles and then bear west.

Historical Periods and Events

One essay question dealt with the Battle of the Bulge in World War II.

Races, Nations, Nationalities

The census form asked whether I was Caucasian, Native Canadian, or Asian.
Last summer I hitchhiked through Italy, France, and Germany.
The city is a melting pot for Koreans, Vietnamese, and Tamils.

But: Use small letters when referring to *whites* or *blacks*.

Both whites and blacks supported our mayor in the election.

Opening and Closing of a Letter

Dear Sir:	Sincerely yours,
Dear Madam:	Truly yours,

Note: Capitalize only the first word in a closing.

Practice: Finding Incorrect Capitalization

Cross out the words that need capitals in the following sentences. Then write the capitalized forms of the words in the spaces provided. The number of spaces tells you how many corrections to make in each case.

1.   When aunt esther died, she left all her money to her seven cats and nothing to my uncle.

   _____   _____

2. This fall I'm taking night courses in french and aerobic exercise I.

   _____   _____   _____

3. Tony was referred to dr. purdy's office because his regular dentist was on vacation.

   _____   _____

4. The french-canadian family in the apartment upstairs has just moved here from the gaspé.

   _____   _____

5. My accounting courses are giving me less trouble than intermediate math 201.

   _____   _____

UNNECESSARY USE OF CAPITALS

Practice: Using Capital Letters Correctly

Many errors in capitalization are caused by adding capitals where they are not needed. Cross out the incorrectly capitalized letters in the following sentences and write the correct forms in the spaces provided. The number of spaces tells you how many corrections to make in each sentence.

1. During the Summer I like to sit in my backyard, Sunbathe, and read Magazines like *Flare* and *Chatelaine*.

   _____   _____   _____

2. Every Week I seem to be humming another Tune. Lately I have been humming the Melody for the latest Pepsi commercial on television.

   _____   _____   _____

3. After High School I travelled to eight Provinces, including Newfoundland, and then I decided to enrol in a local College.

   _____   _____   _____   _____

4. The Title of my Paper was "The End of the War of 1812." My Teacher did not give me a good Grade for it.

   _____   _____   _____   _____

5. My Friend Roger said, "People no longer have to go to College and get a Diploma in order to find a good job and succeed in Life."

   _____   _____   _____   _____

■ Review Test 1

Cross out the words that need capitals in the following sentences. Then write the capitalized forms of the words in the spaces provided. The number of spaces tells you how many corrections to make in each sentence.

Example   During half-time of the ~~saturday~~ afternoon football game, my sister said, "~~let's~~ get some hamburgers from ~~harvey's~~ or put a pizza in the oven."

     <u>Saturday</u>   <u>Let's</u>   <u>Harvey's</u>

1. Stanley was disgusted when he was told he couldn't order mother parker's tea at the chinese restaurant.

   _____   _____

2. When my grandfather came to canada from the ukraine, which was then a part of russia, he spoke no english.

   _____   _____   _____   _____

3. Ellen said, "i've been working as a server at the red lobster since last march."

   _____   _____   _____   _____

4. My math 101 course meets on tuesdays in champlain hall.

   _____   _____   _____   _____

5. Every election Day, my mother takes a day off from her job as a nurse at memorial hospital to serve as an enumerator for the Liberals.

   _____   _____   _____

6. Crystal said, "my favourite episode of the original *star trek* is the one in which Mr. Spock falls in love."

   _____   _____   _____

7. At the corner of thirteenth and market streets is a newsstand where people can buy magazines from as far away as france.

   _____   _____   _____   _____   _____

8. When aunt esther's pontiac finally broke down, she decided to get a toyota.

   _____   _____   _____   _____

9. The college is showing the movie *stagecoach* on friday night as part of its john wayne film festival.

   _____   _____   _____   _____

10. On our trip to ottawa, we visited the national arts centre, sat through a session of the Canadian parliament, and then fell asleep on a bench at the national gallery.

_____   _____   _____

_____   _____   _____

■ Review Test 2

On separate paper, write:

- ■ Seven sentences demonstrating the seven main uses of capital letters.
- ■ Eight sentences demonstrating the eight other uses of capital letters.

NUMBERS AND ABBREVIATIONS

NUMBERS

Rule 1:   Spell out numbers that take no more than two words. Otherwise, use numerals—the numbers themselves.

> Last year Tina bought nine new CDs.
>
> Ray struck out fifteen batters in Sunday's softball game.

But

> Tina now has 114 CDs in her collection.
>
> Already this season Ray has recorded 168 strikeouts.

You should also spell out a number that begins a sentence:

> One hundred fifty first-graders throughout the city showed flu symptoms today.

Rule 2:   Be consistent when you use a series of numbers. If some numbers in a sentence or paragraph require more than two words, then use numbers themselves throughout the selection.

> This past spring, we planted 5 rhodos, 15 azaleas, 50 summersweet, and 120 myrtle around our house.

Rule 3:   Use numbers to show dates, times, addresses, percentages, exact sums of money, and parts of a book.

> My birth date is July 22, 1967.
>
> My job interview was set for 10:15. (*But:* Spell out numbers before *o'clock.* For example: The time was then changed to eleven o'clock.)
>
> Janet's new address is 118 North 35th Street.
>
> Almost 40 per cent of my meals are eaten at fast-food restaurants.
>
> The cashier rang up a total of $18.35. (*But:* Round amounts may be expressed as words. For example: The movie has a five-dollar admission charge.)
>
> Read Chapter 6 in your math textbook and answer questions 1 to 5 on page 250.

Practice: Using Correct Citation for Numbers

Use the three rules to make the corrections needed in these sentences.

  1. Why do I always wind up with 5 exams in 3 days?

2. 2 teenage girls were responsible for the shoplifting.

3. My appointment was for eight-thirty in the evening.

4. However, the doctor didn't arrive until 9 o'clock.

5. I worked overtime last week and received a paycheque for two hundred and eighty-two dollars.

6. Steve lives at twenty-three West Pine Street.

7. Fred and Martha were married on May thirty-first, nineteen-fifty-six.

8. Our son has decorated his room with two wall posters, five album covers, and over 215 baseball cards.

9. Eaton's fifty per cent–off sale on certain items ends on Friday.

10. Our team was penalized 5 yards for having 12 men on the field.

ABBREVIATIONS

While abbreviations are a helpful time-saver in note-taking, you should avoid most abbreviations in formal writing. Listed below are some of the few abbreviations that can acceptably be used in compositions. Note that a period is used after most abbreviations.

1 Mr., Mrs., Ms., Jr., Sr., and Dr. when used with proper names:

Mr. Rollin   Ms. Peters   Dr. Langille

2 Time references:

A.M. or a.m.   P.M. or p.m.   B.C.E. or C.E.

3 First or middle initial in a signature:

T. Alan Parker   Linda M. Evans

4 Organizations, technical words, and trade names known primarily by their initials:

CBC   YMCA   UNESCO   GM   CIBC   LTD

Practice: Using Abbreviations Correctly

Cross out the words that should not be abbreviated and correct them in the spaces provided.

1. My cous. moved into her own apt. after she had a fight with her parents.

   _____   _____

2. The only station I get on my old telev. is CBC.

   _____

3. Linda gets depressed when all her charge acct. bills arrive before the first of the mo.

   _____   _____

4. After the mov. men broke my recliner, I wrote an angry letter to the pres. of the co.

   _____   _____   _____

5. Fran has lost five kilo. on the diet she started three wks. ago.

   _____   _____

6. My favour. actor is George C. Scott, esp. in old movies like *Dr. Strangelove.*

   _____   _____

7. That sec. from the temp. agency can process seventy-eight words a min.

   _____   _____   _____

8. My younger bro. is a drum major with his h. s. marching band.

   _____   _____   _____

9. Our new Honda gets ten kilometres a lit. on city sts.

   _____   _____

10. At 11:15 a.m., Dr. Brooks came out of the hosp. operating rm. and told me that my wife was fine.

    _____   _____

■ Review Test

Cross out the mistake or mistakes in numbers and abbreviations and correct them in the spaces provided.

1. All that was left in the refrigerator were 2 over-ripe pears.

   _____

2. As usual, the train pulled into the sta. forty min. late.

   _____   _____

3. On Saturdays, the hardware store on Portage Street doesn't open until ten-fifteen.

   _____

4. Even though I had paid all my premiums on time, my insur. co. refused to reimburse me for my loss.

   _____   _____

5. Dr. Engler's driver's lic. was revoked after he got into a traffic accident on Wayne Ave.

   _____   _____

6. I can still remember when it cost only 8 cents to mail a first-class letter and three cents for a postcard.

   _____

7. Last Wed. I fell asleep at 9 p.m. watching the p.m. address parliament on television.

   _____   _____

8. My little brother has had bronchitis six times this year and has missed 32 days of school.

   _____

9. The nice thing about double feat. is that you can see two mov. for the price of one.

   _____   _____

10. Can you believe that the thrift shop on Hastings Street is selling two-hundred-and-fifty-dollar down coats for $49.95?

    _____

END MARKS

A sentence always begins with a capital letter. It always ends with a period, a question mark, or an exclamation point.

PERIOD (.)

Use a period after a sentence that makes a statement.

> More single parents are adopting children.
> It has rained for most of the week.

Use a period after most abbreviations.

Mr. Brady	B.A.	Dr. Ballard
Ms. Peters	a.m.	Tom Ricci, Jr.

QUESTION MARK (?)

Use a question mark after a *direct* question.

> When is your paper due?
> How is your cold?
> Tom asked, "When are you leaving?"
> "Why doesn't everyone take a break?" Rosa suggested.

Do not use a question mark after an *indirect* question (a question not in the speaker's exact words).

> She asked when the paper was due.
> He asked how my cold was.
> Tom asked when I was leaving.
> Rosa suggested that everyone take a break.

EXCLAMATION POINT (!)

Use an exclamation point after a word or sentence that expresses strong feeling.

> Come here!
> Ouch! This pizza is hot!
> That truck just missed us!

Note: Be careful not to overuse exclamation points.

Practice: Using Correct Punctuation Marks

Add a period, a question mark, or an exclamation point, as needed, to each of the following sentences.

1. How long will the store sale continue

2. Watch out for that bump in the road

3. The copper bracelet on her arm helps her arthritis

4. Does Barbara's room always look as if a hurricane came for a visit

5. Dr. Kirby specializes in acupuncture of the wallet

6. Manny, Moe, and Jack are always working on their cars

7. Watch out or you'll step on my sunglasses

8. He asked if I had read Tolkien's *The Lord of the Rings*

9. "It will take hours to clean up this mess " Ellen cried.

10. Little Alan asked his uncle, "Is your moustache a wig "

APOSTROPHES

INTRODUCTORY PROJECT

1. You're the kind of person who believes he's going to be a big success without doing any hard work, but the world doesn't work that way.

    What is the purpose of the apostrophe in *You're*, *he's*, and *doesn't*?

    _____

2. the eagle's nest
    Fred's feet
    my mother's briefcase
    the children's drawings
    Jacques Plante's mask

    What is the purpose of the *'s* in all the examples above?

    _____

3. The piles of old books in the attic were starting to decay. One book's spine had been gnawed away by mice.
    Two cars were stolen yesterday from the mall parking lot. Another car's antenna was ripped off.

    In the sentence pairs above, why is the *'s* used in each second sentence but not in the first?

    _____

    _____

Answers are on page 487.

The two main uses of the apostrophe are:

1 To show the omission of one or more letters in a contraction
2 To show ownership or possession

Each use is explained on the pages that follow.

APOSTROPHES IN CONTRACTIONS

A contraction is formed when two words are combined to make one word. An apostrophe is used to show where the word is *contracted*; where letters are omitted in forming the contraction. Here are two contractions:

have + not = haven't (the *o* in *not* has been omitted)
I + will = I'll (the *wi* in *will* has been omitted)

The following are some other common contractions:

I + am	= I'm		it + is	= it's
I + have	= I've		it + has	= it's
I + had	= I'd		is + not	= isn't
who + is	= Who's		could + not	= couldn't
do + not	= don't		I + would	= I'd
did + not	= didn't		they + are	= they're
let + us	= let's		there + is	= there's

Note: *will* + *not* has an unusual contraction: *won't*.

Practice 1: Forming Contractions

Combine the following words into contractions. One is done for you.

he + is = ___*he's*___   we + are = _____

are + not = _____   has + not = _____

you + are = _____   who + is = _____

they + have = _____   does + not = _____

would + not = _____   where + is = _____

Practice 2: Creating Contractions

Write the contraction for the words in parentheses.

Example He (could not) _____ *couldn't* _____ come.

1. (I will) _____ be with you shortly if (you will) _____ just wait a minute.

2 (It is) _____ such a long drive to the ballpark that Damian (would not) _____ go there if you paid him.

3. You (should not) _____ drink any more if (you are) _____ hoping to get home safely.

4. Alice's husband (is not) _____ the aggressive type, and her former husbands (were not) _____ either.

5. (I would) _____ like to know (who is) _____ in charge of the cash register and why (it is) _____ taking so long for this line to move.

Note: Even though contractions are common in everyday speech and in written dialogue, usually it is best to avoid them in formal writing.

Practice 3

Write five sentences using the apostrophe in different contractions.

1. _____

2. _____

3. _____

4. _____

5. _____

Four Contractions to Note Carefully

Four contractions that deserve special attention are *they're*, *it's*, *you're*, and *who's*. Sometimes these contractions are confused with the **possessive words** *their*, *its*, *your*, and *whose*. The chart on the following page shows the difference in meaning between the contractions and the possessive words.

Contractions	*Possessive Words*
they're (means *they are*)	their (means *belonging to them*)
it's (means *it is* or *it has*)	its (means *belonging to it*)
you're (means *you are*)	your (means *belonging to you*)
who's (means *who is*)	whose (means *belonging to whom*)

Note: Possessive words are explained further on page 167.

Practice: Identifying Contractions and Possessive Forms

Underline the correct form (the contraction or the possessive word) in each of the following sentences. Use the contraction whenever the two words of the contraction (*they are, it is, you are, who is*) would also fit.

1. (They're, Their) going to hold the party in (they're, their) family room.
2. (You're, Your) not going to be invited if you insist on bringing (you're, your) accordion.
3. (Who's, Whose) going with us and (who's, whose) car are we taking?
4. (It's, Its) too early to go to bed and (it's, its) too late in the day to take a nap.
5. If (your, you're) not going to drive by (they're, their) house, (it's, its) going to be impossible for them to get home tonight.

APOSTROPHES TO SHOW OWNERSHIP OR POSSESSION

To show ownership or possession, we can use such words as *belongs to, owned by,* or (most commonly) *of.*

> the knapsack *that belongs to* Crystal
> the house *owned by* my mother
> the sore arm *of* the pitcher

But the apostrophe plus *s* (if the word does not end in *-s*) is often the quickest and easiest way to show possession. Thus we can say:

> Crystal's knapsack
> my mother's house
> the pitcher's sore arm

Points to Remember

1 The *'s* goes with the owner or possessor (in the examples given, *Crystal*, *mother*, and *pitcher*). What follows is the person or thing possessed (in the examples given, *knapsack*, *house*, and *sore arm*). An easy way to determine the owner or possessor is to ask the question "Whom does it belong to?" In the first example, the answer to the question "Whom does the knapsack belong to?" is *Crystal*. Therefore, the *'s* goes with *Crystal*.

2 There should always be a break between the word and the *'s*.

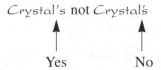

Crystal's not Crystals

    ↑   ↑

   Yes   No

Practice 1: Using Possessive Forms

Rewrite the italicized part of each of the sentences listed below, using the *'s* to show possession. Remember that the *'s* goes with the owner or possessor.

Examples   *The motorcycle owned by Louis* is a frightening machine.

           Louis' motorcycle

           The room-mate of my brother is a sweet and friendly person.

           My brother's room-mate

1. *The sneakers owned by Crystal* were stolen.

2. As a joke, he put on *the lipstick that belongs to Melanie*.

3. The *house of his brother* was burglarized.

4. *The tires belonging to the car* are badly worn.

5. *The bicycle owned by Jan* was stolen from the bike rack outside school.

6. I discovered the *nest of the blue jay* while pruning the tree.

7. I don't like *the title of my paper*.

_____

8. *The arthritis of my mother* gets progressively worse.

_____

9. *The boyfriend belonging to my sister* is an odd-looking man.

_____

10. It is a *game belonging to anybody* at this point.

_____

Practice 2: Finding and Correcting Possessive Forms

Underline the word in each sentence that needs an *'s*. Then write the word correctly in the space at the left. One is done for you as an example.

children's   1. The <u>children</u> voices carried downstairs.

_____ 2. Georgia husband is not a take-charge guy.

_____ 3. My friend computer is also a typewriter.

_____ 4. When the teacher anger became apparent, the class quickly grew quiet.

_____ 5. His girlfriend apple pie made his stomach rebel.

_____ 6. Albert dog looks like a porcupine without its quills.

_____ 7. Under the couch were several of our daughter toys.

_____ 8. My boss car was stolen.

_____ 9. That wine tastes like last night rain.

_____ 10. The dentist charged $50 to fix our son tooth.

Practice 3: Forming Possessive Nouns

Add an *'s* to each of the following words to make it the possessor or owner of something. Then write sentences using the words. Your sentences can be serious or playful. One is done for you as an example.

1. Cary _____ *Cary's* _____

   Cary's hair is bright red. _____

2. neighbour _____

   _____

3. car _____

_____

4. sister _____

_____

5. doctor _____

_____

Apostrophes versus Possessive Pronouns

Do not use an apostrophe with possessive pronouns. They already show ownership. Possessive pronouns include *his*, *hers*, *its*, *yours*, *ours*, and *theirs*.

Correct	*Incorrect*
The bookstore lost its lease.	The bookstore lost its' lease.
The racing bikes were theirs.	The racing bikes were theirs'.
The change is yours.	The change is yours'.
His problems are ours, too.	His' problems are ours', too.
His skin is more tanned than hers.	His' skin is more tanned than hers'.

Apostrophes versus Simple Plurals

When you want to make words plural, just add an *s* or an *es* at the end of the word. Do *not* add an apostrophe. For example, the plural of the word *movie* is *movies*, not *movie's* or *movies'*. Look at this sentence:

When Sally's cat began catching birds, the neighbours called the police.

The words *birds* and *neighbours* are simple plurals, meaning more than one bird, more than one neighbour. The plural is shown by adding *-s* only. (More information about plurals starts on page 213.) On the other hand, the *'s* after *Sally* shows possession—that Sally owns the cat.

Practice: Distinguishing Between Possessive Forms and Plurals

In the space provided under each sentence, add the one apostrophe needed and explain why the other words ending in *s* are simple plurals.

* Words that end in *s*, whether singular or plural, have the possessive apostrophe placed *after* the final *s*.

Example   Sarahs yard is full of gophers.

Sarahs: _Sarah's, meaning "yard of Sarah"_

gophers: _simple plural meaning more than one gopher_

1. The sharp odour of the cheese and onions made Rons eyes water.

    onions: _____

    Rons: _____

    eyes: _____

2. My mothers recipe for potato stuffing is famous among our relatives and friends.

    mothers: _____

    relatives: _____

    friends: _____

3. Sailors ran to their battle stations; the ships alarm had sounded.

    Sailors: _____

    stations: _____

    ships: _____

4. The kites string broke when it got caught in the branches of a tree.

    kites: _____

    branches: _____

5. We met two other girls after our colleges football game and went with them to the movies that night.

    girls: _____

    colleges: _____

    movies: _____

6. Originally the cuffs of mens pants were meant for cigar ashes.

    cuffs: _____

    mens: _____

    pants: _____

    ashes: _____

7. We almost drowned when our inner tubes turned over in the rivers rushing currents.

   inner tubes: _____

   rivers: _____

   currents: _____

8. That movie directors specialty is films about vampires.

   directors: _____

   films: _____

   vampires: _____

9. The secretary made copies of the companys tax returns for the previous three years.

   copies: _____

   companys: _____

   returns: _____

   years: _____

10. Scientists are exploring Africas Congo region for living relatives of the dinosaurs.

   Scientists: _____

   Africas: _____

   relatives: _____

   dinosaurs: _____

Apostrophes with Plural Words Ending in -s

Plurals that end in -s show possession simply by adding the apostrophe, rather than an apostrophe plus s.

Both of my *neighbours'* homes have been burglarized recently.

The many *workers'* complaints were ignored by the company.

All the *campers'* tents were damaged by the hailstorm.

Practice: Finding Plural Possessive Forms

In each sentence, cross out the one plural word that needs an apostrophe. Then write the word out correctly, with the apostrophe, in the space provided.

Example _____ bosses' _____ My two <u>bosses</u> tempers are much the same: explosive.

_____ 1. Icy water from the hose froze on many of the firefighters coats.

_____ 2. Other drivers mistakes have led to my three car accidents.

_____ 3. Two of my friends cars have been stolen recently.

_____ 4. My grandparents television has a 75-centimetre screen.

_____ 5. All of the soldiers uniforms will be replaced.

■ Review Test 1

In each sentence cross out the two words that need apostrophes. Then write the words correctly in the spaces provided.

1. Youre right and Im wrong, though I hate to admit it.

   _____   _____

2. The divers stomach began to cramp as he struggled to the waters surface.

   _____   _____

3. A baby birds throat muscles wont work when its stomach is full.

   _____   _____

4. In the rabbits frenzy to escape the traps hold, it chewed off its hind leg.

   _____   _____

5. If youre rich and caught speeding in Finland, youll pay a stiffer fine than someone who is poorer.

   _____   _____

6. In *The Wild One*, Marlons motorcycle gang roared down Main Street and terrorized the small towns inhabitants.

   _____   _____

7. Im amazed by my sisters perfect recall of how much she has weighed for every important social event.

   _____   _____

8. A golfers chance of making a hole-in-one is nearly ten times better than a bowlers chance of bowling a perfect game.

   _____   _____

9. If youre thinking of entering the contest, youll need to pay an admission fee of $10.

   _____   _____

10. I flinched as someones hands covered my eyes and a voice said, "Dont turn around."

_____   _____

■ Review Test 2

Rewrite the following sentences, changing the underlined words into either (1) a contraction or (2) a possessive.

1. I <u>do not</u> think <u>the diet of Marie</u> has helped her lose weight.

_____

_____

2. <u>I have</u> been warned by friends about <u>the false charms of Michael</u>.

_____

_____

3. <u>The house of the Murphys</u> uses the <u>rays of the sun</u> as a heating source.

_____

_____

4. <u>The bill of the plumber</u> was very high, but his work <u>was not</u> very good.

_____

_____

5. <u>The menu of the restaurant</u> <u>is not</u> very extensive.

_____

_____

QUOTATION MARKS

INTRODUCTORY PROJECT

Read the following scene and underline all the words enclosed within quotation marks. Your teacher may also have you dramatize the scene, with one person reading the narration and two persons acting the two speaking parts of Louis and Sam. The two speakers should imagine the scene as part of a stage play and try to make their words seem as real and true-to-life as possible.

In the registration line-up for elective courses at Granville College, Crystal and Maria became annoyed with Fred, Tony, and Damian. "Tony," Fred said, "take the Canadian Culture course. It's a breeze, I hear." Damian said, "All I want is a course with no heavy reading and only multiple-choice tests. I don't care about the content."

"Canadian culture *is* important," argued Crystal, "because most of our TV and news is dominated by American culture. I *want* to take this course to find out more about what we are as Canadians."

"Who cares," asked Tony. "So long as there's no eighty-dollar textbook, and the course times don't interfere with my hockey practice schedule."

"Right," answered Damian, "raising a kid and working part-time don't leave me time for anybody's culture. I hate reading, so why do more of it?"

Fred, an older student, and Maria's husband, said, "I don't really know what's on the course outline, but I think C.C. consists of a lot of newspaper-article hand-outs and watching videotapes of Canadian TV shows."

"Fred, are you suffering from memory loss?" asked Maria. "I took the course last year, and we had two texts. We had to keep journals of what we watched and read, write our own editorials, and do a final research paper."

"That sounds great." said Crystal. "I read a couple of papers a day anyway, and I'm a big supporter of Canadian talent. I have pretty strong opinions about us as people."

"So do I," answered Tony. "Wayne Gretzky and Shania Twain get my support anytime."

Crystal, annoyed by the trend in the conversation, turned her back on the three men, and returned to reading the Canadian Culture course description.

1. On the basis of the above selection, what is the purpose of quotation marks?

   _____

2. Do commas and periods that come after a quotation go inside or outside the quotation marks?

   _____

Answers are on page 489.

The two main uses of quotation marks are:

1 To set off the exact words of a speaker or writer
2 To set off the titles of short works

Each use is explained on the pages that follow.

QUOTATION MARKS TO SET OFF THE WORDS OF A SPEAKER OR WRITER

Use quotation marks when you want to show the exact words of a speaker or writer:

> "Who left the cap off the toothpaste?" Crystal demanded.
> (Quotation marks set off the exact words that Crystal spoke.)
>
> Stephen Leacock wrote, "Many a man in love with a dimple makes the mistake of marrying the whole girl."
> (Quotation marks set off the exact words that Stephen Leacock wrote.)
>
> "You're never too young," my Aunt Fern often tells me, "to have a heart attack."
> (Two pairs of quotation marks are used to enclose the aunt's exact words.)
>
> Maria complained, "I look so old some days. Even makeup doesn't help. I feel as though I'm painting a corpse!"
> (Note that the end quotes do not come until the end of Maria's speech. Place quotation marks before the first quoted word of a speech and after the last quoted word. As long as no interruption occurs in the speech, do not use quotation marks for each new sentence.)

Punctuation Hint: In the four examples above, notice that a comma sets off the quoted part from the rest of the sentence. Also observe that commas and periods at the end of a quotation always go *inside* quotation marks.

Complete the following statements that explain how capital letters, commas, and periods are used in quotations. Refer to the four examples as guides.

■ Every quotation begins with a _____ letter.

■ When a quotation is split (as in the sentence about Aunt Fern), the second part does not begin with a capital letter unless it is a _____ sentence.

■ _____ are used to separate the quoted part of a sentence from the rest of the sentence.

■ Commas and periods that come at the end of a quote go _____ quotation marks.

The answers are *capital*, *new*, *Commas*, and *inside*.

Practice 1: Placing Quotation Marks

Insert quotation marks where needed in the sentences that follow.

1. Have more trust in me, Crystal said to her mother.
2. The teacher asked Sharon, Why are your eyes closed?
3. Christ said, I come that you may have life, and have it more abundantly.
4. I refuse to wear those itchy wool pants! Jesse shouted at his parents.
5. His father replied, We should give all the clothes you never wear to the Salvation Army.
6. The nervous boy whispered hoarsely over the telephone, Is Linda home?
7. When I was ten, Crystal said, I spent my entire summer playing Monopoly.
8. Tony said, When I was ten, I spent my whole summer playing basketball.
9. The critic wrote about the actor, She runs the gamut of emotions from A to B.
10. The best way to tell if a mushroom is poisonous, the doctor solemnly explained, is if you find it in the stomach of a dead person.

Practice 2: Correctly Citing Quotations

Rewrite the following sentences, adding quotation marks where needed. Use a capital letter to begin a quotation and use a comma to set off a quoted part from the rest of the sentence.

Example   I'm getting tired Sally said.

"I'm getting tired," Sally said.

1. Fred said I'm going with you.

_____

2. Everyone passed the test the teacher informed them.

_____

3. My parents asked where were you?

_____

4. I hate that commercial he muttered.

_____

5. If you don't leave soon, he warned, you'll be late for work.

_____

Practice 3

1. Write three quotations that appear in the first part of a sentence.

   Example "Let's go shopping," I suggested.

   a. _____

   b. _____

   c. _____

2. Write three quotations that appear at the end of a sentence.

   Example Bob asked, "Have you had lunch yet?"

   a. _____

   b. _____

   c. _____

3. Write three quotations that appear at the beginning and end of a sentence.

   Example "If the bus doesn't come soon," Mary said, "we'll freeze."

   a. _____

   b. _____

   c. _____

Indirect Quotations

An indirect quotation is a rewording of someone else's comments rather than a word-for-word direct quotation. The word *that* often signals an indirect quotation.

Direct Quotation	***Indirect Quotation***
George said, "My son is a dare-devil."	George said that his son is a dare-devil.
(George's exact spoken words are given, so quotation marks are used.)	(We learn George's words *in*directly, so no quotation marks are used.)
Carol's note to Arnie read, "I'm at the neighbours'. Give me a call."	Carol left a note for Arnie that said she would be at the neighbours' and he should give her a call.
(The exact words that Carol wrote in the note are given, so quotation marks are used.)	(We learn Carol's words *in*directly, so no quotation marks are used.)

Practice 1: Changing Indirect Quotations to Direct Quotations

Rewrite the following sentences, changing words as necessary to convert the sentences into direct quotations. The first one is done for you as an example.

1. Nick asked Lisa if she had mailed the party invitations.

   Nick asked Lisa, "Have you mailed the party invitations?"

2. Lisa replied that she thought Nick was going to write them this year.

   _____

   _____

3. Nick said that writing invitations was a woman's job.

   _____

   _____

4. Lisa exclaimed that Nick was crazy.

   _____

   _____

5. Nick replied that she had much better handwriting than he did.

   _____

   _____

Practice 2: Changing Direct Quotations into Indirect Quotations

Rewrite the following sentences, converting each direct quotation into an indirect statement. In each case you will have to add the word *that* or *if* and change other words as well.

Example   The barber asked Fred, "Have you noticed how your hair is thinning?"

   The barber asked Fred if he had noticed how his hair was

   thinning.

1. He said, "As the plane went higher, my heart sank lower."

   _____

2. The designer said, "Shag rugs are back in style."

   _____

3. The supervisor asked Jake, "Have you ever operated a lift truck?"

   _____

4. My nosy neighbour asked, "Were Cosmo and Ellen fighting?"

_____

5. Maria complained, "I married a man who eats Tweeties cereal for breakfast."

_____

_____

QUOTATION MARKS TO SET OFF THE TITLES OF SHORT WORKS

Titles of short works are usually set off by quotation marks, while titles of long works are underlined. Use quotation marks to set off the titles of such short works as articles in books, newspapers, or magazines; chapters in a book; short stories; poems; and songs. On the other hand, you should underline the titles of books, newspapers, magazines, plays, movies, CDs, and television shows. See the examples on the next page.

Note: In printed form the titles of long works are set off by italics—slanted type that looks *like this.*

Quotation Marks	*Underlines*
the article "The Toxic Tragedy"	in the book Who's Contaminating Canada
the article "New Cures for Headaches"	in the newspaper The Globe and Mail
the article "When the Patient Plays Doctor"	in the magazine Family Health
the chapter "Connecting with Kids"	in the book Straight Talk
the story "The Dead"	in the book Dubliners
the poem "Cain"	in the book Collected Poems by Irving Layton
the song "Please Forgive Me"	in the album So Far So Good
	the television show The X Files
	the movie Twelve Monkeys

Practice

Use quotation marks or underlines as needed.

1. The young couple opened their brand-new copy of Cooking Made Easy to the chapter titled Meat Loaf Magic.

2. Annabella borrowed Hawthorne's novel The Scarlet Letter from the library because she thought it was about Demi Moore.

3. Did you know that the musical West Side Story is actually a modern version of Shakespeare's tragedy Romeo and Juliet?

4. I used to think that Richard Connell's short story The Most Dangerous Game was the scariest piece of suspense fiction in existence—until I began reading Bram Stoker's classic novel Dracula.

5. Every year at Easter we watch a movie like The Robe on television.

6. During the past year, Canadian Geographic featured an article about mosquitoes titled Biting Flies: Plagues With a Purpose.

7. My father still remembers the way that Julie Andrews sang I Could Have Danced All Night in an early Toronto production of My Fair Lady.

8. As I stand in the supermarket check-out line, I always look at a feature titled Life in Canada Today in Maclean's.

9. My favourite Nylons song is Under the Boardwalk, which can be found in their album Illustrious.

10. Absent-mindedly munching a Dorito, Donna opened the latest issue of Toronto Life to its cover story, Where to Get Stuff Cheap.

OTHER USES OF QUOTATION MARKS

1   To set off special words or phrases from the rest of a sentence:

Many people spell the words "all right" as one word, "alright," instead of correctly spelling them as two words.
I have trouble telling the difference between "principal" and "principle."

2   To mark off a quote within a quote. For this purpose, single quotes (' ') are used:

Stephen Leacock said, "The Lord said, 'let there be wheat' and Saskatchewan was born."
"If you want to have a scary experience," Nick told Lisa, "read Stephen King's story 'The Mangler' in his book *Night Shift*."

3   Periods, question marks, and other final punctuation marks are put *inside* quotation marks.

■ **Review Test 1**

Place quotation marks around the exact words of a speaker or writer in the sentences that follow.

1. Is something wrong with your car again? the mechanic asked Fred.

2. Murphy's law states, Whatever can go wrong, will.

3. Wilfrid Laurier once said, The twentieth century belongs to Canada.

4. The sign read, Be careful how you drive. You may meet a fool.

5. Maria said, Turn on the burglar alarm when you leave the house, Fred.

6. Tony asked the struggling old lady if he could help with her heavy bag. Go to blazes, you masher, she said.

7. Listen, I confided to my sister, Neil told me he is going to ask you to go out with him.

8. The sign in the tough Western saloon read, Carry out your own dead.

9. When the puck hit Doug Gilmour in the helmet and bounced into the crowd, Eric remarked, That was a heads-up play.

10. A woman who was one of Winston Churchill's political enemies once remarked to him, If you were my husband, I would put poison in your coffee. Churchill's reply was, Madam, if I were your husband, I would drink it.

■ **Review Test 2**

1. Write a sentence in which you quote a favourite expression of someone you know. Identify the relationship of the person to you.

   Example   <u>My brother Sam often says after a meal, "That wasn't bad</u>
   <u>at all."</u>

   _____

   _____

2. Write a quotation that contains the words *Tony asked Crystal*. Write a second quotation that includes the words *Crystal replied*.

   _____

   _____

   _____

3. Write a line or sentence that interests or amuses you from a book or poem or song. Identify the title and author of the book.

    Example   *In his poem "The Only Tourist in Havana," Leonard*

    Cohen says, "Let us threaten to join the U.S.A. and pull out

    at the last moment ..."

    _____

    _____

    _____

4. Write a sentence that interests you from a newspaper. Identify the title and the author (if given) of the article.

    _____

    _____

    _____

5. Write a sentence that interests you from a magazine. Identify the title and the author of the article.

    _____

    _____

    _____

■ Review Test 3

Go through the comics section of a newspaper to find a comic strip that amuses you. Be sure to choose a strip where two or more characters are speaking to each other. Write a full description that will enable people who have not read the comic strip to visualize it clearly and appreciate its humour. Describe the setting and action in each panel and enclose the words of the speakers in quotation marks.

COMMAS

INTRODUCTORY PROJECT

A comma often (though not always) signals a minor break or pause in a sentence. Each of the six pairs of sentences below illustrates one of six main uses of the comma. Read each pair of sentences aloud and place a comma wherever you feel a slight pause occurs.

1. a. Joel watched the eleven o'clock news a movie a *Forever Knight* rerun and the station sign-off.

    b. Please endorse your cheque write your account number on the back and fill out a deposit slip.

2. a. Even though I was safe indoors I shivered at the thought of the bitter cold outside.

    b. To start the car depress the accelerator and then turn the ignition key.

3. a. The opossum an animal much like the kangaroo carries its young in a pouch.

    b. George Derek who was recently arrested was a high school class-mate of mine.

4. a. I had enrolled in the course during pre-registration but my name did not appear on the class list.

    b. A police cruiser blocked the busy intersection and an ambulance pulled up on the sidewalk near the motionless victims.

5. a. Emily said "Why is it so hard to remember your dreams the next day?"

    b. "After I left the interview " said David "I couldn't remember a word I had said."

6. a. Mike has driven over 1000000 accident-free kilometres in his job as a long-distance trucker.

    b. The Gates Trucking Company of 1800 Industrial Boulevard Pierrefonds gave Mike an award on October 23 1994 for his superior safety record.

Answers are on pages 490–491.

SIX MAIN USES OF THE COMMA

Commas are used mainly as follows:

1 To separate items in a series
2 To set off introductory material
3 On both sides of words that interrupt the flow of thought in a sentence
4 Between two complete thoughts connected by *and*, *but*, *for*, *or*, *nor*, *so*, *yet*
5 To set off a direct quotation from the rest of a sentence
6 For certain everyday material

You may find it helpful to remember that the comma often marks a slight pause, or break, in a sentence. These pauses or breaks occur at the points where the six main comma rules apply. Read aloud the sentence examples given on the following pages for each of the comma rules and listen for the minor pauses or breaks that are signalled by commas.

At the same time, you should keep in mind that commas are far more often overused than underused. As a general rule, you should *not* use a comma unless a given comma rule applies or unless a comma is otherwise needed to help a sentence read clearly. A good rule of thumb is that "when in doubt" about whether to use a comma, it is often best to "leave it out."

After reviewing each of the comma rules that follow, you will practise adding commas that are needed and omitting commas that are not needed.

1 Commas between Items in a Series

Use a comma to separate items in a series.

> Magazines, paperback novels, and textbooks crowded the shelves.
> Hard-luck Sam needs a loan, a good-paying job, and a close friend.
> Pat sat in the doctor's office, checked her watch, and fidgeted nervously.
> Crystal bit into the ripe, juicy apple.
> More and more people entered the crowded, noisy stadium.

Note:

A comma is used between two descriptive words in a series only if *and* inserted between the words sounds natural. You could say:

> Crystal bit into the ripe *and* juicy apple.
> More and more people entered the crowded *and* noisy stadium.

But notice in the following sentences that the descriptive words do not sound natural when *and* is inserted between them. In such cases, no comma is used.

The model wore a light sleeveless blouse. ("A light *and* sleeveless blouse" doesn't sound right, so no comma is used.)

Dr. Van Helsing noticed two tiny puncture marks on his patient's neck. ("Two *and* tiny puncture marks" doesn't sound right, so no comma is used.)

Practice 1: Placing Commas in a Series

Place commas between items in a series.

1. Maria brought a cake iced with a red flag white snow and green maple leaves to the Canada Day picnic.
2. My brother did the laundry helped clean the apartment waxed the car and watched CBC's *Air Farce*.
3. You can make a Big Mac by putting two all-beef patties special sauce lettuce cheese pickles and onions on a sesame-seed bun.

Practice 2: Correctly Placing Commas

Cross out the one comma that is not needed. Add the one comma that is needed between items in a series.

1. Cold eggs burnt bacon, and watery orange juice are the reasons, I've never returned to that diner for breakfast.
2. Bill relaxes, by reading Donald Duck Archie, and Bugs Bunny comic books.
3. Tonight I've got to work at the restaurant for three hours finish writing a paper, and study, for an exam.

2 Commas after Introductory Material

Use a comma to set off introductory material.

Fearlessly, Crystal picked up the slimy slug.

Just to annoy Tony, she let it crawl along her arm.

Although I have a black belt in karate, I decided to go easy on the demented bully who had kicked sand in my face.

Mumbling under her breath, the woman picked over the tomatoes.

Note:

a If the introductory material is brief, the comma is sometimes omitted. In the activities here, you should include the comma.

b A comma is also used to set off extra material placed at the end of a sentence. Here are two earlier sentences in the book where this comma rule applied:

I spent all day at the employment office, trying to find a job that suited me.
Tony has trouble accepting criticism, except from Crystal.

Practice 1: Placing Commas after Introductory Material

Place commas after introductory material.

1. When I didn't get my paycheque at work I called up the business office. According to the office computer I was dead.
2. After seeing the accident Susan wanted to stop driving forever. Even so she went driving to work next morning over the ice-covered roads.
3. To get her hair done Faye goes to a hairdresser all the way across town. Once there she enjoys listening to the gossip in the hairdresser's shop. Also she likes looking through *Chatelaine* and other magazines in the shop.

Practice 2: Correctly Placing Commas

Cross out the one comma that is not needed. Add the one comma that is needed after introductory material.

1. Even though Tina had an upset stomach she went bowling, with her husband.
2. Looking back over the last ten years I can see several decisions I made, that really changed my life.
3. Instead of going with my family to the mall I decided to relax at home, and to call up some friends.

3   Commas around Words Interrupting the Flow of Thought

Use a comma on both sides of words that interrupt the flow of thought in a sentence.

The car, cleaned and repaired, is ready to be sold.
Maria, our new neighbour, used to work as a bouncer at Rexy's Tavern.
Taking long walks, especially after dark, helps me sort out my thoughts.

Usually you can "hear" words that interrupt the flow of thought in a sentence. However, if you are not sure if certain words are interrupters, remove them from the sentence. If it still makes sense without the words, you know the words are interrupters and that the information they give is nonessential. Such nonessential information is set off with commas. In the following sentence,

Cecile Lalonde, who is my best friend, won a new car in the *Vancouver Sun* sweepstakes.

the words *who is my best friend* are extra information, not needed to identify the subject of the sentence, Cecile Lalonde. Put commas around such nonessential information. On the other hand, in the sentence

The woman who is my best friend won a new car in the *Vancouver Sun* sweepstakes.

the words *who is my best friend* supply essential information needed for us to identify the woman. If the words were removed from the sentence, we would no longer know which woman won the sweepstakes. Commas are not used around such essential information.

Here is another example:

Blood Pact, a novel by Tanya Huff, is the scariest book I've ever read.

Here the words *a novel by Tanya Huff* are extra information, not needed to identify the subject of the sentence, *Blood Pact*. Commas go around such nonessential information. On the other hand, in the sentence

Tanya Huff's novel *Blood Pact* is the scariest book I've ever read.

the words *Blood Pact* are needed to identify the novel. Commas are not used around such essential information.

Most of the time you will be able to "hear" words that interrupt the flow of thoughts in a sentence and will not have to think about whether the words are essential or nonessential.*

Practice 1: Placing Commas Around Interrupters

Add commas to set off interrupting words.

1. Friday is the deadline the absolute final deadline for your papers to be turned in.
2. The nursery rhyme told how the cow a weird creature jumped over the moon. The rhyme also related how the dish who must also have been strange ran away with the spoon.

* Some instructors refer to nonessential or extra information that is set off by commas as a *nonrestrictive clause*. Essential information that interrupts the flow of thought is called a *restrictive clause*. No commas are used to set off a restrictive clause.

3. Tod voted the most likely to succeed in our high school graduating class has just made the front page of our newspaper. He was arrested with other members of the Cruisers a local motorcycle gang for creating a disturbance in the park.

Practice 2: Correctly Placing Commas

Cross out the one comma that is not needed. Add the two commas that are needed to set off interrupting words.

1. My sister's cat which she got from the animal shelter woke her, when her apartment caught on fire.
2. A bulging biology textbook its pages stuffed with notes, and handouts lay on the path to the college parking lot.
3. A baked potato with its crispy skin and soft insides rates as one of my all-time favourite, foods.

4 Commas between Complete Thoughts Connected by a Joining Word

Use a comma between two complete thoughts connected by *and*, *but*, *for*, *or*, *nor*, *so*, *yet*.

My parents threatened to throw me out of the house, so I had to stop playing the drums.

The polyester bed sheets had a gorgeous design on them, but they didn't feel as comfortable as plain cotton sheets.

The teenage girls walked the hot summer streets, and the teenage boys drove by in their shined-up cars.

Notes

a The comma is optional when the complete thoughts are short ones:

Tranh relaxed but Bob kept working.
The pop was flat so I poured it away.
We left school early for the furnace broke down.

b Be careful not to use a comma in sentences having *one* subject and a *double* verb. The comma is used only in sentences made up of two complete thoughts (two subjects and two verbs). In the sentence

Mary lay awake that stormy night and listened to the thunder crashing.

there is only one subject (*Mary*) and a double verb (*lay* and *listened*). No comma is needed. Likewise, the sentence

The quarterback kept the ball and plunged across the goal line for a touchdown.

has only one subject (*quarterback*) and a double verb (*kept* and *plunged*); therefore, no comma is needed.

Practice: Placing Commas Before a Conjunction Between Independent Thoughts

Place a comma before a joining word that connects two complete thoughts (two subjects and two verbs). The four sentences that have only one subject and a double verb do not need commas.

1. The outfielder raced to the warning track and caught the fly ball over his shoulder.
2. The sun set in a golden glow behind the mountain and a single star sparkled in the night sky.
3. Quentin often tries to cut back on his eating but he always gives up after a few days.
4. Her voice became very dry during the long speech and beads of perspiration began to appear on her forehead.
5. Cheryl learned two computer languages in high school and then began writing her own programs.
6. I spent all of Saturday morning trying to fix my car but I still wound up taking it to a garage in the afternoon.
7. She felt like shouting but didn't dare open her mouth.
8. He's making a good living selling cosmetics to hairdressers but he still has regrets about not having gone to college.
9. Crazy Bill often goes into bars and asks people to buy him a drink.
10. He decided not to take the course in advanced math for he wanted to have time for a social life during the semester.

5 Commas with Direct Quotations

Use a comma to set off a direct quotation from the rest of a sentence.

"Please take a number," said the deli clerk.
Fred told Maria, "I've just signed up for a self-assertiveness course."

"Those who sling mud," a famous politician once said, "usually lose ground."

"Reading this book," complained Stan, "is about as interesting as watching paint dry."

Note: A comma or a period at the end of a quotation goes inside quotation marks. See also page 173.

Practice 1: Setting Off Quotations with Commas

Add commas to set off quotations from the rest of the sentence.

1. "I can't wait to have a fish filet and some fries" said Crystal to Tony as she pulled into the order lane at the fast-food restaurant. She asked "What can I get you, Tony?"
2. "Two quarter-pounders with cheese, two large fries, and a large Coke" responded Tony.
3. "Good grief" said Crystal. "It's hard to believe you don't weigh three hundred pounds. In fact" she continued "how much do you weigh?"

Practice 2: Correctly Placing Commas

Cross out the one comma that is not needed. Add the commas that are needed to set off a quotation from the rest of a sentence.

1. "You'd better hurry" Lucy's mother warned "or you're going to miss the last bus, of the morning."
2. "It really worries me" said Dwayne "that you haven't seen a doctor, about that strange swelling under your arm."
3. The student sighed in frustration, and then raised his hand. "My computer has crashed again" he called out to the teacher.

6   Commas with Everyday Material

Use a comma with certain everyday material as shown in the following sections.

Persons Spoken To

Sally, I think that you should go to bed.

Please turn down the stereo, Mark.

Please, sir, can you spare a dollar?

Dates

Our house was burglarized on October 28, 1992, and two weeks later on November 11, 1992.

Addresses

Crystal's sister lives in Markville Acres, 242 Dawnrose Drive, Goderich, Ontario N7A 4C2.

Note: No comma is used before the postal code.

Openings and Closings of Letters

Dear Marilyn,   Sincerely,
Dear John,   Yours Truly,

Note: In formal letters, a colon is used after the opening:

Dear Sir:
Dear Madam:

Numbers

Government officials estimate that Canadians spend about 40,000,000 hours a year filling out federal forms.

Practice: Placing Commas Correctly

Place commas where needed.

1. I am sorry Sir but you cannot sit at this table.
2. On May 6 1954 Roger Bannister became the first person to run a mile in under four minutes.
3. Redeeming the investment certificate before June 30 1996 will result in a substantial penalty.
4. A cash refund of one dollar can be obtained by sending proof of purchase to Cat Heaven 3257 Dunmore Road S.E. Medicine Hat Alberta T1A 7E6.
5. Leo turn off that TV set this minute!

UNNECESSARY USE OF COMMAS

Remember that if no clear comma rule applies for using a comma, it is usually better not to use a comma. As stated earlier, "When in doubt, leave it out." Following are some typical examples of unnecessary commas.

Sharon told me, that my socks were different colours.
(A comma is not used before *that* unless the flow of thought is interrupted.)

The union negotiations, dragged on for three days.
(Do not use a comma between a simple subject and verb.)

I waxed all the furniture, and cleaned the windows.
(Use a comma before *and* only with more than two items in a series or when *and* joins two complete thoughts.)

Sharon carried, the baby into the house.
(Do not use a comma between a verb and its object.)

I had a clear view, of the entire robbery.
(Do not use a comma before a prepositional phrase.)

Practice: Eliminating Unneeded Commas

Cross out the one comma that does not belong in each sentence. Do not add any commas.

1. When I arrived to help with the moving, Jerome said to me, that the work was already done.
2. After the flour and milk have been mixed, eggs must be added, to the recipe.
3. Because my sister is allergic to cat fur, and dust, our family does not own a cat or have any dust-catching drapes or rugs.
4. The guys on the corner, asked, "Have your ever taken karate lessons?"
5. As the heavy Caterpillar tractor, rumbled up the street, our house windows rattled.
6. Windsor, Vancouver, Montreal, and Toronto, are the four places she has worked as a bartender.
7. Thomas Farley, the handsome young man, who just took off his trousers, is an escaped mental patient.
8. Tranh wanted to go to medical school, but he does not have the money, and was not offered a scholarship.
9. Joyce reads, a lot of fiction, but I prefer stories that really happened.
10. Because Mary is single, her married friends do not invite her, to their parties.

■ Review Test 1

Insert commas where needed. In the space provided under each sentence, summarize briefly the rule that explains the use of the comma or commas.

1. After I fell and fractured my wrist I decided to sell my skateboard.

   _____

2. She asked her son "Are you going to church with me tomorrow?"

   _____

3. The weather bureau predicts that sleet fire or brimstone will fall on Ottawa today.

   _____

4. The ignition system in his car as well as the generator was not working properly.

   _____

5. Tony asked Crystal "Have you ever had nightmares in which some kind of monster was ready to swallow you?"

   _____

6. They attacked their bathroom with Lysol Comet and Fantastik.

   _____

7. The pan of bacon fat heating on the stove burst into flame and he quickly set a lid on the pan to put out the fire.

   _____

8. Damian's bad cough which he had had for almost a week began to subside.

   _____

9. I wear thick socks while hiking but I still return from a trip with blistered feet.

   _____

10. When they found pencil shavings in the soup the guests decided they were not hungry.

   _____

■ Review Test 2

1. Write a sentence telling of three items you want to get the next time you go to the store. _____

   _____

2. Write a sentence that describes three things you would like to get done this week. _____

_____

3. Write two sentences, starting the first one with *If a prowler came into my bedroom* and the second one with *Also.* _____

_____

_____

_____

4. Write two sentences describing how you relax after getting home from school or work. Start the first sentence with *After* or *When*. Start the second sentence with *Next.* _____

_____

_____

_____

5. Write a sentence about a selfish or generous person you know. Use the words *a selfish person* or *a generous person* right after his or her name.

_____

_____

6. Write a sentence that tells something about your favourite magazine or television show. Use the words *which is my favourite magazine* or *which is my favourite television show* after the name of the magazine or show.

_____

_____

7. Write two complete thoughts about foods you enjoy. Use *and* to join the two complete thoughts. _____

_____

8. Write two complete thoughts about a person you know. The first thought should tell of something you like about the person. The second thought should tell of something you don't like. Join the thoughts with *but.*

_____

_____

_____

9. Invent a line that Crystal might say to Tony. Use the words *Crystal said* in the sentence. _____

_____

10. Write a remark that you made to someone today. Use the words *I said* somewhere in the middle of the sentence. _____

_____

■ Review Test 3

On a separate sheet of paper, write six sentences, with each sentence demonstrating one of the six main comma rules.

OTHER
PUNCTUATION
MARKS

INTRODUCTORY PROJECT

Each of the sentences below needs one of the following punctuation marks:

;   —   -   ( )   :

Insert the correct mark in each case.

1. The following singers were nominated by the Genie Awards Committee for Best Female Artist Alannah Myles, Alanis Morissette, Shania Twain, k.d. lang, and Celine Dion.

2. A life size statue of her cat adorns the living room of Diana's penthouse.

3. Sigmund Freud, the pioneer psychoanalyst 1856–1939 , was a habitual cocaine user.

4. As children, we would put pennies on the railroad track we wanted to see what they would look like after being run over by a train.

5. The stuntwoman was battered, broken, barely breathing but alive.

Answers are on page 493.

COLON (:)

The colon is a mark of introduction. Use the colon at the end of a complete statement to do the following:

1 Introduce a list.

My little brother has three hobbies: playing video games, racing his Hot Wheels cars all over the floor, and driving me crazy.

2 Introduce a long quotation.

Janet's paper was based on a passage from George Eliot's novel *Middlemarch*: "If we had a keen vision and feeling of all ordinary human life, it would be like hearing the grass grow and the squirrel's heart beat, and we should die of that roar which lies on the other side of silence. As it is, the quickest of us walk about well wadded with stupidity."

3 Introduce an explanation.

There are two ways to do this job: the easy way and the right way.

Two minor uses of the colon are after the opening in a formal letter (*Dear Sir or Madam:*) and between the hour and the minute when writing the time (*The bus will leave for the game at 11:45*).

Practice

Place colons where needed.

1. Lisa had an excellent excuse for being late for work an early-morning power failure that stopped her alarm clock.
2. I ordered the following items from The Bay two pairs of jeans, four plaid flannel shirts, and a wide leather belt.
3. In her speech, Mrs. Wagner quoted William Hazlitt "Man is the only animal that laughs and weeps, for he is the only animal that is struck with the difference between what things are and what they ought to be."

SEMI-COLON (;)

The semi-colon signals more of a pause than the comma alone but not quite the full pause of a period. Use a semi-colon to do the following:

1   Join two complete thoughts that are not already connected by a joining word such as *and*, *but*, *for*, or *so*.

The chemistry lab blew up; Professor Thomas was fired.
I once stabbed myself with a pencil; a black mark has been under my skin ever since.

2   Join two complete thoughts that include a transitional word such as *however*, *otherwise*, *moreover*, *furthermore*, *therefore*, or *consequently*.

I cut and raked the grass; moreover, I weeded the lawn.
Sally finished processing the paper; however, she forgot to bring it to class.

Note: The first two uses of the semi-colon are treated in more detail on pages 43–44.

3   Mark off items in a series when the items themselves contain commas.

This fall I won't have to work on Labour Day, September 3; Remembrance Day, November 11; or Thanksgiving Day, October 14.
At the final Weight Watchers' meeting, prizes were awarded to Sally Wong, for losing 10 kilos; Irving Ross, for losing 12 kilos; and Betty McNulty, the champion loser, who lost 40 kilos.

Practice

Place semi-colons where needed.

1. There's an old saying about law school: in the first year, they scare you to death in the second year, they work you to death and in the third year, they bore you to death.
2. I find some television commercials for soap ads ridiculous for example, people are always grinning as the shower spray pelts their teeth.
3. The following persons have been elected to the National Board of Bank Executives: Ellen Green, Canadian National Bank Jay Hunt, Alberta Co op Bank and M. O. Granby, Farmers' Regional Trust.

DASH (—)

A dash signals a degree of pause longer than a comma but not as complete as a period. Use the dash to set off words for dramatic effect.

I suggest—no, I insist—that you stay for dinner.

The prisoner walked toward the electric chair—grinning.

A meaningful job, a loving wife, and a car that wouldn't break down all the time—these are the things he wanted in life.

Practice

Place dashes where needed.

1. The car is in excellent condition except that the brakes don't always work.
2. I can be ready in ten minutes in fact, I'm ready now.
3. Hunting, fishing, and doing odd jobs around the house rather than going to work these are the activities I enjoy.

HYPHEN (-)

Use a hyphen in the following ways:

1 With two or more words that act as a single unit describing a noun.

The society ladies nibbled at the deep-fried grasshoppers.
A white-gloved server then put some snails on their table.

Note: Your dictionary will often help when you are unsure about whether to use a hyphen between words.

2 To divide a word at the end of a line of writing or typing.

Although it had begun to drizzle, the teams decided to play the championship game that day.

Note: Line-justification in word processing eliminates the need to break words into syllables.

3 Certain Canadian spellings, such as "semi-colon" or "room-mate," are hyphenated.

Notes

a Always divide a word between syllables. Use your dictionary (see page 202) to be sure of correct syllable divisions.
b Do not divide words of one syllable.
c Do not divide a word if you can avoid dividing it.

Practice

Place hyphens where needed.

1. I went food shopping with about sixty five dollars in my pocket and came back with about sixty five cents.
2. The ten year old girl was remarkably self confident when she was giving her speech.
3. My wife's aunt and uncle, who live in a split level house, have been unable to prevent mildew from forming on the walls of the lower level.

PARENTHESES ( )

Use parentheses to do the following:

1   Set off extra or incidental information from the rest of a sentence.

The chapter on drugs in our textbook (pages 142–178) contains some frightening statistics.

The normal body temperature of a cat (30–32°C) is 1°C higher than the temperature of its owner.

2   Enclose letters or numbers that signal items in a series.

Three steps to follow in previewing a textbook are to (1) study the title, (2) read the first and last paragraphs, and (3) study the headings and subheadings.

Note: Do not use parentheses too often in your writing. Parentheses tend to de-emphasize the importance of words placed within them.

Practice

Add parentheses where needed.

1. For tomorrow we must study the charts pages 16–20 in the first chapter of our biology text.
2. To make better use of your time, you should prepare 1 a daily list of things to do and 2 a weekly study schedule.
3. A recent study revealed that people who are heavy coffee drinkers five or more cups a day suffer many more ill effects than those whose coffee intake is less.

■ Review Test 1

At the appropriate spot or spots, place the punctuation mark shown in the margin.

 Example   **;**   The singles dance was a success; I met several people I wanted to see again.

:

1. Before you go anywhere, finish your chores the laundry, the dishes, and the vacuuming.

—

2. The Easter Bunny, Santa Claus, and the Tooth Fairy these were the idols of my youth.

-

3. Tom's self important manner makes him boring to be with.

( )

4. The two most important steps in writing an effective paper are 1 to make a point of some kind and 2 to provide specific evidence to support that point.

:

5. Albert Einstein once said "It is in fact nothing short of a miracle that the modern methods of instruction have not yet entirely strangled the holy curiosity of inquiry; for this delicate little plant, aside from stimulation, stands mainly in need of freedom; without this it goes to wrack and ruin without fail."

;

6. Damian bought a remote-control unit for his television set as a result, he can switch off the sound during commercials.

—

7. I asked the server to return the steak which seemed to consist of more fat than meat to the kitchen.

-

8. Fred always brings a pair of wide angle binoculars to the football games.

( )

9. The television set is relatively new having been bought only a year ago but has been to the repair shop three times.

;

10. Angelo had a lot of studying to do: for sociology, he had to read two articles for his math course, he had to interpret an entire page of graphs and for English, he had to catch up on his journal.

■ Review Test 2

On a separate sheet of paper, write two sentences for each of the following punctuation marks: colon, semi-colon, dash, hyphen, parentheses.

DICTIONARY USE

INTRODUCTORY PROJECT

The dictionary is an indispensable tool, as will be apparent if you try to answer the following questions *without* using the dictionary.

1. Which one of the following words is spelled incorrectly?

    fortutious   macrobiotics   stratagem

2. If you wanted to hyphenate the following word correctly, at which points would you place the syllable divisions?

    h i e r o g l y p h i c s

3. What common word has the sound of the first *e* in the word *chameleon*?

4. Where is the primary accent in the following word?

    o c t o g e n a r i a n

5. What are two separate meanings of the word *earmark*?

Your dictionary is a quick and sure authority on all these matters: spelling, syllabication, pronunciation, and word meanings. And as the chapter ahead will show, it is a source for many other kinds of information as well.

Answers are on page 493.

The dictionary is a valuable tool. To take advantage of it, you need to understand the main kinds of information that a dictionary gives about a word. Look at the information provided for the word *dictate* in the following entry from the *Oxford Advanced Learner's Dictionary.**

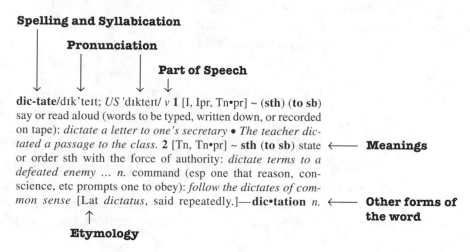

SPELLING

The first bit of information, in the **boldface** (heavy type) entry itself, is the spelling of *dictate*. You probably already know the spelling of *dictate*, but if you didn't, you could find it by pronouncing the syllables in the word carefully and then looking it up in the dictionary.

Use your dictionary to correct the spelling of the following words:

alright _____	elavater _____
assosiation _____	plesure _____
awkwerd _____	balence _____
diferent _____	beleiving _____
omited _____	libary _____
opinyon _____	apetite _____
critikal _____	happyness _____
embarasment _____	usualy _____
probaly _____	suprise _____

* *Oxford Advanced Learner's Dictionary.* Copyright © Oxford University Press 1948, 1963, 1974, 1989, 1990.

SYLLABICATION

The second bit of information that the dictionary gives, also in the boldface entry, is the syllabication of *dic•tate*. Note that a dot separates each syllable (or part) of the word.

Use your dictionary to mark the syllable divisions in the following words. Also indicate how many syllables are in each word.

be lieve   (_____ syllables)

treach er ous   (_____ syllables)

dis sat is fied   (_____ syllables)

un prec e dent ed   (_____ syllables)

Noting syllable divisions will enable you to *hyphenate* a word: divide it at the end of one line of writing and complete it at the beginning of the next line. You can correctly hyphenate a word only at a syllable division, and you may have to check your dictionary to make sure of a particular word's syllable divisions.

PRONUNCIATION

The third bit of information in the dictionary entry is the pronunciation of *dictate*: (dɪkˈteɪt) or (dɪkteɪt). You already know how to pronounce *dictate*, but if you did not, the information within the parentheses would serve as your guide. Use your dictionary to complete the following exercises that relate to pronunciation.

Vowel Sounds

You will probably use the pronunciation key in your dictionary mainly as a guide to pronouncing different vowel sounds (vowels are the letters *a, e, i, o,* and *u*). Here is a section of the pronunciation key that appears in the paperback *Oxford Advanced Learner's Dictionary*:

æ as in **hat** /hæt/   ɪ as in **sit** /sɪt/

ɑ as in **arm** /ɑːm/   aɪ as in **five** /faɪv/

eɪ as in **page** /peɪdʒ/

e as in **ten** /ten/

iː as in see /siː/

The key tells you, for example, that the sound of the short *a* (= æ) is pronounced like the *a* in *hat*, the sound of the long *a* is like the *a* (= eɪ) in *page*, and the sound of the short *e* is like the *e* in *ten*.

Now look at the pronunciation key in your dictionary. The key is probably located in the front of the dictionary or at the bottom of every page. What common word in the key tells you how to pronounce each of the following sounds?

[ĕ] _____   [aʊ] _____

[ɑ] _____   [ɔɪ] _____

[ʊ] _____   [u] _____

(Note that the long vowel always has the sound of its own name.)

The Schwa (ə)

The symbol [ə] looks like an upside-down *e*. The International Phonetic Alphabet calls this symbol a *schwa*, and it stands for the unaccented sound in such words as *about*, *item*, *edible*, *gallop*, and *circus*. More approximately, it stands for the sound *uh*—like the *uh* that speakers sometimes make when they hesitate in their speech. Perhaps it would help to remember that *uh*, as well as ə, could be used to represent the schwa sound.

Here are some of the many words in which the sound appears: *socialize* (sō′ shə līz or sō′ shuh līz); *legitimate* (lə jĭt′ ə mĭt or luh jĭt′ uh mĭt); *oblivious* (ə blĭv′ ē əs or uh blĭv′ ē uhs). Open your dictionary to any page, and you will almost surely be able to find three words that make use of the schwa in the pronunciation in parentheses after the main entry. Write three such words and their pronunciations in the following spaces:

1. _____

2. _____

3. _____

Accent Marks

Some words contain both a primary accent, shown by a heavy stroke (′), and a secondary accent, shown by a lighter stroke (′). For example, in the word *vicissitude* (vɪ′sɪsitju:d′), the stress, or accent, goes chiefly on the first syllable (vɪ′), and, to a lesser extent, on the last syllable (tju:d′).

Use your dictionary to add stress marks to the following words:

soliloquy (sə′lɪləkwɪ)

diatribe (dī ə trīb)

rheumatism (roō mə tĭz əm)

representation (rĕp rĭ zĕn tā shən)

Note: Dictionaries will vary in their notation of vowel sounds and of consonant pronunciation. The first example shows the Oxford notation; the other three examples show other standard notation systems.

Full Pronunciation

Use your dictionary to write out the full pronunciation (the information given in parentheses) for each of the following words:

1. enigma _____
2. inveigle _____
3. tenacious _____
4. salient _____
5. permeate _____
6. epitome _____
7. cognizant _____
8. indigenous _____

9. insouciant _____
10. neuralgia _____
11. ethereal _____
12. capricious _____
13. fastidious _____
14. pejorative _____
15. camaraderie _____

Now practise pronouncing each word. Use the pronunciation key in your dictionary as an aid to sounding out each syllable. Do *not* try to pronounce a word all at once; instead, work on mastering *one syllable at a time.* When you can pronounce each of the syllables in a word successfully, then say them in sequence, add the accent, and pronounce the entire word.

OTHER INFORMATION ABOUT WORDS

Parts of Speech

The dictionary entry for *dictate* includes the abbreviation *v.* This means that the meanings of *dictate* as a verb will follow. The abbreviation *n.* is then followed by the meaning of *dictate* as a noun.

At the front of your dictionary, you will probably find a key that will explain the meanings of abbreviations used in the dictionary. Use the key to fill in the meanings of the following abbreviations:

pl. = _____   adj. = _____

sing. = _____   adv. = _____

Principal Parts of Irregular Verbs

Dictate is a regular verb and forms its principal parts by adding *-d*, *-d*, and *-ing* to the stem of the verb. When a verb is irregular, the dictionary lists its principal parts. For example, with *begin* the present tense comes first (the entry itself, *begin*). Next comes the past tense (*began*), and then the past participle (*begun*)— the form of the verb used with such helping words as *have*, *had*, and *was*. Then comes the present participle (*beginning*)—the *-ing* form of the word.

Look up the principal parts of the following irregular verbs and write them in the spaces provided. The first one has been done for you.

Present Tense	Past Tense	Past Participle	Present Participle
see	saw	seen	seeing
go	_____	_____	_____
ride	_____	_____	_____
speak	_____	_____	_____

Plural Forms of Irregular Nouns

The dictionary supplies the plural forms of all irregular nouns (regular nouns form the plural by adding *-s* or *-es*). Give the plurals of the following nouns:

cemetery _____

knife _____

veto _____

neurosis _____

Note: See page 220 for more information about plurals.

Meanings

When there is more than one meaning to a word, the meanings are numbered in the dictionary, as with the verb *dictate*. In many dictionaries, the most common meanings are presented first. The introductory pages of your dictionary will explain the order in which meanings are presented.

Use the sentence context to try to explain the meaning of the underlined word in each of the following sentences. Write your definition in the space provided.

Then look up and record the dictionary meaning of the word. Be sure you pick out the meaning that fits the word as it is used in the sentence.

1. The surgeons first <u>flushed</u> the patient's chest cavity with sterile fluid.

   Your definition: _____

   Dictionary definition: _____

2. Several well-known actors make <u>cameo</u> appearances in the director's first movie.

   Your definition: _____

   _____

   Dictionary definition: _____

   _____

3. The spy story was so <u>riveting</u> I stayed awake till 2:00 a.m. reading it.

   Your definition: _____

   Dictionary definition: _____

Etymology

Etymology refers to the history of a word. Many words have origins in foreign languages, such as Greek (Gk) or Latin (L). Such information is usually enclosed in brackets and is more likely to be present in a large-format dictionary than in a compact one. Good dictionaries include the following:

> *The Gage Canadian Dictionary*
> *The Oxford Advanced Learner's Dictionary*
> *The Concise Oxford Dictionary*
> *Funk & Wagnall's Canadian College Dictionary*

A good dictionary may tell you, for example, that the word *cannibal* derives from the name of the man-eating tribe, the Caribs, that Christopher Columbus encountered on his arrival on Cuba and Haiti. Cannibalism, however, was *never* limited to any *one* group; many cultures practised it as a ritual.

See if your dictionary says anything about the origins of the following words.

bikini _____

_____

sandwich _____

_____

tantalize _____

_____

breakfast _____

_____

* Find three other interesting new word origins and share them with your class.

Usage Labels

As a general rule, use only standard English words in your writing. If a word is not standard English, your dictionary will probably give it a usage label like one of the following: *informal, nonstandard, slang, vulgar, obsolete, archaic, rare.*

Look up the following words and record how your dictionary labels them. Remember that a recent large-format dictionary will always be the best source of information about usage.

break (meaning *a stroke of luck*) _____

cop out _____

uptight _____

ritzy _____

gripe _____

Synonyms

A *synonym* is a word that is close in meaning to another word. Using synonyms helps you avoid unnecessary repetition of the same word in a paper. A paperback dictionary is not likely to give you synonyms for words, but a good desk dictionary will. (You might also want to own a *thesaurus*, a book that lists synonyms and antonyms. An *antonym* is a word approximately opposite in meaning to another word.)

Consult a good dictionary that gives synonyms for the following words, and write the synonyms in the spaces provided.

fear _____

answer _____

love _____

■ Review Test

Use your dictionary to answer the following questions.

1. How many syllables are in the word *cinematography*? _____

2. Where is the primary accent in the word *domesticity*? _____

3. In the word *oppressive*, the *o* is pronounced like
   a. schwa
   b. short *o*
   c. long *u*
   d. long *o*

4. In the word *culpable*, the *a* is pronounced like
   a. short *a*
   b. long *a*
   c. short *i*
   d. schwa

5. In the word *negotiate*, the first *e* is pronounced like
   a. short *e*
   b. long *e*
   c. schwa
   d. short *i*

Items 6–10: There are five misspelled words in the following sentence. Cross out each misspelled word and write the correct spelling in the spaces provided.

The college I plan to transferr to will accept my psikology credits, the counseler told me, but I will not recieve credit for my courses in introductory mathamatics and basic English.

6. _____

7. _____

8. _____

9. _____

10. _____

SPELLING
IMPROVEMENT

INTRODUCTORY PROJECT

Circle the word that is misspelled in each of the following pairs:

akward	*or*	awkward
exercise	*or*	exercize
business	*or*	buisness
worried	*or*	worryed
shamful	*or*	shameful
begining	*or*	beginning
partys	*or*	parties
sandwichs	*or*	sandwiches
heroes	*or*	heros

Answers are on page 494.

Poor spelling often results from bad habits developed in early school years. With work, such habits can be corrected. If you can write your name without misspelling it, there is no reason that you can't do the same with almost any word in the English language. Following are seven steps you can take to improve your spelling.

STEP 1: USING THE DICTIONARY

Get into the habit of using the dictionary. When you write a paper, allow yourself time to look up the spelling of all those words you are unsure about. Do not overlook the value of this step just because it is such a simple one. Just by using the dictionary, you can probably make yourself a 95 per cent better speller.

STEP 2: KEEPING A PERSONAL SPELLING LIST

Keep a list of words you misspell and study the words regularly. Use the space on the inside front cover of this book as a starter. When you accumulate additional words, you may want to use a back page of your English notebook.

Hint: When you have trouble spelling long words, try to break each word down into syllables and see whether you can spell the syllables. For example, *mis-demeanour* can be spelled easily if you can hear and spell in turn its four syllables: *mis-de-mean-our*. The word *formidable* can be spelled easily if you hear and spell in turn its four syllables: *for-mi-da-ble*. Remember, then: try to see, hear, and spell long words in terms of their syllable parts.

STEP 3: MASTERING COMMONLY CONFUSED WORDS

Master the meanings and spellings of the commonly confused words on pages 224–238. Your instructor may assign twenty words for you to study at a time and give you a series of quizzes until you have mastered all the words.

STEP 4: USING ELECTRONIC AIDS

There are three electronic aids that may help your spelling. First, the word-processing program you use with either your computer or the computers at your college undoubtedly has a *spell-checker* as part of its capabilities. Making use of the spell-checker for every document you prepare will enable you to identify incorrectly spelled words and to select from suggested correct spellings. Spell-checking systems cannot differentiate between unintentional mistakes in word usage, though. "Same sound" words, homonyms like *its* and *it's* or *there*, *their*, and *they're*, spelled correctly but used incorrectly, cannot be corrected by a spell-checker. You may want to highlight these words on your processor screen and double-check your intended meaning and spelling with the dictionary.

Second, *electronic spell-checkers* are pocket-size devices that look much like pocket calculators. They are among the latest examples of how technology can help the learning process. Electronic spellers can be found in the computer and electronics sections of most department, office supplies, or electronics stores. The checker includes a tiny keyboard. You type out the word the way you think it is spelled, and the checker supplies the correct spelling of related words. Some checkers even *pronounce* the word aloud for you. Canadian students will want to ask whether British/Canadian or American spelling systems are programmed into the spell-checker they select, and should find out whether or not instructors permit the use of these devices in classes and exams.

Third, many *electronic typewriters* on the market today will beep automatically when you misspell or mistype a word. They include built-in dictionaries that will then give you the correct spelling.

STEP 5: UNDERSTANDING BASIC SPELLING RULES

Explained briefly here are three rules that may improve your spelling. While exceptions sometimes occur, the rules hold true most of the time.

1   *Change y to i.*   When a word ends in a consonant plus *y*, change *y* to *i* when you add an ending.

try	+ ed = tried	marry + es	= marries
worry	+ es = worries	lazy	+ ness = laziness
lucky	+ ly = luckily	silly	+ est	= silliest

2   *Final silent e.*   Drop a final *e* before an ending that starts with a vowel (the vowels are *a*, *e*, *i*, *o*, and *u*).

hope + ing = hoping	sense + ible = sensible
fine + est = finest	hide + ing = hiding

Keep the final *e* before an ending that starts with a consonant.

use + ful = useful	care + less = careless
life + like = lifelike	settle + ment = settlement

3 *Doubling a final consonant.*   Double the final consonant of a word when all the following are true:

a   The word is one syllable or is accented on the last syllable.
b   The word ends in a single consonant preceded by a single vowel.
c   The ending you are adding starts with a vowel.

sob   + ing = sobbing   big   + est = biggest
drop + ed = dropped   omit + ed = omitted
admit + ing = admitting   begin + ing = beginning

Practice

Combine the following words and endings by applying the three rules above.

1. study + ed = _____
2. advise + ing = _____
3. carry + es = _____
4. stop   + ing = _____
5. terrify + ed = _____

6. compel + ed = _____
7. retire   + ing = _____
8. hungry + ly = _____
9. expel   + ing = _____
10. judge   + es = _____

A NOTE ABOUT CANADIAN SPELLING

Canadian spelling has become a subject of contention. Many Canadian newspapers use what we think of as "American" forms of words like *neighbor* or *color*. These are choices made by their style guides. Canadian spelling is neither British nor American spelling; it is a "hybrid," or mixture of the two. Student confusion is understandable.

Check for your instructor's preference, but choose *one* spelling system, and **be consistent**. Choose an Oxford dictionary, which this text uses, or a Canadian dictionary, like *Gage* or *Penguin*. If your word-processing program's spell-check system allows you to choose between British or American spelling, choose British, which is sometimes called "UK Lex."

This text uses the Canadian "hybrid" or mixture of spelling styles. The main differences between American and Canadian spellings are such words as the *-or/our* words, like *honour*, *neighbour*, *labour*, *flavour*, the *-er/-re* endings on words like *theatre*, *litre*, *centre*, *fibre*, and the *-se/-ce* word endings such as *defence*, *licence*, and *offence*.

Many Canadian spellings use double "l's" where American spellings do not. Examples are words like "tranqui*ll*izer" and "counse*ll*or." Past tenses of some verbs ending in "l" double the final "l" in Canadian spelling: for example, "travelled," "cancelled."

This text does *not* maintain certain spellings which are currently regarded as "British": for example, *analyse*, *emphasise*, and *programme*. Current Canadian style guides and dictionaries now prevail in favour of *analyze*, *emphasize*, and *program*.

STEP 6: UNDERSTANDING PLURALS

Most words form their plurals by adding *-s* to the singular.

Singular	*Plural*
blanket	blankets
pencil	pencils
street	streets

Some words, however, form their plurals in special ways, as shown in the rules that follow.

1 Words ending in *-s, -ss, -z, -x, -sh,* or *-ch* usually form the plural by adding *-es*.

kiss	kisses		inch	inches
box	boxes		dish	dishes

2 Words ending in a consonant plus *y* form the plural by changing *y* to *i* and adding *-es*.

party	parties		county	counties
baby	babies		city	cities

3 Some words ending in *f* change the *f* to *v* and add *-es* in the plural.

leaf	leaves		life	lives
wife	wives		yourself	yourselves

4 Some words ending in *o* form their plurals by adding *-es*.

potato	potatoes		mosquito	mosquitoes
hero	heroes		tomato	tomatoes

5 Some words of foreign origin have irregular plurals. When in doubt, check your dictionary.

antenna   antennae   crisis   crises
criterion criteria   medium   media

6 Some words form their plurals by changing letters within the word.

man   men   foot   feet
tooth teeth   goose   geese

7 Combined words (words made up of two or more words) form their plurals by adding -s to the main word.

brother-in-law   brothers-in-law
passer-by   passersby

Note: The importance of spelling correctly will not decline with technological advances in, and changes to, the workplace. The Internet and other international communications systems will be part of your personal and professional future. Clear and understandable communication relies on standardized spelling. In the twenty-first century, individual illiteracy bounced off satellites and transmitted through fibre-optic cable becomes an international liability to employers and private citizens alike.

Practice: Forming Correct Plurals

Complete these sentences by filling in the plural of the word at the left.

grocery   1. I carried six bags of _____ into the house.

town   2. How many _____ did you visit during the tour?

supply   3. While the Lone Ranger waited at the campsite, Tonto rode into town to get some _____.

body   4. Because the gravediggers were on strike, _____ piled up in the morgue.

lottery   5. She plays two provincial _____ in hopes of winning a fortune.

pass   6. Dave caught six _____ in a losing cause.

tragedy   7. That woman has had to endure many _____ in her life.

watch   8. I have found that cheap _____ work better for me than expensive ones.

suit   9. To help himself feel better, he went out and bought two _____.

boss   10. I have not one but two _____ to worry about every day.

STEP 7: MASTERING A BASIC WORD LIST

Make sure you can spell all the words in the following list. They are some of the words used most often in English. Again, your instructor may assign twenty words for you to study at a time and give you a series of quizzes until you have mastered the words.

ability	bargain	daily	general
absent	beautiful	danger	grocery
accident	because	daughter	guess
across	become	decide	happy
address	before	death	heard
advertise	begin	deposit	heavy
advice	being	describe	height
after	believe	different	himself
again	between	direction	holiday
against 40	bottom	distance 100	house
all right	breathe	doubt	however
almost	building	dozen	hundred
a lot	business	during	hungry
always	careful	each	important
although	careless	early	instead
among	cereal	earth	intelligence
angry	certain	education	interest
animal	change	either	interfere
another	cheap	English	kitchen
20 answer	chief 80	enough	knowledge
anxious	children	entrance	labour
apply	church	everything	language
approve	cigarette	examine	laugh
argue	clothing	exercise	leave
around	collect	expect	length
attempt	colour	family	lesson
attention	comfortable	flower	letter
awful	company	foreign	listen
awkward	condition	friend	loneliness
balance 60	conversation	garden 120	making

marry	ought	restaurant	through
match	pain	ridiculous	ticket
matter	paper	said	tired
measure	pencil	same	today
medicine	people	sandwich	together
middle	perfect	send	tomorrow
might	period	sentence	tongue
million	personal	several	tonight
minute	picture	shoes	touch
mistake	160 place	should	220 travel
money	pocket	since	truly
month	possible	sleep	understand
morning	potato	smoke	unity
mountain	president	something	until
much	pretty	soul	upon
needle	problem	started	usual
neglect	promise	state	value
newspaper	property	straight	vegetable
noise	psychology	street	view
140 none	public	200 strong	visitor
nothing	question	student	voice
number	quick	studying	warning
ocean	raise	success	watch
offer	ready	suffer	welcome
often	really	surprise	window
omit	reason	teach	would
only	receive	telephone	writing
operate	recognize	theory	written
opportunity	remember	thought	year
original	180 repeat	thousand	240 yesterday

■ Review Test

Use the three spelling rules to spell the following words.

1. cry   + es   = _____

2. believe + able = _____

3. bury   + ed   = _____

4. date   + ing = _____

5. lonely + est = _____

6. large   + er   = _____

7. skim   + ed   = _____

8. rare   + ly   = _____

Circle the correctly spelled plural in each pair.

 9. beliefs   believs

10. churchs   churches

11. bullys   bullies

12. countries   countrys

13. womans   women

14. potatos   potatoes

Circle the correctly spelled word (from the basic word list) in each pair.

15. foreign   foriegn

16. condicion   condition

17. restarant   restaurant

18. opportunity   oportunity

19. entrance   enterance

20. surprise   surprize

OMITTED WORDS
AND LETTERS

Be careful not to leave out words or letters when you write. The omission of words like *a*, *an*, *of*, *to*, or *the* or the -*s* ending needed on nouns or verbs may confuse and irritate your readers. They may not want to read what they regard as careless work.

FINDING OMITTED WORDS AND LETTERS

Finding omitted words and letters, like finding many other sentence-skills mistakes, is a matter of careful proofreading. You must develop your ability to look carefully at a page to find places where mistakes may exist.

The exercises here will give you practice in finding omitted words and omitted -*s* endings on nouns. Another section of this book (pages 54–55) gives you practice in finding omitted -*s* endings on verbs.

Practice: Adding Omitted Words

Add the missing word (*a*, *an*, *the*, *of*, or *to*) as needed.

Example Some people regard television as ˄*a* tranquillizer that provides temporary relief from ˄*the* pain and anxiety ˄*of* modern life.

1. When I began eating box of chicken I bought at the fast-food restaurant, I found several pieces that consisted of lot crust covering nothing but chicken bones.

2. Sally had teacher who tried light a piece of chalk, thinking it was cigarette.

3. In his dream, Harry committed perfect crime: he killed his enemy with icicle, so murder weapon was never found.

4. Dr. Yutzer told me not worry about sore on my foot, but I decided to get second opinion.

5. As little girl ate vanilla sugar cone, ice cream dripped out hole at the bottom onto her pants.

6. When thick black clouds began form and we felt several drops rain, we knew picnic would be cancelled.

7. After spending most her salary on new clothes, Susan looks like something out of fashion magazine.

8. As wasps buzzed around room, I ran for can of Raid.

9. Sam put pair wet socks in oven, for he wanted dry them out quickly.

10. Because weather got hot and stayed hot for weeks, my flower garden started look like dried flower arrangement.

The Omitted *-s* Ending

The plural form of regular nouns usually ends in *-s*. One common mistake that some people make with plurals is to omit this *-s* ending. People who drop the ending from plurals when speaking also tend to do it when writing. This tendency is especially noticeable when the meaning of the sentence shows that a word is plural.

> Ed and Mary pay two hundred dollar a month for an apartment that has only two room.

The *-s* ending has been omitted from *dollars* and *rooms*.

The activities that follow will help you correct the habit of omitting the *-s* endings from plurals.

Practice 1: Forming Plurals

Add *-s* endings where needed.

Example   Bill beat me at several game͜ₛof darts.

1. When Naheed's two boyfriend met each other last night, they almost came to blow.

2. My brother let out a choice selection of curse when he dropped his watch in the sand.

3. We were expected to write an essay of several paragraph on key event leading up to the War of 1812.

4. Sunlight reflected off the windshield of the many car in the parking lot.

5. A number of house along the elevated subway route have been torn down to make room for two new highway that are being built.

6. Rainy day depress me, especially during those time when I am depressed already.

7. Our drive along the shoreline was marred by the billboard that seem to have popped up everywhere.

8. There were no folding chair in the room; instead, people were asked to sit on pillow spread around the floor.

9. From the top of either of those watchtower, you can see three Maritime provinces.

10. Motorist waited restlessly as several tow truck worked to remove the tractor trailer spread-eagled across the highway.

Practice 2: Creating Sentences Which Use Correct Plurals

Write sentences that use plural forms of the following pairs of words.

Example   girl, bike   <u>The little girls raced their bikes down the street.</u>

1. paper, grade _____

   _____

2. pillow, bed _____

   _____

3. sock, shoe _____

   _____

4. day, night _____

   _____

5. game, loss _____

   _____

Note: People who drop the *-s* ending on nouns also tend to omit endings on verbs. Pages 53–54 will help you correct the habit of dropping endings on verbs.

■ Review Test 1

In each of the following sentences, two small connecting words are needed. Write them in the spaces provided, and write a caret (∧) at each place in the sentence where a connecting word should appear.

_____   1. Like ostriches, the two men hunched over car's hood buried their heads in the
_____   engine.

_____   2. Each time I put my bare foot down on hot asphalt road, I think I left layer of
_____   skin behind.

_____ 3. Lisa sneaked out of diner when the server wasn't looking; she didn't have enough money leave a tip.
_____

_____ 4. Vince held lighted match to his car door, trying unfreeze the lock.
_____

_____ 5. I can't remember the name the book we were assigned read for Friday's class.
_____

■ Review Test 2

Add the two -*s* endings needed in each sentence.

_____ 1. Fred keeps two giant jar of multicoloured vitamin on the counter.
_____

_____ 2. The grimy fingerprint of the workers had smudged the electric switchplate in the living and dining rooms.
_____

_____ 3. If I could just get together a thousand dollar, I think all my money problem could be solved.
_____

_____ 4. Crystal had big plan for the weekend, but all Tony wanted to do was watch a series of football game on television.
_____

_____ 5. When Eddie opened the package of shirt from the laundry, he discovered that many button were missing.
_____

COMMONLY CONFUSED WORDS

INTRODUCTORY PROJECT

Circle the five words that are misspelled in the following passage. Write their correct spellings in the spaces provided.

If your a resident of a temperate climate, you may suffer from feelings of depression in the winter and early spring. Scientists are now studying people who's moods seem to worsen in winter, and there findings show that the amount of daylight a person receives is an important factor in "seasonal depression." When a person gets to little sunlight, his or her mood darkens. Its fairly easy to treat severe cases of seasonal depression; the cure involves spending a few hours a day in front of full-spectrum fluorescent lights that contain all the components of natural light.

1. _____

2. _____

3. _____

4. _____

5. _____

Answers are on pages 495–496.

HOMONYMS

The commonly confused words shown below (also known as *homonyms*) have the same sounds but different meanings and spellings. Complete the activities for each set of words, and check off and study the words that give you trouble.

all ready	pair	threw
already	pear	through
brake	passed	to
break	past	too
		two
coarse	peace	
course	piece	wear
		where
hear	plain	
here	plane	weather
		whether
hole	principal	
whole	principle	whose
		who's
its	right	
it's	write	your
		you're
knew	than	
new	then	
know	their	
no	there	
	they're	

all ready   completely prepared
already   previously; before

   We were *all ready* to go, for we had eaten and packed *already* that morning.

Fill in the blanks: I was _____ to start ordering breakfast when I found out that the restaurant had _____ shifted to its luncheon menu.

Write sentences using *all ready* and *already*.

_____

_____

brake   stop
break   come apart

Delia slams the *brake* pedal so hard that I'm afraid I'll *break* my neck in her car.

Fill in the blanks: Al tried to put the _____ on his appetite, but the luscious rum cake made him _____ all his resolutions.

Write sentences using *brake* and *break*.

_____

_____

coarse   rough
course   part of a meal; a school subject; direction; certainly (with *of*)

During the *course* of my career as a server, I've dealt with some very *coarse* customers.

Fill in the blanks: Weaving a wall hanging with _____ yarns is part of the arts and crafts _____ .

Write sentences using *coarse* and *course*.

_____

_____

hear   perceive with the ear
here   in this place

If I *hear* another insulting ethnic joke *here*, I'll leave.

Fill in the blanks: My mother always says, "Come _____ if you can't _____ what I'm saying."

Write sentences using *hear* and *here*.

_____

_____

hole   an empty spot
whole   entire

If there is a *hole* in the tailpipe, I'm afraid we will have to replace the *whole* exhaust assembly.

Fill in the blanks: The _____ in the wallboard gives the _____ living room a neglected look.

Write sentences using *hole* and *whole*.

_____

_____

its belonging to it
it's the shortened form for *it is* or *it has*

The kitchen floor has lost *its* shine because *it's* been used as a roller-skating rink by the children.

Fill in the blanks: _____ the chemistry course with _____ lab requirement that worries me.

Write sentences using *its* and *it's*.

_____

_____

knew past tense of *know*
new not old

We *knew* that the *new* television comedy would be cancelled quickly.

Fill in the blanks: If you _____ in advance all the _____ turns your life would take, you might give up.

Write sentences using *knew* and *new*.

_____

_____

know to understand
no a negative

I never *know* who might drop in even though *no* one is expected.

Fill in the blanks: When that spoiled boy's parents say _____ to him, we all _____ a temper tantrum is likely to result.

Write sentences using *know* and *no*.

_____

_____

pair   a set of two
pare   to peel
pear   a fruit

The dessert consisted of a *pair* of thin biscuits topped with vanilla ice cream and poached *pear* halves.

Fill in the blanks: The _____ grove is one of the places where the

_____ of escaped convicts was spotted last week.

Write sentences using *pair* and *pear*.

_____

_____

passed   went by; succeeded in; handed to
past   by, as in "I drove past the house"; a time before the present

After Eliza *passed* the driver's test, she drove *past* all her friends' houses and honked the horn.

Fill in the blanks: In her _____ jobs, Lucy had _____
up several opportunities for promotion because she did not want to seem aggressive.

Write sentences using *passed* and *past*.

_____

_____

peace   calm
piece   a part

The *peace* of the little town was shattered when a *piece* of a human body was found in the town dump.

Fill in the blanks: The judge promised to give the troublemaker more than

just a _____ of his mind if the boy ever disturbed the

_____ again.

Write sentences using *peace* and *piece*.

_____

_____

plain   simple
plane   aircraft

The *plain* box contained a very expensive model *plane* kit.

Fill in the blanks: That _____-looking man boarding the

_____ is actually a famous movie director.

Write sentences using *plain* and *plane*.

_____

_____

principal   main; a person in charge of a school; amount of money borrowed
principle   a law or standard

My *principal* goal in child rearing is to give my daughter strong *principles* to live by.

Fill in the blanks: The school _____ defended the school's

_____ regarding a dress code for students.

Write sentences using *principal* and *principle*.

_____

_____

Note: It might help to remember that the *e* in *principle* is also in *rule*—the meaning of *principle*.

right   correct; opposite of *left*
write   what you do in English

It is my *right* to refuse to *write* my name on your petition.

Fill in the blanks: Ellen wanted to _____ and thank Steve for his

flowers, but she didn't think it _____ to keep leading him on.

Write sentences using *right* and *write*.

_____

_____

than   used in comparisons
then   at that time

I glared angrily at my boss, and *then* I told him our problems were more serious *than* he suspected.

Fill in the blanks: I went to the front porch to get my newspaper, and _____ I made my breakfast. The news on the front page was no more cheerful _____ it had been the day before.

Write sentences using *than* and *then*.

_____

_____

Note: It might help to remember that *then* is also a time signal.

their belonging to them
there at that place; a neutral word used with verbs like *is*, *are*, *was*, *were*, *have*, and *had*
they're the shortened form of *they are*

The tenants *there* are complaining because *they're* being cheated by *their* building owners.

Fill in the blanks: Some Canadian tribes once lived _____, building unique lives in _____ longhouses; now _____ gone.

Write sentences using *their*, *there*, and *they're*.

_____

_____

_____

threw past tense of *throw*
through from one side to the other; finished

When a character in a movie *threw* a cat *through* the window, I had to close my eyes.

Fill in the blanks: My favourite sweat socks went _____ hundreds of washings before they started to disintegrate; then my mother _____ them away.

Write sentences using *threw* and *through*.

_____

_____

to   a verb part, as in *to smile*; toward, as in "I'm going to heaven."
too   overly, as in "The pizza was too hot"; also, as in "The coffee was hot, too."
two the number 2

> Crystal drove to the store to get some ginger ale. (The first *to* means *toward*; the second *to* is a verb part that goes with *get*.)
>
> The sport jacket is *too* tight; the slacks are tight, *too*. (The first *too* means *overly*; the second *too* means *also*.)
>
> The *two* basketball players leaped for the jump ball. (2)

Fill in the blanks: _____ Ayesha, the _____ holidays just meant _____ much company and _____ little rest.

Write sentences using *to*, *too*, and *two*.

_____

_____

_____

wear   to have on
where in what place

> I work at a nuclear reactor, *where* one must *wear* a radiation-detection badge at all times.

Fill in the blanks: If you _____ your jacket buttoned up, no one will see _____ the stain is.

Write sentences using *wear* and *where*.

_____

_____

weather atmospheric conditions
whether if it happens that; in case; if

> Because of the threatening *weather*, it's not certain *whether* or not the game will be played.

Fill in the blanks: The _____ is glorious, but I don't know _____ the water is warm enough for swimming.

Write sentences using *weather* and *whether.*

_____

_____

whose   belong to whom
who's   the shortened form for *who is* and *who has*

> The man *who's* the author of the latest diet book is a man *whose* ability to cash in on the latest craze is well known.

Fill in the blanks: Don is determined to find out _____ van is in the street and _____ been watching him from it with binoculars.

Write sentences using *whose* and *who's.*

_____

_____

your   belonging to you
you're   the shortened form of *you are*

> Since *your* family has a history of heart disease, *you're* the kind of person who should take extra health precautions.

Fill in the blanks: When _____ always the last person chosen for a team, _____ self-confidence dwindles away.

Write sentences using *your* and *you're.*

_____

_____

OTHER WORDS FREQUENTLY CONFUSED

Following is a list of other words that people frequently confuse. Complete the activities for each set of words, and check off and study the ones that give you trouble.

a	beside	fewer
an	besides	less
accept	can	former
except	may	latter
advice	clothes	loose
advise	cloths	lose
affect	desert	quiet
effect	dessert	quite
among	does	though
between	dose	through

a   Both *a* and *an* are used before other words to mean, approximately, *one*.
an

Generally you should use *an* before words starting with a vowel (*a, e, i, o, u*), or before words starting with a vowel sound:

  an absence   an exhibit   an idol   an offer   an upgrade

Generally you should use *a* before words starting with a consonant (all other letters), or with a consonant sound:

  a pen   a ride   a digital clock   a movie   a neighbour

Fill in the blanks: Crystal bought her mother _____ orchid and

_____ slinky nightgown for her birthday.

Write sentences using *a* and *an*.

_____

_____

accept   receive; agree to
except   exclude; but

  If I *accept* your advice, I'll lose all my friends *except* you.

Fill in the blanks: _____ for one detail, my client is willing to

_____ this offer.

Write sentences using *accept* and *except*.

_____

_____

advice   a noun meaning *an opinion*
advise   a verb meaning *to counsel, to give advice*

> Jake never listened to his parents' *advice*, and he ended up listening to a cop *advise* him of his rights.

Fill in the blanks: Maria Grimaldi's doctor said, "I _____ you to follow my diet rather than take the _____ of the minister who promised you could lose weight through prayer."

Write sentences using *advice* and *advise*.

_____

_____

affect   a verb meaning *to influence*
effect   a verb meaning *to bring about something*; a noun meaning *result*

> My sister Sally cries for *effect*, but my parents caught on and her act no longer *affects* them.

Fill in the blanks: The loud music began to _____ my hearing, creating a high-pitched ringing _____ in my ears.

Write sentences using *affect* and *effect*.

_____

_____

among   implies three or more
between implies only two

> We selfishly divided the box of candy *between* the two of us rather than *among* all the members of the family.

Fill in the blanks: _____ the twenty-five girls on the camping trip, arguments developed only _____ the two counsellors.

Write sentences using *among* and *between*.

_____

_____

beside   along the side of
besides   in addition to

> Fred sat *beside* Maria. *Besides* them, there were ten other people at the Tupperware party.

Fill in the blanks: I love this class; _____ the fact that the course has thought-provoking content, I sit _____ a Michael J. Fox lookalike.

Write sentences using *beside* and *besides*.

_____

_____

can   refers to the ability to do something
may   refers to permission or possibility

> If you *can* work overtime on Saturday, you *may* take Monday off.

Fill in the blanks: When she _____ speak English fluently, she _____ be eligible for that job.

Write sentences using *can* and *may*.

_____

_____

clothes   articles of dress
cloths   pieces of fabric

> I tore up some old *clothes* to use as polishing *cloths*.

Fill in the blanks: I keep some _____ next to me to wipe up any food spills before they reach the baby's _____.

Write sentences using *clothes* and *cloths*.

_____

_____

desert   a stretch of dry land; to abandon one's post or duty
dessert   last part of a meal

Don't *desert* us now; order a sinful *dessert* along with us.

Fill in the blanks: When it's time to order _____, that man's appetite will never _____ him.

Write sentences using *desert* and *dessert*.

_____

_____

does   a form of the verb *do*
dose   an amount of medicine

Maria *does* not realize that a *dose* of brandy is not the best medicine for the flu.

Fill in the blanks: _____ she understand the importance of taking only the prescribed _____?

Write sentences using *does* and *dose*.

_____

_____

fewer   used with things that can be counted
less   refers to amount, value, or degree

I missed *fewer* classes than Rafael, but I wrote *less* effectively than he did.

Fill in the blanks: I've had _____ attacks of nerves since I began drinking _____ coffee.

Write sentences using *fewer* and *less*.

_____

_____

former   refers to the first of two items named
latter   refers to the second of two items named

I turned down both the service-station job and the shipping-clerk job; the *former* involved irregular hours and the *latter* offered very low pay.

Fill in the blanks: Howard doesn't like babies or dogs: the _____ cry when they see him and the _____ try to bite him.

Write sentences using *former* and *latter*.

_____

_____

Note: Be sure to distinguish *latter* from *later* (meaning *after some time*). Very often people will use the word *latter* when in fact they mean *later*.

loose   not fastened; not tight-fitting
lose   misplace; fail to win

   I am afraid I'll *lose* my ring: it's too *loose* on my finger.

Fill in the blanks: Crystal told Tony, "You look dumpy when you wear a _____-fitting shirt. You _____ all the wonderful lines of your chest."

Write sentences using *loose* and *lose*.

_____

_____

quiet   peaceful
quite   entirely; really; rather

   After a busy day, the children were not *quiet*, and their parents were *quite* tired.

Fill in the blanks: My friends regarded Bob as _____ a catch, but he was just too _____ for me.

Write sentences using *quiet* and *quite*.

_____

_____

though   despite the fact that
thought   past tense of *think*

   Though I enjoyed the dance, I *thought* the cover charge of $5 was too high.

Fill in the blanks: _____ Pam is now content, she once
_____ her unhappiness would never end.

Write sentences using *though* and *thought*.

_____

_____

INCORRECT WORD FORMS

Following is a list of incorrect word forms that people sometimes use in their writing. Complete the activities for each word, and check off and study the words that give you trouble.

being that	could of	would of
can't hardly	must of	irregardless
couldn't hardly	should of	

being that   **Incorrect!** Use *because* or *since*.

                           because
I'm going to bed now ~~being that~~ I must get up early tomorrow.

Correct the following sentences.

1.   Being that she's a year older than I am, Mary thinks she can run my life.

2.   I think school will be cancelled, being that the bus drivers are on strike.

3.   Being that I didn't finish the paper, I didn't go to class.

can't hardly   **Incorrect!** Use *can hardly* or *could hardly*.
couldn't hardly

                         can
Small store owners ~~can't~~ hardly afford to offer large discounts.

Correct the following sentences.

1.   I can't hardly understand why Nelson would cut class when he's madly in love with the teacher.

2. You can't hardly imagine how I felt when I knocked over my aunt's favourite plant.

3. You couldn't hardly see last night because of the heavy fog.

could of   **Incorrect!** Use *could have*, *must have*, *should have*, *would have*
must of
should of
would of

                have
I should ~~of~~ applied for a loan when my credit was good.

Correct the following sentences.

1. Anita must of gone home from work early.

2. I should of started reading the textbook early in the semester.

3. If the game had been cancelled, they would of been very disappointed.

4. If Mary had wanted to, she could of come with us.

irregardless   **Incorrect!** Use *regardless*.

      Regardless
~~Irregardless~~ of what anyone says, he will not change his mind.

Correct the following sentences.

1. They decided to buy the house irregardless of the price.

2. That company insures people irregardless of their age or state of health.

3. Irregardless of the risk, I started mountain climbing as a hobby.

■ Review Test 1

These sentences check your understanding of *its*, *it's*; *there*, *their*, *they're*; *to*, *too*, *two*; and *your*, *you're*. Underline the correct word in the parentheses. Rather than guess, look back at the explanations of the words when necessary.

1. Some stores will accept (your, you're) credit card but not (your, you're) money.

2. I know (its, it's) late, but (its, it's) important to get this job done properly.

3. (There, Their, They're) is a good baseball game down at the playground, but (there, their, they're) (to, too, two) busy to walk down (there, their, they're).

4. (Its, It's) been an hour since I put the TV dinner in the oven, but (its, it's) still not ready.

5. (There, Their, They're) going to be away for (to, too, two) weeks and want me to go over to (there, their, they're) yard to water (there, their, they're) rose bushes.

6. (Your, You're) going to have to do a better job on (your, you're) final exam if you expect to pass the course.

7. That issue is (to, too, two) hot for any politician (to, too, two) handle.

8. If (your, you're) hoping to get good grades on (your, you're) essay tests, you need to improve (your, you're) handwriting.

9. (There, Their, They're) planning to trade in (there, their, they're) old car for a new one before taking (there, their, they're) vacation.

10. (Your, You're) going to have to put aside individual differences and play together for the benefit of (your, you're) team.

■ Review Test 2

The sentences that follow check your understanding of a variety of commonly confused words. Underline the correct word in the parentheses. Rather than guess, look back at the explanations of the words when necessary.

1. I try to get (through, threw) each day without a cigarette. I (through, threw) away my old magazine collection because their tempting cigarette ads were (affecting, effecting) my resolve.

2. We weren't sure (whether, weather) or not a storm was brewing until several hours had passed. (Then, Than) the air became (quiet, quite), clouds formed, and we (knew, new) enough to run indoors.

3. (Being that, Since) "Stormy (Weather, Whether)" is her favourite song, I (should of, should have) gotten her an album with that song on it.

4. Take my (advice, advise) and hurry down (to, too, two) the radio station. You'll get a (pair, pear) of free tickets to the rock concert.

5. For Crystal the (principal, principle) (course, coarse) of the meal—a (desert, dessert) of French vanilla ice cream and blueberry pie—was yet (to, too, two) come.

6. (Its, It's) obvious why (know, no) one is eating the cheese; (there, their, they're) frightened by (its, it's) unusual smell.

7. The first (course, coarse) of the meal was soup. Its (principal, principle) ingredient was onion, to which I'm allergic. Trying to be polite, I ate one mouthful, but (than, then) I began to sneeze uncontrollably.

8. As he (passed, past) by the church, he (though, thought) of the Sunday mornings he had spent (there, their, they're) in the (passed, past).

9. The night after I watched the horror movie, I dreamed that (a, an) gigantic (hole, whole) opened up in the earth, swallowed a whole city, and (than, then) tried to swallow me, (to, too, two).

10. "I'm going to let you be my (knew, new) woman," the man declared. "(Your, You're) my (peace, piece) of property from now on."

"(Whose, Who's) messed up (your, you're) head?" the woman replied. "I can't believe I (hear, here) you (right, write). (Where, Wear) are you at? I think you have been (affected, effected) by the sun."

■ Review Test 3

On separate paper, write short sentences using the ten words shown below.

there	then	you're	affect	who's
past	advise	too (meaning *also*)	its	break

EFFECTIVE WORD CHOICE

INTRODUCTORY PROJECT

Put a check mark beside the sentence in each pair that you feel makes more effective use of words.

1. After the softball game, we wolfed down a few burgers and drank a couple of brews. _____

   After the softball game, we ate hamburgers and drank beer. _____

2. A little birdie told me you're getting married next month. _____

   Someone told me you're getting married next month. _____

3. The personality-adjustment inventories will be administered on Wednesday. _____

   Psychological tests will be given on Wednesday. _____

4. The referee in the game, in my personal opinion, made the right decision in the situation. _____

   I think the referee made the right decision. _____

Now, circle the correct number in each case:

Pair (1, 2, 3, 4) contains a sentence with slang; pair (1, 2, 3, 4) contains a sentence with a cliché; pair (1, 2, 3, 4) contains a sentence with pretentious words; and pair (1, 2, 3, 4) contains a wordy sentence.

Answers are on pages 496–497.

Choose your words carefully when you write. Always take the time to think about your word choices rather than simply using the first word that comes to mind. You want to develop the habit of selecting words that are appropriate and exact for your purposes. One way you can show your sensitivity to language is by avoiding slang, clichés, pretentious words, and wordiness.

SLANG

We often use slang expressions when we talk because they are so vivid and colourful. However, slang is usually out of place in formal writing. Here are some examples of slang expressions:

> The party was a *real horror show*.
>
> I don't want to *lay a guilt trip* on you.
>
> Our boss is not *playing with a full deck*.
>
> Dad *flipped out* when he learned that Jan had *totalled* the car.

Slang expressions have a number of drawbacks. They go out of date quickly, they become tiresome if used excessively in writing, and they may communicate clearly to some readers but not to others. Also, the use of slang can be an evasion of the specific details that are often needed to make one's meaning clear in writing. For example, in "The party was a real horror show," the writer has not provided the specific details about the party necessary for us to understand the statement clearly. Was it the setting, the food and drink (or lack of same), the guests, the music, the hosts, the writer, or what that made the party such a dreadful experience? In general, then, you should avoid the use of slang in your writing. If you are in doubt about whether an expression is slang, it may help to check a recently published large-format dictionary.

Practice: Creating More Appropriate Tone through Word-Choice

Rewrite the following sentences, replacing the italicized slang words with more formal ones.

Example   My friend had *wheels*, so we decided to *cut out* of the *crummy* dance.

We decided to use my friend's car to leave the boring dance.

1. If you don't *get your act together* in this course, you're going to be *blown away* by the midterm exam.

   _____

   _____

2. Living with a room-mate is a *drag*, but the *extra bread* helps when the rent is due.

   _____

   _____

3. The football game was a *real wipeout*; we *got our butts kicked*.

   _____

   _____

4. If people keep *bad-mouthing* Gene, soon no one will *hang out* with him.

   _____

   _____

5. I *pushed the panic button* when the teacher called on me. My brain went *out to lunch*.

   _____

   _____

CLICHÉS

Clichés are expressions that have been worn out through constant use. Some typical clichés are:

all work and no play	saw the light
at a loss for words	short but sweet
better late than never	sigh of relief
drop in the bucket	singing the blues
easier said than done	taking a big chance
had a hard time of it	time and time again
in the nick of time	too close for comfort
in this day and age	too little, too late
it dawned on me	took a turn for the worse
it goes without saying	under the weather
last but not least	where he/she is coming from
make ends meet	word to the wise
on top of the world	work like a dog
sad but true	

Clichés are common in speech but make your writing seem tired and stale. Also, they are often an evasion of the specific details that you must work to provide in your writing. You should, then, avoid clichés and try to express your meaning in fresh, original ways.

Practice 1: Choosing More Precise Wording

Underline the cliché in each of the following sentences. Then substitute specific, fresh words for the trite expression.

> **Example**   My parents supported me through some <u>trying times</u>.
> *rough years*

1. The physical exam didn't shed any light on why I was getting headaches.

   _____

2. I heaved a sigh of relief when I learned my final grade for the course was a B.

   _____

3. The CD began selling like hotcakes as soon as it was released.

   _____

4. Helen could not have cared less whom Pete was dating.

   _____

5. Since my mother was feeling under the weather, she didn't go to work.

   _____

Practice 2

Write a short paragraph describing the kind of day you had. Try to put as many clichés as possible into your writing. For example, "I had a long hard day. I had a lot to get done, and I kept my nose to the grindstone." By making yourself aware of clichés in this way, you should lessen the chance that they will appear in your writing.

PRETENTIOUS WORDS

Some people feel they can improve their writing by using fancy and elevated words rather than more simple and natural words. They use artificial and stilted language that more often obscures their meaning than communicates it clearly. Here are some unnatural-sounding sentences:

> The football combatants left the gridiron.
> His instructional technique is a very positive one.
> At the counter, we inquired about the arrival time of the aircraft.
> I observed the perpetrator of the robbery depart from the retail establishment.

The same thoughts can be expressed more clearly and effectively by using plain, natural language, as below:

The football players left the field.

He is a good teacher.

At the counter, we asked when the plane would arrive.

I saw the robber leave the store.

Here is a list of some other inflated words and the simple words that could replace them.

Inflated Words	Simpler Words
component	part
delineate	describe
facilitate	help
finalize	finish
initiate	begin
manifested	shown
subsequent to	after
to endeavour	to try
transmit	send

Practice: Making Clear and Specific Word Choices

Cross out the artificial words in each sentence. Then substitute clear, simple language for the artificial words.

Example   Sally was ~~terminated~~ from her ~~employment~~.

Sally was fired from her job.

1. My television receiver is not operative.

    _____

2. We made an expedition to the mall to see the new fall apparel.

    _____

3. Vince indicated an aversion to fish.

    _____

4. The fans expressed their displeasure when the pitcher threw the ball erratically.

    _____

5. How long have you resided in that municipality?

    _____

WORDINESS

Wordiness — using more words than necessary to express a meaning — is often a sign of lazy or careless writing. Your readers may resent the extra time and energy they must spend when you have not done the work needed to make your writing direct and concise. Here are examples of wordy sentences:

At this point in time in our large urban areas, the amount of violence seems to be increasing every day.

I called to the children repeatedly to get their attention, but my shouts did not get any response from them.

Omitting needless words improves the sentences:

Violence is increasing in large cities in Canada.

I called to the children repeatedly, but they didn't respond.

Here is a list of some wordy expressions that could be reduced to single words.

Wordy Form	*Short Form*
a large number of	many
a period of a week	a week
arrive at an agreement	agree
at an earlier point in time	before
at the present time	now
big in size	big
due to the fact that	because
during the time that	while
five in number	five
for the reason that	because
good benefit	benefit
I personally	I
in every instance	always
in my own personal opinion	I think
in the event that	if
in the near future	soon
in this day and age	today
is able to	can
large in size	large
plan ahead for the future	plan
postponed until later	postponed
red in colour	red
return back	return

Practice: Eliminating Unneeded Words

Rewrite the following sentences, omitting needless words.

Example   Starting as of the month of June, I will be working at the store on a full-time basis.

As of June, I will be working at the store full time.

1. Because of the fact that it was raining, I didn't go shopping.

    _____

2. As far as I am concerned, in my opinion I do not feel that prostitution should be legalized.

    _____

3. Please do not hesitate to telephone me if you would like me to come into your office for an interview.

    _____

4. During the time that I was sick and out of school, I missed a total of three math tests.

    _____

5. Well-paying jobs are all too few and far between unless a person has a high degree of training.

    _____

■ Review Test 1

Certain words are italicized in the following sentences. In the space provided, identify whether the words are slang (*S*), clichés (*C*), or pretentious words (*PW*). Then replace them with more effective words.

_____   1. If the boss starts *putting heat* on me again, I'm going to quit.

    _____

_____   2. Because of the rain, I wore a jacket that *has seen better days*.

    _____

_____   3. Ted won't help us unless we offer *a monetary reward*.

    _____

_____   4. When my younger brother did not get home from the party until 2:00 a.m., my mother decided *to put her foot down*.

    _____

_____   5. My upset stomach was *alleviated* by the antacid.

    _____

_____ 6. The vacation spot was a *total rip-off*; the weather and the food were both *the pits*.

_____

_____ 7. Stan *saw the error of his ways* and began to work harder.

_____

_____ 8. I needed *a respite from my exertions* after I finished typing the long report.

_____

_____ 9. I *jumped for joy* when I heard about the promotion.

_____

_____ 10. *You could have wiped me off the floor* when I learned my old girlfriend was on drugs.

_____

■ Review Test 2

Rewrite the following sentences, omitting needless words.

1. At this point in time, I cannot say with any degree of certainty that I am planning to participate in the blood drive.

    _____

    _____

2. Due to the fact that there was no consensus of opinion, the committee agreed that it should meet again.

    _____

    _____

3. As far as Jason is concerned, he thinks that a working day of eight hours of work is too demanding for the average Canadian worker.

    _____

    _____

4. For the price of $600, you can purchase outright this car of mine.

    _____

    _____

5. Without a doubt, the importance of the question of abortion as an issue cannot be denied.

    _____

    _____

PART TWO

REINFORCEMENT
OF THE SKILLS

INTRODUCTION

To reinforce the sentence skills presented in Part One, this part of the book consists of mastery tests, combined mastery tests, proofreading tests, and editing tests. Four *mastery tests* appear for each of the skills where errors occur most frequently; two *mastery tests* are provided for each of the remaining skills. A series of *combined mastery tests* measures your understanding of important related skills. *Editing* and *proofreading tests* offer practice in finding and correcting one kind of skills error in a brief passage. *Combined editing tests* then offer similar practice—except that the passages contain a variety of skills mistakes. Both the editing and proofreading tests will help you become a skilful editor and proofreader. All too often, students can correct mistakes in practice sentences but are unable to do so in their own writing. They must learn to look carefully for skills errors and to make such close checking a habit.

Appendix C provides progress charts that will help you keep track of your performance on these tests.

MASTERY TESTS

SUBJECTS AND VERBS

■ Mastery Test 1

Draw one line under the subjects and two lines under the verbs. Cross out prepositional phrases where needed to help find subjects. (Be sure to underline all the parts of a verb. Also, remember that you may find more than one subject and one verb in a sentence.)

1. My son pours chocolate milk on his cereal.

2. A solution to the problem popped suddenly into my head.

3. The salad and potatoes fed only half the guests.

4. That man on the corner may ask you for a quarter.

5. The fallen power line jumped and sparked on the street.

6. Crystal likes to walk barefoot across the campus.

7. Nick and Lisa sang together and banged on the piano.

8. The flashing lights of the police car appeared unexpectedly in my rear-view mirror.

9. Julio often plays the stereo but almost never watches television.

10. We sat by a large rock, munched peanuts, and talked for hours.

Score: Number correct _____ × 10 = _____%

SUBJECTS AND VERBS

■ Mastery Test 2

Draw one line under the subjects and two lines under the verbs. Cross out prepositional phrases where needed to help find subjects. (Be sure to underline all the parts of a verb. Also, remember that you may find more than one subject and one verb in a sentence.)

1. I may hitchhike to the Calgary Stampede this year.

2. Those tulips make my eyes itch.

3. Carol will be studying all day for the test.

4. Strange behaviour in our house is the norm rather than the exception.

5. The prices of jewelry items in that specialty store have been reduced.

6. Fred and Maria refuse to drive their car at night.

7. I walked out to the garage last night and ran into a rug on the clothesline.

8. The rising tide will start to wash away that sandcastle.

9. Harriet buys clothing impulsively, sends off for lots of mail-order items, and in general quickly spends her money.

10. The girls paddled their canoe across the lake and visited some boys at the camp on the other side.

Score: Number correct _____ × 10 = _____%

SUBJECTS AND VERBS

■ Mastery Test 3

Draw one line under the subjects and two lines under the verbs. Cross out prepositional phrases where needed to help find subjects. (Be sure to underline all the parts of a verb. Also, remember that you may find more than one subject and one verb in a sentence.)

1. Crystal believes in extrasensory perception.

2. The drawer of the dresser sticks on rainy days.

3. The little boy squirmed impatiently in his father's arms.

4. The window fan made a clanking sound and kept them awake at night.

5. The shrubs are starting to grow too close to the side of the house.

6. Three members of the basketball team have been suspended from school.

7. Jerry began to study seriously before final exams.

8. The newspaper seller shouted out the headlines and soon sold all the papers.

9. They won a lifetime supply of dish detergent on the game show but do not have any room for it in their house.

10. The shattered glass, cracked foundations, and fallen signs throughout the city resulted from earthquake tremors.

Score: Number correct _____ × 10 = _____%

SUBJECTS AND VERBS

■ Mastery Test 4

Draw one line under the subjects and two lines under the verbs. Cross out prepositional phrases where needed to help find subjects. (Be sure to underline all the parts of a verb. Also, remember that you may find more than one subject and one verb in a sentence.)

1. The nail under the rug barely missed my toe.

2. I have studied over eight hours for my biology test.

3. Tony and Crystal just bought matching sweatshirts.

4. The game has been postponed because of bad weather.

5. Our families played badminton and volleyball at the picnic.

6. Behind all that mud you will see my daughter's face.

7. The beginning of that movie should not be missed.

8. Fred began to exercise seriously after his heart attack.

9. Jack has been thinking about the job offer but has not made a decision yet.

10. The people on the tour bus dozed, read magazines, talked to each other, or snapped pictures.

Score: Number correct _____ × 10 = _____%

SENTENCE FRAGMENTS

■ Mastery Test 1

Each word group in the student paragraph below is numbered. In the space provided, write *C* if a word group is a complete sentence; write *Frag* if it is a fragment. You will find ten fragments in the paragraph.

1. _____
2. _____
3. _____
4. _____
5. _____
6. _____
7. _____
8. _____
9. _____
10. _____
11. _____
12. _____
13. _____
14. _____
15. _____
16. _____
17. _____
18. _____
19. _____
20. _____

[1] I was seventeen on the night I died. [2] In the spring of 1995. [3] I had a severe case of the flu. [4] And had spent the first three days of my illness in bed. [5] Running a temperature between 35°C and 37°C. [6] Only getting up to take care of the necessities of life. [7] On Friday, the sixth day of my illness, rain from early morning on. [8] The wind howled outside, the house was damp and chilly, and my fever seemed higher than ever. [9] In late afternoon, I took my pillow and blanket into the living room. [10] Because I was sick of bed and had decided to lie on the sofa and watch television. [11] I watched Camilla's talk show and read a magazine for a while. [12] Then I must have fallen asleep. [13] When I was suddenly conscious again. [14] I was in the middle of total darkness. [15] And total silence. [16] I was absolutely terrified. [17] Because I was sure that I had died. [18] Then, somewhere in the blackness ahead of me, I saw and recognized a small, dissolving spot of light. [19] I slowly realized it was coming from the television set. [20] And that there had been a power failure.

Score: Number correct _____ × 5 = _____%

SENTENCE FRAGMENTS

■ Mastery Test 2

Underline the fragment in each selection. Then make whatever changes are needed to turn the fragment into a sentence.

> ***Example***   In grade school, I didn't want to wear glasses~~.~~ <u>~~A~~nd avoided having to get them by memorizing the eye chart.</u>

1. I rang their doorbell for ten minutes. Finally deciding no one was home. I stalked away in disgust.

2. According to the latest weather report. Heavy rains will fall for the next twenty-four hours. Flash floods are expected.

3. A ceiling should be painted a very light colour. Such as white or pale beige. Then, the room will seem larger.

4. My classes all being in the afternoon this semester. I can sleep until noon every day. My room-mate hates me for it.

5. The plumber told us she could fix the leak in our shower. But would not be able to come until next month.

6. I spent an hour in the mall parking lot yesterday. Looking for my grey compact car. There were hundreds of other cars just like it in the lot.

7. Tony filled in the three-page application. Then he waited to see the Human Resources manager. Who would interview him for the position.

8. Suddenly the pitcher turned around. And threw to first base. But the runner was already standing on second.

9. Staggering under the weight of the heavy laundry basket. Nick stumbled down the basement steps. Then he discovered the washer was not working.

10. My brother spends a lot of time at the mall. There is an arcade there called Space Port. Where he meets his friends and plays video games.

> ***Score:***   Number correct _____ × 10 = _____%

SENTENCE FRAGMENTS

■ Mastery Test 3

Underline the fragment in each selection. Then make whatever changes are needed to turn the fragment into a sentence.

1. Susie turned in her exam book. Then she walked out of the room. Wondering if she had passed.

2. The coach was fined $1,000. He had sworn at the referee. And thrown his stick across the ice.

3. Crystal's printer cartridge was giving her trouble. Every *y* was losing it tail. And looked like a *v*.

4. My little brother enjoys playing practical jokes. On anyone who visits our house. He even tells people that our house is haunted.

5. Because she had not studied for the exam. Cecile was very nervous. If she got a passing grade, it would be a miracle.

6. Customers were lined up ten-deep at every entrance. Waiting for the store to open. Everything was on sale at 50 per cent off.

7. Lisa often goes to sleep early. Sometimes as early as eight o'clock. She says she thinks most clearly in the mornings.

8. We loaded the car with camping gear. Including a four-burner propane stove and a portable television.

9. Frank has a terrible problem. Unless he can scrape together a hundred dollars for his monthly instalment. He will lose his new Honda.

10. The unusual meeting began at 3:00 p.m. But adjourned at 3:05 p.m. Nobody could think of anything to talk about.

Score: Number correct _____ × 10 = _____ %

SENTENCE FRAGMENTS

■ Mastery Test 4

Underline and then correct the ten fragments in the following passage.

When my mother was a young girl. She spent several summers on her aunt and uncle's Manitoba farm. To this day she has vivid memories of the chores she did on the farm. Such as shucking corn for dinners and for canning. As she pulled off the moist brown cornsilk. Yellow worms would wiggle on the ear or drop off into my mother's lap. Another task was stringing yellow beans. Which had to be picked over before the beans would be cooked. My mother and her aunt spent hours snapping the ends off the beans. And tossing each one into a large basin. But the chore my mother remembers most clearly is preparing a chicken for Sunday dinner. Her aunt would head for the chicken yard. Somehow, the chickens seemed to know her purpose. They ran wildly in all directions. Fluttering and squawking, or fleeing into the hen house. When Aunt Helen found the right chicken. She picked it up and gave its neck a quick twist. Killing it instantly. Back in the kitchen, she and my mother would gut the chicken. And pluck its feathers out, down to the last tiny pinfeather. One special treat came out of this bloody chore. My mother always got the chicken feet to play with. Their long white tendons still attached. As my mother pulled on the tendons, the claws opened and closed like mechanical toys. My mother loved to terrorize her friends with these moving claws.

Score: Number correct _____ × 10 = _____%

RUN-ONS

■ Mastery Test 1

In the space provided, write *R-O* beside run-on sentences. Write *C* beside sentences that are punctuated correctly. Some of the run-ons have no punctuation between the two complete thoughts; others have only a comma.

Correct each run-on by using (1) a period and a capital letter, (2) a comma and a joining word, or (3) a semi-colon. Do not use the same method of correction in each sentence.

Examples

<u>R-O</u> I applied for the job, _∧but I never got called in for an interview.

<u>R-O</u> Carla's toothache is getting worse, ^Sshe should go to a dentist soon.

_____ 1. I had a very bad headache I felt light-headed and feverish as well.

_____ 2. Our children have the newest electronic games the house sounds like a video arcade.

_____ 3. Two men held up the ski shop, they were wearing bank tellers' masks.

_____ 4. Swirls of dust flew across the prairie field good topsoil vanished into the distance.

_____ 5. I cannot get a definite commitment from Beth I decided not to count on her.

_____ 6. The soup was too hot to eat, so I dropped in two ice cubes and cooled it off quickly.

_____ 7. The course on the history of UFOs sounded interesting it turned out to be very dull.

_____ 8. That clothing store is a strange place to visit, you keep walking up to dummies that look like real people.

_____ 9. Maria throws out old pieces of soap, for she can't stand the sharp edges of the worn-down bars.

_____ 10. The oil warning light came on Jermaine foolishly continued to drive the car.

Score: Number correct _____ × 10 = _____%

RUN-ONS

■ Mastery Test 2

Correct the run-on in each sentence by using subordination. Choose from among the following dependent words:

after	before	unless
although	even though	until
as	if	when
because	since	while

Example   The bus drivers are on strike, I had to walk to work today.

Because the bus drivers are on strike, I had to walk to work today.

1. Nick pulled the cellophane off the cake, the icing came along with it.

   _____

   _____

2. Sherrie was late for the job interview she still got the job.

   _____

   _____

3. I threw some potatoes in the oven I then prepared the salmon loaf.

   _____

   _____

4. Winters in Kapuskasing are very cold Cindy decided to move to Leamington.

   _____

   _____

5. I've been using a calculator for a year, I've almost forgotten the multiplication tables.

   _____

   _____

Score: Number correct _____ × 20 = _____%

RUN-ONS

■ Mastery Test 3

In the space provided, write *R-O* beside run-on sentences. Write *C* beside sentences that are punctuated correctly. Some of the run-ons have no punctuation between the two complete thoughts; others have only a comma.

Correct each run-on by using (1) a period and capital letter, (2) a comma and a joining word, or (3) a semi-colon. Do not use the same method of correction in each sentence.

_____ 1. Crystal does yoga exercises every morning she strongly believes in a healthy body.

_____ 2. Fast cars and fast people can be lots of fun, but they can also be very dangerous.

_____ 3. I wondered why the time was passing so slowly then I realized my watch had stopped.

_____ 4. Bill can crush walnuts with his teeth he is also good at biting the caps off of beer bottles.

_____ 5. At one time Bill used to bend nails with his teeth this practice ended when a wise guy slipped him a tempered nail.

_____ 6. My dentist teaches part-time in a neighbourhood clinic he refers to himself as a drill instructor.

_____ 7. An improperly placed goldfish bowl can start a house fire, sunlight reflects and magnifies through the bowl glass.

_____ 8. At the crack of dawn, our neighbours start up their lawnmowers and weed-whippers and the Saturday-morning symphony begins.

_____ 9. Fred had a bad headache yesterday, moreover, his arthritis was bothering him.

_____ 10. As a little girl, she pretended she was a hairdresser her closet was full of bald dolls.

Score: Number correct _____ × 10 = _____%

RUN-ONS

■ Mastery Test 4

Correct the run-on in each sentence by using subordination. Choose from among the following dependent words:

after	before	unless
although	even though	until
as	if	when
because	since	while

1. My boss needs me to work overtime, I can't study for the test.

   _____

   _____

2. A storm was predicted for later in the day we still decided to go for a hike.

   _____

   _____

3. Fred's shirt sleeve caught on fire, his wife quickly dumped a pitcher of iced tea on it.

   _____

   _____

4. I was very tired at the end of the day, I still managed to complete a paper for my English class.

   _____

   _____

5. Marilyn took a year of accounting courses in school she decided to switch to another program.

   _____

   _____

Score: Number correct _____ × 20 = _____%

STANDARD ENGLISH VERBS

■ Mastery Test 1

Underline the correct words in the parentheses.

1. The radio announcer said that traffic (is, are) tied up for three kilometres because of an accident that just (happen, happened) on the highway.

2. My new pen (scratch, scratches) when I write with it; it (make, makes) little cuts in the paper.

3. Before I (mail, mailed) the letter, the postage went up, so I (need, needed) an extra stamp.

4. Nick (have, has) a new tuxedo that (make, makes) him look just like a movie star.

5. They (do, does) not plan to give a New Year's Eve party this year, for they (have, has) too painful memories of last year's.

6. Tim (is, be) terrific at home repairs; for example, he (fix, fixes) broken appliances just like a professional.

7. Just as Stanley (walk, walked) around the corner, he saw someone trying to steal his bicycle, so he (yell, yelled) for the police.

8. Little Danny (pile, piled) the blocks into a tower, but it (collapse, collapsed) with a loud crash, with the blocks scattering all over the floor.

9. We (suspect, suspected) from the start that it (was, were) the neighbour's boy who took our lawn furniture.

10. My two sisters (was, were) thrilled when I (turn, turned) up with three tickets to the Tragically Hip concert.

Score: Number correct _____ × 5 = _____%

STANDARD ENGLISH VERBS

■ Mastery Test 2

Cross out the nonstandard verb form and write the correct form in the space provided.

_____seems_____   ***Example***   The job offer ~~seem~~ too good to be true.

_____   1. When I was learning how to drive, I strip the gears on my father's car.

_____   2. My parents is going to throw me a big party when I graduate.

_____   3. Bill prefer riding his motorcycle to just about any other activity.

_____   4. Vince do well on every exam he takes.

_____   5. Lucille change into comfortable clothes right after she gets home from a day of work.

_____   6. I remember how my mittens used to steam when I place them on the living-room radiator.

_____   7. It was so cold that my breath turn into sharp white puffs of smoke when I exhaled.

_____   8. When Ida have her work breaks during the day, she often reads a magazine.

_____   9. Tea contain so much theobromine that it stimulates some people more than coffee.

_____   10. When I were little, my father would punish me just for expressing my opinion.

Score: Number correct _____ × 10 = _____%

STANDARD ENGLISH VERBS

■ Mastery Test 3

Part 1: Fill in each blank with the appropriate standard verb form of *to be*, *to have*, or *to do* in present or past tense.

People _____ really funny at amusement parks. They

1
_____ to prove that they _____ absolutely fearless,

2   3
so they _____ crazy things such as stand up while the roller coaster

4
_____ on its way downhill at fifty kilometres per hour. A normally

5
careful driver _____ accidents on purpose; he _____

6   7
this to see how many cars he can hit in the Bumper Cars. I wonder if our parents
_____ equally crazy things when they _____

8   9
young kids and needed to prove to the world that they _____

                                                        10
courage.

Part 2: Fill in each blank with the appropriate form of the regular verb shown in parentheses. Use present or past tense as needed.

When Joanne (*rush*) _____ she often gets in trouble. Last

                           11
Monday, while in a hurry to catch her GO Train, she (*park*) _____

                                                        12
her car too close to a shiny green Saturn that was in the next space on the lot. When
she (*arrive*) _____ at the station in the afternoon and (*open*)

                              13
_____ her car door, Joanne (*realize*) _____ she could

14   15
not back out of the parking space without hitting the other car. In addition, its
driver was waiting impatiently and (*scowl*) _____ as she (*watch*)

                                              16
_____ Joanne struggling with the wheel. Joanne finally got out of the

17
space, but she (*scrape*) _____ a two-inch strip off the Saturn's fender.

                             18
The angry driver of the other car (*calm*) _____ down only when Joanne

                                              19
(*agree*) _____ to pay.

                  20

Score: Number correct _____ × 5 = _____%

STANDARD ENGLISH VERBS

■ Mastery Test 4

Part 1: Fill in each blank with the appropriate standard verb form of *to be*, *to have*, or *to do* in the present or past tense.

My cousin Naheed _____ determined to lose five kilos, so
                                    1
she _____ put herself on a rigid diet that _____
        2   3
not allow her to eat anything that she enjoys. Last weekend while the family
_____ at Aunt Aliyah's house for dinner, all Naheed
        4
_____to eat _____a can of Aylmer diet peaches.
        5   6
We _____convinced that Naheed meant business when she joined
        7
an exercise club whose members _____to work out on enormous
                                            8
machines and _____ fifty sit-ups just to get started. If Naheed
                    9
succeeds, we _____going to be proud.
                    10

Part 2: Fill in each blank with the appropriate form of the regular verb shown in parentheses. Use present or past tense as needed.

Have you ever (*notice*) _____what (*happen*) _____
                                11   12
at a children's playground? Very often one child (*struggle*) _____
                                                                    13
with another to be first on the slide, while a third child (*compete*) _____
                                                                            14
with a fourth for the sandbox. Meanwhile, parents (*wait*) _____
                                                                15
patiently on a nearby park bench and (*ignore*) _____their offspring.
                                                        16
Just yesterday, I saw a young father whose daughter had (*drag*) _____
                                                                        17
him to the playground. He (*stare*) _____at his watch while she
                                        18
(*scream*) _____happily from the top of the jungle gym. He must
                19
have been counting the minutes until they (*return*) _____home.
                                                            20

Score: Number correct _____ × 5 = _____%

IRREGULAR VERBS

■ Mastery Test 1

Underline the correct word in the parentheses.

1. Julio had (wrote, written) me five times before the letters stopped.
2. Did you see the damage that maniac (did, done) to the laundromat?
3. The fever made me hallucinate, and I (saw, seen) monkeys at the foot of my bed.
4. After dicing the vegetables, Sarah (freezed, froze) them.
5. I (drank, drunk) at least six cups of coffee while working on the paper.
6. That last commercial (came, come) close to making me scream.
7. The supervisor asked why I had (went, gone) home early from work the day before.
8. I should have (wore, worn) heavier clothes to the picnic.
9. If I hadn't (threw, thrown) away the receipt, I could have gotten my money back.
10. Willy (brang, brought) his volleyball to the picnic.
11. I would have (become, became) very angry if you had not intervened.
12. I was exhausted because I had (swam, swum) two lengths of the pool.
13. Albert (eat, ate) four slices of almond fudge cake before he got sick.
14. How long has your watch been (broke, broken)?
15. If we had (knew, known) how the weather would be, we would not have gone on the trip.
16. The children had (did, done) the dishes as a surprise for their mother.
17. Teresa has (rode, ridden) all over the city looking for an apartment.
18. The burglar (ran, run) like a scared rabbit when he heard the alarm.
19. Chili had (took, taken) the wrong coat from the restaurant rack.
20. The trucker (drived, drove) all night; his eyes looked like poached eggs.

Score: Number correct _____ × 5 = _____%

IRREGULAR VERBS

■ Mastery Test 2

Cross out the incorrect verb form. Write the correct form in the space provided.

_____ 1. The mop that I left by the door has froze stiff.

_____ 2. My car was stole, and I had no way of getting to school.

_____ 3. Someone leaved a book in the classroom.

_____ 4. Our gym teacher speaked on physical fitness, but we slept through the lecture.

_____ 5. That sweater was tore yesterday.

_____ 6. After I had loose weight, the pants fit perfectly.

_____ 7. Ellen awaked from a sound sleep with the feeling there was someone in the house.

_____ 8. Life has dealed Lonnell a number of hard moments.

_____ 9. Father begun to yell at me as I walked in the door.

_____ 10. The sick puppy laid quietly on the veterinarian's table.

_____ 11. The teacher didn't remember that I had spoke to him.

_____ 12. While Alec sung in the church choir, his mother beamed with pride and pleasure.

_____ 13. I would have went on vacation this week, but my boss asked me to wait a month.

_____ 14. When the boys throwed water balloons at us, we decided to throw some back.

_____ 15. I blowed up the balloon until it exploded in my face.

_____ 16. The body that the men taked out of the water was a terrible thing to see.

_____ 17. Rich breaked the video game that I lent him.

_____ 18. If the phone had rang once more, my mother would have tossed a pot at it.

_____ 19. A sudden banging on the door shaked me out of sleep.

_____ 20. Granny has wore the same dress to every wedding and funeral for twenty years.

Score: Number correct _____ × 5 = _____%

IRREGULAR VERBS

■ Mastery Test 3

Write in the space provided the correct form of the verb shown in the margin.

sink   1. The fishing rod slipped out of his hand and _____ to the bottom of the pond.

choose   2. I _____ the blueberry pie for dessert because the pudding looked watery.

write   3. Pat had _____ the essay three times, but it still needed revision.

lie   4. As soon as I _____ down to take a nap, the phone rang.

catch   5. Fred _____ a cold while defrosting the refrigerator.

sell   6. The brothers worked on their old station wagon for a month and then _____ it for twice as much as they paid for it.

ride   7. Eric _____ the bucking bronco for a full thirty seconds before he was tossed into the sawdust.

hide   8. How did my little brother ever guess where his Christmas present was _____?

speak   9. If I _____ only when I was spoken to, I'd never get a word into conversations.

shake   10. Cecile's hands _____ as she handed in her paper.

Score: Number correct _____ × 10 = _____%

IRREGULAR VERBS

■ Mastery Test 4

Write in the space provided the correct form of the verb shown in the margin.

ring　　1. Sometimes the doorbell has _____ for several minutes before my grandfather notices the sounds.

shrink　2. My new designer jeans _____ three sizes in the wash.

lend　　3. Stella _____ someone her notebook and then forgot who had borrowed it.

rise　　4. Had taxes not _____ so much this year, I could have afforded a vacation.

sleep　5. I turned in my term paper and then _____ for ten hours.

sting　6. Kim didn't see the bee in her sleeve and was _____ the moment she put her jacket on.

wear　　7. Nick jogs ten kilometres a day and has _____ out three pairs of running shoes this year.

burst　8. Crystal blew the biggest bubble I have ever seen. Then it _____, leaving shreds of pink bubblegum all over her face.

keep　　9. I should have _____ my old coat instead of contributing it to the church rummage sale.

drive　10. We _____ for fifty kilometres without seeing a single gas station.

Score:　Number correct _____ × 10 = _____%

SUBJECT-VERB AGREEMENT

■ Mastery Test 1

Underline the correct verb in the parentheses. Note that you will first have to determine the subject in each sentence. To help find subjects in certain sentences, you may find it helpful to cross out prepositional phrases.

1. The four flights of stairs up to my apartment (is, are) as steep as the Rockies sometimes.
2. The sweater and the books on the table (belongs, belong) to Sid.
3. One of their sons (has, have) been expelled from school.
4. My brother and I (has, have) season tickets to the games.
5. Nick and Lisa (enjoys, enjoy) watching old movies on television.
6. Either of the television sets (gives, give) excellent picture quality.
7. There (is, are) about ten things I must get done today.
8. Hurrying down the street after their father (was, were) two small children.
9. Here (is, are) the screwdriver you were looking for all weekend.
10. No one in this world (is, are) going to get out alive.
11. The plywood under your carpets (is, are) rotting.
12. Sex and violence (is, are) the mainstays of many action movies.
13. Jill is one of those people who (loses, lose) their temper quickly.
14. Not only the manager but also the owners of the ball club (is, are) responsible for the poor performance of the team.
15. There (is, are) a great deal of work yet to be done.
16. One of the women on the bowling team (has, have) won a thousand dollars in the provincial lottery.
17. The study of statistics (is, are) important for a psychology major.
18. My father is a person who (cares, care) more about time with his family than about success in his job.
19. The carpenter and the electrician (is, are) working at the house today.
20. I tug and pull, but the line of supermarket carts (seems, seem) welded together.

Score: Number correct _____ × 5 = _____%

SUBJECT-VERB AGREEMENT

■ Mastery Test 2

In the space provided, write the correct form of the verb shown in the margin.

is, are   1. The chain-link fence surrounding the school grounds _____ ready to collapse.

plays, play   2. I envy people who _____ a musical instrument well.

is, are   3. Inside the bakery-shop carton _____ your favourite pastries.

has, have   4. Someone on the team _____ forgotten her warm-up jacket.

wants, want   5. Because I spilled a beaker of sulphuric acid, nobody in my chemistry lab

_____ to work with me.

is, are   6. At the end of the long movie line _____ about twenty people who will not get into the next show.

looks, look   7. Neither of the coats _____ good on you.

is, are   8. A little time for rest and relaxation _____ what I need right now.

was, were   9. The shirts that she thought _____ too expensive are now on sale.

shops, shop   10. Janet and her mother _____ together on Thursday nights.

Score: Number correct _____ × 10 = _____%

SUBJECT-VERB AGREEMENT

■ Mastery Test 3

Cross out the incorrect form of the verb. In addition, underline the subject that goes with the verb. Then write the correct form of the verb in the space provided. Mark the one sentence that is correct with a *C*.

_____ 1. The price of the computer games have been reduced.

_____ 2. The marigolds that was planted yesterday were accidentally mowed over today.

_____ 3. Many tables at the auction was covered with very old books.

_____ 4. Brenda checked with the employment agencies that was helping her look for a job.

_____ 5. Trucks and cars uses our street heavily since road construction began.

_____ 6. The old woman rooting through those garbage bins have refused to enter a nursing home.

_____ 7. The vicious gossip about our new neighbour have begun to anger me.

_____ 8. Sam is one of those people who rips pages out of library books rather than copy them on a photocopy machine.

_____ 9. The plastic slipcovers on their furniture has started to turn yellow.

_____ 10. Either my willpower or my lust for chocolate has to win out.

Score: Number correct _____ × 10 = _____%

SUBJECT-VERB AGREEMENT

■ Mastery Test 4

Cross out the incorrect form of the verb. In addition, underline the subject that goes with the verb. Then write the correct form of the verb in the space provided. Mark the one sentence that is correct with a *C*.

_____   1. Why has Cindy and Karen quit their jobs as telephone repairpersons?

_____   2. One actor at the rehearsals have become ill from the heat.

_____   3. The buildings across the street is all going to be demolished.

_____   4. Those old coats in your closet has dust lying on their shoulders.

_____   5. Archery and soccer is the new sports at our school.

_____   6. If only there was more hours in the day, I could get all my work done.

_____   7. Two pieces of dry toast and a soft-boiled egg is all Naheed is allowed to eat for breakfast.

_____   8. One of the servers at the restaurant have just won a free trip to Vancouver.

_____   9. Crystal's long red silk scarf and her lipstick match perfectly.

_____   10. Anything that parents tell their children usually get ignored.

Score: Number correct _____ × 10 = _____%

CONSISTENT VERB TENSE

■ Mastery Test 1

In each selection one verb must be changed so that it agrees in tense with the other verbs. Cross out the inconsistent verb and write the correct form in the space provided.

_____ 1. After he bought a stereo and collects a lot of CDs, my brother wound up listening mostly to his FM radio.

_____ 2. The little boy raced his model train too fast, so that it topples off the track when it rounded a curve.

_____ 3. She let her mother cut her hair until her friends began saying that her hairstyle looks very strange.

_____ 4. The air pollution is so bad that the weather bureau urges people not to exercise outside until it cleared.

_____ 5. Sandy greeted the postal carrier and flips quickly through the letters he handed her to see if there was a letter from her boyfriend.

_____ 6. After the truck overturned, passing motorists parked their cars on the side of the road and walk back to look at the damage.

_____ 7. The lights went out and we all jump because we were watching a horror movie at the time.

_____ 8. The wind came up quickly, knocks down a lot of dead tree branches, and blew in the front window of the bank across the street.

_____ 9. After the wolf unsuccessfully huffed and puffed at the little pigs' brick house, he realizes he would have to hire a demolition contractor.

_____ 10. While in the hospital, she read lots of magazines, watched daytime television, shuffles up and down the corridor, and generally felt very bored.

Score: Number correct _____ × 10 = _____ %

CONSISTENT VERB TENSE

■ Mastery Test 2

In each selection one verb must be changed so that it agrees in tense with the other verbs. Cross out the inconsistent verb and write the correct form in the space provided.

_____ 1. Crystal likes to use lip gloss but hates the way it stains her fingers and never seemed to come off.

_____ 2. Tony reached way down into the bread bag. He skipped the first couple of pieces and grabs one of the fresher, bigger pieces from the middle.

_____ 3. Eric believes he is smarter than we are; he tried to show this all the time.

_____ 4. When I noticed the way my mother cocked her head, I realize that she had an earache.

_____ 5. When we asked for a fresh tablecloth, the server looks as though we were speaking Russian.

_____ 6. As the tourists walked through the forest, they check the trail markers that were posted periodically.

_____ 7. My eyes always close and my fingers get numb when I listened to an afternoon lecture in Professor Snorrel's class.

_____ 8. Billy graduated from Pembina High School, works as a plumber's assistant for two years, and then returned to school.

_____ 9. At holiday dinners, many people continue to stuff themselves even when it seemed obvious that they are already full.

_____ 10. I wiped my hands on my trousers before I walk in for the job interview. I did not want the Human Resources officer to know my palms were sweating.

Score: Number correct _____ × 10 = _____%

PRONOUN REFERENCE, AGREEMENT, AND POINT OF VIEW

■ Mastery Test 1

Underline the correct word in the parentheses.

1. I realized that each of the coaches had done (her, their) best to motivate me.
2. Either of the television sets has (its, their) good and bad features.
3. I hated my job as an office mail carrier because (I, you) got taken advantage of by everyone.
4. A player on the hockey team broke (his, their) arm last week.
5. I stopped my pottery classes because (it, the ceramic dust) made me sneeze.
6. If (a person goes, people go) barefoot through the store, he or she can expect to meet a security guard.
7. We went to West Edmonton Mall on a Sunday, and (you, we) had to wait an hour for every ride.
8. My cat got hold of a lollipop, and (it, the cat) got very sticky.
9. When Jack argues with Theo, (he, Theo) always gets in the last word.
10. One of my sisters has decided to separate from (her, their) husband.
11. I've been taking cold medicine and now (it, the cold) is better.
12. The ten girls in our cabin developed a closeness that (you, we) could feel grow as the summer at camp progressed.
13. Sarah was nervous about her speech, but (it, the nervousness) didn't show.
14. Each of the men was asked to put (his, their) name on the petition.
15. When we reached the station, (you, we) realized that the train had left.
16. Has everybody in the sorority finished (her, their) work for the committee?
17. I went fishing yesterday and caught three (of them, fish).
18. No one in the men's dorm felt (he, they) had taken very good notes at the lecture.
19. When the Leafs met the Canadiens in the playoff game, (they, the Leafs) won.
20. If students work with irresponsible lab partners, (you, they) will find it difficult to get a good grade.

Score: Number correct _____ × 5 = _____%

PRONOUN REFERENCE, AGREEMENT, AND POINT OF VIEW

■ Mastery Test 2

In the space provided, write *PE* beside sentences that contain pronoun errors. Write *C* beside the two sentences that use pronouns correctly. Then cross out each pronoun error and write the correction above it.

PE _____ ***Example*** Each of the boys explained ~~their~~ ^{his} project.

_____ 1. Crystal loves to run, but Tony's not interested in it.

_____ 2. My deepest thoughts and feelings are ones that you can hide easily.

_____ 3. If I don't have my activities for the day planned in advance, I waste too much time deciding what to do next.

_____ 4. My cousin is a religious man and has devoted much of his life to it.

_____ 5. They take too many taxes out of my weekly paycheque.

_____ 6. I have a carton full of pencils and pens here; where do you want me to put them?

_____ 7. One of the best swimmers on the team has badly sprained her back.

_____ 8. As we watched the lightning storm, you were in awe.

_____ 9. Elaine told Sue that she was being selfish.

_____ 10. Each of the women had pinned a gardenia in their hair.

Score: Number correct _____ × 10 = _____%

PRONOUN REFERENCE, AGREEMENT, AND POINT OF VIEW

■ Mastery Test 3

In the space provided, write *PE* beside sentences that contain pronoun errors. Write *C* beside the two sentences that use pronouns correctly. Then cross out each pronoun error and write the correction above it.

_____   1. A person should always be extremely careful when driving their snowmobile.

_____   2. Many people flick on the television as soon as they get in the house, which is a bad habit for you to get into.

_____   3. After I joined the music club, they began sending me stacks of junk mail.

_____   4. Many toys on the market today can both entertain children and educate them as well.

_____   5. The custard pie was so good that you kept going back for more.

_____   6. Crystal told her mother that she was too impatient.

_____   7. A student in a late-afternoon class often has difficulty attending to their teacher.

_____   8. No one except a police officer is allowed to turn their car around on a divided highway.

_____   9. When my broken wrist was set, I could feel the bones grinding against each other.

_____   10. At the bookstore in the mall, they have all the best-sellers in racks at the front.

Score: Number correct _____ × 10 = _____%

PRONOUN REFERENCE, AGREEMENT, AND POINT OF VIEW

■ **Mastery Test 4**

In the space provided, write *PE* beside sentences that contain pronoun errors. Write *C* beside the two sentences that use pronouns correctly. Then cross out each pronoun error and write the correction above it.

_____   1. When the picture tube on the television burned out, I had to get a new one.

_____   2. People will enjoy the movie if they don't mind a sentimental ending.

_____   3. Everyone who donates their time for the project will receive free admission to the union picnic.

_____   4. People should never go for a job interview if you don't prepare in advance.

_____   5. If a person intends to pass a chemistry course, you have to be good at math.

_____   6. Melissa told her mother she needed a new pair of shoes.

_____   7. We wanted to see the exhibit, but you couldn't push through the crowds.

_____   8. Everyone in the class should be ready to deliver her report by next Monday.

_____   9. I enjoyed the volleyball match even though I'm not very good at it.

_____   10. I wanted a free pencil sharpener, but you first had to buy five dozen pencils.

Score: Number correct _____ × 10 = _____%

PRONOUN TYPES

■ Mastery Test 1

Underline the correct word in the parentheses.

1. Hang pretended to be at ease, but he didn't fool Susan or (me, I).
2. (This, This here) tree is full of sparrows at night.
3. I believe that coat is (hers', hers).
4. Talking intimately, Ellen and (I, me) didn't see Fred walking up to our front porch.
5. The two of you must give (yourself, yourselves) another chance.
6. Al and (I, me) are equally poor in math.
7. My car's front tires, (who, which) vibrate at high speeds, need to be realigned.
8. (Those, Them) newspapers have to be carried down to the recycling bin.
9. That last hamburger on the grill is (yours', yours) if you want it.
10. Though the furry black weasel was in a cage, it still scared Bill and (I, me).
11. Whenever our neighbour sees me on the porch, he invites (hisself, himself) over.
12. You are getting more of your work done than (I, me).
13. Theo (hisself, himself) takes full responsibility for the accident.
14. The teacher glared at Sarah and (I, me) and then dismissed the class.
15. Though younger than (I, me), Andrea acts like my superior.
16. When I miss class, I get together later with a student (who, whom) takes good notes.
17. Of all the children in the class, Doreen and (he, him) are the least reliable.
18. The teacher asked Enzo and (I, me) to volunteer.
19. I recently met a friend of (her, hers).
20. (Those, Them) boots weren't made for walking.

Score: Number correct _____ × 5 = _____%

PRONOUN TYPES

■ Mastery Test 2

Cross out the incorrect pronoun in each sentence and write the correct form in the space provided.

_____   1. The coach's decision didn't suit Charlie or I.

_____   2. Our teacher gave us homework in all of those there books.

_____   3. That rabbit of yours' just became a mother again.

_____   4. Joel won because he has played chess much longer than her.

_____   5. Our brothers were very proud of themself when they caught the vandal in our neighbourhood.

_____   6. The women whom filed the class action suit were initially fired by the company.

_____   7. The mail carrier says that Paul and me get more mail than all the other people on the block combined.

_____   8. Lee never gets tired of talking about hisself.

_____   9. Even Canada Post gets things done faster than her.

_____   10. This here toothbrush looks like someone used it to scrub potatoes.

_____   11. Angela and me go hiking together each fall.

_____   12. The firefighters theirselfs were puzzled by the source of the smoke in my basement.

_____   13. Our garden is more cared for than theirs'.

_____   14. The stone barely missed we and the children.

_____   15. Them mosquitoes will bite you faster than you can blink your eyes.

_____   16. If you want that old garden shovel, it's yours'.

_____   17. I heard that her and her sister were expelled from school.

_____   18. Julio is looking for someone to who he can sell his car.

_____   19. Pete jogs on a more regular basis than me.

_____   20. The pages are torn in many of them books.

> *Score:*   Number correct _____ × 5 = _____ %

ADJECTIVES AND ADVERBS

■ Mastery Test 1

Part 1:   Cross out the incorrect adjectival or adverbial form in each sentence. Then write the correct form in the space provided.

_____   1. My mother spoke bluntly to the salesperson, and he responded aggressive.

_____   2. The spade cut sharp and severed the tree root.

_____   3. Because the children were quietly during the movie, their parents were happy to buy them some ice cream.

_____   4. Our powerful singing rang out noisy in the packed theatre.

_____   5. Your cupcakes taste so well that they are rapidly disappearing.

Part 2:   Cross out the error in comparison in each sentence. Then write the correct form in the space provided.

_____   6. Andy considers himself importanter than other people.

_____   7. Crystal's hair is the most shortest that she has ever worn it.

_____   8. Despite the reviews, I think *The Killer Frogs* was the entertainingest movie released this year.

_____   9. Earthworms are less likelier to make me squeamish than are spiders.

_____   10. I always do a more good job in making a meal than my brother does.

Score: Number correct _____ × 10 = _____%

ADJECTIVES AND ADVERBS

■ Mastery Test 2

Part 1:   Cross out the incorrect adjectival or adverbial form in each sentence. Then write the correct form in the space provided.

_____   1. For a week after his accident, Carlo could not walk steady.

_____   2. I didn't think the instructor had graded my paper fair.

_____   3. The sharp blade slipped easy between the chicken's bumpy skin and satiny flesh.

_____   4. My father was thoughtfully as he looked at the pictures in the old family album.

_____   5. Waitressing was easy for Natalie, but since my co-ordination was not as well as hers, I was fired.

Part 2:   Add to each sentence the correct form of the word in the margin.

strong   6. Jerry, whose nickname is Goliath, is probably the _____ player on the football team.

graceful 7. The _____ sport at the Olympics is the figure-skating competition.

hard   8. My science exam was the _____ of my two tests.

little   9. That is the _____ of my many worries.

bad   10. I can't decide what to do; the _____ thing, though, would be to do nothing.

Score: Number correct _____ × 10 = _____%

MISPLACED MODIFIERS

■ Mastery Test 1

Underline the misplaced word or words in each sentence. Then rewrite the sentence, placing related words together and making the meaning clear.

1. Every six hours the doctor told me to take a pill.

   _____

   _____

2. I bought a watch at the flea market that I wear every day.

   _____

   _____

3. Crystal dozed by the pool growing redder by the minute.

   _____

   _____

4. We need another player on the team who can catch badly.

   _____

   _____

5. Elena almost got an A in every subject.

   _____

   _____

6. Mike signed a letter of intent to play football at the University of Manitoba in the family kitchen.

   _____

   _____

7. I threw the potatoes in the pot and tore open a box of peas in a bad mood.

   _____

   _____

8. My uncle bought a house from an elderly real estate agent with a large bay window.

   _____

   _____

Score: Number correct _____ × 12.5 = _____%

MISPLACED MODIFIERS

■ Mastery Test 2

Underline the misplaced word or words in each sentence. Then rewrite the sentence, placing related words together and making the meaning clear.

1. Lisa was attacked by a stray dog working in the yard.

    _____

    _____

2. I will never ride another horse wearing shorts.

    _____

    _____

3. Everyone we invited almost came to the party.

    _____

    _____

4. The boy struggled to reel in the large fish with shaking hands.

    _____

    _____

5. I bought a tire from an auto shop that flattened overnight.

    _____

    _____

6. Judy bought sheepskin seat covers for her Toyota that cost only thirty dollars.

    _____

    _____

7. Breakfast is served at the school cafeteria from 8:00 a.m. until the end of the school year.

    _____

    _____

8. Finding their house burglarized, the Murphys called the police when they came back from vacation.

    _____

    _____

Score: Number correct _____ × 12.5 = _____%

DANGLING MODIFIERS

■ Mastery Test 1

Underline the dangling modifier in each sentence. Then rewrite the sentence, correcting the dangling modifier.

1. Feeling extra lucky, the black cat didn't scare Diana.

   _____

   _____

2. After waiting all day, the moving truck finally arrived at our apartment.

   _____

   _____

3. Hot and sizzling, Crystal bit into the apple tart.

   _____

   _____

4. Having faulty plumbing, we decided not to rent the apartment.

   _____

   _____

5. Waiting in line to be seated, the head server finally called our names.

   _____

   _____

6. Out late the night before, Naheed's eyes were red and strained.

   _____

   _____

7. Having won the championship game, the locker room was filled with cheering players.

   _____

   _____

8. While walking through the shopping mall, my head suddenly began to pound.

   _____

   _____

Score: Number correct _____ × 12.5 = _____%

DANGLING MODIFIERS

■ Mastery Test 2

Underline the dangling modifier in each sentence. Then rewrite the sentence, correcting the dangling modifier.

1. While cutting the lawn, five mosquitoes bit me.

    _____

    _____

2. Smoking in the washroom, my math teacher caught Fred and me.

    _____

    _____

3. Shortly before giving birth, the doctor gave his wife a sedative.

    _____

    _____

4. Quickly taking the sheets off the clothesline, rain pelted our faces.

    _____

    _____

5. Dripping with perspiration, the air-conditioned store offered us relief.

    _____

    _____

6. While shopping at the store, my bike was stolen.

    _____

    _____

7. Hurrying to class, my English paper fell out of my notebook into a puddle.

    _____

    _____

8. After watching two movies at the Cineplex, my stomach began rumbling for pizza.

    _____

    _____

Score: Number correct _____ × 12.5 = _____%

PARALLELISM

■ Mastery Test 1

The unbalanced part of each sentence is italicized. Rewrite this part so that it matches the rest of the sentence.

1. Long box office lines, *T-shirts that are overpriced*, and overcrowded parking lots—these are what I dislike about going to a rock concert.

   _____

2. My sister can do her math homework, cut my hair, and *be planning a party* while she watches television.

   _____

3. The sky got dark, a wind sprang up, and *there was a drop in the temperature*.

   _____

4. My magazines sometimes arrive torn, dirty, and *being late*.

   _____

5. Between work and dinner, she picked up her son at school, *was stopping at the drugstore*, and dropped the dog off at the vet's office.

   _____

6. The flowers that Robin entered in the show were healthy-looking, brilliantly coloured, and *smelled sweet*.

   _____

7. I'd play golf day and night if it weren't for eating and *to have to sleep*.

   _____

8. The crowd showed excitement, happiness, and *there was patriotic spirit*.

   _____

9. If it weren't for Marie's indecision and *being insecure*, she could accomplish great things in the business world.

   _____

10. My nephew's career plans centre on becoming a provincial police officer, training for the city police, or *to join the RCMP*.

   _____

Score: Number correct _____ × 10 = _____%

PARALLELISM

■ Mastery Test 2

Draw a line under the unbalanced part of each sentence. Then rewrite the unbalanced part so that it matches the other items in the sentence.

1. My bedridden little brother asked for a bowl of cereal, a glass of orange juice, and to have a comic book to read.

   _____

2. Science fiction, popular music, and sports that are on television are the things my father enjoys most.

   _____

3. My sister's peculiar habits included yelling in her sleep and to do her homework in the bathtub.

   _____

4. That new blond-haired boy is both handsome as he is personable.

   _____

5. Crystal enjoys novels, shopping for new clothes, and meeting new people.

   _____

6. Shoppers stop in pet stores to buy a pet, to pick up pet supplies, or just looking at the animals.

   _____

7. Our children can watch television, talk on the phone, and their homework all at the same time.

   _____

8. Frustrated, annoyed, and feeling depression, Steve returned to work after the strike.

   _____

9. Thelma likes people who have thoughtfulness and are unselfish.

   _____

10. His headache was so bad that Andy was ready to give all his money or the confessing of all his secrets to anyone who would stop the pain.

    _____

Score: Number correct _____ × 10 = _____%

CAPITAL LETTERS

■ Mastery Test 1

Cross out the two capitalization errors in each of the following sentences. Then write the corrections in the spaces provided.

_____
_____ 1. Our local nightspot, studio 84, will admit only people dressed in designer Jeans.

_____
_____ 2. Lisa complained, "this pearl bracelet I bought at biway has started to turn green."

_____
_____ 3. Though howard no longer lives on third Street, he likes to return there on weekends to visit old friends.

_____
_____ 4. Joe and Leslie love british Columbia, but we prefer quebec.

_____
_____ 5. The statue in the Upper Town is supposed to represent all the soldiers killed during the Battle of the plains of abraham.

_____
_____ 6. I hired a lawyer after my Dodge caravan was sideswiped by a canpar delivery truck.

_____
_____ 7. Jack often works overtime on saturdays and sundays to help keep up with his bills.

_____
_____ 8. Our neighbour, mr. charles Reynolds, accidentally backed into our maple tree today.

_____
_____ 9. "last week I bought Adidas sneakers and a jogging sweatshirt," Janey said. "But my asthma is so bad that my Doctor won't let me start running."

_____
_____ 10. I don't like instant coffee, but that's all that's served at the weight watchers' meetings on Wednesday nights.

Score: Number correct _____ × 5 = _____%

CAPITAL LETTERS

■ Mastery Test 2

Cross out the two capitalization errors in each of the following sentences. Then write the corrections in the spaces provided.

_____   1. I asked the clerk, "do you have any italian olives?"
_____

_____   2. the third-grade children sang "Jingle Bells" during the school Christmas
_____   assembly.

_____   3. I drove lance to the auto shop to get the estimate on repairs to his 1970
_____   thunderbird.

_____   4. "because of the bad weather conditions," said the manager, "our Store will
_____   be closing at four o'clock."

_____   5. I can't decide whether to buy the boots I saw at butler's or to see if I can find
_____   a better pair at Eaton's on laurier Street.

_____   6. I am so brainwashed by Advertising that I always want to buy both kraft and
_____   President's Choice peanut butter.

_____   7. Linda works at the Manitoba Co op Trust in dauphin on Mondays, Wednesdays,
_____   and Fridays.

_____   8. He got low grades in his Math courses but straight A's in English and Spanish.
_____

_____   9. When the company transferred Rick's mother to the West coast, he wound up
_____   as a student at Kitsilano High school.

_____ 10. The epitaph on W. C. Fields' tombstone reads, "on the whole, I'd rather be
_____   in philadelphia."

_____
_____
_____
_____
_____

CAPITAL LETTERS

■ Mastery Test 3

Cross out the two capitalization errors in each of the following sentences. Then write the corrections in the spaces provided.

_____

_____ 1. My Uncle, a guide at Banff National Park, wrote a pamphlet titled "a Guide to Banff's Wild Flowers."

_____

_____ 2. Last summer I visited my aunt in israel and had a chance to learn some Hebrew and French, since she spoke both Languages.

_____

_____ 3. During the college's festival of marx brothers movies, Jean saw *Duck Soup* for the first time.

_____

_____ 4. The book titled *A Study in Human Dignity* tells the story of john merrick, a terribly deformed young man.

_____

_____ 5. Dave studied at the Canadian Culinary Institute before joining the staff at the greenbrier inn.

_____

_____ 6. As soon as his father came in the door, Frankie cried, "Who won, Dad? i'll bet the expos did."

_____

_____ 7. After visiting the royal ontario museum in Toronto, we headed for a Chinese restaurant recommended by friends.

_____

_____ 8. Although he is a christian scientist, Harold Phipps decided to let the doctors treat his son with antibiotics.

_____

_____ 9. After the game we stopped off to get an early supper at a nearby swiss chalet.

_____

_____ 10. Bryan Adams' "Forgive Me" is tony's all-time favourite Song.

_____

Score: Number correct _____ × 5 = _____%

CAPITAL LETTERS

■ Mastery Test 4

Cross out the two capitalization errors in each of the following sentences. Then write the corrections in the spaces provided.

_____ 1. "Why subscribe to *TV guide*," said Nick to Fran, "when there's a perfectly
_____   good TV listing in the saturday paper?"

_____ 2. Someone smashed into Claude's toyota when it was parked on Pine street and
_____   stole all his CDs.

_____ 3. Sherry came home from work hungry and devoured three mars bars and a bag
_____   of fritos; then she asked what was for supper.

_____ 4. "You ought to quit smoking those players," said Maria to her husband.
_____   "Even old Ports would be less harmful."

_____ 5. Mike was watching a soap opera, *General hospital*, on TV when a woman
_____   from bell Telephone called.

_____ 6. I had no sooner sat down in dr. Stein's office last tuesday evening than his
_____   beeper began to sound.

_____ 7. My Mother's first job was as a real estate salesperson for remax.
_____

_____ 8. To Sam, labour day means staying up all night to watch the CTV Telethon.
_____

_____ 9. the remodelling work is completed, our psychology classes will be held in
_____   wister hall.

_____ 10. The dirty Sign on the back of the speeding truck read, "this driver is a
_____   professional."

Score: Number correct _____ × 5 = _____%

NUMBERS AND ABBREVIATIONS

■ Mastery Test 1

Cross out the mistake in numbers or abbreviations in each sentence and correct it in the space provided.

_____ 1. In a panic, William grabbed the phone book and looked in the inside cover for the emergency number of the fire dept.

_____ 2. Did you know that an two hundred and fifty millilitre glass of tomato juice has only 50 calories?

_____ 3. Rod finally entered the ladies' room to investigate after he had waited a half hr. for his girlfriend.

_____ 4. By the time I graduated from high school, I had written 3 term papers, thirty-two book reports, and 120 spelling tests.

_____ 5. The federal govt. had to reimburse the citizens whose land was being incorporated into a protected wilderness area.

_____ 6. The basketball ref. called a technical foul on the screaming coach who had run out onto the court.

_____ 7. It took Sam all evening to do the twenty problems on page eighty-seven.

_____ 8. In Silvia's backyard were 125 old tires, 263 yards of rusty barbed wire, and three cast-iron bathtubs.

_____ 9. To discourage burglars, our automatic timer turns on a light and radio at 8 o'clock every night.

_____ 10. The overjoyed couple had won a thousand dollars a wk. for life in one of the provincial lottery draws.

Score: Number correct _____ × 10 = _____%

NUMBERS AND ABBREVIATIONS

■ Mastery Test 2

Cross out the mistake in numbers or abbreviations in each sentence and correct it in the space provided. Mark the one sentence that is correct with a *C*.

_____ 1. A delivery van was carelessly blocking the entrance to the hosp. emergency room.

_____ 2. From five potted tomato plants on the patio, Ruth harvested over ninety-five tomatoes.

_____ 3. Whenever I catch a cold, I take 2 aspirins every four hours.

_____ 4. Mrs. Green stood patiently in line at the P.O. waiting to mail a package and several letters.

_____ 5. As she did, she studied the faces of the "Ten Greatest Canadian p.m.'s" on the CPC poster.

_____ 6. After joining Weight Watchers, Maria lost thirty-two pounds in only 17 weeks.

_____ 7. I hurried to answer the phone, but it was only someone from the Rescue Squad requesting a contrib.

_____ 8. One of the actual questions on the test was when the War of Eighteen Twelve was fought.

_____ 9. By mid-nineteen-ninety-five, employment in service industries is expected to increase by 30 per cent.

_____ 10. The trouble with Ms. Ryder, my history prof., is that she never gives any examples when she lectures.

Score: Number correct _____ × 10 = _____%

END MARKS

■ Mastery Test 1

Add a period, a question mark, or an exclamation point, as needed, to each of the following sentences.

Note: End marks always go *inside* the quotation marks that appear in some sentences.

1. Even today women earn, on the average, only 59 per cent of men's salaries

2. Are you going to watch the Miss Canada pageant this year

3. After interrupting the program, the radio announcer hurried to assure us, "This was only a test "

4. The strange meal consisted of sausage, potato chips, and watermelon

5. When will daylight saving time end this year

6. Karen screamed, "I don't ever want to see you again "

7. That tree has been attacked by some kind of insect

8. Watch out for an incoming Frisbee

9. Sometimes I get depressed and wonder if I will ever get my diploma

10. Do you know how many cups of coffee it took me to finish this paper

11. The man threw open the window and yelled, "I'm mad at the world and I'm not going to take it any more "

12. My little brother is always working on ways to be more obnoxious

13. In bold red letters, the ad proclaimed, "You too can be a star "

14. My Uncle Jack is so budget-conscious that the only book he ever reads is his bank book

15. How much time do we have left to finish the test

16. Stanley yelled at the top of his voice, "Turn that stereo down before I break it "

17. Lisa asked, "Nick, will you type my sociology paper "

18. Get inside quickly or that dog will bite you—hurry

19. "One of the strangest phobias people have," said the professor, "is the fear of peanut butter sticking to the roof of the mouth "

20. Have you heard the one about the fellow at the shopping mall who wanted to buy the escalator because it was marked down

Score: Number correct _____ × 5 = _____ %

END MARKS

■ Mastery Test 2

Add a period, a question mark, or an exclamation point, as needed, to each of the following sentences.

Note: End marks always go *inside* the quotation marks that appear in some sentences.

1. Uncle Arthur's moustache makes him look like a walrus
2. Do coleslaw and French fries come with every order
3. From the airplane window, the clouds looked like mashed potatoes
4. A voice from the stands screamed, "Hustle your butts "
5. How can you hold down two jobs and still go to college
6. With a loud crack, the rotted branch broke and fell from the tree
7. "On your way over," asked Lisa, "could you pick up a case of Cokes "
8. Every time I take a shower, the kitchen ceiling begins to drip
9. The teacher asked me whether I had studied for the exam
10. "Somebody's been squeezing the bottom of the chocolates without eating them " Maria cried.
11. Annie wanted to know if I had finished bathing the dog
12. Why do I always get thirsty in the middle of the night
13. You're going to knock the vase off the table—watch out
14. I often wonder why more people don't buy live Christmas trees and plant them in their yards afterward
15. Must all our house guests bring screaming kids with them
16. The minute Aunt Agatha thought she had won, she jumped out of her seat and yelled "Bingo "
17. I'd jump into boiling oil before I took one of his courses again
18. The gas company wants to know if it can replace the meter in our basement
19. Have you tried that new Indian fast-food restaurant, Cash and Curry
20. It is better to keep one's mouth closed and be thought a fool than to open it and remove all doubt

Score: Number correct _____ × 5 = _____%

APOSTROPHES

■ Mastery Test 1

Cross out the word in each sentence that needs an apostrophe. Then write the word correctly in the space provided.

_____   1. I walked casually around the parking lot, trying to conceal the fact that Id no idea where I left my car.

_____   2. Maria ignored the police motorcycle officers siren and ended up in jail last night.

_____   3. The man insisted that his name was Elmer Fudd, but I didnt believe him.

_____   4. The blue whales tongue weighs about as much as forty men.

_____   5. Crystals mother put on designer jeans and went along with Crystal to the rock concert.

_____   6. Tony had to remove wood ticks from his hair after a walk through the field behind his uncles house.

_____   7. The womens room in that service station is always clean.

_____   8. Youre going to cause trouble for yourself if your temper gets out of hand.

_____   9. Some of the most violent crime years in Canadas history occurred during the Great Depression.

_____   10. Since apartheids collapse in South Africa, great cultural and economic advantages have happened for that country.

Score: Number correct _____ × 10 = _____%

APOSTROPHES

■ Mastery Test 2

In the space provided under each sentence, add the one apostrophe needed and explain why the other word ending in *s* is a simple plural.

Example   Joans hair began to fall out two days after she dyed it.

Joans: <u>Joan's, meaning "the hair belonging to Joan"</u>

days: <u>simple plural meaning more than one day</u>

1. The students gradually got used to the professors Japanese accent.

   students: _____

   professors: _____

2. Our tough mayors campaign promise is that he'll replace the parking meters with bicycle lock-ups.

   mayors: _____

   meters: _____

   lock-ups: _____

3. My little sisters habit of sucking in noodles makes her an unpleasant dining companion.

   sisters: _____

   noodles: _____

4. When the students complained about the teachers assignment, he said, "You're not in high school any more."

   students: _____

   teachers: _____

5. A football-sized nest of wasps hung menacingly under the roofs rain gutter.

   wasps: _____

   roofs: _____

Score: Number correct _____ × 10 = _____%

APOSTROPHES

■ Mastery Test 3

In each sentence two apostrophes are missing or are used incorrectly. Cross out the two errors and write the corrections in the spaces provided.

_____
_____

1. Freds day started going sour when he noticed that everyone in the doughnut shop had gotten fatter doughnuts' than he did.

_____
_____

2. While the team was in the showers, someone tied all the players sneakers' together.

_____
_____

3. If youll check the noise in the attic, Ill stand by the phone in case you scream.

_____
_____

4. Despite the drivers warning that smoking was not allowed, several people lit cigarettes' in the back of the bus.

_____
_____

5. When I sat on the fender of Teds car, he stared darts' at me until I slid off.

_____
_____

6. My brothers car phone was stolen by vandals' who broke his car window.

_____
_____

7. Sallys word processing might improve if shed cut an inch off her nails.

_____
_____

8. Maria has been in Freds bad books since she revealed that he sleeps with his' socks on.

_____
_____

9. The police officers face was stem as he told me that my drivers licence had expired.

_____
_____

10. I never ride any more in my uncles station wagon; its like being on a roller coaster.

_____

Score: Number correct _____ × 5 = _____%

APOSTROPHES

■ Mastery Test 4

In each sentence two apostrophes are missing or are used incorrectly. Cross out the two errors and write the corrections in the spaces provided.

_____   1. I was shocked when the movie stars toupee blew off; I hadnt realized he was
_____   completely bald.

_____   2. The skirts cheap lining puckered and scorched even though Christines iron
_____   was set at the lowest possible heat level.

_____   3. The two boys boat capsized in the rivers rushing current.
_____

_____   4. Theos work always ends up on someone elses desk.
_____

_____   5. People in the dentists waiting room squirmed uneasily as a childs cries echoed
_____   down the hall.

_____   6. When Jeans voice cracked during her solo, I thought shed faint with
_____   embarrassment.

_____   7. Didnt you know that school will be closed next week because of a teachers
_____   conference?

_____   8. My youngest sisters goldfish has jumped out of its' bowl many times.
_____

_____   9. "Its the muffler," the mechanic explained, crawling from under Freds car.
_____

_____   10. Kevin knew he was headed for trouble when his dates father said that hed like
_____   to come along.

Score: Number correct _____ × 5 = _____%

QUOTATION MARKS

■ Mastery Test 1

Place quotation marks where needed.

1. A friend of mine used to say, There's nothing wrong with you that a few birthdays won't cure.

2. The food critic wrote, The best test of a fast-food hamburger is to eat it after all the trimmings have been taken off.

3. After I finished Stephen Leacock's story My Financial Career, I started to write a paper on it.

4. When I'm finished exercising in the morning, said Crystal, there's a smoky fragrance to my skin.

5. Well, this is just fine, he mumbled. The recipe calls for four eggs and I have only two.

6. Eating Crystal's chili, Tony whispered, is a breathtaking experience.

7. After Bill pulled the flip-top cap off the can, he noticed that the label said, Shake well before drinking.

8. How would you feel, the teacher asked the class, if I gave you a surprise quiz today?

9. In a tired voice, Damian asked, Did you ever wonder why kids have more energy at the end of a long day than they had when they got up?

10. When Dick Cavett first met Groucho Marx on a street corner, he said, Hello, Groucho, I'm a big fan of yours. Groucho's response was, If it gets any hotter, I could use a big fan.

Score: Number correct _____ × 10 = _____%

QUOTATION MARKS

■ Mastery Test 2

Place quotation marks or underlines where needed.

1. The tag on the pillow read, Do not remove under penalty of law.

2. You two kids had better stop fighting this minute! ordered Aunt Esther in her most severe tone of voice.

3. If we don't hurry, we'll miss the beginning of the movie, Nick reminded Lisa.

4. Honest people, said the cranky old man, are scarcer than the feathers on a frog.

5. The most famous line from George Orwell's novel 1984 is, Big Brother is watching you.

6. It never fails, complained Maria. Just as I lie down to take a nap, the telephone rings.

7. I know I'm getting old, Grandfather said. When I walked past the cemetery today, two guys ran after me with shovels.

8. There is a sign in the grocery store that reads, All shoplifters will be accompanied by a police officer. If you don't have your own, we'll provide one for you.

9. When Damian got home from work, he said, At times I feel I'm in a rat race and the rats are winning. Angela consoled him by saying that everyone feels that way from time to time.

10. In a Canadian Consumer article titled What's Inside Frozen Dinners? the editors write, The filth we discovered is not a health hazard. But it's unpleasant to discover that these pies contain big and little parts of aphids, flies, moths, weevils, cereal beetles, and rodent hairs.

Score: Number correct _____ × 10 = _____%

QUOTATION MARKS

■ Mastery Test 3

Place quotation marks or underlines where needed.

1. Northrop Frye wrote, There is only one way to degrade mankind and that is to destroy language.

2. k.d. lang's song Constant Craving is one of my all-time favourites.

3. Are you positive you locked the front door? asked Vince for the third time.

4. You know, Bill said to the bartender, there are times in my life when I kind of panic. I want to go to bed and never get up again.

5. When I know I have a long day ahead, Judy said, I always have trouble sleeping well the night before.

6. Cracking his knuckles, Harry complained, I wish people didn't have so many annoying habits.

7. Look out, you idiot! screamed the frightened pedestrian. Are you trying to kill somebody?

8. Immanuel Kant once wrote: Two things fill me with constantly increasing admiration and awe the longer and more earnestly I reflect on them—the starry heavens without and the moral law within.

9. The saying we learned in school was, Do unto others as you would have them do unto you. The saying that I now have on the wall of my study reads, Remember the golden rule: she who has the gold makes the rules.

10. One of the questions on Sharon's Canadian literature test was to identify the poem in which the following line appears: Suzanne takes you down to a place by the river. . .

Score: Number correct _____ × 10 = _____%

QUOTATION MARKS

■ Mastery Test 4

Place quotation marks or underlines where needed.

1. Tony's uncle likes to say to him, You're never too young to have a heart attack.

2. The preacher began his sermon with the words, Nobody will ever get out of this world alive.

3. I won't get nervous. I won't get nervous, Terry kept repeating to herself as she walked into the exam room.

4. The honest politician proclaimed to the crowd, I haven't the slightest idea of what I'm talking about.

5. Tony said to Crystal, Guess how many jellybeans I can hold in my mouth at one time?

6. Bill complained, No one wants to go with me to Maniac for Hire, the new movie at the Cineplex.

7. If an infielder makes a mistake during a softball game, Darryl yells from the bench, You're a disgrace to your base!

8. As a child I was ugly, said the comedian. Once my old man took me to the zoo. The guy at the gate thanked him for returning me.

9. Don't let your paintbrushes dry up, advises the book Saving Money Around the House. Instead, store them in motor oil.

10. I agree that the public has a right to know what is in a hot dog, said the president of the meat company. But does the public really want to know what's in a hot dog?

Score: Number correct _____ × 10 = _____%

COMMAS

■ Mastery Test 1

Add commas where needed. Then refer to the box below to write, in the space provided, the letter of the one comma rule that applies in each sentence.

a. Between items in a series	d. Between complete thoughts
b. After introductory material	e. With direct quotations
c. Around interrupters	

_____ 1. The hot dogs that we bought tasted delicious but they reacted later like delayed time bombs.

_____ 2. Because it was the thing to do Tony pretended he had dated a lot of women when he talked with the guys.

_____ 3. Damian had no idea what his weight was but Angela always knew hers.

_____ 4. Crystal a good athlete surprised Tony by making forty-six of fifty foul shots.

_____ 5. The child's eyes glowed at the sight of the glittering tree colourful packages and stuffed stockings.

_____ 6. "Before you crack open another walnut" Tony's father warned him "remember that we're going to be eating shortly."

_____ 7. When she got back from the supermarket, she realized she had forgotten to get cereal grape jelly and Drano.

_____ 8. The old graveyard was filled with vampires werewolves crooked politicians and other monsters.

_____ 9. The problem with you David is that you take criticism personally.

_____ 10. Fred chose the shortest waiting line at the post office but the man in front of Fred suddenly began pulling a number of tiny packages out of his pocket.

Score: Number correct _____ × 10 = _____%

COMMAS

■ Mastery Test 2

Add commas where needed. Then refer to the box below to write, in the space provided, the letter of the one comma rule that applies in each sentence.

a. Between items in a series	d. Between complete thoughts
b. After introductory material	e. With direct quotations
c. Around interrupters	

_____ 1. As soon as Sam finished the difficult problem he let out a satisfied grunt.

_____ 2. On Saturday if it doesn't rain we plan to take the kids to the splatter-ball game.

_____ 3. I don't care if I never see you your family or your vacation pictures again.

_____ 4. Tony quit his part-time job at a local gas station for he was being paid only $3.25 an hour.

_____ 5. "Aunt Agatha is so forgetful" my mother observed "that whenever she ties a string around her finger as a reminder, she forgets to look at the string."

_____ 6. The Toronto, Ontario zoo purchases 20,000 kilos of meat 6,500 loaves of bread 114,000 live crickets and other foods for its animals each year.

_____ 7. My Aunt Esther loves watching the silly childish antics of the contestants on *Let's Make a Deal*.

_____ 8. Although my classes don't begin until ten o'clock I still have trouble getting to the lecture hall on time.

_____ 9. A flock of whooping cranes their shiny wings flashing in the sun flew above the marshlands.

_____ 10. Mike brought a tape recorder to class for he had broken two fingers and couldn't take notes.

Score: Number correct _____ × 10 = _____%

COMMAS

■ Mastery Test 3

Add commas where needed. Then refer to the box below to write, in the space provided, the letter of the one comma rule that applies in each sentence.

a.	Between items in a series	d.	Between complete thoughts
b.	After introductory material	e.	With direct quotations
c.	Around interrupters		

_____ 1. Damian and Angela took Gabriel their son to see Walt Disney's *Bambi*.

_____ 2. The film covers the birth of Bambi the loss of his mother his escape from a forest fire and his growth to young fatherhood.

_____ 3. Just before the film started Damian decided to get a giant box of licorice bits.

_____ 4. While he was at the refreshment counter, the houselights dimmed the stage curtains opened and the movie started.

_____ 5. Damian hurried back down the dark aisle almost stumbling and he slipped into the empty aisle seat that he thought was his.

_____ 6. While Damian popped licorice bits into his mouth the woman next to him rested her head on his shoulder.

_____ 7. Damian's eyes grew accustomed to the dark and he became aware suddenly of an elderly man standing near him in the aisle.

_____ 8. "Excuse me, Sir" the man said. "You're in my seat."

_____ 9. Hearing the man's voice, the woman looked up saw Damian next to her and screamed.

_____ 10. "I'm really sorry, Madam," Damian said. He got up quickly and saw just in front of him waving and laughing his wife and son.

Score: Number correct _____ × 10 = _____%

COMMAS

■ Mastery Test 4

Do three things: 1) cross out the one comma that is not needed; 2) add the one comma that is needed; 3) in the space provided, write the letter of the one comma rule that applies in each sentence.

a.   Between items in a series
b.   After introductory material
c.   Around interrupters
d.   Between complete thoughts
e.   With direct quotations

_____   1. On Friday, my day off I went, to get a haircut.

_____   2. "When I have a headache" my aunt explained, "I simply close my eyes, and take several deep breaths."

_____   3. The aliens in the science-fiction film visited our planet in peace but we greeted them, with violence.

_____   4. A neat appearance warm smile, and positive attitude, will make an employer respond to you.

_____   5. "Even, the greatest creations," the sign said "start from small seeds."

_____   6. Frank does not like, cooked carrots and he cares even less for lima beans.

_____   7. According to rumours our school janitor has made himself a millionaire, through real estate investments.

_____   8. Helena was not happy, about having to drop the math course but there were too many other demands being made on her time.

_____   9. A jar of split-pea soup, which was all Bill had in the refrigerator did not make, for a very satisfactory meal.

_____   10. Although Maria is normally, a careful and defensive driver she drives reck-lessly if she is in a bad mood.

Score: Number correct _____ × 10 = _____%

OTHER PUNCTUATION MARKS

■ Mastery Test 1

At the appropriate spot (or spots), place the punctuation mark shown in the margin.

— 1. Maria screamed when she saw a water bug the kind that can travel a hundred kilometres an hour race across her bathroom floor.

; 2. A canary's claws must be carefully clipped it is important not to nick the little veins in each one.

— 3. Chapleau is so far north that it has only two seasons winter and August.

: 4. A search of Danny's pockets revealed these items a two-centimetre-long piece of wire, a crumpled baseball card, three small stones, and a dead grasshopper.

( ) 5. The incoming line section should be a rigid dead-front type, completely encased with metal and self-supporting see diagram *A* .

- 6. "Don't Cry for Me Argentina" is a tear jerking, heart tugging solo from the international hit *Evita.*

( ) 7. Our country's national parks especially famous ones like Banff and Nahanni must now deal with major crimes committed by summer visitors.

; 8. Native Canadians have many unique characters in their belief systems for instance the evil Wendigo and the playful Nanabush.

- 9. The slightly built burglar was well known as the most talented "second storey" man in town.

: 10. *Canadian Consumer* concludes its article on wood stoves by stating "You should first ask yourself if you *need* a wood stove to help lower your home-heating costs. Are you sure you've done as much as you can to save energy in other ways? Are you prepared for the inconveniences, major and minor, that a stove entails?"

Score: Number correct _____ × 10 = _____ %

OTHER PUNCTUATION MARKS

■ Mastery Test 2

Add colons, semi-colons, dashes, hyphens, or parentheses as needed. Each sentence requires only one of the five kinds of punctuation marks.

1. Bargain hunters swarmed around the entrance to the store the manager quickly opened the doors.
2. The diagram of the reproductive cycle pages 24–25 must also be studied for the test.
3. Self centred people are often very insecure individuals.
4. There is one sure way to get in trouble with that teacher ask too many questions.
5. Tarzan, Superman, the Lone Ranger these were the heroes of his boyhood.
6. George Orwell has written "On the whole, human beings want to be good, but not too good, and not quite all the time. … Society has always to demand a little more from human beings than it will get in practice."
7. Two squirrels there they are on top of the fence are building a nest in the storage shed.
8. The three required books on our psychology reading list are *Towards a Psychology of Being*, by Abraham Maslow *On Becoming a Person*, by Carl Rogers and *Love and Will*, by Rollo May.
9. I don't know why the door to the gas station washroom is locked perhaps the owner is afraid someone will get inside to clean it.
10. This do it yourself repair book will save homeowners a lot of money.

Score: Number correct _____ × 10 = _____%

DICTIONARY USE

■ Mastery Test 1

Use your dictionary to answer the following questions.

1. How many syllables are in the word *decontaminate?* _____

2. Where is the primary accent in the word *interpretation?* _____

3. In the word *posterity*, the *i* is pronounced like
   a. short *e*
   b. short *i*
   c. long *i*
   d. schwa

4. In the word *secularize*, the *u* is pronounced like
   a. schwa
   b. short *a*
   c. short *u*
   d. long *u*

5. In the word *erratic*, the *e* is pronounced like
   a. short *e*
   b. long *e*
   c. short *i*
   d. schwa

Items 6–10: There are five misspelled words in the following sentence. Cross out each misspelled word and write in the correct spelling in the spaces provided.

The canidate for mayor promised to reduce subway fares by a nickle, to crack down on criminels, and to bring new businesses to the city by ofering tax breaks.

6. _____   8. _____   10. _____

7. _____   9. _____

Score: Number correct _____ × 10 = _____%

DICTIONARY USE

■ Mastery Test 2

Use your dictionary to answer the following questions.

1. How many syllables are in the word *rationalize?* _____

2. Where is the primary accent in the word *dilapidated?* _____

3. In the word *vicarious*, the second *i* is pronounced like
   a. long *e*
   b. short *i*
   c. long *i*
   d. schwa

4. In the word *cumbersome*, the *o* is pronounced like
   a. schwa
   b. short *a*
   c. short *o*
   d. long *o*

5. In the word *esoteric*, the second *e* is pronounced like
   a. short *e*
   b. long *e*
   c. short *i*
   d. schwa

Items 6–10: There are five misspelled words in the following sentence. Cross out each misspelled word and write the correct spelling in the space provided.

My mother's most precious possesion is her collection of crystel animals; she keeps them in a specal cabinet in the dineing room and won't allow anyone to handel them.

6. _____   8. _____   10. _____

7. _____   9. _____

Score: Number correct _____ × 10 = _____%

SPELLING IMPROVEMENT

■ Mastery Test 1

Use the three spelling rules to spell the following words.

1. debate + able = _____
2. run   + ing = _____
3. thorny + est = _____
4. woe   + ful = _____
5. swim + er   = _____
6. happy + ly   = _____
7. hate   + ful = _____
8. infer   + ed = _____

Circle the correctly spelled plural in each pair.

9. knifes   knives   12. stories   storys
10. wishes   wishs   13. heros   heroes
11. decoys   decoies   14. ourselfs   ourselves

Circle the correctly spelled word (from the basic word list) in each pair.

15. possible   possable   18. success   sucess
16. exercize   exercise   19. rediculous   ridiculous
17. receive   recieve   20. acident   accident

Score: Number correct _____ × 5 = _____%

SPELLING IMPROVEMENT

■ Mastery Test 2

Use the three spelling rules to spell the following words.

1. equip   + ed   = _____
2. excite   + ment = _____
3. heavy   + ly   = _____
4. flat   + est   = _____
5. carry   + ed   = _____
6. begin   + er   = _____
7. surprise + ing   = _____
8. crazy   + ness   = _____

Circle the correctly spelled plural in each pair.

9. issues   issus   12. loaves   loafs
10. partys   parties   13. halfs   halves
11. worries   worrys   14. father-in-laws fathers-in-law

Circle the correctly spelled word (from the basic word list) in each pair.

15. measure   meazure   18. psycology   psychology
16. knowlege   knowledge   19. awkward   akward
17. alright   all right   20. receive   recieve

Score: Number correct _____ × 5 = _____%

OMITTED WORDS AND LETTERS

■ Mastery Test 1

Part 1: In the spaces provided, write in the two small connecting words needed in each sentence. Use carets (∧) within the sentences to show where these words belong.

_____

_____   1. With only inning left play, the score was three to two.

_____

_____   2. In middle of the night, I heard a loud crash jumped out of bed, trembling.

_____

_____   3. Whenever Lisa puts a Tony Bennett record on stereo, Nick goes to sleep.

_____

_____   4. If Maria thinks she is coming down with cold, she drinks a cup tea with honey.

_____

_____   5. The young actor slowly got out of the limousine, clutching small white poodle that resembled animated mop.

_____

Part 2: In the spaces provided, write in the two words that need *-s* endings in each sentence. Be sure to add the *s* to each word.

_____

_____   6. Our expense were getting out of control, so my husband and I began keeping a record of all our purchase.

_____

_____   7. All the section of two course Tony wanted were closed.

_____

_____   8. We had forgotten to make extra ice cube, so Melissa volunteered to pick up two bag at the corner store.

_____

_____   9. A young couple in the laundromat started to roll their sock into ball and lob them at each other.

_____

_____   10. After several attempt, Vince was finally able to press 100 kilos.

_____

Score: Number correct _____ × 5 = _____%

OMITTED WORDS AND LETTERS

■ Mastery Test 2

Part 1: In the spaces provided, write in the two small connecting words needed in each sentence. Use carets (∧) within the sentences to show where these words belong.

_____ 1. Jean called cable company when picture on her set resembled a crazy quilt.
_____

_____ 2. When ten centimetres rain fell in one day, our backyard resembled swimming pool.
_____

_____ 3. I have lost track how many parties our neighbour has given in past year.
_____

_____ 4. Even though Bill ate three sandwiches lunch, he began eat a bag of doughnuts at three o'clock.
_____

_____ 5. The quarterback would have had better completion record if backs had not dropped so many passes this year.
_____

Part 2: In the spaces provided, write in the two words that need *-s* endings in each sentence. Be sure to add the *s* to each word.

_____ 6. The music store in the mall has two trade-in day a month when used CD are purchased for cash.
_____

_____ 7. The pattern had worn off the linoleum floor in many place, and the wall were water-stained.
_____

_____ 8. Like small black freight train, long lines of ant moved across the sidewalk.
_____

_____ 9. The director's chair on Larry's porch are imprinted with the name of the family members.
_____

_____ 10. Everything, from a group of stuffed parrot to several antique bicycle, hung from the ceiling of the restaurant.
_____

> *Score:* Number correct _____ × 5 = _____%

COMMONLY CONFUSED WORDS

■ Mastery Test 1

Choose the correct words in each sentence and write them in the spaces provided.

_____

_____

1. Last year the (hole, whole) publishing industry seemed to concentrate on turning out (knew, new) romantic novels.

_____

_____

2. (To, Too, Two) test our snowmobiles, we headed (strait, straight) into the blustery weather.

_____

_____

3. The mechanic did not (know, no) what caused the (break, brake) in the fuel line of Fred's car.

_____

_____

4. My dog lost (its, it's) tail when run over by a truck that had lost its (brakes, breaks).

_____

_____

5. (Irregardless, Regardless) of what her co-workers think, Susan always wears plain (clothes, cloths) to work.

_____

_____

6. Pete (could of, could have) used the money, but he refused to (accept, except) the cheque his parents offered him.

_____

_____

7. Morris can't stand to (hear, here) advice. He lives by the (principal, principle), "If I make my own decisions, I have only myself to praise or blame."

_____

_____

8. Kevin and Judy have to make (there, their, they're) handwriting neater and more legible if (there, their, they're) after good grades.

_____

_____

9. Just (among, between) us, I'd advise you not to take Dear Abby's (advice, advise) as gospel.

_____

_____

10. That lion over (there, their, they're) clawed at the attendant cleaning (it's, its) cage.

Score: Number correct _____ × 5 = _____%

COMMONLY CONFUSED WORDS

■ Mastery Test 2

Choose the correct words in each sentence and write them in the spaces provided.

_____
_____
1. Laurie is going to (lose, loose) her job even though she was (among, between) the ten best salespeople in the company last year.

_____
_____
2. The (affect, effect) of the medication is that all my symptoms (accept, except) for a slight cough have disappeared.

_____
_____
3. (Its, It's) hard to deny the fact that (there, their, they're) are many fools in the world.

_____
_____
4. I (would of, would have) tried out for that role, but the director told me that she had (already, all ready) filled the part.

_____
_____
5. (Being that, Because) you never studied for the course, you (can hardly, can't hardly) blame the instructor for your F.

_____
_____
6. (There, Their, They're) are only (to, too, two) days left to take advantage of the store's January white sale.

_____
_____
7. Tony pushed the mower (through, threw) the heavy underbrush on the back lawn and (than, then) manoeuvred it past a huge pile of rocks.

_____
_____
8. (It's, Its) very peaceful and (quite, quiet) along the stretch of the river that passes near our town.

_____
_____
9. The (weather, whether) was so bad that it caused a one-hour (brake, break) in the game.

_____
_____
10. Marilyn changed her seat to get away from the (to, too, two) (coarse, course) people on the bus.

Score: Number correct _____ × 5 = _____%

COMMONLY CONFUSED WORDS

■ Mastery Test 3

Cross out the two mistakes in usage in each sentence. Then write the correct words in the spaces provided.

_____

_____
1. A stranger in an black suit knocked on my neighbour's door and handed him a plane manila envelope.

_____

_____
2. Its not easy to find food in that refrigerator because it's shelves are crowded and poorly lit.

_____

_____
3. If this cough syrup dose its job, your going to be feeling better very soon.

_____

_____
4. Our psychology teacher should of cancelled the last class before the holiday, for less than six students showed up.

_____

_____
5. Do you know that the cactus plant over their is the basis for a delicious desert?

_____

_____
6. When he tries to learn her how to drive, she sets up a mental block and refuses to except his instructions.

_____

_____
7. One affect of the strong wind is that some lose roof shingles have blown off the house.

_____

_____
8. Too get to the Brock Monument, you must ride two buses and take a long walk, to.

_____

_____
9. I can't hardly recommend you buy that house, for there are termite wholes in the basement studs.

_____

_____
10. If the principle ingredient in that stew is octopus, I don't know whether I'll accept you're invitation to try it.

Score: Number correct _____ × 5 = _____%

COMMONLY CONFUSED WORDS

■ Mastery Test 4

Cross out the two mistakes in usage in each sentence. Then write the correct words in the spaces provided.

_____   1. Beside the twins, the Fosters have three other children—more then anyone
_____   else on the block.

_____   2. Larry should of realized by now that he could have past the course by study-
_____   ing harder.

_____   3. Its to bad that the pair of you didn't apply for the job there.
_____

_____   4. Nothing was less appealing to Joel then the possibility of excepting the advice
_____   I had given him.

_____   5. Regardless of what you say, I believe we could of learned our collie how to
_____   be a good watchdog.

_____   6. I pursue both rug making and gardening: the latter allows me to be creative
_____   and the former allows me to enjoy the peace of nature.

_____   7. I'll be quiet surprised if the promise of a delicious desert doesn't make my
_____   little sister agree to be quiet.

_____   8. Being that it's sinking into the water, their must be too many people in the boat.
_____

_____   9. You're new car has been inspected and registered, so it's already to drive.
_____

_____   10. Whether or not I take that course depends on whose teaching it and how much
_____   righting is required.

_____
| ***Score:***   Number correct _____ × 5 = _____% |
_____

EFFECTIVE WORD CHOICE

■ Mastery Test 1

Certain words are italicized in the following sentences. In the space at the left, identify whether the words are slang (*S*), clichés (*C*), or pretentious words (*PW*). Then replace the words with more effective diction.

_____   1. The man in the house on the corner *kicked the bucket* last night.

_____   2. That book is by a millionaire who *didn't have a dime to his name* as a boy.

_____   3. Marty has always *endeavoured* to excel in his college courses.

_____   4. The boss told Bob to *get his act together* or to resign.

_____   5. I have a *large quantity* of chores to do this weekend.

_____   6. Our team's chances of winning the league championship are *as dead as a doornail*.

_____   7. The players were nervous; they didn't want to *blow* the championship game.

_____   8. Donna *came out of her shell* after she joined the theatre group at school.

_____   9. When Julie's marriage *hit the rocks*, she decided to see a therapist.

_____   10. Many people today *entertain anxieties* about our country's economy.

Score: Number correct _____ × 10 = _____%

EFFECTIVE WORD CHOICE

■ Mastery Test 2

Certain words are italicized in the following sentences. In the space at the left, identify whether the words are slang (*S*), clichés (*C*), or pretentious words (*PW*). Then replace the words with more effective diction.

_____ 1. Joanna thought it was *too good to be true* when the boss told her to go home early.

_____

_____ 2. I won't be coming; line dancing just *isn't my thing*.

_____

_____ 3. Passing the course is *contingent* upon my grade in the final exam.

_____

_____ 4. I am *sick and tired of* her dog's digging up my backyard.

_____

_____ 5. If the boss starts *putting heat on me* again, I'm going to ask for a transfer.

_____

_____ 6. Long political speeches *bore me to tears*.

_____

_____ 7. I got so tired at Neil's party that I had to *sack out* on his living-room couch.

_____

_____ 8. Nick scrubbed the countertop with Vim until it was *clean as a whistle*.

_____

_____ 9. Monique is embarrassed about the fact that, after high school, she did not go on to *an institution of higher learning*.

_____

_____ 10. My husband and I have both lost weight as a result of our *reducing regimens*.

_____

Score: Number correct _____ × 10 = _____%

EFFECTIVE WORD CHOICE

■ Mastery Test 3

The following sentences include examples of wordiness. Rewrite the sentences in the space provided, omitting needless words.

1. The fact of the matter is that I did not remember that I had an appointment to meet with you.

   _____

   _____

2. To make a long story short, my brother and his wife are going to get a divorce.

   _____

   _____

3. At our company there are at present two coffee breaks, with each of them fifteen minutes long.

   _____

   _____

4. At this point in time, Lou would be wise to start working on the paper he has to write for English.

   _____

   _____

5. Permit us to take this opportunity to inform you that your line of credit has been increased.

   _____

   _____

Score: Number correct _____ × 20 = _____%

EFFECTIVE WORD CHOICE

■ Mastery Test 4

The following sentences include examples of wordiness. Rewrite the sentences in the space provided, omitting needless words.

1. In my opinion, I think that all people, men and women both, should be treated exactly alike.

    _____

    _____

2. The exercises that Susan does every day of the week give her more energy with which to deal with everyday life.

    _____

    _____

3. I hereby wish to inform you in this letter that I will not be renewing my lease for the apartment.

    _____

    _____

4. All Canadian citizens should consider it their duty to go out and vote on the day that has been scheduled to be Election Day.

    _____

    _____

5. In view of the fact that miracle drugs exist in our science today, our lifetimes will be extended longer than our grandparents'.

    _____

    _____

Score: Number correct _____ × 20 = _____%

COMBINED MASTERY TESTS

SENTENCE FRAGMENTS AND RUN-ONS

■ Combined Mastery Test 1

Each of the word groups below is numbered. In the space provided, write *C* if a word group is a complete sentence, write *F* if it is a fragment, and write *R-O* if it is a run-on. Then correct the errors.

1. _____

2. _____

3. _____

4. _____

5. _____

6. _____

7. _____

8. _____

9. _____

10. _____

11. _____

12. _____

13. _____

14. _____

15. _____

16. _____

17. _____

18. _____

19. _____

20. _____

[1] The cheap motel room smelled musty.[2] As if the window had never been opened.[3] I snapped on the light, a roach sauntered across the floor.[4] Although the bed looked lumpy.[5] I flopped on it gratefully, totally exhausted.[6] I needed about ten hours' sleep.[7] Then I would get something to eat.[8] And start to plan on how to get my life going in the right direction again.

[9] As the rest of the class scribbled furiously during the lecture.[10] Gene doodled in his notebook.[11] Weird stick figures marched across the page odd flowers blossomed on its borders.[12] Because he was so involved in his fantasy world.[13] Gene continued to draw.[14] After the lecture had ended.

[15] Gripping the scissors in one hand and her son's shoulder in the other.[16] Margaret attempted to give the squirming toddler a haircut.[17] Waving his fist angrily.[18] The boy knocked the shears out of his mother's hand.[19] The shears skidded across the floor they headed for the family's unsuspecting dog.[20] Who jumped backward suddenly and began to bark loudly.

Score: Number correct _____ × 5 = _____%

SENTENCE FRAGMENTS AND RUN-ONS

■ Combined Mastery Test 2

In the space provided, indicate whether each item below contains a fragment (*F*) or a run-on (*R-O*). Then correct the error.

_____   1. Since the game ended in a tie. The teams had to go into sudden-death over-time. Not a single fan left the stadium.

_____   2. Nick and Lisa buy only name brands at the store, they feel economy brands are lower not just in price but in quality. I disagree with them.

_____   3. The fire drills in school gave a welcome break to the daily routine. Students moved quickly and obediently. Clearing the building in a hurry.

_____   4. Because the miracle soles on Fred's shoes have never worn down. He has used the same pair for the last four years. Maria is sick of looking at them.

_____   5. An astrologer read my chart I didn't believe her. My friend was born on the same day, but we have completely different personalities.

_____   6. My sister parked her cart in the check-out line at the market. Then dashed off to get final items on her list. I hate people who do that.

_____   7. When Laurie left for college, her mother was devastated, she was not used to a lonely house. Her solution was to return to school herself.

_____   8. Nick and Lisa didn't have time to cook dinner. They stopped at a Tim Horton's. To pick up Timbits.

_____   9. Because Dave is only five feet three inches, he has trouble getting dates. He often fantasizes about being an incredibly tall basketball player then all the women in the world would look up to him.

_____ 10. Until I was twelve, I believed there really was a tooth fairy. She would leave a dollar under my pillow. Whenever I lost a tooth.

Score: Number correct _____ × 10 = _____%

VERBS

■ Combined Mastery Test 1

Each sentence contains a mistake involving (1) standard English or irregular verb forms, (2) subject-verb agreement, or (3) consistent verb tense. Cross out the incorrect verb and write the correct form in the space provided.

_____ 1. The quarterback had broke most of the school's passing records by grade twelve.

_____ 2. The cost of the transmission and brake repairs are more than the car's worth.

_____ 3. The more my instructor tried to explain the material and the more he writes on the board, the more confused I got.

_____ 4. Nobody on the police force know the identity of the informer.

_____ 5. Crystal likes to use lip gloss but hated the way it stains her fingers and never seems to come off.

_____ 6. Each of Anita's boyfriends think he is the only man in her life.

_____ 7. The socks I bought at that store have wore thin after only three months.

_____ 8. Out of my little brother's mouth comes some of the most amazing words I have ever heard.

_____ 9. As soon as the store opened, customers race through the doors and hurried to the bargain racks.

_____ 10. We have not ate out at a restaurant since my wife lost her job.

Score: Number correct _____ × 10 = _____%

VERBS

■ Combined Mastery Test 2

Each sentence contains a mistake involving (1) standard English or irregular verb forms, (2) subject-verb agreement, or (3) consistent verb tense. Cross out the incorrect verb and write the correct form in the space provided.

_____ 1. Crystal was stang by some kind of bug during her hike in the woods.

_____ 2. My sister and I often gets into an argument at the dinner table.

_____ 3. The mechanic told me my car was going to be ready by noon, but he finishes working on it at five o'clock.

_____ 4. I had not did my math homework, so I was sure my teacher would give a surprise quiz.

_____ 5. Roaring down a quiet street at ninety kilometres an hour were Daisy on her new Honda.

_____ 6. You should have knowed better than to trust your little brother to deliver the message.

_____ 7. Carlo watched suspiciously as a strange car drives back and forth in front of his house.

_____ 8. I should have brung an extra pen to the exam.

_____ 9. When Crystal saw the children skipping home from school clutching their drawings, she remembered when she use to do the same thing.

_____ 10. Rob Revolting, lead singer of the Deadly Poisons, wears a black satin jumpsuit with a silver skull and crossbones on the front when he perform.

Score: Number correct _____ × 10 = _____%

PRONOUNS

■ Combined Mastery Test 1

Choose the sentence in each pair that uses pronouns correctly. Then write the letter of that sentence in the space provided.

_____ 1. a. When I took my son to his first basketball game, he was amazed at how tall they were.
　　　　　 b. When I took my son to his first basketball game, he was amazed at how tall the players were.

_____ 2. a. You can't play the new software on the Macintosh because it's defective.
　　　　　 b. You can't play the new software on the Macintosh because the software is defective.

_____ 3. a. None of the players on the women's softball team felt proud about her performance in the championship game.
　　　　　 b. None of the players on the women's softball team felt proud about their performance in the championship game.

_____ 4. a. I've learned a lot about biking from Eddie, who is a much better biker than me.
　　　　　 b. I've learned a lot about biking from Eddic, who is a much better biker than I.

_____ 5. a. I wanted to browse through the store, but in every department a salesperson came up and asked to help you.
　　　　　 b. I wanted to browse through the store, but in every department a salesperson came up and asked to help me.

_____

Score:　Number correct _____ × 20 = _____%

PRONOUNS

■ Combined Mastery Test 2

In the space provided, write *PE* beside each of the nine sentences that contain pronoun errors. Write *C* beside the sentence that uses pronouns correctly. Then cross out each pronoun error and write the correction above it.

_____   1. Diane received in the mail an ad that said you could make $600 a month addressing envelopes.

_____   2. We refereed the game ourselfs, for no officials were available.

_____   3. Before any more time is wasted, you and me must have a serious talk.

_____   4. One of the Boy Scouts left some live embers burning in his campfire.

_____   5. Everyone who works in the company must have their chest X-rayed every two years.

_____   6. The teacher gave George and I a warning look.

_____   7. Gina wanted to run in for some bread and milk, but it was so crowded that she decided not to bother.

_____   8. If them eggs have a bad smell, throw them away.

_____   9. When I visited a friend at the hospital, you had to pay two dollars just to use the parking lot.

_____   10. Alex called Franco at work to say that his father had had an accident.

Score: Number correct _____ × 10 = _____%

FAULTY MODIFIERS AND PARALLELISM

■ Combined Mastery Test 1

In the space provided, indicate whether each sentence contains a misplaced modifier (*MM*), a dangling modifier (*DM*), or faulty parallelism (*FP*). Then correct the error in the space under the sentence.

_____ 1. My parents like to visit auctions, eat Mexican food, and watching horror movies.

_____

_____ 2. An old wreck of wars past, Admiral Hawkeye inspected the ship.

_____

_____ 3. I notified the police that my house had been burglarized by phone.

_____

_____ 4. Dulled by Novocaine, the dentist pulled my tooth.

_____

_____ 5. With sweaty hands and a voice that trembled, Alice read her paper aloud.

_____

_____ 6. At the age of six, my mother bought me a chemistry set.

_____

_____ 7. Cut and infected, Reggie took his dog to the vet.

_____

_____ 8. My neighbour mowed the lawn shirtless.

_____

_____ 9. Mariel decided to start a garden while preparing dinner.

_____

_____ 10. To earn extra money, Terry processes term papers and is working at the Point Grill.

_____

Score: Number correct _____ × 10 = _____%

FAULTY MODIFIERS AND PARALLELISM

■ Combined Mastery Test 2

In the space provided, indicate whether each sentence contains a misplaced modifier (*MM*), a dangling modifier (*DM*), or faulty parallelism (*FP*). Then correct the error in the space under the sentence.

_____   1. By studying harder, Barry's grades improved.

    _____

_____   2. We put the food back in the knapsack that we had not eaten.

    _____

_____   3. My doctor advised extra sleep, nourishing food, and that I should exercise regularly.

    _____

_____   4. Smelling up the room, I quickly put the trout in the freezer.

    _____

_____   5. Buying a foreign car will cause more family arguments for me than to buy a Canadian car.

    _____

_____   6. Marty is the guy carrying packages with curly brown hair.

    _____

_____   7. My hopes for retirement are good health, having plenty of money, and beautiful companions.

    _____

_____   8. Filled with cigarette butts and used tea bags, I washed the disgusting cups.

    _____

    _____

_____   9. I asked Bonnie to see a movie with me nervously.

    _____

_____   10. Frightened by the rising crime rate, an alarm system was installed in the house.

    _____

> ***Score:***   Number correct _____ × 10 = _____%

CAPITAL LETTERS AND PUNCTUATION

■ Combined Mastery Test 1

Each of the following sentences contains an error in capitalization or punctuation. Refer to the box below to write, in the space provided, the letter identifying the error. Then correct the error.

a. Missing capital	c. Missing quotation marks
b. Missing apostrophe	d. Missing comma

_____ 1. I wanted desperately to scratch the scab on my hand but I didn't want to take the risk of infecting it.

_____ 2. "Don't drive too close to the edge of the prairie, the old prospector warned the tourists, "or you're liable to fall off."

_____ 3. Did you know they're going to tear down the old school on second Street and put a Swiss Chalet there?

_____ 4. The hamsters eyes glowed when some fresh lettuce was put into its cage.

_____ 5. Because the electric can opener was broken Fred was unable to make himself some chicken noodle soup.

_____ 6. Its not going to be easy to find a job that both pays well and involves interesting work.

_____ 7. The woman was asked why she wanted to be a mortician. "I enjoy working with people, she replied.

_____ 8. For my lonely Uncle Russ, holidays are the worst time of the year.

_____ 9. Some people believe that voting should be mandatory not merely encouraged, in Canada.

_____ 10. Maria said to the woman behind her in the theatre, "will you shut your mouth, please?"

Score: Number correct _____ × 10 = _____%

CAPITAL LETTERS AND PUNCTUATION

■ Combined Mastery Test 2

Each of the following sentences contains an error in capitalization or punctuation. Refer to the box below to write, in the space provided, the letter identifying the error. Then correct the error.

a. Missing capital	c. Missing quotation marks
b. Missing apostrophe	d. Missing comma

_____ 1. There is nothing on the menu of that restaurant," Nick said, "that would not cause nausea in laboratory mice."

_____ 2. If you'll hold this package shut for me I'll be able to do a better job of taping it closed.

_____ 3. Crystals yoga class has been cancelled this week, so she's decided to go running instead.

_____ 4. Lisa said, "the directions called for a pinch of sugar in the stew, but I accidentally added a teaspoon."

_____ 5. Roger just got a good job offer today so he won't have to stand in the UIC line any more.

_____ 6. Unless I start studying soon, I'm going to have to repeat sociology 101.

_____ 7. "Did you hear the news? Maria asked Fred. "A man who was attempting to walk around the world drowned today."

_____ 8. If youre going to stay up late, be sure to turn down the heat before going to bed.

_____ 9. I was able to return the vacuum, even though I hadn't saved the receipt to the Canadian Tire catalogue store.

_____ 10. The company has to pay double time when it calls workers in to work an extra shift on sunday.

Score: Number correct _____ × 10 = _____ %

WORD USE

■ Combined Mastery Test 1

Each of the following sentences contains a mistake identified in the left-hand margin. Underline the mistake and then correct it in the space provided.

Slang

1. Ralph was canned from his job yesterday for sleeping at his desk.

_____

Wordiness

2. I'm in college for the purpose of getting a diploma in data processing.

_____

Cliché

3. Nick and Lisa were able to depend upon their parents in their hour of need.

_____

Pretentious language

4. Eric improved his math skills by utilizing the tutoring centre at school.

_____

Adverb error

5. Betty has not done bad in her math course, even though she missed a week of class because of illness.

_____

Error in comparison

6. This year my garden has been producing the abundantest crop of weeds in human history.

_____

Confused word

7. It's the second time our dog has broken it's chain and run away.

_____

Confused word

8. The doctor was concerned that the new allergy drug would effect my sense of balance.

_____

Confused word

9. There not too friendly in that store, but their merchandise is sold at bargain prices.

_____

Confused word

10. Whitney plans to move to an efficiency apartment hear in the city.

_____

> ***Score:*** Number correct _____ × 10 = _____%

WORD USE

■ Combined Mastery Test 2

Each of the following sentences contains a mistake identified in the left-hand margin. Underline the mistake and then correct it in the space provided.

Slang
1. That company has spent millions to hype its new shampoo.

_____

Wordiness
2. I plan to quit my job because of the fact that my boss treats me unfairly.

_____

Cliché
3. The catcher and pitcher had a sneaking suspicion their signs were being stolen.

_____

Pretentious language
4. Bonnie wants to procure a VCR as soon as she has the money.

_____

Adverb error
5. Phil and Nancy are taking their relationship too serious, considering that they're still teenagers.

_____

Error in comparison
6. The book report for my psychology class is the most bad paper I've ever written.

_____

Confused word
7. Football has always been the principle sport at our school.

_____

Confused word
8. You're children are the ones who broke my front gate, so you're going to pay for the damage.

_____

Confused word
9. Whose the professor whose courses involve a lot of field trips?

_____

Confused word
10. Classes in college are far less regimented then the ones in high school.

_____

Score: Number correct _____ × 10 = _____%

EDITING AND PROOFREADING TESTS

The passages in this section can be used in either of two ways:

1 *As Editing Tests:* Each passage contains a number of mistakes involving a single sentence skill. For example, the first passage on page 341 contains five sentence fragments. Your instructor may ask you to proofread the passage to locate the five fragment errors. Spaces are provided at the bottom of the page for you to indicate which word groups are fragments. Your instructor may also have you correct the errors, either in the text itself or on separate paper. Depending on how you do, you may also be asked to edit the second and third passages for fragments.

There are three passages for each skill area, and there are twelve skills covered in all. Here is a list of the skill areas:

Test 1   Sentence fragments
Test 2   Run-ons (fused sentences)
Test 3   Run-ons (comma splices)
Test 4   Standard English verbs
Test 5   Irregular verbs
Test 6   Misplaced and dangling modifiers
Test 7   Faulty parallelism
Test 8   Capital letters
Test 9   Apostrophes
Test 10 Quotation marks
Test 11 Commas
Test 12 Commonly confused words

2 As Guided Composition Activities: To give practice in proof-reading as well, your instructor may ask you to do more than correct the skill mistakes in each passage. You may be asked to rewrite the passage, correcting it for skill mistakes *and also* copying perfectly the rest of the passage. Should you miss one skill mistake or make even one copying mistake (for example, omitting a word, dropping a verb ending, misspelling a word, or misplacing an apostrophe), you may be asked to rewrite a different passage that deals with the same skill.

Here is how you would proceed. You would start with sentence fragments, rewriting the first passage, proofreading your paper carefully, and then showing it to your instructor, who will check it quickly to see that all the fragments have been corrected and that no copying mistakes have been made. If the passage is error-free, the instructor will mark and initial the appropriate box in the progress chart on pages 500–501 and you can move on to run-ons.

If even a single mistake is made, the instructor may question you briefly to see if you recognize and understand it. (Perhaps your instructor will put a check mark beside the line in which the mistake appears and then ask if you can correct it.) You may then be asked to write the second passage under a particular skill. If necessary, you will remain on that skill and rewrite the third passage (and even perhaps go on to repeat the first and second passages) as well. You will complete the program in guided composition when you successfully work through all twelve skills. Completing the twelve skills will strengthen your understanding of the skills, increase your chances of transferring the skills to actual writing situations, and markedly improve your proofreading ability.

In doing the passages, note the following points:

a For each skill you will be told the number of mistakes that appear in the passages. If you have trouble finding the mistakes, turn back and review the pages in this book that explain the skill in question.

b Here is an effective way to go about correcting a passage. First, read it over quickly. Look for and mark off mistakes in the skill area involved. For example, in your first reading of a passage that has five fragments, you may locate and mark only three fragments. Next, reread the passage carefully so you can find the remaining errors in the skill in question. Finally, make notes in the margin about how to correct each mistake. Only at this point should you begin to rewrite the passage.

c Be sure to proofread with care after you finish a passage. Go over your writing word for word, looking for careless errors. Remember that you may be asked to do another passage involving the same skill if you make even one mistake.

Test 1: Sentence Fragments

Mistakes in each passage: 5

Passage A

¹I am only thirty, but a trip to the movies recently made me realize my youth is definitely past. ²The science-fiction movie had attracted a large audience of younger kids and teenagers. ³Before the movie began. ⁴Groups of kids ran up and down the aisles, laughing, giggling, and spilling popcorn. ⁵I was annoyed with them. ⁶But thought, "At one time, I was doing the same thing. ⁷Now I'm acting like one of the adults." ⁸The thought was a little depressing, for I remembered how much fun it was not to care what the adults thought. ⁹Soon after the movie began, a group of teenagers walked in and sat in the first row. ¹⁰During the movie, they vied with each other. ¹¹To see who could make the loudest comment. ¹²Or the most embarrassing noise. ¹³Some of the adults in the theatre complained to the usher, but I had a guilty memory about doing the same thing myself a few times. ¹⁴In addition, a teenage couple was sitting in front of me. ¹⁵Occasionally, they held hands or the boy put his arm around the girl. ¹⁶A few times, they sneaked a kiss. ¹⁷Realizing that my wife and I were long past this kind of behaviour in the movies. ¹⁸I again felt like an old man.

Word groups with fragments: _____ _____ _____ _____ _____

Passage B

¹For her biology class, Ann lay stretched out on the grass in the park. ²Taking notes on the insect life she observed around her. ³First off, a clear-winged bug sat down from the heat. ⁴And swayed on a blade of grass nearby. ⁵Next, landing suddenly on her hand, a ladybug. ⁶Ann could count the number of dots on its tiny, speckled body as it crawled around and under her fingers. ⁷When the ladybug left, Ann picked up a low, flat rock. ⁸Three black crickets slithered quickly away. ⁹Seeking shelter under other rocks or leaves. ¹⁰She watched one camouflage itself under a leaf. ¹¹Carefully, she removed the leaf and watched the cricket dig deeper into the underbrush. ¹²It kept crawling away from the light. ¹³Ann moved her eyes away for a second as a car went by. ¹⁴When she looked back. ¹⁵The cricket had disappeared.

Word groups with fragments: _____ _____ _____ _____ _____

Passage C

¹One factor that causes you to forget is lack of motivation. ²If you have no reason for remembering certain information. ³You will probably forget it. ⁴Dr. Joyce Brothers, a prominent psychologist, relates how she memorized facts on boxing. ⁵To win $64,000 on a television quiz show. ⁶She and her husband were college students at the time. ⁷And, like most students, could use some extra money. ⁸She was not as interested in boxing as she was in winning the money. ⁹After she had won the money and used her memorized information for its purpose. ¹⁰She promptly forgot the facts. ¹¹Another factor in forgetting is interference. ¹²Previous learning can interfere with new learning. ¹³Especially if there are similarities between the two. ¹⁴If you have previously studied traditional math, you may experience difficulty learning the new math.

Word groups with fragments: _____ _____ _____ _____ _____

■ Test 2: Run-Ons (Fused Sentences)

Mistakes in each passage: 5

Passage A

¹Someday soon you may not have to get up in the morning and go to work you will, instead, work at home in front of your very own computer. ²Already many thousands of Canadian workers are "telecommuters" they do at home what they used to do in the office. ³For instance, one secretary takes dictation from the manager over the telephone. ⁴Then she types the letters on her computer terminal. ⁵Stockbrokers or salespeople can place orders and keep records right in their living rooms all they need is a computer hookup. ⁶A few banks and consulting firms give their employees a choice of working in the office or at home many other businesses as well plan to try this idea. ⁷Telecommuting has many advantages some of them are no commuting time, no expensive lunch hours, and an extra income tax deduction for a home office. ⁸You also have a chance to do your work without worrying about the boss looking over your shoulder.

Sentences with run-ons: _____ _____ _____ _____ _____

Passage B

¹Have you ever wondered what the hotels of the future might look like? ²You need not wonder any longer a hotel in Japan will give you a preview. ³The name of this hotel is the Capsule Inn its rooms rent for eleven dollars a night. ⁴Each room comes with a radio, a television set, and an alarm clock in addition, all the rooms are air-conditioned, but here any resemblance to a twentieth-century hotel ends. ⁵The rooms are small plastic capsules each capsule is about two metres high by two metres wide by three metres deep. ⁶The capsules are stacked in a double layer guests have to crawl into bed through a large porthole entrance. ⁷Bathrooms and washing facilities, and couches, chairs, and vending machines are located in common areas in other parts of the hotel. ⁸Believe it or not, this hotel is almost always full, perhaps because the price of the rooms is as small as the rooms themselves.

Sentences with run-ons: _____ _____ _____ _____ _____

Passage C

The paperback book that we take for granted is a fairly new invention. ²At one time, the only books available were hardcover ones that cost a few dollars—an expensive purchase for the average working person. ³Then, in the 1930s, one publisher decided that there was a large market for a light, portable, inexpensive book the book would be cheaper to manufacture because it would have paper covers and a glued spine. ⁴The publisher was right it took several years for the books to catch on. ⁵World War II gave paperbacks the push they needed. ⁶The Canadian government gave armed forces editions of paperbacks to men and women serving overseas the books were light enough to carry in a pack. ⁷Many soldiers survived dull or frightening times by turning to the tattered books in their kits after the war, they brought the paperback habit home with them. ⁸In the fifties, however, paperbacks suffered a loss of respectability they were linked with trashy detective stories or soft-core sex. ⁹Now, paperbacks are bought by almost everyone, and readers can find everything from best-selling novels to works of philosophy enclosed in soft covers.

Sentences with run-ons: _____   _____   _____   _____   _____

■ Test 3: Run-Ons (Comma Splices)

Mistakes in each passage: 5

Passage A

[1]"Typhoid Mary" is the name that was given to a woman who unknowingly spread death throughout New York City at the turn of the century. [2]Typhoid is caused by a virus and is highly infectious, it causes fever, diarrhea, and often death. [3]Mary was a carrier of the disease, but she herself was unaffected by it. [4]Unfortunately, Mary worked as a cook, so she passed the disease to others through the food she touched. [5]Mary would take a job as cook to a household. [6]A few weeks later, several members of the family would become ill, sometimes typhoid would break out over a whole neighbourhood. [7]After this happened several times, Mary became frightened, death appeared wherever she went, but she did not understand why or how. [8]Eventually, Mary was tracked down and arrested by public health authorities. [9]When she promised not to work as a cook again, she was released, she then vanished into the city. [10]But there were rumours that she continued to work as a cook, whenever typhoid broke out in the city for years afterward, "Typhoid Mary" was blamed.

Sentences with run-ons: _____ _____ _____ _____ _____

Passage B

[1]The worst summer job I ever had was as a packager in the Saskatoon Laundry. [2]First of all, I hated the hours, I had to get up at five in the morning and work from six until two-thirty in the afternoon. [3]Second, the work was boring. [4]All day long, I folded clothes, wrapped them in brown paper, and sealed them with tape that never stuck to the paper. [5]Also, the heat in the "hole," which is what the workers called the place, was unbearable. [6]There were two little fans in the front of the store, they didn't help, however, because I was in the middle of twelve hot dryers. [7]It was always ten degrees hotter inside than it was out, on prairie summer days the temperature inside was at least forty degrees! [8]But I think the main reason I hated the job was Harry, my boss, Harry's favourite lines were, "My, you look tired today" and "All right, let's keep moving because there's a lot to do today." [9]I badly wanted to slug Harry or curse him, I did not control my temper easily. [10]Because he was always around watching me, I was never able to take

little breaks along the way. ¹If I had had a chance to rest now and then, the job might have been more bearable.

Sentences with run-ons: _____   _____   _____   _____   _____

Passage C

¹People are fond of pointing out how much there is wrong with television programming, and many shows do leave much to be desired. ²But there is also much that is good about television, to begin with, television offers us an escape from our daily problems. ³No matter what is bothering us, we can rest our brains for a while and enjoy some mindless fun, this only becomes a problem if we leave our minds asleep for hours on end. ⁴Another positive aspect of television is the wide choice of programs we have to choose from, it wasn't long ago in Canada that there were only three network channels. ⁵If you didn't find something you liked on one of those three, you had no other choices. ⁶Since the development of cable television, it is not uncommon for a viewer to have more than thirty different channels to choose from, this means more interests and tastes are being served. ⁷The best thing about television, though, is the service it performs for all of us. ⁸It keeps us in touch with what is happening around the world, we have therefore learned more about other Canadians and people from different places and cultures. ⁹In fact, millions of people have at times worked together to aid others whose misfortunes they learned about on television news.

Sentences with run-ons: _____   _____   _____   _____   _____

■ Test 4: Standard English Verbs

Mistakes in each passage: 5

Passage A

[1]Sal should have stayed in bed yesterday. [2]He knew it when he tried to shut off his alarm and accidentally pushed the clock to the floor. [3]Sal decide to brave fate anyway. [4]He dressed and headed for the breakfast table. [5]After putting two slices of bread into the toaster, he went out to get the paper. [6]Rain hurtled down from a dark sky. [7]The paper was not under the shelter of the porch but was sitting, completely soak with water, on the walk. [8]"Thanks a lot, paper carrier," Sal said to himself as he left the paper where it was and return to the kitchen. [9]After eating quickly, he gathered his books and ran down to the bus stop. [10]No one was there, which meant he had miss the bus. [11]As he stood for twenty minutes waiting for the next bus, his pants were splashed by two cars that went by. [12]When the bus finally pulled up, Sal reached into his pocket for the fare. [13]Two tokens slipped out of his fingers and fell into the water at the curb. [14]After fishing out the tokens and paying his fare, Sal discovered there were no empty seats on the bus. [15]Standing there, he wonder what other kinds of bad luck awaited him at school.

Sentences with nonstandard verbs: _____   _____   _____   _____   _____

Passage B

[1]Keeping cities clean became more difficult as cities grew larger. [2]Some ancient cities solve the cleanliness problem: for example, inhabitants of ancient Rome had waterborne sewage systems and public baths. [3]But during the Middle Ages, these health-supporting systems disappear from the cities of Europe. [4]Sewage and garbage were dump in yards and streets, and bathing in the river was considered to be bad for one's health. [5]It was not surprising that a great plague, the Black Death, rage through Europe during this period, killing about one-fourth of its inhabitants. [6]Eventually sanitary facilities improve, and in modern cities, many social agencies take care of removing sewage, disposing of garbage, and sweeping the streets.

Sentences with nonstandard verbs: _____   _____   _____   _____   _____

Passage C

¹The river rambles for many kilometres around trees and bushes. ²At one point, children throw small rocks and laugh at the splashes they make. ³Farther along, factories dump litres of slime and pollutants in the water. ⁴Away from the factories, the river seem to smile as it ripples over stones. ⁵A waterfall appears near a clump of trees. ⁶Romantic couples sit there in the spring. ⁷Occasionally, people fishing try their luck at the river's edge. ⁸A kilometre or two past the waterfall, the river roar angrily along. ⁹It rush noisily. ¹⁰Boys and girls pretend they are captains of many fleets. ¹¹They sail paper ships and watch them sink. ¹²Where the river widen and grows calm once more, someone always seems to be paddling a canoe. ¹³Where a bridge stretch across the river, old men stand and look out over the water. ¹⁴The river never gets lonely, for someone is always there to use it.

Sentences with nonstandard verbs: _____   _____   _____   _____   _____

■ Test 5: Irregular Verbs

Mistakes in each passage: 10

Passage A

¹When the game-show contestant learned she had chose the box with only a penny in it, she was badly shaken. ²She begun to cry and the game-show host for a minute was froze with fear. ³Then he taked her hand and said, "You have not gotten to the end of the line yet, Mrs. Waterby. Cheer up." ⁴When she learned she was going to be given one more chance, Mrs. Waterby stopped crying. ⁵At the host's signal, a tray was brang onto the stage and placed in front of Mrs. Waterby. ⁶On the tray sat three shells. ⁷One shell, the host told her, covered the key to a new Infiniti. ⁸Mrs. Waterby was to choose the shell she thoughted had the key under it. ⁹There was a long pause, and she gived her answer, "Number three." ¹⁰The host lifted up the third shell; the key was underneath. ¹¹Mrs. Waterby danced about the stage, just as she had been instructed to do if she winned. ¹²Her husband run up on stage and embraced her. ¹³They had realized the great Canadian dream: they had gotten something for nothing.

Sentences with irregular verbs (write down the number of a sentence twice if it contains two irregular verbs):

_____ _____ _____ _____ _____

_____ _____ _____ _____ _____

Passage B

¹Occasionally when I have drove to work, I have gotten behind a slow driver. ²This usually occurs when I have leaved the house late. ³I have tried to pass such drivers, but traffic always seems too heavy in the opposite direction. ⁴At this point, I have spoke to myself or sung to myself, trying to forget how slowly I was travelling. ⁵I have never understood the reason for going 15 kilometres per hour in a 40-kilometre-per-hour zone. ⁶Once past the stage of trying to keep calm, I have always expressed my anger to the fullest. ⁷I have shook the steering wheel and sayed the foulest words I know. ⁸I have imagined stealing a phaser on *Star Trek* and blasting the slow driver with it. ⁹After I have wore myself out, I have gritted my teeth and waited for my sanity to return. ¹⁰Usually about a kilometre from my office, the driver in front of me has turned off and has rode out of sight. ¹¹Then I have forgetted all about it and have went on with my day.

Sentences with irregular verbs (write down the number of a sentence twice if it contains two irregular verbs):

_____ _____ _____ _____ _____

_____ _____ _____ _____ _____

Passage C

¹Pete Langlois had knew the meaning of fear before, like the time he got a cramp while swimming. ²Luckily, he had been saved from drowning then by a friend he always swum with. ³But Pete admits that his first job interview brang an even greater fear. ⁴On the morning of the interview, his stomach felt as if he had ate a block of concrete the night before. ⁵In his throat, a lump had grew to the size of a soccer ball, and he wondered if he would be able to speak at all. ⁶His mother realized Pete was nervous. ⁷She drove him to the interview office and then burst out laughing. ⁸"Pete," she said, "this is just an interview for a job at Swiss Chalet." ⁹Pete was angry at first with his mother for laughing, but when she apologized he forgave her. ¹⁰He also knowed his mother was right. ¹¹He was just going to be interviewed for a job cutting chicken. ¹²He kepted his composure during the interview and came through it with ease.

Sentences with irregular verbs (write down the number of a sentence twice if it contains two irregular verbs):

_____ _____ _____ _____ _____

_____ _____ _____ _____ _____

■ Test 6: Misplaced and Dangling Modifiers

Mistakes in each passage: 5

Passage A

[1]The best vacation I ever had was when my friends and I rented a big old cottage in Port Stanley. [2]Having four rooms, each of us had plenty of room to ourselves. [3]The cottage was nearly located right on the beach, so all we had to do in the morning was walk a few steps to be right in the middle of the action. [4]Playing volleyball and lying in the sun, the days passed by in a blur of contentment. [5]For lunch we strolled up to the boardwalk to buy foot-long hot dogs from a vendor with "the works" heaped on top. [6]After lunch we returned to our spot on the beach to read or take a nap. [7]When the sun got too hot in the afternoon, we retreated to the cottage, where we sat in comfortable old rocking chairs on the porch. [8]Sitting there, we could relax and watch the action on the beach. [9]With a cool drink in hand, the summer felt as if it just might last forever.

Sentences with misplaced modifiers: _____ _____

Sentences with dangling modifiers: _____ _____ _____

Passage B

[1]Last Saturday I tried to be a good friend and agreed to help my friend Levon move into his new apartment. [2]What was supposed to take only an hour or two ended up lasting the entire day. [3]Levon's idea was to save money by doing the job himself, but I think he almost spent as much as it would have cost to hire professionals. [4]Robert and Brent and I arrived at Levon's apartment at eight o'clock, but he was still sound asleep. [5]After pounding on the door, he finally let us in. [6]Stumbling around with his eyes half closed, a half hour was wasted before Levon finally got ready. [7]Then he and I drove to the truck-rental agency. [8]Before he knew what had happened to him, Levon agreed to buy packing cartons, tape, and twine. [9]He also paid extra for a dolly to use in moving the refrigerator. [10]Finally seated behind the wheel of the rental truck, it wouldn't start, so the attendant had to come out and start it for us. [11]On the way back to the apartment, Levon stopped to borrow money to pay for the truck at his parents' house. [12]By the time we returned to his apartment, the curb was lined with packing boxes, and Robert and Brent were sitting

on the front step. [13]The rest of the day moved a little faster than the morning. [14]But it was dark by the time we finished, and I was left wondering where my Saturday had gone.

Sentences with misplaced modifiers: _____ _____

Sentences with dangling modifiers: _____ _____ _____

Passage C

[1]One of the best jobs I ever had was in Port Huron as a stock expediter in a Saint Lawrence Seaway shipyard. [2]There were always some materials that had been ordered and paid for but never received by the shipyard, which it was my job to find. [3]Using the original invoice as a starting point, my work in finding lost items would begin. [4]Most items were found very quickly, but there were always a few that seemed to have disappeared. [5]Those were the cases I liked the most. [6]Several items had been missing for several years, and I devoted my attention to these whenever I had a spare moment. [7]Wandering through some of the old warehouses, luck would often come my way. [8]Sitting in a damp corner covered with mouse droppings, I once found a box of sheet metal screws. [9]I wrote down the number of the box on a notepad and checked it against my lists. [10]Sure enough, the box was one of the items I had been searching for. [11]It had been ordered three years earlier! [12]I felt like a very shrewd detective who had just cracked a difficult case at moments like that.

Sentences with misplaced modifiers: _____ _____

Sentences with dangling modifiers: _____ _____ _____

■ Test 7: Faulty Parallelism

Mistakes in each passage: 5

Passage A

¹People who do not want to pay for air-conditioning can find other ways to keep a house cool during the hot weather. ²One way is to plant trees and shrubs and the use of awnings. ³As a result, outside walls and windows are kept cool. ⁴Another method is to get rid of the hot air that builds up in attic spaces by installing attic vents and power fans. ⁵In addition, window fans can be used at night to push out the hot daytime air and pull in the air that is cool in the evening. ⁶In the morning, when the house is still cool, the windows should be closed and draw the drapes. ⁷The windows and drapes can be opened if a breeze begins or a sudden drop in temperature. ⁸A final method of keeping the house cool is to water areas outside occasionally, such as paved areas, driveways and decks, that tend to collect heat and reflecting it against the house. ⁹Wet these every hour or so with a sprinkler or hose to prevent heat buildup.

Sentences with faulty parallelism:

_____   _____   _____   _____   _____

Passage B

¹Human beings attempt to protect themselves psychologically as well as in physical ways. ²If someone harms you physically, your first instinct may be to fight back. ³To guard yourself psychologically, you may use defence mechanisms. ⁴You may be unaware of your real motives in adjusting to a situation that is undesirable or a threat.

⁵Three common defence mechanisms are regression, rationalization, and trying to compensate. ⁶Regression means returning to an earlier form of behaviour. ⁷A person who regresses temporarily rejects the "hard cruel world" and is seeking the greater sensitivity of childhood. ⁸Rationalization is making excuses. ⁹A student not wanting to study for a test decides that she doesn't know what to study. ¹⁰Compensation is a form of substitution. ¹¹If a person wants a better education but cannot attend school, she may try studying on her own or to learn more through experience.

Sentences with faulty parallelism:

_____   _____   _____   _____   _____

Passage C

[1]In shopping for a good used car, be cautious and have suspicion. [2]Remember that the previous owner had some reason for getting rid of the car. [3]The reason may have been that the owner wanted to buy a new car or the avoidance of costly repairs. [4]A car that appears to have a "dirt-cheap" price may turn out to have "sky-high" costs. [5]Remember, too, that the older a car is, the chances are better that it will soon require major repairs. [6]If you buy an older car, be sure that repair parts and service facilities are available in your area. [7]Try to pick a used car with the fewest kilometres on the odometer, the best overall condition, and that the dealer guarantees for the longest time. [8]There are several ways to protect yourself from a falsified odometer. [9]You should ask for a kilometre disclosure statement, examine closely the condition of the vehicle, and contacting the previous owner. [10]Some provinces now have resale certification requirements.

Sentences with faulty parallelism:

_____   _____   _____   _____   _____

■ Test 8: Capital Letters

Mistakes in each passage: 10

Passage A

¹Red Riding Hood decided to visit her grandmother in sarnia. ²Old Mrs. Hood had just been released from huron hospital, where she had spent the entire month of september recovering from a broken hip. ³Red Riding Hood's mother gave her daughter a container of vegetable soup to bring to Grandma Hood. ⁴Red entered the bus station on lasalle avenue, and when the bus pulled in, she boarded it. ⁵Suddenly, a young man approached Red. ⁶He resembled a wolf with his long, greasy hair and beard, and he said, "what a foxy face you've got, little girl. ⁷I'd like to eat you up." ⁸"Take off," said Red. ⁹"I'm a student of martial arts and I know how to defend myself." ¹⁰When he tried to touch Red, she flipped the copy of *The Life of Bruce Lee* she was reading into his face to distract him. ¹¹Then she delivered a quick karate chop with her hand. ¹²The man staggered backward and an elderly woman then batted him with a large box of alcan aluminum foil from her shopping bag. ¹³The bus entered the station and Red Riding Hood stepped over the wolflike man, who lay groaning on the floor. ¹⁴"Maybe this will teach you to let decent people ride the bus in peace," she said as she stepped through the doors.

Sentences with missing capitals (write the number of a sentence as many times as it contains capitalization mistakes):

_____ _____ _____ _____ _____

_____ _____ _____ _____ _____

Passage B

¹Although I'm much older now, I still remember the day I found out santa claus was a fake. ²I was seven years old, and my brother Neil was five-and-a-half. ³That evening, Mother told us, "be sure you go to bed early, and don't try any tricks, or you won't get your Christmas present till *next* december." ⁴So we quickly put on our pyjamas, brushed our teeth with mclean's toothpaste, and got under the covers. ⁵I didn't even finish the Wonder Woman comic book I was halfway through. ⁶We whispered for a while about whether we'd get the irish setter puppy we wanted so badly, or if we'd just get another boring game like tinkertoys that was supposed to be "educational." ⁷Then we went to sleep, but in the middle of the night I woke up with a horrible thought. ⁸What if Santa

didn't know that we lived at 7201 ouellette avenue? [9]He might bring our puppy to the wrong house! [10]I ran into my parents' bedroom to ask them if he knew where we lived, but they weren't there. [11]Then I heard noises coming from the living room. [12]I tiptoed downstairs—and there were my parents, putting something wrapped in green paper and tied with red ribbon under the tree. [13]To this day, I don't know what hurt more—getting a Scrabble set the next morning or finding out that the jolly fat man in a red suit and white beard was only Mom and Dad.

Sentences with missing capitals (write the number of a sentence as many times as it contains capitalization mistakes):

_____   _____   _____   _____   _____

_____   _____   _____   _____   _____

Passage C

[1]Credit cards have been abused by both the people who own them and the companies that issue them. [2]Some people fall into the habit of using their visa charge card for hotels and meals, their petrocan card for gasoline, and other cards for department store purchases. [3]The danger in this, as was pointed out recently on the CBC television program *W5*, is that people can quickly reach a point where they cannot meet the monthly payments on their charge cards. [4]Such people can appreciate the warning in a b.c. newspaper, "it isn't buying on time that's difficult, it's paying on time." [5]Organizations such as Canadian consumer groups have published articles alerting people to the high interest charges involved. [6]And magazines such as *Maclean's* and *report on business* have also pointed out how quickly people lose a sense of their financial resources with charge cards. [7]Perhaps charge cards should carry the message, "excessive use of this card may be hazardous to your economic health."

Sentences with missing capitals (write the number of a sentence as many times as it contains capitalization mistakes):

_____   _____   _____   _____   _____

_____   _____   _____   _____   _____

■ Test 9: Apostrophes

Mistakes in each passage: 10

Passage A

[1]Working as a house packer for Assiniboine Moving Service was an enjoyable job for me. [2]First of all, almost no other job allows you to go into peoples houses and see at close range how they live. [3]I encountered a lot of interesting surprises. [4]For example, one womans house was as neat as a display room in a museum, but her basement was as littered as our towns dump. [5]Another person had converted a bedroom into a small library. [6]The rooms four walls contained storage shelves, all filled with books and magazines like *Saturday Night* and old *Star Weeklies*. [7]I also liked the job because people would give me things they didnt want any more. [8]For instance, I received a lot of childrens toys and a complete set of tools. [9]In fact, my mothers cellar started filling with items I received from customers cellars. [10]Im planning to work again for Assiniboine next year.

Sentences with missing apostrophes (write down the number of a sentence twice if it contains two missing apostrophes):

_____   _____   _____   _____   _____

_____   _____   _____   _____

Passage B

[1]Mrs. Bartlett is our towns strangest person. [2]She has lived in the big house on Pine Street, without once setting foot outside, for more years than most people remember. [3]In her yard she keeps several cocker spaniels thatll rip your pants in a second. [4]While the regular postal carriers face is familiar to the dogs, they treat a substitute postie like a juicy bone. [5]In addition to the dogs, there are dozens of tame blackbirds perched in the trees. [6]Hitchcocks movie *The Birds* could have been made using her yard and house as a setting. [7]If you are on her good side, Mrs. B. (everyones name for her) will invite you in for tea. [8]Her gardener, Willy, watches the dogs while you hurry to the porch. [9]Willys job, by the way, is also to serve as night security guard. [10]Since he's almost two metres tall, its not surprising that no prowlers have troubled the property. [11]Inside the house, a maid named Tina will take your coat. [12]A curiosity-seekers question will get only a scowl from the close-mouthed Tina and a short, "Thats not your business." [13]People in general seem to respect this answer, and no ones challenged the right of Mrs. B. to live life her own way.

Sentences with missing apostrophes (write down the number of a sentence twice if it contains two missing apostrophes):

_____ _____ _____ _____ _____

_____ _____ _____ _____ _____

Passage C

[1]In a small park near the centre of Millville, a group of bronze statues stands in a circle. [2]Most of them are models of the individual rich men who provided money for the towns beginning. [3]The centre of the circle is occupied by a nameless man. [4]Citizens call him Joe because hes a symbol of the common man. [5]Joes clothes appear tattered, but his body seems strong. [6]His face looks tired, but his eyes look proud. [7]Each person Joe represents couldnt give money to the town but gave strength and sweat instead. [8]A farmers back worked to keep the town in food. [9]A womans hands wove, knitted, and sewed clothes. [10]A blacksmiths arms struggled to provide horseshoes and tools. [11]Joes eyes must talk to passers-by. [12]People seem to realize that without the ordinary mans help, that circle of rich men wouldnt exist.

Sentences with missing apostrophes (write down the number of a sentence twice if it contains two missing apostrophes):

_____ _____ _____ _____ _____

_____ _____ _____ _____ _____

■ Test 10: Quotation Marks

Quotation marks needed in each passage: 10 pairs

Passage A

[1]When my friend Brad asked me what I wanted to drink at the party, I said, Pepsi, if there is any. I don't drink.

[2]Very funny, Joe. Now what do you want? he asked. [3]He was truly shocked when I repeated my words. [4]I think he was even a little embarrassed that he had brought me to the party. [5]Later the subject of drinking came up when I was talking to a young woman I met.

[6]You must be in training, she assumed. [7]Or is it that you're on medication?

[8]Neither—I just don't like to drink, I answered patiently.

[9]Oh, I see. You're one of those who proves himself different by playing the role of Mr. Nonconformist.

[10]That's partly it, I agreed. [11]I don't want to be an average Joe.

[12]But you can drink and still be yourself, an individual. Just be comfortable with yourself, she asserted.

[13]I responded, I do feel comfortable with myself. But I wouldn't if I drank just to be like everyone else here.

Sentences or sentence groups with missing quotation marks:

_____ _____ _____ _____ _____

_____ _____ _____ _____ _____

Passage B

[1]Tony and Crystal were standing in the express line at the A&P supermarket. [2]Crystal pointed to a sign above the check-out counter that read, Express line—ten items or less. [3]She then said to Tony, Look at that guy in front of us. He has at least seventeen items in his cart. He shouldn't be in the express line.

[4]Be quiet, said Tony. [5]If you're not, he'll hear you.

[6]I don't mind if he does hear me, Crystal replied. [7]People like that think the world owes them a favour. I hope the cashier makes him go to another lane.

[8]The man in front of them suddenly turned around. [9]Stop acting as if I've committed a federal crime, he said. [10]See those five cans of Dr. Ballard's—that counts as one item. See those four packs of Vachon cakes—that's one item.

[11]Let's just say this, Crystal replied. [12]You have an interesting way of counting.

Sentences or sentence groups with missing quotation marks:

_____ _____ _____ _____ _____

_____ _____ _____ _____ _____

Passage C

[1]Once when I was walking down a lonely street, three boys came up to me. [2]Hey, Mister! one of them said. [3]Will you give us a nickel?

[4]I'm sorry, fellows, I replied. [5]I don't have any change to spare.

[6]All we want are three nickels, Mister, they said and suddenly surrounded me.

[7]Get out of my way, will you? I asked, trying to be polite. [8]I'm in a hurry.

[9]At this point the boy in front of me said, Stop trying to walk over me, Mister.

[10]As I raised my arm to move him aside, I felt a hand going into my back pocket. [11]I spun around and yelled, Give me that wallet! to the boy who had taken it. [12]I grabbed the wallet and the coin purse snapped open, with change spilling out over the sidewalk. [13]The boys scooped up the coins, chanting, Thanks for the change, Mister. [14]I wanted to chase them but decided it would be safer to walk quickly away.

Sentences or sentence groups with missing quotation marks:

_____ _____ _____ _____ _____

_____ _____ _____ _____ _____

■ Test 11: Commas

Mistakes in each passage: 10

Passage A

[1]Going to a big arena for a sporting event or musical performance means being bombarded by hard selling. [2]The pitches begin on the road into the parking areas. [3]As lines of cars wait to enter the lot salespeople will walk past the crawling cars. [4]They will hawk programs souvenirs T-shirts and even droopy carnations. [5]The ticket-holders may pass up these items but they are only the first assault on their sales resistance. [6]Near the arena's ticket gates are more vendors. [7]In addition to the same programs and souvenir items they hawk CDs and different kinds of snacks. [8]Inside the enormous building is a chain of concessionaires' booths with everything from hot dogs to cheap jewelry. [9]People who continue to resist the hard sell have one last hurdle for there are still the hawkers who roam the aisles. [10]Their voices can be heard crying out all across the rows of seats "Pop here!" or "Peanuts while they last!" [11]The last holdouts especially if they have children with them usually give in at this point. [12]They fork over several dollars for a tiny bag of chips and a watery pop.

Sentences with missing commas (write down the number of a sentence as many times as it contains comma mistakes):

_____ _____ _____ _____ _____

_____ _____ _____ _____ _____

Passage B

[1]If you want to become a better note-taker you should keep in mind the following hints. [2]Most important you should attend class on a regular basis. [3]The instructor will probably develop in class all the main ideas of the course and you want to be there to write the ideas down. [4]Students often ask "How much should I write down?" [5]By paying close attention in class you will probably develop an instinct for the material that you must write down. [6]You should record your notes in outline form. [7]Start main points at the margin indent major supporting details and further indent more subordinate material. [8]When the speaker moves from one aspect of a topic to another show this shift on your paper by skipping a line or two. [9]A final hint but by no means the least is to write down any points your teacher repeats or takes the time to put on the board.

REINFORCEMENT OF THE SKILLS

Sentences with missing commas (write down the number of a sentence as many times as it contains comma mistakes):

_____ _____ _____ _____ _____

_____ _____ _____ _____ _____

Passage C

[1]Studies have found that people have a psychological need for plants. [2]People who grew up in Canadian cities one survey revealed often mentioned the presence or absence of lawns in their neighbourhood. [3]One person observed "I realized how much I missed lawns and trees after living in a city where concrete covered everything." [4]Unfortunately the city is a difficult environment for plants. [5]The soil of the city is covered mostly with buildings and pavements so there is little space for plants to grow. [6]Plants that are present are often hurt by haze smog and air pollution. [7]Some plants are more sensitive to pollution than others; Peace Lilies thrive but snapdragons for example do poorly in polluted air. [8]When planners choose the kind of plants to place in urban areas they must consider the plants' chances for survival under the difficult growing conditions of city streets.

Sentences with missing commas (write down the number of a sentence as many times as it contains comma mistakes):

_____ _____ _____ _____ _____

_____ _____ _____ _____ _____

■ Test 12: Commonly Confused Words

Mistakes in each passage: 10

Passage A

[1]Recently, I was driving across Edmonton in heavy city traffic. [2]Cars followed one another bumper-to-bumper, and their were bicyclists and pedestrians darting threw the streets. [3]Beside the heavy traffic, it had begun to rain, making the traffic situation even worse. [4]I was driving cautiously, keeping three metres or so from the rear of the car in front of me. [5]Than, in my rear-view mirror, I noticed the woman behind me. [6]Her car was so close our bumpers were almost locked. [7]Her face was red and angry, and she tapped impatiently on her steering wheel. [8]Suddenly, she saw a five-second brake in the traffic. [9]She past me with a roar and squeezed in ahead of me. [10]I though angrily, "Your a complete idiot!" and honked my horn. [11]She honked back at me and lifted her hand in an obscene gesture. [12]I am a little ashamed at the affect this had on me—I was so enraged I wanted to stop my car and hers to give her a lecture. [13]It took me more than an hour to calm down completely and except the fact that the incident had been a very minor one.

Sentences with commonly confused words (write down the number of a sentence twice if it contains two commonly confused words):

_____ _____ _____ _____ _____

_____ _____ _____ _____ _____

Passage B

[1]Anyone whose stayed up all night studying for a test knows the dizzy, foggy feeling you're head gets. [2]Although I have had this terrible experience more than once, I can't seem to discipline myself enough to avoid it. [3]As a result, I always have to cram at exam time, and I am up righting notes and studying all through the night.

[4]Hear are some of the techniques I use to stay awake. [5]I drink large doses of coffee. [6]I take Vitamin C, to, if I feel that the coffee begins to lose its affect on me. [7]And I eat candy bars, though the fewer the better, for they can upset my stomach. [8]There are also two study methods that really help me. [9]First, I take regular little brakes—about ten minutes an hour, I lie down for a few minutes' peace. [10]Second, I pace like a tiger when I'm studying. [11]The principle value of this study method is that I don't get sleepy if I am

physically moving about. [12]Its probably a strange sight to see me walking up and down the hallway reciting notes to myself, but the plane fact is that the technique works.

Sentences with commonly confused words (write down the number of a sentence twice if it contains two commonly confused words):

_____ _____ _____ _____ _____

_____ _____ _____ _____ _____

Passage C

[1]If at all possible, try to take you're summer vacation any time accept during the summer. [2]First, by scheduling your vacation at another time of the year, you will avoid the crowds. [3]You will not have to fight the traffic around resort areas or drive passed dozens of motels and bed-and-breakfasts with "No Vacancy" signs. [4]Beaches and campsites will be quite, to. [5]By vacationing out of season, you will also see many areas at there most beautiful, without the bother of summer's heat, thunderstorms, and insects. [6]Weather you go in spring or fall, you can travel by car without feeling stuck to your seat or to exhausted to explore the city or park. [7]Finally, an off-season trip can save you money. [8]Before and after the summer, prices at resorts drop, for fewer people are demanding reservations. [9]Its possible to stay too weeks for the price of one; or you might stay in a luxury hotel you might not otherwise be able to afford.

Sentences with commonly confused words (write down the number of a sentence twice if it contains two commonly confused words):

_____ _____ _____ _____ _____

_____ _____ _____ _____ _____

COMBINED EDITING TESTS

EDITING FOR SENTENCE-SKILLS MISTAKES

The twelve editing tests in this section will give you practice in finding a variety of sentence-skills mistakes. People often find it hard to edit a paper carefully. They have put so much work into their writing, or so little, that it's almost painful for them to look at the paper one more time. You may have to simply *force* yourself to edit. Remember that eliminating sentence-skills mistakes will improve an average paper and help ensure a strong grade on a good paper. Further, as you get into the habit of editing your papers, you will get into the habit of using the sentence skills consistently. They are a basic part of clear and effective writing.

The first two tests check your understanding of the correct format to use when writing and handing in a paper. The remaining tests check your ability to identify a variety of sentence-skills mistakes, especially sentence fragments and run-ons. In tests three through eight, the spots where errors occur have been underlined; your job is to identify each error. In the last four tests, you must locate as well as identify the errors. Use the progress chart on page 502 to keep track of your performance on these tests.

■ Combined Editing Test 1

Identify the five mistakes in paper format in the student paper that follows. From the box below, choose the letters that describe the five mistakes and write those letters in the spaces provided.

a. The title should not be underlined.

b. The title should not be set off in quotation marks.

c. There should not be a period at the end of a title.

d. All the major words in a title should be capitalized.

e. The title should just be several words and not a complete sentence.

f. The first line of a paper should stand independently of the title.

g. A line or two lines of a processed paper should be skipped between the title and the first line of the paper.

h. The first line of a paper should be indented or tabbed five spaces.

i. The right-hand margin should not be crowded.

j. Hyphenation should occur only between syllables.

	"Nervous times"
	There are three different times that I feel nervous. First of all, if
	I'm in a classroom full of students I don't know and I'm asked to
	answer a question, I may begin to stutter. Or I may know the
	answer, but my mind will just block out. Second, if I'm going out
	on a date with someone for the first time, I won't eat. Eating when
	I'm nervous makes my fork tremble, and I'm likely to drop food on
	my clothes. Finally if I'm going to a job interview, I will practise
	at home what I'm going to say. But as soon as I'm alone with the
	interviewer, and she asks me if there's anything I'd like to say, I
	say something dumb like "I'm a people person, you know." One day
	I hope to overcome these nervousness problems.

1. _____   2. _____   3. _____   4. _____   5. _____

■ Combined Editing Test 2

Identify the five mistakes in paper format in the student paper that follows. From the box below, choose the letters that describe the five mistakes and write those letters in the spaces provided.

a. The title should not be underlined.

b. The title should not be set off in quotation marks.

c. There should not be a period at the end of a title.

d. All the major words in a title should be capitalized.

e. The title should just be several words and not a complete sentence.

f. The first line of a paper should stand independently of the title.

g. A line or two lines of a processed paper should be skipped between the title and the first line of the paper.

h. The first line of a paper should be indented or tabbed five spaces.

i. The right-hand margin should not be crowded.

j. Hyphenation should occur only between syllables.

<u>coming down with the flu.</u>

I could tell that I was coming down with it. For one th-ng, my nose and throat were shutting down. I could not breathe through my nose at all, while my nose was running nonstop, so that I soon went through a box of tissues. My throat was sore, and when I was brave enough to speak, my voice sounded horrible. Another reason I knew I had the flu was fever and chills. The thermometer registered 35 degrees. My chills were so bad that to get warm I had to put on sweat socks, flannel pyjamas, and a heavy robe, and I then had to get under two blankets and a sheet. Finally, I was extremely fatigued. After I got into bed, I slept for eight hours straight. When I woke up I was still so tired that I couldn't get out of bed. My eyelids felt like they weighed a hundred kilograms each, and I could not lift my head off the pillow. Too tired to think, I drifted back to sleep with hazy thoughts of my mother's homemade chicken soup.

1. _____   2. _____   3. _____   4. _____   5. _____

■ Combined Editing Test 3

Identify the sentence-skills mistakes at the underlined spots in the selection that follows. From the box below, choose the letter that describes each mistake and write it in the space provided. The same mistake may appear more than once.

a.	Sentence fragment	d.	Missing comma
b.	Run-on	e.	Faulty parallelism
c.	Missing apostrophe	f.	Misplaced modifier

On the day when her divorce papers came. Roz tried to feel something. She wanted
<u>   1   </u>
to be very happy or feel sadness. However, she felt nothing a part of her life had simply
                 2   3
ended. She didnt care about Don any more, and that disturbed her. She felt guilty about
       4
not caring. Until she remembered that she had a right to happiness, too.
               5

When I was four years old I had the first traumatic experience of my life. My family
              6
was staying at my Winnipeg aunts old house at Clear Lake. I was chasing my cousin
              7
Michelle toward the steps with untied shoelaces. Running too quickly I tripped and fell.
              8   9
My mouth hit the bottom of the wooden steps. I thought I would die I must have cried
                    10
for hours. To this day, I still have a bump on my lower lip.

1. _____ 3. _____ 5. _____ 7. _____ 9. _____
2. _____ 4. _____ 6. _____ 8. _____ 10. _____

■ Combined Editing Test 4

Identify the sentence-skills mistakes at the underlined spots in the selection that follows. From the box below, choose the letter that describes each mistake and write it in the space provided. The same mistake may appear more than once. In one case, there is no mistake.

a. Sentence fragment	d. Missing capital letter
b. Run-on	e. Missing comma
c. Dropped verb ending	f. No mistake

The worst thing that <u>happen</u> to me recently was when I <u>decide</u> to play a quick game

          1   2

of shinny with some friends. I felt good physically when the game was over. The next

morning, <u>however I</u> learned that I was not in the shape I thought I was. <u>When I tried to</u>

            3   4

<u>get out of bed but couldn't.</u> After my wife <u>help</u> me out of <u>bed I</u> felt a little better. But all

                                             5   6

during the day I had to struggle whenever I got in or out of my car. I thought the "<u>monday</u>

                                                                           7

soreness" was the end of it. <u>Until the next morning, when my wife had to help me put</u>

                                                               8

<u>my shoes on.</u> I could barely walk all <u>day, I</u> even needed help getting out of my car.

                                                  9

<u>My body has delivered a loud and clear message to me, forcing me to reconsider my</u>

                                              10

<u>imagined physical prowess.</u>

1. _____   3. _____   5. _____   7. _____   9. _____

2. _____   4. _____   6. _____   8. _____   10. _____

■ Combined Editing Test 5

Identify the sentence-skills mistakes at the underlined spots in the selection that follows. From the box below, choose the letter that describes each mistake and write it in the space provided. The same mistake may appear more than once. In one case, there is no mistake.

a. Sentence fragment	e. Irregular verb mistake
b. Run-on	f. Missing comma
c. Dangling modifier	g. No mistake
d. Mistake in subject-verb agreement	

When I was a child, my brother took advantage of my fear of ghosts. I would be taking a shower, and my brother would open the <u>door turn</u> out the lights and start
1
"wooing" until I began to cry. Then he would almost suffocate from laughing. Other times, he would make moaning sounds through the keyhole of my bedroom door. <u>Rattling the doorknob as well.</u> One night he did the worst thing of <u>all he</u> took out the main
2   3
fuse in the fuse box, and all the lights in the house went out. Neither one of my parents <u>were</u> home at the <u>time, and I</u> was so petrified that at first I couldn't move. But I sure did
4   5
move when my brother came running down the hall with a white sheet over his head. <u>Screaming at the top of his lungs.</u> He must have chased me around the house for almost
6
a half hour. I finally <u>stopped grabbed</u> an apple out of the fruit basket, and <u>throwed</u> it at
7   8
him as hard as I could. I missed him but not the kitchen window. <u>Telling my parents what
9
happened later,</u> they grounded my brother for two weeks. But thanks to him, I can't walk down a dark street today. <u>Without thinking there is someone behind me.</u>
10

1. _____   3. _____   5. _____   7. _____   9. _____

2. _____   4. _____   6. _____   8. _____   10. _____

■ Combined Editing Test 6

Identify the sentence-skills mistakes at the underlined spots in the selection that follows. From the box below, choose the letter that describes each mistake and write it in the space provided. The same mistake may appear more than once.

---

a. Sentence fragment   e. Missing capital letter
b. Run-on   f. Missing comma
c. Irregular verb mistake   g. Faulty parallelism
d. Apostrophe mistake

People often wonder why they have <u>spended</u> so much money at the supermarket.
1

<u>On things they didn't intend to buy in the first place.</u> A recent survey indicates that 75
2

per cent of all grocery <u>shoppers'</u> make at least one impulse purchase. They might not have
3

<u>ate</u> recently and reach for a package of <u>breton</u> crackers to munch on while they go up
4   5

and down the aisles. They may be lured by an eye-catching display or a colourful <u>package</u>
6

<u>over</u> one-third of all impulse purchases are made because the item is temptingly wrapped.

When shoppers are waiting in the check-out <u>line a</u> final surge of buying fever often comes
7

over them. They'll buy <u>magazines candy,</u> and other small items on the racks next to the
8

check-out counter. There are ways of avoiding impulse buying and <u>to save</u> money on
9

groceries. Shoppers should make a list and stick to <u>it buy</u> no-frills brands, and eat well
10

before going shopping.

---

1. _____   3. _____   5. _____   7. _____   9. _____

2. _____   4. _____   6. _____   8. _____   10. _____

■ Combined Editing Test 7

Identify the sentence-skills mistakes at the underlined spots in the selection that follows. From the box below, choose the letter that describes each mistake and write it in the space provided. The same mistake may appear more than once. In one case, there is no mistake.

a. Sentence fragment	e. Missing quotation marks
b. Run-on	f. Missing comma
c. Dangling modifier	g. No mistake
d. Faulty parallelism	

I have never understood why my parents each felt so differently about me. They are both dead now, I guess I will never have the answer. I am convinced that my father did
<u>   1</u>
not love me. Although never physically cruel, there was little affection for me. He used
                2
to say, I love all my children, but I don't like them all." He once looked at me when he
             3
said this, adding, "You know what I mean, Karen." He never seemed proud of me nor
was there an interest in what I was doing. My report cards, for example. He skipped the
        4   5
class plays I appeared in and rarely asked anything personal. He didn't say, "Do you have
a boyfriend? What's he like?" Instead, he would grunt, "Don't be late or you know what'll
                                   6
happen." On the other hand my mother seemed to care for me more than anyone. Maybe
           7
she wanted to make it up to me for my father's behaviour. She made clothes for me on
her sewing machine and decorating my room the way I wanted it. Also, driving me places
                     8   9
in the car. She asked me about school and about my friends. She would get my father
out of the house so that I could have a party, she would save her money to buy me special
                                        10
birthday and Christmas presents. Without my mother's special love, I think I would never have survived my father's indifference.

1. _____   3. _____   5. _____   7. _____   9. _____

2. _____   4. _____   6. _____   8. _____   10. _____

■ Combined Editing Test 8

Identify the sentence-skills mistakes at the underlined spots in the selections that follow. From the box below, choose the letter that describes each mistake and write it in the space provided. The same mistake may appear more than once. In one case, there is no mistake.

a. Sentence fragment	e. Dangling modifier
b. Mistake in subject-verb agreement	f. Missing capital letter
	g. No mistake
c. Subject-pronoun mistake	
d. Dropped *-ly* ending (adverb mistake)	

Cindy had a weird but fascinating dream last night. <u>Simply by turning the dial on</u>
1

<u>her magical television set.</u> She could see what anyone in the world was doing at the time.

On one channel she could see her English teacher. He was sitting <u>quiet</u> by himself in a
2

small room. <u>Watching a late movie.</u> On another channel, she could see the prime minister
3

of Canada fast asleep with his wife in a Sussex Drive bedroom. Turning <u>to another</u>
4

<u>channel, the first</u> boyfriend Cindy ever had <u>were</u> on <u>screen.</u> <u>Him</u> and a <u>young</u> woman were
5   6

having a conversation at a singles' bar.

My brother and <u>I</u> <u>was</u> always different when we were little boys. Once my parents
7 8

took us to see Santa Claus. <u>Who was at the local department store instead of the North Pole.</u>
9

My brother asked Santa for a red wagon and world peace. I asked Santa, "<u>how</u> much
10

money do you make?"

1. _____   3. _____   5. _____   7. _____   9. _____

2. _____   4. _____   6. _____   8. _____   10. _____

■ Combined Editing Test 9

Locate and correct the ten sentence-skills mistakes in the following passage. The mistakes are listed in the box below. As you locate each mistake, write the number of the sentence containing that mistake. Use the spaces provided.

3 sentence fragments _____	1 mistake in pronoun point of
_____ _____	view _____
3 run-ons _____ _____	1 missing set of quotation marks
_____	_____
1 dangling modifier _____	1 missing comma _____

¹The main problem in my work as a substitute Canada Post carrier is contending with dogs. ²Who are used to the regular carrier but not to me. ³The route I was assigned to last week featured a German shepherd. ⁴The dog had been hit once while chasing a car and had lost a leg. ⁵Even though he had only three legs, he still chased cars. ⁶As I walked up the lawn of the house where the German shepherd stood guard I felt very uneasy. ⁷I could see the dog, who was sitting in the side yard, out of the corner of my eye. ⁸Giving me a hateful stare. ⁹As I opened the screen door of the house, he let out several vicious snarls and barks. ¹⁰I could see his teeth showing. ¹¹His owner appeared to get the mail, she yelled at him, You stay right where you are, Rex. ¹²I felt like asking the woman to stand there and watch Rex until I was back on the sidewalk; however, I didn't want to seem afraid. ¹³I headed back away from the house. ¹⁴Walking slowly but eagerly, I heard the door click behind me, and you knew the owner had gone back into the house. ¹⁵I wished that I felt as confident as she did that her dog would behave. ¹⁶When I was almost at the sidewalk, Rex began to bark again. ¹⁷Then his barking became louder and closer. ¹⁸I turned around and saw Rex coming at me in full, three-legged stride. ¹⁹With only three legs, I was sure that I could outrun him at least up to the corner. ²⁰I felt foolish, but that didn't stop me from running just as fast as I could. ²¹Rex was tearing at my pants as I reached the corner, I slid behind a hedge, using it as a shield to frustrate Rex. ²²Rex hurled himself at the hedge several times then he backed off when his owner began to call. ²³After catching my breath, I resolved not to return to the dog's place again. ²⁴At least not without a can of pepper spray.

■ Combined Editing Test 10

Locate and correct the ten sentence-skills mistakes in the following passage. The mistakes are listed in the box below. As you locate each mistake, write the number of the sentence containing that mistake. Use the spaces provided.

---

3 sentence fragments _____

_____ _____

1 mistake in subject-verb
agreement _____

1 mistake in verb tense _____

1 subject-pronoun mistake

_____

1 missing apostrophe _____

1 missing capital letter _____

2 missing sets of quotation
marks _____ _____

---

¹Steve Miller is a stingy friend of mine. ²When he comes to work, he never brings any money. ³But always asks me if I have a quarter or two to lend him so that he can buy cookies or a small bag of potato chips. ⁴One time he asked me to lend him a dollar so he could buy a ticket from another employee for the thanksgiving turkey draw. ⁵I refused at first, but he practically begged me. ⁶Resulting in my giving him the money. ⁷As I expected, he never offered to return my dollar. ⁸When I'd remind him, he'd say, Oh yeah, I'll get it to you soon, but he never did. ⁹Another example of Steves stinginess were the time he and me and two of our friends decided to go out and eat during our lunch hour at the Red Rooster, a new restaurant. ¹⁰Steve suggested that we take his car, and as we were driving to the restaurant, he said his gas tank was empty. ¹¹I couldn't believe he would have the nerve to ask us for gas money. ¹²With only a total of eight kilometres to the restaurant and back. ¹³However, he pulls into a Petrocan gas station and cheerfully said that a dollar for gas from each of us would be fine. ¹⁴I was really fuming because I could see that his gas tank was at least a quarter full. ¹⁵After we pulled into the restaurant parking lot, Steve informed us that he would wait in the car while the rest of us ate. ¹⁶I asked him with a hard voice, Don't you have any money? ¹⁷Steve's reply was, "Yeah, but I'm not going to spend it eating out when I can go home and eat for nothing."

5

10

15

■ Combined Editing Test 11

Locate and correct the ten sentence-skills mistakes in the following passage. The mistakes are listed in the box below. As you locate each mistake, write the number of the sentence containing that mistake. Use the spaces provided.

2 sentence fragments _____ _____	2 missing commas after introductory words _____ _____
2 run-ons _____ _____	
1 irregular verb mistake _____	2 missing commas in a series
1 inconsistent pronoun point of view _____	_____ _____

[1]While shopping in Byward Market one Saturday morning, I passed an interesting-looking character on the street. [2]I was puzzled and, along with several other people, stopped and turned around after I passed him. [3]In order to stare in fascination. [4]The gentleman, in full evening dress reached suddenly into his pocket. [5]And took out a small felt roll bound in ribbon containing a full setting of formal cutlery as well as a large dinner napkin. [6]Bowing to one of the vendors as he took out a fork he leaned over and began to prod the tomatoes on her display. [7]Soon he made his selection. [8]The gentleman then wiped his fork on a linen napkin and stood silently for a moment, perhaps thinking of his next menu item. [9]Then, without any apparent hesitation but seeming to feel a great sense of purpose, he strode briskly to a booth selling herbs and oils. [10]He snatched down several bunches of fresh herbs sniffed each with care and enjoyment and sampled a few of the leaves. [11]A man working at the next stall shouted, "What are you doing, you crazy man." [12]However, he didn't try to stop the street gourmet's enjoyment of his basil leaves. [13]He shook his head, looked for agreement from other watchers, and turned his attention to a nearby customer. [14]The tuxedoed gentleman suddenly seemed to become aware of the fascinated crowd of watchers he heard someone applauding, and he began to smile, and applauded back to the crowd, but louder. [15]At the same time, his face creased into a wide smile. [16]You suddenly felt guilty and also delighted for having watched him. [17]As I turned and walked away I heard the elegant visitor's warm laughter echoing through the market alleys.

■ Combined Editing Test 12

Locate and correct the ten sentence-skills mistakes in the following passage. The mistakes are listed in the box below. As you locate each mistake, write the number of the sentence containing that mistake. Use the spaces provided.

3 sentence fragments _____ _____ _____	2 dropped verb endings _____ _____
3 run-ons _____ _____ _____	1 missing capital letter _____
	1 homonym mistake _____

¹When I met a girl named Barbara, my life started to change. ²Our relationship began one lonely night this past winter. ³I was sitting in the Dewdrop Inn near Niagara-on-the-Lake with a friend. ⁴We were having a couple of beers and shooting a game of darts. ⁵The place was almost empty, I guess there were about four people at the bar. ⁶Then Barbara and her friend walk in. ⁷Passing in front of us. ⁸At the jukebox they played some tunes. ⁹On there way to the bar, I asked Barbara if she and her friend would like to play some darts. ¹⁰To my surprise, she said, "yes, we would." ¹¹I still can't believe what happened then. ¹²They beat us.

¹³The night went on until Barbara and her friend said they had to go home. ¹⁴I felt sort of sad. ¹⁵I walked with her to her car, kissed her good-night, and made a date to go bowling on Saturday afternoon. ¹⁶However, I didn't show up for our date. ¹⁷Because I was afraid she wouldn't be there. ¹⁸I went to the auto races in Cayuga with a buddy instead. ¹⁹A couple of days went by before I saw her again. ²⁰I didn't think that she would talk to me. ²¹But she fool me. ²²We made another date, and this time I kept it.

²³We started to see each other several nights a week. ²⁴Becoming closer and closer to one another. ²⁵It's hard to explain what I felt about her. ²⁶When she met me, I was often drinking from early in the morning to late at night. ²⁷I did not have a job, I felt as though I had nothing to work for. ²⁸She changed me. ²⁹I went out and got a job and did well at it.

³⁰Then I applied to Mohawk college, and I am now in school trying to learn and do well in life. ³¹Barbara is helping me out as I try to achieve these goals, we are married and are happy. ³²In this strange world of ours, if a man has something to work for, he will do his best in order to achieve. ³³I can honestly say that I now have a meaning in my life.

5

10

15

20

PART THREE

SENTENCE VARIETY THROUGH COMBINING ACTIVITIES

INTRODUCTION

Part One of this book gives you practice in skills needed to write clear sentences. Part Two helps you work on reinforcing those skills. The purpose of this part of the book is to provide you with methods for writing varied and interesting sentences. Through the technique of sentence combining, you will learn about the many different options open to you for expressing a given idea. At the same time, you will develop a natural instinct and "ear" for choosing the option that sounds best in a particular situation. By the end of Part Three, you will be able to compose sentences that bring to your writing style a greater variety and ease. You will also be able to write sentences that express more complex thoughts.

How Sentence Combining Works: The combining technique used to help you practise various sentence patterns is a simple one. Two or more short sentences are given and then combined in a particular way. You are then asked to combine other short sentences in the same way. Here is an example:

- The diesel truck chugged up the hill.
- It spewed out black smoke.

  Spewing out black smoke, the diesel truck chugged up the hill.

The content of most sentences is given to you, so that instead of focusing on *what* you will say, you can concentrate on *how* to say it.

The sentence-combining activities are presented in a three-section sequence. The first section describes the four traditional sentence patterns in English and explains the important techniques of co-ordination and subordination central to these patterns. The second section presents other patterns that can be used to add variety to writing. And the last section provides a number of practice units in which you can apply the combining patterns you have learned as well as compose patterns of your own.

FOUR TRADITIONAL SENTENCE PATTERNS

Sentences have been traditionally described in English as being simple, compound, complex, or compound-complex. This section explains and offers practice in all four sentence types. The section also describes co-ordination and subordination—the two central techniques you can use to achieve different kinds of emphasis in your writing.

THE SIMPLE SENTENCE

A simple sentence has a single <u>subject</u>-<u>verb</u> combination.

> <u>Children</u> <u>play</u>.
> The <u>game</u> <u>ended</u> early.
> My <u>car</u> <u>stalled</u> three times last week.
> The <u>lake</u> <u>has been polluted</u> by several neighbouring streams.

A simple sentence may have more than one subject:

> <u>Crystal</u> and <u>Tony</u> <u>drove</u> home.
> The <u>wind</u> and <u>water</u> <u>dried</u> my hair.

or more than one verb:

> The <u>children</u> <u>smiled</u> and <u>waved</u> at us.
> The <u>lawnmower</u> <u>smoked</u> and <u>sputtered</u>.

or several subjects and verbs:

> <u>Manny</u>, <u>Moe</u>, and <u>Jack</u> <u>lubricated</u> my car, <u>replaced</u> the oil filter, and <u>cleaned</u> the spark plugs.

Activity

On separate paper, write:

> Three sentences, each with a single subject and verb
> Three sentences, each with a single subject and a double verb
> Three sentences, each with a double subject and a single verb

In each case, underline the subject once and the verb twice. (See page 10 if necessary for more information on subjects and verbs.)

THE COMPOUND SENTENCE

A compound, or "double," sentence is made up of two (or more) simple sentences. The two complete statements in a compound sentence are usually connected by a comma plus a joining word (*and*, *but*, *for*, *or*, *nor*, *so*, *yet*).

A **compound sentence** is used when you want to give **equal weight to two closely** related ideas. The technique of showing that ideas have equal importance is called *co-ordination*.

Following are some compound sentences. Each sentence contains two ideas that the writer considers equal in importance.

The rain increased, so the officials cancelled the game.

Maria wanted to go shopping, but Fred refused to drive her.

Tom was watching television in the family room, and Maria was upstairs on the phone.

I had to give up wood carving, for my arthritis had become very painful.

Activity 1: Forming Compound Sentences

Combine the following pairs of simple sentences into compound sentences. Use a comma and a logical joining word (*and*, *but*, *for*, *so*) to connect each pair.

Note: If you are not sure what *and*, *but*, *for*, and *so* mean, review page 41.

Example   ■   We hung up the print.
             ■   The wall still looked bare.
             We hung up the print, but the wall still looked bare.

1. ■   My cold grew worse.
    ■   I decided to see a doctor.

    _____

    _____

2. ■   My uncle always ignores me.
    ■   My aunt gives me kisses and presents.

    _____

    _____

3. ■ We played ball hockey in the afternoon.
   ■ We went to a movie in the evening.

   _____

   _____

4. ■ I invited Richard to sleep overnight.
   ■ He wanted to go home.

   _____

   _____

5. ■ Police raided the club.
   ■ They had gotten a tip about illegal drugs for sale.

   _____

   _____

Activity 2: Creating Compound Sentences

On separate sheet of paper, write five compound sentences of your own. Use a different joining word (*and*, *but*, *for*, *or*, *nor*, *so*, *yet*) to connect the two complete ideas in each sentence.

THE COMPLEX SENTENCE

A complex sentence is made up of a simple sentence (a complete statement) and a statement that begins with a dependent word.* Here is a list of common dependent words:

after	if, even if	when, whenever
although, though	in order that	where, wherever
as	since	whether
because	that, so that	which, whichever
before	unless	while
even though	until	who
how	what, whatever	whose

* The two parts of a complex sentence are sometimes called an independent clause and dependent clause. A *clause* is simply a word group that contains a subject and a verb. An *independent clause* expresses a complete thought and can stand alone. A *dependent clause* does not express a complete thought in itself and "depends on" the independent clause to complete its meaning. Dependent clauses always begin with a dependent or subordinating word.

A **complex sentence** is used when you want to **emphasize one idea over another** in a sentence. Look at the following complex sentence:

Because I forgot the time, I missed the final exam.

The idea that the writer wishes to emphasize here—*I missed the final exam*—is expressed as a complete thought. The less important idea—*Because I forgot the time*—is subordinated to the complete thought. The technique of giving one idea less emphasis than another is called *subordination*.

Following are other examples of complex sentences. In each case, the part starting with the dependent word is the less emphasized part of the sentence.

While Sue was eating breakfast, she began to feel sick.

I checked my money *before* I invited Tom for lunch.

When Jerry lost his temper, he also lost his job.

Although I practised for three months, I failed my driving test.

Activity 1: Forming Complex Sentences

Use logical dependent words to combine the following pairs of simple sentences into complex sentences. Place a comma after a dependent statement when it starts the sentence.

Examples
- I obtained a credit card.
- I began spending money recklessly.

  When I obtained a credit card, I began spending money recklessly.

- Alan stuffed the turkey.
- His brother greased the roasting pan.

  Alan stuffed the turkey while his brother greased the roasting pan.

1.
   - The teacher announced the quiz.
   - The class groaned.

   _____

2.
   - Gene could not fit any more groceries into his cart.
   - He decided to go to the check-out counter.

   _____

   _____

3. ■   Your car is out of commission.
   ■   You should take it to Otto's Transmission.

   _____

   _____

4. ■   I finished typing the paper.
   ■   I proofread it carefully.

   _____

5. ■   We owned four cats and a dog.
   ■   No one would rent us an apartment.

   _____

   _____

Activity 2: Using Subordination to Form Complex Sentences

Rewrite the following sentences, using subordination rather than co-ordination. Include a comma when a dependent statement starts a sentence.

Example   The hair dryer was not working right, so I returned it to the store.
   Because the hair dryer was not working right, I returned it
   to the store.

1. Ruth turned on the large window fan, but the room remained hot.

   _____

   _____

2. The plumber repaired the hot-water heater, so we can take showers again.

   _____

   _____

3. I washed the sheets and towels, and I scrubbed the bathroom floor.

   _____

   _____

4. You should go to a doctor, for your chest cold may get worse.

   _____

   _____

5. The fish tank broke, and guppies were flopping all over the carpet.

_____

_____

Activity 3: Forming Complex Sentences

Combine the simple sentences on the pages below and following into complex sentences. Omit repeated words. Use the dependent words *who*, *which*, and *that*.

Notes

a The word *who* refers to persons.

b The word *which* refers to things.

c The word *that* refers to persons or things.

Use commas around the dependent statement only if it seems to interrupt the flow of thought in the sentence. (See also pages 184–185.)

Examples ■ Damian picked up a hitchhiker.
  ■ The hitchhiker was travelling around the world.
      Damian picked up a hitchhiker who was travelling around the world.

  ■ Larry is a sleepwalker.
  ■ Larry is my brother.
      Larry, who is my brother, is a sleepwalker.

1. ■ The magazine article was about abortion.
    ■ The article made me very angry.

_____

_____

2. ■ The woodshed has collapsed.
    ■ I built the woodshed myself.

_____

3. ■ The power drill is missing.
    ■ I bought the power drill at half price.

_____

4. ■ Rita Haber was indicted for bribery.
   ■ Rita Haber is our mayor.

   _____

5. ■ The chicken pies contain dangerous preservatives.
   ■ We ate the chicken pies.

   _____

Activity 4: Using Subordination to Create Complex Sentences

On separate sheet of paper, write eight complex sentences, using, in turn, the dependent words *unless*, *if*, *after*, *because*, *when*, *who*, *which*, and *that*.

THE COMPOUND-COMPLEX SENTENCE

The compound-complex sentence is made up of two (or more) simple sentences and one (or more) dependent statements. In the following examples, a solid line is under the simple sentences and a dotted line is under the dependent statements.

> When the power line snapped, Jack was listening to the stereo, and Linda was reading in bed.
>
> After I returned to school following a long illness, the math teacher gave me make-up work, but the history teacher made me drop her course.

Activity 1: Forming Compound-Complex Sentences

Read through each sentence to get a sense of its overall meaning. Then insert a logical joining word (*and*, *or*, *but*, *for*, or *so*) and a logical dependent word (*because*, *since*, *when*, or *although*).

1. _____ he suffered so much during hay fever season, Pete bought an air-conditioner, _____ he swallowed allergy pills regularly.

2. _____ I put on my new flannel shirt, I discovered a button was missing, _____ I angrily went looking for a replacement button in the sewing basket.

3. _____ the keyboard was just repaired, the return key still sticks, _____ certain other keys keep jamming.

4. _____ I have lived all my life in the Maritimes, I felt uncomfortable during a West Coast vacation, _____ I kept thinking that the ocean was on the wrong side.

5. _____ water condensation continues in your basement, you should either buy a dehumidifier, _____ you should cover the masonry walls with waterproof paint.

Activity 2: Creating Compound-Complex Sentences

On separate paper, write five compound-complex sentences.

REVIEW OF CO-ORDINATION AND SUBORDINATION

Remember that co-ordination and subordination are ways of showing the exact relationship of ideas within a sentence. Through co-ordination we show that ideas are of equal importance. When we co-ordinate, we use the words *and*, *but*, *for*, *or*, *nor*, *so*, and *yet*. Through subordination we show that one idea is less important than another. When we subordinate, we use dependent words like *when*, *although*, *since*, *while*, *because*, and *after*. A list of common dependent words is given on page 385.

Activity: Developing Varied Sentence Structures

Use co-ordination or subordination to combine the groups of simple sentences on the next pages into one or more longer sentences. Omit repeated words. Since a variety of combinations is possible, you might want to jot several combinations on separate paper. Then read them aloud to find the combination that sounds best.

Keep in mind that, very often, the relationship among ideas in a sentence will be clearer when subordination rather than co-ordination is used.

Example
- My car is not starting on cold mornings.
- I think the battery needs to be replaced.
- I already had it recharged once.
- I don't think it would help to charge it again.

  Because my car is not starting on cold mornings, I think the battery needs to be replaced. I already had it recharged once, so I don't think it would help to charge it again.

Comma Hints

a   Use a comma at the end of a word group that starts with a dependent word (as in "Because my car is not starting on cold mornings, ...").

b   Use a comma between independent word groups connected by *and*, *but*, *for*, *or*, *nor*, *so*, or *yet* (as in "I already had it recharged once, so. ...").

1. ■   Louise used a dandruff shampoo.
   ■   She still had dandruff.
   ■   She decided to see a dermatologist.

   _____

   _____

   _____

2. ■   Al's parents want him to be a doctor.
   ■   Al wants to be a salesperson.
   ■   He impresses people with his charm.

   _____

   _____

   _____

3. ■   The teacher conducted a discussion period.
   ■   Jack sat at his desk with his head down.
   ■   He did not want the teacher to call on him.
   ■   He had not read the assignment.

   _____

   _____

   _____

4. ■   Crystal wanted to get a quick lunch at the cafeteria.
   ■   All the sandwiches were gone.
   ■   She had to settle for a cup of yogurt.

   _____

   _____

   _____

5. ■   I was leaving to do some shopping in town.
   ■   I asked my son to water the back lawn.
   ■   He seemed agreeable.

- ■ I returned three hours later.
- ■ The lawn had not been watered.

_____

_____

_____

_____

_____

6. ■ I ate too quickly.
   ■ My stomach became upset.
   ■ It felt like a war combat zone.
   ■ I took two antacid tablets.

_____

_____

_____

7. ■ Jennifer is always buying plants and flower seeds.
   ■ She enjoys growing things.
   ■ Not many things grow well for her.
   ■ She doesn't know why.

_____

_____

_____

8. ■ My car was struck from behind yesterday.
   ■ I slowed suddenly for a red light.
   ■ The driver of the truck behind me slammed on his brakes.
   ■ He didn't quite stop on time.

_____

_____

_____

9. ■ Ed skimmed through the help-wanted ads.
■ Nothing was there for him.
■ He desperately needed a job.
■ He would have to sell his car.
■ He could no longer keep up the payments.

_____

_____

_____

_____

10. ■ The meat loaf didn't taste right.
■ The mashed potatoes had too much salt in them.
■ We sent out for a pizza.
■ It was delivered late.
■ It was cold.

_____

_____

_____

_____

OTHER PATTERNS THAT ADD VARIETY TO WRITING

This section gives you practice in other patterns or methods that can add variety and interest to your sentences. The patterns can be used with any of the four sentence types already explained. Note that you will not have to remember the grammar terms that are often used to describe the patterns. What is important is that you practise the various patterns extensively, so that you increase your sense of the many ways available to you for expressing your ideas.

-*ING* WORD GROUPS (PRESENT PARTICIPLE PHRASES)

Use an -*ing* word group at some point in a sentence. Here are examples:

> The doctor, *hoping* for the best, examined the X-rays.
> *Jogging* every day, I soon raised my energy level.

More information about -*ing* words, also known as *present participles*, appears on page 88.

Activity 1: Beginning Sentences with Present Participle Phrases

Combine each pair of sentences below into one sentence by using an -*ing* word and omitting repeated words. Use a comma or commas to set off the -*ing* word group from the rest of the sentence.

Example   ■ The diesel truck chugged up the hill.
　　　　　　　 ■ It spewed out smoke.
　　　　　　　 　Spewing our smoke, the diesel truck chugged up the hill.

　　　　　　or　The diesel truck, spewing out smoke, chugged up the hill.

1. ■ Ginger refused to get out of bed.
   ■ She pulled the blue blanket over her head.

   _____

   _____

2. ■ Dad is able to forget the troubles of the day.
   ■ He putters around in his basement workshop.

   _____

   _____

3. ■ The crowd of dancers moved as one.
   ■ They swayed to the music.

   _____

   _____

4. ■ George tried to protect himself from the dampness of the room.
   ■ He wrapped a scarf around his neck.

   _____

   _____

5. ■ The woman listened intently to the earnest young man.
   ■ She caressed her hair.

   _____

   _____

Activity 2: Creating Sentences with Present Participle Phrases

On separate sheet of paper, write five sentences of your own that contain *-ing* word groups.

-*ED* WORD GROUPS (PAST PARTICIPLE PHRASES)

Use an *-ed* word group at some point in a sentence. Here are examples:

> *Tired* of studying, I took a short break.
> Mary, *amused* by the joke, told it to a friend.
> I opened my eyes wide, *shocked* by the red "F" on my paper.

More information about *-ed* words, also known as *past participles*, appears on page 88.

Activity: Forming Sentences with Past Participle Phrases

Combine each of the following pairs of sentences into one sentence by using an *-ed* word and omitting repeated words. Use a comma or commas to set off the *-ed* word group from the rest of the sentence.

Example ■ Tim woke up with a start.
             ■ He was troubled by a dream.

<u>Troubled by a dream, Tim woke up with a start.</u>

or <u>Tim, troubled by a dream, woke up with a start.</u>

1. ■ I called an exterminator.
   ■ I was bothered by roaches.

   _____

2. ■ Sam grew silent.
   ■ He was baffled by what had happened.

   _____

3. ■ The crowd began to file slowly out of the stadium.
   ■ They were stunned by the last-minute touchdown.

   _____

   _____

4. ■ I tried to stifle my grin.
   ■ I was amused but reluctant to show how I felt.

   _____

   _____

5. ■ Cindy lay on the couch.
   ■ She was exhausted from working all day.

   _____

   _____

APPOSITIVES

Use appositives. An *appositive* is a word group that renames a noun (any person, place, or thing). Here is an example:

Renée, a good friend of mine, works as a police officer.

The word group *a good friend of mine* is an appositive that renames the word Renée.

Activity 1: Forming Sentences Using Appositives

Combine each of the following pairs of sentences into one sentence by using an appositive and omitting repeated words. Most appositives are set off by commas.

Example ■ Alan Thorn got lost during the hiking trip.

■ He is a former Army Cadet.

Alan Thorn, a former Army Cadet, got lost during the hiking trip.

1. ■ Calgary is a rapidly growing city.
   ■ Calgary is my hometown.

   _____

   _____

2. ■ Roger refused to get involved in the argument.
   ■ Roger is a gentle man.

   _____

   _____

3. ■ My little brother wallpapered his room with monster pictures.
   ■ My little brother is a horror-movie fan.

   _____

   _____

4. ■ High Park is where I go to think.
   ■ High Park is a shady retreat.

   _____

   _____

5. ■ The bungalow did not look safe enough to enter.
   ■ The bungalow is a tilted structure with a sagging roof.

   _____

   _____

Activity 2: Creating Sentences Using Appositives

On separate sheet of paper, write five sentences of your own that contain appositives. Use commas as necessary to set off the appositives.

-LY OPENERS

Use an -ly word to open a sentence. Here are examples:

Gently, he mixed the chemicals together.
Anxiously, the contestant looked at the game clock.
Skilfully, the quarterback rifled a pass to his receiver.

More information about -ly words, which are also known as *adverbs*, appears on pages 117–118.

Activity 1: Forming Sentences Beginning with Adverbs

Combine each pair of sentences below into one sentence by starting with an -ly word and omitting repeated words. Place a comma after the opening -ly word.

Example   ■   I gave several yanks to the starting cord of the lawnmower.
           ■   I was angry.
           Angrily, I gave several yanks to the starting cord of the
           lawnmower.

1. ■   The burglars carried the television out of the house.
    ■   They were quiet.

    _____

    _____

2. ■   Lizette squirmed in her seat as she waited for her turn to speak.
    ■   She was nervous.

    _____

    _____

3. ■   I reinforced all the coat buttons with a strong thread.
    ■   I was patient.

    _____

    _____

4. ■   He finished answering the last question on the test.
    ■   He was quick.

    _____

    _____

5. ■ I tore the wrapping off the present.
   ■ I was excited.

_____

Activity 2: Creating Sentences with Adverbial Openers

On separate sheet of paper, write five sentences of your own that begin with -*ly* words.

TO OPENERS (INFINITIVE PHRASES)

Use a *to* word group to open a sentence. Here are examples:

To succeed in that course, you must attend every class.
To help me sleep better, I learned to quiet my mind through meditation.
To get good seats, we went to the game early.

The *to* in such a group is also known as an *infinitive*, as explained on page 87.

Activity 1: Forming Sentences Beginning with Infinitive Phrases

Combine each of the following pairs of sentences into one sentence by starting with a *to* word group and omitting repeated words. Use a comma after the opening *to* word group.

Example ■ I fertilize the grass every spring.
■ I want to make it greener.
   To make the grass greener, I fertilize it every spring.

1. ■ Doug ran five kilometres a day all summer.
   ■ He wanted to prepare for the track season.

   _____

2. ■ You should meet Al's parents.
   ■ This will help you understand him better.

   _____

3. ■ She wants to get the stain off her hand.
   ■ She will have to use an abrasive soap.

   _____

   _____

4. ■ I left the house early.
   ■ I had to get to the church on time.

   _____

   _____

5. ■ I punched in my PIN number.
   ■ I did this to make the automatic banking machine work.

   _____

   _____

Activity 2: Creating Sentences Beginning with Infinitive Phrases

On separate sheet of paper, write five sentences of your own that begin with *to* word groups.

PREPOSITIONAL PHRASE OPENERS

Use prepositional phrase openers. Here are examples:

> *From* the beginning, I disliked my boss.
> *In spite of* her work, she failed the course.
> *After* the game, we went to a movie.

Prepositional phrases include words like *in*, *from*, *of*, *at*, *by*, and *with*. A full list is on page 13.

Activity 1: Forming Sentences Beginning with Prepositional Phrases

Combine each of the following groups of sentences into one sentence by omitting repeated words. Start each sentence with a suitable prepositional phrase and place the other prepositional phrases in places that sound right. Generally you should use a comma after the opening prepositional phrase.

Example   ■   A fire started.
             ■   It did this at 5:00 a.m.
             ■   It did this inside the garage.
             <u>At 5:00 a.m., a fire started inside the garage.</u>

1.   ■   I sat napping.
    ■   I did this during my work break.
    ■   I did this in the lunchroom corner.
    ■   I did this with my head on my arm.

    _____

    _____

2.   ■   We played basketball.
    ■   We did this in the church gym.
    ■   We did this during the winter.
    ■   We did this on many evenings.

    _____

    _____

3.   ■   Fred Grimaldi studies his bald spot.
    ■   He does this with grave concern.
    ■   He does this in the bathroom mirror.
    ■   He does this before going to bed.

    _____

    _____

4.   ■   The car skidded.
    ■   It did this on an oil slick.
    ■   It did this on a sharp curve.
    ■   It did this during the race.

    _____

    _____

5.   ■   The teenage driver raced his car to the busy intersection.
    ■   He did this without slowing down.
    ■   The intersection is in the heart of town.

    _____

    _____

Activity 2: Creating Sentences with Prepositional Phrase Openers

On separate sheet of paper, write five sentences of your own that begin with prepositional phrases and that contain at least one other prepositional phrase.

SERIES OF ITEMS

Use a series of items. Following are two of the many items that can be used in a series: adjectives and verbs.

Adjectives in Series

Adjectives are descriptive words. Here are examples:

The *husky young* man sanded the *chipped, weather-worn* paint off the fence.

Husky and *young* are adjectives that describe *man*; *chipped* and *weather-worn* are adjectives that describe *paint*. More information about adjectives appears on page 115.

Activity 1: Forming Sentences with Adjectives in Series

Combine each of the following groups of sentences into one sentence by using adjectives in a series and omitting repeated words. Use commas between adjectives only when *and* inserted between them sounds natural.

Example
- I sewed a set of buttons onto my coat.
- The buttons were shiny.
- The buttons were black.
- The coat was old.
- The coat was green.

    I sewed a set of shiny black buttons onto my old green coat.

1. - The boy stomped on the bug.
    - The boy was little.
    - The boy was angry.
    - The bug was tiny.
    - The bug was red.

    _____

    _____

2. ■ The man slowly wiped his forehead with a bandanna.
   ■ The man was tall.
   ■ The man was thin.
   ■ His forehead was sweaty.
   ■ His bandanna was dirty.
   ■ His bandanna was blue.

   _____

   _____

3. ■ My sister is intelligent.
   ■ My sister is good-natured.
   ■ My sister is humorous.

   _____

4. ■ The boy looked at the girl.
   ■ The boy was shy.
   ■ The boy was timid.
   ■ The girl was grinning.
   ■ The girl was curly-haired.

   _____

   _____

5. ■ The man wearing work clothes strode into the tavern.
   ■ The man was short.
   ■ The man was muscular.
   ■ The man was bald.
   ■ The work clothes were wrinkled.
   ■ The work clothes were green.
   ■ The tavern was noisy.
   ■ The tavern was smoke-filled.

   _____

   _____

   _____

Activity 2: Creating Sentences with Adjectives in Series

On separate paper, write five sentences of your own that contain a series of adjectives.

Verbs in Series

Verbs are words that express action. Here are examples:

In my job as a cook's helper, I *prepared* salads, *sliced* meat and cheese, and *made* all kinds of sandwiches.

Basic information about verbs appears on pages 10–11.

Activity 1: Combining Sentences Using Verbs in Series

Combine each group of sentences below into one sentence by using verbs in a series and omitting repeated words. Use a comma between verbs in a series.

Example ■ In the dingy bar Sam shelled peanuts.
 ■ He sipped a beer.
 ■ He talked up a storm with friends.

 In the dingy bar Sam shelled peanuts, sipped a beer, and
 talked up a storm with friends.

1. ■ When the popular comedian walked from behind the curtain, the crowd applauded.
 ■ The crowd raised their fists.
 ■ The crowd grunted, "Ooh … ooh … ooh!"

   _____

   _____

2. ■ Everywhere in the cafeteria students were pulling on their coats.
 ■ They were scooping up their books.
 ■ They were hurrying off to class.

   _____

   _____

3. ■ By 6:00 a.m., I had read the textbook chapter.
 ■ I had taken notes on it.
 ■ I had studied the notes.
 ■ I had drunk eight cups of coffee.

   _____

   _____

4. ■ I pressed the Weetabix into the bowl.
   ■ I poured milk on them.
   ■ I waited for the milk to soak the cereal.

   _____

   _____

5. ■ I am afraid the dentist's drill will slip off my tooth.
   ■ I am afraid it will bite into my gum.
   ■ I am afraid it will make me jump with pain.

   _____

   _____

Activity 2: Creating Sentences with Verbs in a Series

On separate sheet of paper, write five sentences of your own that use verbs in a series.

Note: The section on parallelism (pages 134–138) gives you practice in some of the other kinds of items that can be used in a series.

SENTENCE-COMBINING EXERCISES

This section provides a series of combining exercises. The exercises are made up of a number of short sentence units, each of which can be combined into one sentence. (Occasionally, you may decide that certain sentences are more effective if they are not combined.) The patterns you have already practised will suggest combining ideas for the units that you work on. However, do not feel limited to previous patterns. Use your own natural instinct to explore and compose a variety of sentence combinations. It will help if you write out possible combinations and then read them aloud. Choose the one that sounds best. You will gradually develop an ear for hearing the option that reads most smoothly and clearly and that sounds most appropriate in the context of surrounding sentences. As you continue to practise, you will increase your ability to write more varied, interesting, and sophisticated sentences.

Here is an example of a short sentence unit and some possible combinations:

- Maria moved in the desk chair.
- Her moving was uneasy.
- The chair was hard.
- She worked at her assignment.
- The assignment was for her English class.

> Maria moved uneasily in the hard desk chair, working at the assignment for her English class.
>
> Moving uneasily in the hard desk chair, Maria worked at the assignment for her English class.
>
> Maria moved uneasily in the hard desk chair as she worked at the assignment for her English class.
>
> While she worked at the assignment for her English class, Maria moved uneasily in the hard desk chair.

Note: In combining short sentence clusters into one sentence, omit repeated words where necessary. Use separate paper.

1 Stray Dog

- A dog trots down the street.
- The dog is a stray.
- The dog is hungry.

- He has a lovable face.
- He has a healthy coat.
- But someone has abandoned him.

- He approaches a house.
- He smells a garbage can.
- The can is filled with smelly delights.

- The dog knocks the can over.
- Garbage spills to the ground.

■ Inside the house, the owner is alerted.
■ He is alerted by the sound of the falling can.

■ The dog digs into his find.
■ He doesn't hear the owner coming.

■ The owner opens his back door.
■ He yells at the dog.
■ The dog is quickly scared off.

■ The owner cleans up the mess.
■ The dog appears out of the shadows.
■ The dog is hungry.

■ The owner feels sorry for the dog.
■ He returns to his house.
■ He gets the dog some real food.

■ **2   April Fool**

■ April Fool's Day is an occasion.
■ It happens yearly.
■ It brings out the worst in people.

■ People play tricks.
■ They play tricks on their friends.
■ They send them unordered pizzas.
■ They tell them their cars were stolen.

■ Practical jokers also like to make phone calls.
■ The calls are to the zoo.

■ The zoo answers.
■ The caller asks for someone.
■ The someone has a name.
■ The name is of an animal.

- A caller asks to speak to Mr. Lyon.
- A caller asks to speak to Mr. Bear.
- A caller asks to speak to Ms. Fish.

- One year a joker tried something.
- The something was new.
- He asked for Mr. Tad Pole.

- This year the local zoo is trying an approach.
- The approach is clever.
- The approach will discourage these calls.

- An April Fool's joker calls.
- The zoo will play a recording.
- The recording will say this.

- "Thank you for calling the zoo."
- "Mr. Lyon and his friends are busy."
- "They can't come to the phone."

- "They would prefer a visit."
- "The visit would be from you."
- "Please visit them soon."

■ 3 Department Store Sale

- There's a sale at the large chain store.
- The sale is in all departments.

- Shoppers flood the store.
- They hurry down the aisles.

- People paw through sweaters.
- People paw through shirts.
- The sweaters and shirts are on special sales tables.
- The people do this excitedly.

- Stacks of coffee-makers are snapped up.
- The coffee-makers are reduced by 50 per cent.
- This happens quickly.

- There is a long line of women.
- The women are holding piles of clothes.
- The line is in front of the fitting room.

- Some people buy things they don't need.
- Other people buy things they don't want.

- The manager smiles at the success of the sale.
- His employees don't smile.

- The shoppers mistreat the salespeople.
- The shoppers act like animals.
- The salespeople hate sales.

- The shoppers throw clothes on the floor.
- The shoppers throw dirty looks at each other.

- At the end of the day the store has made money.
- At the end of the day the manager is happy.
- At the end of the day the salespeople feel like quitting.

■ 4 The Garbage Problem

- We have a garbage problem.
- The problem is severe.
- The problem is in Canada.

- This problem has been growing for a long time.
- No one ever wanted to think about it.

- No one wanted to plan ahead for the day the dumps would fill up.
- No one wanted to plan ahead for the day liquid wastes would begin to leak.

- We ignored the problem.
- We did this by covering it up with pleasant-sounding words.

- We call garbage collectors "sanitation engineers."
- We call garbage trucks "sanitation vehicles."
- We call garbage dumps "landfills."

- A landfill is really a pit.
- The pit is full of garbage.
- The garbage is smelly.
- The garbage is decaying.

- The euphemisms we use sound clean.
- They sound harmless.
- They help us forget about the garbage.
- The garbage is piling up in our country.

- Now, we are faced with a crisis.
- The crisis involves buried chemical poisons.
- The crisis involves overflowing garbage dumps.

- Language has helped us avoid this problem.
- The time has come to drop the cover-up.
- The time has come to face the situation honestly.

■ 5   Cocoa and Doughnut

- A cup of cocoa sat on the high-chair tray.
- Half a doughnut sat on the high-chair tray.
- The cocoa was dark brown.
- The doughnut was a white sugar doughnut.

- A little boy was in the high chair.
- He stuck his finger in the cocoa.
- The sticking of his finger was careful.

- Then he picked up the doughnut half.
- He pushed the doughnut into the cup.
- His pushing was deep.

- Cocoa flowed over the top of the cup.
- It ran onto the tray.
- It dropped off the tray onto a tablecloth.
- The tablecloth was white linen.

- The little boy grabbed at the doughnut.
- The doughnut was spongy.
- The doughnut would not come out of the cup.

- The boy pushed at the cup.
- The cup rolled onto its side.
- It rocked back and forth on the plastic tray.
- The rocking was gentle.

- The boy dug his hand into the cup.
- He pulled out a piece of doughnut.

- He pressed the doughnut against the plastic tray.
- He pressed it with his fist.
- The doughnut flattened.
- The flattening was like a pancake.

- The boy shoved the pressed doughnut.
- He shoved most of it off the tray.
- It splattered onto the floor.
- It splattered onto the tablecloth.

- The boy picked up a fistful of doughnut.
- He jammed it into his mouth.

- He sat chewing the doughnut.
- His chewing was contented.

- The boy's father walked into the room.
- The boy looked up at his father.
- The boy was happy.

■ 6   Jack Alone

- Jack entered his apartment.
- He locked the door.
- The muscles in his face began to relax.
- The muscles in his body began to relax.

- He felt happy to be at home.
- He felt happy after an exhausting day at work.
- The work was as a delivery person for Canpar.

- He was carrying a newspaper.
- He was carrying his mail.
- He dropped both of them on the sofa.

- He walked into the kitchen.
- He opened the freezer door.
- He took out a TV dinner.
- The TV dinner was a Maple Leaf chicken pie.

- He placed the dinner in his toaster oven.
- He set the oven at 200°C.

- Then he went into the bedroom.
- He undressed.
- He hung on a chair his heavy brown shirt.
- He hung on a chair his heavy brown pants.
- The hanging was neat.

- In the bathroom he washed his face.
- He washed his arms and hands.
- He brushed the tangles out of his hair.

- His hair was curly.
- His hair was black.

- He put on a corduroy shirt.
- The shirt was soft.
- He pulled on a pair of trousers.
- The trousers were old.
- The trousers were baggy.
- The trousers hung loosely around his waist.

- Then he put on a pair of slippers.
- The slippers were blue.
- The slippers were fleece-lined.

- Jack shuffled back to the kitchen.
- He boiled water.
- He made a large cup of tea.

- To the tea Jack added a tablespoon of honey.
- To the tea Jack added a tablespoon of rye.

- Jack carried the tea to the living room.
- He sat down beside his newspaper and mail.
- He flicked on the television.

- Later Jack might feel lonely.
- Now he was relaxed.
- Now he was comfortable.
- Now he was happy to be by himself.

■ 7 A Surprise for Dracula

- Crystal had a dream.
- The dream was recent.
- The dream was about Dracula.

- Dracula slipped through a window.
- The window was open.

- He approached Crystal.
- Crystal was sleeping.

- Dracula's lip curled back.
- His fangs were revealed.
- The fangs were long.
- The fangs were pointed.
- The pointing was cruel.

- Dracula bent over Crystal.
- Crystal stirred.
- She felt the shadow above her.

- Crystal opened her eyes.
- Dracula grinned down at her.
- He assumed his victim was powerless.

- He bent down to her neck.
- The bending was slow.
- But then something happened.
- What happened was unexpected.

- Crystal's hand flew out.
- She gave him a karate chop.
- The karate chop was quick.
- The karate chop was on the side of his head.

- Dracula was knocked backward.
- He tripped on his cape.
- He fell to the floor.

- Dracula sprang up.
- He made a cry.
- The cry was terrible.
- The cry was chilling.
- The cry was of an incensed beast.

- He leaped at Crystal.
- She held up a crucifix.
- The crucifix was small.
- The crucifix was shining.

- Dracula winced.
- He came to a stop.
- The stop was abrupt.

- The crucifix radiated.
- It radiated an invisible shield.
- The shield was protective.
- Dracula could not penetrate the shield.

- Dracula drew his cape about him.
- He grew smaller in size.
- This happened rapidly.

- He disappeared.
- Only a bat remained.
- The bat was squeaking.

- It flew out of the room.
- Its going was quick.
- It was a bat returning to Hell.

■ 8 Writing a Paper

- Maria has writer's block.
- She can think of nothing to write.

- She scribbles words on the page.
- The words do not develop the subject.
- She crosses out the words.

- Maria is sweating.
- Maria is frustrated.

- She feels bored.
- She feels stupid.

- She pulls at the collar of her blouse.
- She gets up.
- She walks around the room.
- She walks for a couple of minutes.

- She stares out the window.
- She wishes the paper was finished.
- Her wishing is desperate.

- She thinks of what she could be watching on television.
- She thinks of calls she could make to friends.

- Then she sighs.
- She returns to the desk.

- She does two things.
- The things are to break the writer's block.

- First, she writes about her subject.
- She writes whatever comes into her head.
- She does this for twenty minutes.

- Then she reads what she has written.
- She tries to decide on her main point.
- She tries to decide on her support for that point.

- This work helps clear her confusion.
- Her confusion is now not so great.

- She senses the point of her paper.
- She senses how to support that point.
- She senses how to organize the support.

- She works hard for more than an hour.
- The result is the first rough draft of her paper.

- Maria sighs with relief.
- She gets up to take a break.

- She still has a second draft to write.
- She even has a third draft to write.
- But the worst part is over.
- Maria knows she has won the battle.

■ 9   Victim

- The TV van hurried to the scene.
- The scene was of an auto accident.
- The lights of the TV van were flashing.

- An ambulance pulled away from the scene.
- It carried a dead boy.
- It left as the van arrived.

- The boy had backed his car out of a driveway.
- He had done so without looking.

- His car was struck by a truck.
- The truck was oncoming.
- He was killed instantly.

- The mother of the boy stood in the driveway.
- She was sobbing.
- She was talking to neighbours.

- TV lights were focused on her face.
- The focusing was cruel.
- A TV reporter approached her with a microphone.
- He asked her to speak.

- Her friends moved aside.
- Their moving was uncertain.
- Her friends did not stop the TV crew.

- Bystanders jostled in the background.
- Police moved them aside.
- The police did not stop the TV crew.

- The woman began to talk.
- The woman talked about the accident.
- The woman talked about her dead son.

- She began to cry.
- She tried to keep talking.
- The camera continued to roll.

- The reporter looked sympathetic.
- He stood to one side.
- His standing was careful.
- He wanted the camera to have a good angle.

- The woman felt obliged to the TV people.
- She felt obliged to co-operate.
- She should not have.

- The woman did not have to share her grief.
- The grief was private.

- The woman should have said something to the TV people.
- She should have said, "Get out of here."
- She should have said, "My tragedy is none of your business."

- The woman did not do this.
- The camera rolled on.

■ 10 Life in the Canadian Winter

- For many people, Canadian winter is a dead season.
- It is actually full of life.
- The life is hidden.

- For instance, many insects die.
- They do this in autumn.
- They leave life behind.
- It is in the form of eggs.

- The eggs are on tree bark.
- They are on weeds.
- They are in the ground.

- The eggs will hatch.
- This will happen next spring.
- Millions of crickets will emerge.
- Millions of wasps will emerge.
- Millions of spiders will emerge.

- Woolly caterpillars are different.
- They do not die.
- Instead, they find a piece of wood.
- They attach themselves to it.
- They freeze solid during the winter.

- They will defrost.
- They will crawl away.
- This will happen in the spring.

- Other animals bury themselves alive.
- They do this to avoid winter's cold.

- Frogs dig into the mud.
- Turtles dig into the mud.
- They enter a state of hibernation.

- The pond will freeze.
- The frogs and turtles will be alive.
- They will be waiting for spring.

- Woodchucks go into a sleep too.
- The sleep is deep.
- The sleep is months-long.

- The woodchuck enters its den.
- It rolls into a ball.
- The ball is tight.
- The woodchuck's limbs grow rigid.
- This happens when it is ready to hibernate.

- A woodchuck's heart beats eighty times a minute.
- This happens normally.
- The heart slows to five beats a minute.
- This happens during hibernation.

- Life goes on.
- This happens under the deepest snows.
- This happens in the most bitter cold.

PART FOUR

WRITING
ASSIGNMENTS

INTRODUCTION

Part Four provides a series of writing assignments so that you can apply the sentence skills practised in the earlier parts of the book. Applying these skills *in actual writing* is the surest way to achieve mastery of grammar, mechanics, punctuation, and usage rules. Part Four begins with a brief description of four key steps that will help you write effectively. Most of the assignments that follow ask you to write simple paragraphs in which you support an opening point, also known as a topic sentence. Later assignments give you some practice at writing essays in which you support an overall point, also known as a thesis statement.

Note: Make a special effort to apply the sentence skills you have already learned to each assignment. To help you achieve such a transfer, your instructor may ask you to rewrite a paper as many times as necessary for you to correct a sentence-skills mistake. A writing progress chart on pages 503–504 (in Appendix C) will help track your performance.

WRITING EFFECTIVELY

Here are the steps to follow in order to write effectively.

STEP 1: EXPLORE YOUR TOPIC THROUGH INFORMAL WRITING

First of all, explore the topic you want to write about, or that you have been assigned to write about. You can explore your topic through *informal writing*, which usually means one of three things.

You can *freewrite* about your topic for at least ten minutes. In other words, write for ten minutes whatever comes into your head about your subject. Write without stopping, and without worrying at all about spelling or grammar or the like. Simply get down on paper all the information about the topic that occurs to you.

A second thing you can do is to *make a list of ideas and details* that could go into your paper. Simply pile these items up, one after another, like a shopping list, without worrying about putting them in any special order. Accumulate as many details as you can think of.

A third way to explore your topic is to *write down a series of questions and answers* about the topic. Your questions can start with words like *What*, *Why*, *How*, *When*, and *Where*.

Getting your thoughts and ideas down on paper will help you think more about your topic. With some raw material to look at, you are now in a better position to decide on just how to proceed with the topic.

STEP 2: PLAN YOUR TOPIC WITH AN INFORMAL OUTLINE

After using informal writing to explore what you want to write about, plan your paper using an *informal outline*. Do two things:

- *Decide on and write out the point of your paper.* This opening point is also known as a *topic sentence.*
- *List the supporting reasons that back up your point.* In many cases, you should have at least three supporting reasons. Number them 1, 2, and 3.

Check your reasons carefully. Make sure that each reason truly supports and explains your point. Your outline should be the logical backbone of any paper that you write.

STEP 3: USE TRANSITIONS

Once your outline is worked out, you should have a clear "road map" for writing your paper. As you write the early drafts of your paper, use *transitions* to introduce each of the separate reasons you present to back up your point. For example, you might introduce your first supporting reason with the transitional words "First of all." You might begin your second reason with the words "Another reason." And you might indicate your final reason with the words "Last of all" or "A final reason."

STEP 4: EDIT AND PROOFREAD YOUR PAPER

After you have a solid draft, edit and proofread the paper. Ask yourself four questions to evaluate your paper:

1. Is the paper *unified*? Is all the material in the paper on target in support of the opening point?
2. Is the paper *well supported*? Do I have plenty of specific evidence to back up my opening point?
3. Is the paper *clearly organized*? Does the material proceed in a way that makes sense? Do I use transitions to help connect ideas?
4. Is the paper *well written* in terms of sentence skills? When I read the paper aloud, do the sentences flow smoothly and clearly? Have I checked the paper carefully for sentence-skills mistakes?

A number of writing assignments appear on the pages that follow. Most of them are paragraph assignments. A few closing assignments give you some practice with the five-paragraph essay form as well.

WRITING THE PARAGRAPH

The paragraphs you write for these assignments should consist of about eight to twelve sentences. The point or topic sentence typically should be the first sentence of the paragraph. All the sentences that follow should support or develop the point expressed in the topic sentence.

■ 1 Best or Worst Job

Write a paragraph on the best or worst job you ever had. Provide three reasons why your job was a best or worst one, and provide plenty of details to develop each of your three reasons. Look first at the student paper below, and then do the activity that follows.

BATTERY LOADER

The worst job I ever had was working as a loader in a battery plant near my home. For one thing, the work was physically hard. During a nine-hour shift, I had to lift hundreds of assembled batteries off of a steadily moving production belt and place them onto wooden skids. I once figured that I was lifting over 20,000 kilograms of batteries a shift. Another drawback of the job was that my partner was uncooperative. He had a sixth sense for when the boss was near, and only then would he do a fair share of work. Otherwise, he found so many ways to avoid work that I lifted three batteries to every two that he did. But the worst part of the job was the acid vapour always in the air. The vapour irritated my sinuses and often left me with a headache at the end of a shift. I was afraid that some of the battery chemicals I was inhaling would start building up in my body. I wasted no time, then, in finding another job where I could work in a safer environment.

Activity: Creating an "X-Ray" Outline

Complete the following outline of the paragraph. Summarize in a few words the details that develop each reason, rather than writing the details out in full.

Point: _____

_____

Reason 1: _____

    Details that develop reason 1: _____

_____

_____

Reason 2: _____

    Details that develop reason 2: _____

_____

_____

Reason 3: _____

    Details that develop reason 3: _____

_____

_____

How to Proceed

1   Think of a job that might make a promising topic to write about. Then write about that job for ten minutes or so, getting down on paper all the good and bad details about the job that occur to you. Then ask yourself these questions: "Was this mostly a good job or mostly a bad one? What was the best or worst single feature of the job? Do I have enough details here to write about this job, or should I choose another one?"

2   If the job seems like a promising one to write about, express in a clear, direct sentence exactly what the job was and whether it was the best or worst job you ever had. Do NOT begin by just stating what the job was:

NO: I once worked as a loader in a battery plant near my home.

YES: The worst job I ever had was working as a loader in a battery plant near my home.

Your point: _____

_____

3 Work up a brief outline of the reasons why you liked or disliked the job. Here, for example, is the list prepared by the author of the paper above:

The worst job I ever had was working as a loader in a battery plant near my home.

1. Hard work
2. Unco-operative partner
3. Acid smell in air

4 Use your list as a guide to write the first rough draft of your paper. As you write the draft, try to think of details that will make very clear each of your supporting reasons.

For example, the writer above develops the first reason, "hard work," by stating how many kilograms of batteries he lifted every shift. The writer develops his or her second reason, "uncooperative partner," by telling us how the partner would lift two batteries to every three. The student develops the third reason, "acid smell in air," by explaining that the vapour irritated his or her sinuses and caused a headache.

5 Do not expect to finish your paper in one draft! Writing is a *process*: it happens a step at a time, not all at once. Each step from informal writing (also known as prewriting) to scratch outline to rough draft to second draft brings you a little bit closer to where you want to be. One step helps you go on to the next step. Bit by bit, you move toward your goal: a paper that **makes a point**, **supports the point**, **organizes the support**, and **is well written** in terms of sentence skills.

6 Use transitions to introduce each of your supporting reasons. Here are words to use:

To introduce reason 1: *First of all* or *For one thing*
To introduce reason 2: *Second* or *A second reason* or *Another reason*
To introduce reason 3: *Finally* or *Last of all* or *A final reason*

7 Check the next-to-final draft of your paper for sentence-skills mistakes by reading it aloud. Make sure you are reading exactly what is on the page. If there are rough spots where your writing is hard to read, make the changes needed to ensure that the paper reads smoothly and clearly.

If there are any words whose spelling you are unsure about, check their spellings in a dictionary. You should definitely use a recent large-format dictionary and keep it handy nearby.*

* See the chapter on Dictionary Use, pages 200–208, for specific recommendations on dictionaries and spelling tips.

Finally, use the checklist on the inside back cover of this book to proof-read your paper for specific sentence-skills mistakes.

8   Add a title to the paper. The title should give the reader a quick sense of what your paper is about. It should usually be several words rather than a complete thought.

Be sure to skip a line between the title and the first sentence of your paper. Also, make sure that the first sentence of your paper stands on its own, independent of the title:

NO

	Battery Loader
	I once worked as one in a plant near my home.

(The first sentence depends upon the title to make sense; only by looking at the title do we know what "one" refers to.)

YES

	Battery Loader
	I once worked as a battery loader in a plant near my home.

(The first sentence stands on its own, independent of the title.)

Note: You may find that, if you are accustomed to using a computer regularly, or if your classroom is equipped with computers for use in your writing class, using the computer for all stages of the writing process is enjoyable, quick, and efficient.

1.   When you are brainstorming or listing during the *prewriting* stage, you can easily add, subtract, and move words and phrases on the screen before printing anything. You may find that you are better able to sort out the order of your ideas, and their relationships to each other, as well as the relative importance of one detail compared to another.

2.   During the writing of your initial drafts, the computer allows you to change words, phrases, and their order without creating a "nightmare page" of cross-outs and illegible insertions. *Double space* all your drafts, so that when you print, you can make changes easily. Your instructor will appreciate the double-spacing as well; it's very difficult to add helpful comments when there is no space between the lines of print or writing.

3. The final, and most pleasant, advantage which your computer offers you is the use of spellcheck. You need no longer waste mark deductions for most common spelling errors. The computer cannot fix commonly confused words like "accept" and "except," nor does it understand when you mean "it's," rather than "its": these *you* must master on your own. Occasionally, you may also find the thesaurus on your computer of some use, but be wary of using a substitute word you have never seen before: the results may be unintentionally hilarious—words have many shades of meaning which the thesaurus cannot explain to you. Check any new words in your dictionary.

■ **2 Best or Worst Teacher or Boss**

Write a paragraph about one of the best or worst teachers or bosses you have ever had. Give three reasons why that person was a best or worst one, and provide details to develop each reason. Look first at the short paper below.

MY WORST TEACHER

My grade nine algebra teacher, Mrs. Jamison, was the worst teacher I ever had. First of all, she seemed to know little about algebra. If you asked her a question about something that was not in the book, her answer was, "I'm not going to cover things that are not in the book." At least once every other week, the class had to correct mistakes she made in doing equations on the board. Another reason I disliked Mrs. Jamison is that she favoured the girls in the class. She always excused them for the bathroom, but almost never gave permission for the boys. She spoke to the girls in a friendly tone of voice and would smile or say "Thank you" when they gave an answer. On the other hand, she seldom thanked a boy and seemed to regard us in general with suspicion. Finally, Mrs. Jamison was often late or absent. She would usually come into the class about four minutes after the start of the hour. We had more substitute teachers in her class than in any other—about three times a month. And since she seldom left any work for the substitute teacher to give us, we would just sit there and do nothing until the class ended. I was not surprised to hear that Mrs. Jamison was fired at the end of the school year.

Activity: Creating an "X-Ray" Outline

Complete the following outline of the previous paragraph. Summarize in a few words the details that develop each reason rather than writing the details out in full.

Point: _____

_____

Reason 1: _____

Details that develop reason 1: _____

_____

_____

Reason 2: _____

Details that develop reason 2: _____

_____

_____

Reason 3: _____

Details that develop reason 3: _____

_____

_____

How to Proceed

1   Think of a teacher or boss who might make a promising topic to write about. Then make up a list of all the large and small reasons you like or dislike that teacher or boss.

2   Now express in a clear, direct sentence exactly who the teacher or boss was and that he or she was a best or worst teacher or boss. Do NOT begin by just stating who the teacher or boss was:

NO: My grade nine algebra teacher was Mrs. Jamison.

YES: My grade nine algebra teacher, Mrs. Jamison, was the worst teacher I ever had.

Your point: _____

_____

3   Work up a brief outline of the reasons why you liked or disliked the teacher or boss. Here, for example, is the list prepared by the author of the paper above:

My grade nine algebra teacher, Mrs. Jamison, was the worst teacher I ever had.

1.   Didn't know her subject
2.   Favoured the girls
3.   Often late or absent

4 Use your list as a guide to write the first rough draft of your paper. As you write the draft, try to think of details that will make very clear each of your supporting reasons.

For example, the writer above develops his first reason, "didn't know her subject," by telling us about her unwillingness to go outside the book and about her mistakes in class. He develops his second reason, "favoured the girls," by telling us just how she treated the boys differently from the girls. He develops his third reason, "often late or absent," by explaining just how late she came to class and how often substitute teachers were used.

5 Do not expect to finish your paper in one draft! Writing is a *process*: it happens a step at a time, not all at once. Each step from informal writing (also known as prewriting) to scratch outline to rough draft to second draft brings you a little bit closer to where you want to be. One step helps you go on to the next step. Bit by bit, you move toward your goal: a paper that makes a point, supports the point, organizes the support, and is well written in terms of sentence skills.

6 Use transitions to introduce each of your supporting reasons. Here are words to use:

To introduce reason 1: *First of all* or *For one thing*
To introduce reason 2: *Second* or *A second reason* or *Another reason*
To introduce reason 3: *Finally* or *Last of all* or *A final reason*

7 Check the next-to-final draft of your paper for sentence-skills mistakes by reading it aloud. Make sure you are reading exactly what is on the page. If there are rough spots where your writing is hard to read, make the changes needed to ensure that the paper reads smoothly and clearly.

If there are any words whose spelling you are unsure about, check their spellings in a dictionary. You should definitely use a recent large-format dictionary and keep it handy nearby.

Finally, use the checklist on the inside back cover of this book to proofread your paper for specific sentence-skills mistakes.

8 Add a title to the paper. The title should give the reader a quick sense of what your paper is about. It should usually be several words rather than a complete thought. (As a general rule, your title should be no longer than five words.)

Be sure to skip a line between the title and the first sentence of your paper. Also, make sure that the first sentence of your paper stands on its own, independent of the title:

NO

	My Worst Teacher
	This was my grade nine algebra teacher, Mrs. Jamison.

(The first sentence depends upon the title to make sense; only by looking at the title do we know what "This" refers to.)

YES

	My Worst Teacher
	My grade nine algebra teacher, Mrs. Jamison, was the
	worst teacher I ever had.

(The first sentence stands on its own, independent of the title.)

■ 3 Living Where You Do

Do you share an apartment or a dorm? Do you live with your parents or another family member? Do you own your own home? Write a paragraph about three separate advantages or disadvantages of living in the place where you do.

1 First of all, do the activity that follows:

Activity: Making an Outline

Prepare the following outline of the paragraph. (You may want to use scratch paper first as you think on paper about how you might develop the outline.)

Decide on your point from among the choices given. For example, you may decide to write on the disadvantages of living at home.

At the same time, decide on the three reasons you can use to support the point.

Then summarize in a few words the details that develop each reason, rather than writing the details out in full.

Point: There are several advantages (*or* disadvantages) of (sharing an apartment *or* living in a dorm *or* living at home with my family *or* owning my own home).

Reason 1: _____

Details that develop reason 1: _____

_____

_____

Reason 2: _____

Details that develop reason 2: _____

_____

_____

Reason 3: _____

Details that develop reason 3: _____

_____

_____

2 Use your outline as a guide to write the first rough draft of your paper. As you write the draft, try to think of details that will make very clear each of your supporting reasons.

3 Do not expect to finish your paper in one draft! Writing is a *process*: it happens a step at a time, not all at once. Each step from informal writing (also known as prewriting) to scratch outline to rough draft to second draft brings you a little bit closer to where you want to be. One step helps you go on to the next step. Bit by bit, you move toward your goal: a paper that makes a point, supports the point, organizes the support, and is well written in terms of sentence skills.

4 Use transitions to introduce each of your supporting reasons. Here are words to use:

To introduce reason 1: *First of all* or *For one thing*
To introduce reason 2: *Second* or *A second reason* or *Another reason*
To introduce reason 3: *Finally* or *Last of all* or *A final reason*

5 Check the next-to-final draft of your paper for sentence-skills mistakes by reading it aloud. Make sure you are reading exactly what is on the page. If there are rough spots where your writing is hard to read, make the changes needed to ensure that the paper reads smoothly and clearly.

If there are any words whose spelling you are unsure about, check their spellings in a dictionary. You should definitely use a recent large-format dictionary and keep it handy nearby.

Finally, use the checklist on the inside back cover of this book to proofread your paper for specific sentence-skills mistakes.

6 Add a title to the paper. The title should give the reader a quick sense of what your paper is about. It should usually be several words rather than a complete thought. (As a general rule, your title should be no longer than five words.)

Be sure to skip a line between the title and the first sentence of your paper. Also, make sure that the first sentence of your paper stands on its own, independent of the title:

NO

	Advantages of Living at Home
	There are several advantages.

(The first sentence depends upon the title to make sense; only by looking at the title do we know what the "several advantages" refer to.)

YES

	Advantages of Living at Home
	There are several advantages to living at home.

(The first sentence stands on its own, independently of the title.)

■ 4 Owning a Car or Using Public Transportation

Write a paragraph about three separate advantages or disadvantages of your car, or of the public transportation you use to get around.

1 First of all, do the activity that follows:

Activity

Prepare the following outline of the paragraph. (You may want to use scratch paper first as you think on paper about how you might develop the outline.) Decide on your point. At the same time, decide on the three reasons you can use to support the point. Then summarize in a few words the details that develop each reason, rather than writing the details out in full.

Point: There are several advantages (*or* disadvantages) of (my car *or* of using public transportation in my town or city).

Reason 1: _____

   Details that develop reason 1: _____

_____

_____

Reason 2: _____

   Details that develop reason 2: _____

_____

_____

Reason 3: _____

   Details that develop reason 3: _____

_____

_____

2 Use your list as a guide to write the first rough draft of your paper. As you write the draft, try to think of details that will make very clear each of your supporting reasons.

3 Do not expect to finish your paper in one draft! Writing is a *process*: it happens a step at a time, not all at once. Each step from informal writing (also known as prewriting) to informal outline to rough draft to second draft brings you a little bit closer to where you want to be. One step helps you go on to the next step. Bit by bit, you move toward your goal: a paper that makes a point, supports the point, organizes the support, and is well written in terms of sentence skills.

4 Use transitions to introduce each of your supporting reasons. Here are words to use:

To introduce reason 1: *First of all* or *For one thing*
To introduce reason 2: *Second* or *A second reason* or *Another reason*
To introduce reason 3: *Finally* or *Last of all* or *A final reason*

5 Check the next-to-final draft of your paper for sentence-skills mistakes by reading it aloud. Make sure you are reading exactly what is on the page. If there are rough spots where your writing is hard to read, make the changes needed to ensure that the paper reads smoothly and clearly.

    If there are any words whose spelling you are unsure about, check their spellings in a dictionary. You should definitely use a recent large-format dictionary and keep it handy nearby. If you are writing your draft on the computer, run spellcheck on the final draft of your document.

Finally, use the checklist on the inside back cover of this book to proof-read your paper for specific sentence-skills mistakes.

6   Add a title to the paper. The title should give the reader a quick sense of what your paper is about. It should usually be several words rather than a complete thought. (As a general rule, your title should be no longer than five words.)

Be sure to skip a line between the title and the first sentence of your paper. Also, make sure that the first sentence of your paper stands on its own, independent of the title, as illustrated in the previous assignments.

■ 5   Quality of Some Person or Relative

Write a paragraph about one quality of a parent or step-parent, or other member of your family (a brother, sister, uncle, aunt, cousin). Below are some qualities you might consider:

self-centred	trustworthy
other-directed	unreliable
generous	neat
stingy	sloppy
hard-working	honest
lazy	dishonest

The quality you focus on might be one of the above, or any other specific quality.

How to Proceed

1   Decide on and write out the topic sentence of your paper. In the sentence, include the name of the person you want to write about, your relationship to that person, and the specific quality you are focusing on. State your topic (person), your connection to the topic, and your point of view. For example:

My brother Randy is the laziest student I have ever known.

Dolly is an aggressive cousin I know at work.

My sister Vanessa has always been self-centred.

My father, Phil, has always been an even-tempered person.

Write your topic sentence here: _____

_____

2   Make a list of examples that will support your topic sentence. For instance, ask yourself, "What are specific times when Randy really showed what a lazy person he is?" Then write down all the times that you can think of that your brother Randy showed himself to be a lazy person. You may want to freewrite a bit—for ten minutes or so, just write down everything you can think of about that quality in a person without worrying about spelling or grammar or the like.

If you cannot think of enough specific examples that will really *show* readers how lazy Randy is, then you may want to write about another quality. Remember that it is not enough to simply *tell* your reader that a certain person is lazy (or hard-working or impatient or ambitious or whatever). Instead, you must give readers supporting details so that they can *see for themselves* the quality you are writing about. You must provide your readers with the **evidence needed to prove your point** about the person.

3   If you think you have enough material, prepare a scratch outline of your paragraph. Perhaps you will have three examples that show what a lazy person Randy is. Decide which example you will present first, which you will describe second, and which example you will close with. Always close with the strongest and most dramatic example.

4   Use your scratch outline as a guide to write the first rough draft of your paper. As you write, try to think of additional details that will support your topic sentence.

5   Be sure to use transitions as you develop your paper:

One example of Randy's laziness is …
Another instance …
The final and best example of how lazy my brother is …

6   Check the next-to-final draft of your paper for sentence-skills mistakes by reading it aloud. Make sure you are reading exactly what is on the page. If there are rough spots where your writing is hard to read, make the changes needed to ensure that the paper reads smoothly and clearly.

If there are any words whose spelling you are unsure about, check their spellings in a dictionary, or run spellcheck over your document. You should definitely use a recent large-format dictionary and keep it handy nearby.

Finally, use the checklist on the inside back cover of this book to proofread your paper for specific sentence-skills mistakes.

7   Add a title to the paper. The title should give the reader a quick sense of what your paper is about. It should be several words that do at least two things: 1) state the quality (point of view) you are writing about; 2) give the name of the person (topic) you are writing about or your relationship to the person or both.

Here are possible titles for the four sample topic sentences shown above:

My Lazy Brother
An Aggressive Cousin
Self-Centred Vanessa
An Even-Tempered Father

Be sure to skip a line between the title and the first sentence of your paper. Also, make sure that the first sentence of your paper stands on its own, independent of the title, as illustrated in the previous assignments.

■ 6 Writing about an Emotional Experience

Write a paragraph about a time in which you experienced a certain emotion. The emotion might be one of the following, or some other:

disappointment	anger
relief	jealousy
nervousness	rejection
sympathy	sadness
happiness	regret
frustration	surprise
fear	pride

How to Proceed

1 Think of an experience or event in your life in which you felt a certain emotion strongly. Then spend ten minutes freewriting about the experience. Don't worry about spelling or grammar or putting things in the right order. Instead, just try to get down all the details you can think of that may be related to the experience.

2 This preliminary writing will help you decide whether your topic is promising enough to develop further. If it is not, choose another emotion. If it is, do two things:

    a **First**, write out your topic sentence, underlining the emotion you want to focus on. For example:

The time I witnessed a robbery was the <u>most frightening</u> moment of my life.

Taking my driver's test made me <u>more nervous</u> than almost any other experience I can remember.

One of the <u>happiest</u> moments of my life was winning an award in high school.

I had a date several years ago that resulted in an <u>embarrassing</u> moment.

    b **Second**, make up a list of all the details involved in the experience. Then prepare a scratch outline in which you arrange these details in time order. *Time order* simply means that details are listed as they occur in time. *First* this happened; *next* this; *then* this; *after* that, this; and so on. Here is a list of time words that you can use:

        first, then, next, after, as, before, while, during, now, finally

3   Write the first rough draft of your paper. Be sure to use time words to connect details as you move from the beginning to the middle to the end of your story.

Do not expect to finish your paper in one draft. Remember that writing is a *process*: it happens a step at a time, not all at once. Each step from freewriting to list to scratch outline to rough draft to second draft brings you a little bit closer to where you want to be. One step helps you go on to the next step. Bit by bit, you move toward your goal of a finished paper.

4   Check the next-to-final draft of your paper for sentence-skills mistakes by reading it aloud. Make sure you are reading exactly what is on the page. If there are rough spots where your writing is hard to read, make the changes needed to ensure that the paper reads smoothly and clearly.

If there are any words whose spelling you are unsure about, check their spellings in a dictionary, or run spellcheck over your document. You should definitely use a recent large-format dictionary and keep it handy nearby.

Finally, use the checklist on the inside back cover of this book to proofread your paper for specific sentence-skills mistakes.

5   Add a title to the paper. The title should give the reader a quick sense of what your paper is about. It should be several words that state the emotion you are writing about.

Here are possible titles for the four sample topic sentences shown above:

A Frightening Moment

A Nervous Time

A Happy Moment

An Embarrassing Moment

Be sure to skip a line between the title and the first sentence of your paper. Also, make sure that the first sentence of your paper stands on its own, independent of the title, as illustrated in the previous assignments.

■ 7 Describing a Process

Many everyday activities are processes—that is, a series of steps carried out in a definite order. Most of these processes are familiar and automatic; for example, getting dressed, preparing breakfast, or travelling to work or school. We are therefore seldom aware of the steps that make up each activity.

The purpose of this assignment will be to write a paragraph in which all of the steps in a particular process are clearly explained. Write a set of specific instructions on *one* of the following two processes:

■   The steps involved in performing your job effectively. If you are working, imagine that your boss has asked you to write a job description. Detail, a step at a time, the sequence of tasks that you must perform in the course of a typical day on the job.

■ Specific instructions on how to get from your writing classroom to your house. Imagine you are giving these instructions to a stranger who has just come into the room and who wants to deliver a million dollars to your home. You want, naturally, to give *exact* directions, including various landmarks that may guide the way, for the stranger does not know the area.

How to Proceed

1 Write your topic sentence. For example:

There are a series of tasks that a server must carry out during a typical day of work at Larry's Lobster Lounge.

Here is how to get from the Writing Centre at Seneca College, Newnham Campus, to my home at 293 Avondale Avenue, North York, Ontario.

2 Freewrite for at least ten minutes on your topic. Write without stopping and without worrying about spelling or grammar about all the details you can think of that might go into your paper.

Your freewriting gives you a good start; it gets some raw material down on paper. Now, using your freewriting as a base, make up a list of all the different steps you can think of that are part of the process. After completing your list, look it over and then number your items in time order.

3 Use your list as a guide to write the first rough draft of your paper. As you write, try to think of additional details that will support your opening sentence. Don't expect to finish your paper in one draft. You should, in fact, be ready to write at least several drafts.

4 As you develop your paper, use time words like *first*, *then*, *next*, *now*, *during*, *after*, and *finally* to help the reader follow clearly as you move from one step to the next.

5 Check the next-to-final draft of your paper for sentence-skills mistakes by reading it aloud. Make sure you are reading exactly what is on the page. If there are rough spots where your writing is hard to read, make the changes needed to ensure that the paper reads smoothly and clearly.

If there are any words whose spelling you are unsure about, check their spellings in a dictionary, or run spellcheck over your document. You should definitely use a recent large-format dictionary and keep it handy nearby.

Add a title to the paper: several words that give the reader a quick sense of what your paper is about.

Finally, use the checklist on the inside back cover of this book to proof-read your paper for specific sentence-skills mistakes.

■ 8   Examining Causes

Why did Vanessa drop the course? What caused Patrick to start up his own business? Why are jobs so scarce in our town? How has divorce affected Bonnie? Every day we ask questions similar to these and look for answers. We realize that many actions do not take place without causes. By examining the reasons for an action, we seek to understand and explain things that happen in our lives.

How to Proceed

1   In this paragraph, you will analyze the reasons for a certain attitude or behaviour. Read the following topic sentences, and then on separate paper prepare scratch outlines for *two* of them.

There are several reasons why I have stopped smoking.

My relationship with _____ (name a relative or friend) is a good one (*or* not a good one) for several reasons.

Television is a bad influence on my life for several reasons.

There are several causes for my not doing well in high school.

Because of certain things that have happened to me, I am here in college at this time.

People enjoy (*or* do not enjoy) eating at _____ (name a particular dining place) for several reasons.

Probably several factors account for my being (*or* not being) a good reader.

There are several reasons my child is doing well (*or* not doing well) in school.

2   Now choose the scratch outline that you think is most promising to develop. That outline should have *three separate reasons* that back up the point, and *good potential details* to support each of the three reasons. Develop your scratch outline by doing the activity that follows.

Activity: Creating a Formal Outline

Complete the following outline of the paragraph. Summarize in a few words the details that you think can develop each reason, rather than writing the details out in full.

Point: _____

_____

Reason 1: _____

    Details that develop reason 1: _____

_____

_____

Reason 2: _____

    Details that develop reason 2: _____

_____

_____

Reason 3: _____

    Details that develop reason 3: _____

_____

_____

3 Use your outline as a guide to write the first rough draft of your paper. As you write the draft, concentrate on providing good details that will make very clear each of your supporting reasons.

4 Use transitions to introduce each of your supporting reasons. Here are words to use:

To introduce reason 1: *First of all* or *For one thing*

To introduce reason 2: *Second* or *A second reason* or *Another reason*

To introduce reason 3: *Finally* or *Last of all* or *A final reason*

5 Check the next-to-final draft of your paper for sentence-skills mistakes by reading it aloud. Make sure you are reading exactly what is on the page. If there are rough spots where your writing is hard to read, make the changes needed to ensure that the paper reads smoothly and clearly.

If there are any words whose spelling you are unsure about, check their spellings in a dictionary, or run spellcheck over your document. You should definitely use a recent large-format dictionary and keep it handy nearby.

Add a title to the paper: several words that give the reader a quick sense of what your paper is about.

Finally, use the checklist on the inside back cover of this book to proof-read your paper for specific sentence-skills mistakes.

■ 9 Three Paragraph Topics: Personal

Using what you have learned from the previous assignments about how to write effectively, write a paragraph on any one of the following topics:

■ How you take care (*or* don't take care) of yourself physically
■ Times you get nervous
■ A quality or habit that helps make you unique

Be sure to begin with a topic sentence that states what your paragraph will be about. For example:

■ I neglect my health and mistreat my body in several ways.
■ There are three different times I always feel nervous.
■ One quality that makes me unique is that I am a house-cleaning fanatic.

Be sure to provide enough details to develop and support your topic sentence. And after reading your paper aloud for smoothness and clarity, use the checklist on the inside back cover of this book when proofreading your paper for sentence-skills mistakes.

■ 10 Three Paragraph Topics: Persuasive

Using what you have learned from the previous assignments about how to write effectively, write a paragraph on any one of the following topics:

■ Why all family members should share household chores
■ Why students should be given evaluations instead of grades
■ Why spring (or summer, winter, or fall) is the best season of the year

Begin with a topic sentence that states what your paragraph will be about, that answers "why" to any of these statements. Then provide at least three reasons that support your topic sentence. Use word signals such as *first of all*, *second*, and *finally* to introduce each reason. And after reading your paper aloud for smoothness and clarity, use the checklist on the inside back cover of this book when proofreading your paper for sentence-skills mistakes.

■ 11 Writing a Paragraph Summary: I

Making a summary is an excellent way to improve your writing and reading skills. To summarize a selection, you must first read it carefully. Only after you understand fully and clearly what is being said can you reduce a selection to a few sentences. For this assignment, you will be asked to read a selection titled

"Keys to College Success" (on pages 447–449) and condense it to 100 to 125 words. Here are the reading and writing steps you should take to do an effective summary.

Steps to Follow in Summarizing

1   Take a few minutes to preview the work. You can preview an article by taking a quick look at the following:

   a   *Title:* The title often summarizes what the article is about. Think about the title and how it may condense the meaning of an article.

   b   *Subtitle:* A subtitle or caption, if given, consists of words in special print appearing under or next to the title. Such words often summarize the article or provide a quick insight into its meaning.

   c   *First and last paragraphs:* In the first paragraphs, the author may introduce you to the subject and state the purpose of the article. In the last paragraphs, the author may present conclusions or a summary. These previews or summaries can give you a quick overview of what the entire article is about.

2   Read the article for all you can understand the first time through. Don't slow down or turn back. Look for general statements and for details or examples that support those statements. Mark off what appear to be the main points and key supporting details.

3   Go back and reread more carefully the areas you have identified as most important. Also, focus on other key points you may have missed in your first reading.

4   Take notes on the material. After you have formulated what you think is the main idea of the selection, ask yourself the question, "Does all or most of the material in the article support the idea in this statement?" If it does, you have probably identified the main idea. Write it out in a sentence. Then write down the main supporting details for that idea.

5   Remember these points when working on the drafts of your summary:

   a   Express the main idea and supporting ideas **in your own words**. Do not imitate or stay too close to the style of the original work.

   b   Don't write an overly detailed summary. Your goal is **a single paragraph** not less than 100 words and not more than 125 words in length.

   c   **Preserve the balance and proportion of the original work.** If the original devoted 70 per cent of its space to one idea and only 30 per cent to another, your summary should reflect that emphasis.

   d   Use the checklist on the inside back cover of this book to proofread your summary for sentence-skills mistakes, including spelling.

KEYS TO COLLEGE SUCCESS

At the start of Erica's first semester in college, one of her professors handed out a test schedule on the first day of class. The schedule showed that a one-hour exam would be given on October 2—the first test in the course. Erica scanned the sheet, stuck it in one of her textbooks, and promptly forgot about it. She assumed that the professor would give the class several reminders about the test and that he would go over the materials the students needed to know. As time went by, and nothing was said about the test, she assumed the professor had changed his mind. On October 2, Erica received a rude awakening in the form of five closely typed sheets of paper containing fifty tough questions on the assigned readings and on the lectures the professor had given. Erica was in shock. "How could he give us a test without reminding us?" she thought. "It's not fair to announce a test four weeks in advance and expect us to remember the date and study for the test on our own!" Erica was outraged. She didn't do well on the test, to put it kindly.

During that year, Erica learned other shocking things in college, many of them having to do with taking on responsibility without being prompted or reminded. Erica's experiences are similar to those of many other college students. Such students never acquire the necessary keys to college success.

Control Your Time

The first key to succeeding in college is taking control of your time. This means *knowing* what you have to do and *planning* ahead for classes, projects, and tests. One important means of time control is using a large monthly calendar to give you an "at-a-glance" view of due dates and other special events. Keeping the calendar in a place where you will see it often can prevent you from losing track of time and being surprised by the nearness of your term paper due date or biology midterm. Another means of time control is making up a weekly study schedule. In other words, plan specific blocks of time during your week when you will study. In making a weekly schedule, first fill in the hours when you have unbreakable commitments to class time, work time, and so on. Then look for chunks of free time—at least one hour long—that you can use for studying. A study schedule can help you make efficient use of your time by capturing those free hours that would otherwise drift away, leaving you wondering why you accomplished so little. A final method of time control is a "to-do" list. On a "to-do" list, you jot down the goals you want to accomplish during the day, or over the next several days. Such a list might contain reminders on everything from buying a CD to reading Chapter 3 of your psychology text. A "to-do" list brings together all the stray "I have to …" ideas that cross your mind each day. Crossing items off a "to-do" list can give you a real feeling of satisfaction. You also have the pleasant sensation that you are controlling your tasks and responsibilities, not the other way around.

Get Off to a Strong Start

Making a strong start at the beginning of each new semester is another key to college success. Wasting time at the start of the term and then trying to play "catch-up" is a sure route to failure in college. Making a strong start means being disciplined enough to study, read, and initiate time-control measures even though "It's only the first week" or "I don't have a test for three weeks." You have to go prepared to those first classes by being ready to take notes. You should buy your books right away, despite the long line at the bookstore. In addition, you should find out the names and phone numbers of one or two people in each class so you can borrow their notes if you miss class. Another part of making a strong start is giving some thought to those end-of-the-semester papers and projects, even if December or May seems incredibly far away. It takes additional energy to do some early research in the library, and it takes some initiative to discuss a term paper idea early on with a professor, but getting off to a quick start has important benefits. You space out your work, for one thing, so that you don't face a marathon week of putting together a project or paper. And you relieve the psychological pressure you feel when you put off tasks until the job seems overwhelming.

Apply Study Skills

A third key to success in college is to brush up on—or learn—study skills. Study skills include knowing how to take class notes; how to read texts skilfully by previewing, marking, and taking notes on them; and how to study for objective or essay exams. Without these vital skills, the time you spend attending class and studying may be of little help in earning a good grade. Just as you have to learn new skills on a job, you have to learn the skills needed to do well in college. Some students know these skills by the time they arrive on a college campus—they may have been taught them in high school or "picked them up" on their own. Other students slide by in high school without knowing these skills and, because they have grade twelve or an OAC, feel they are equipped for college. They aren't. College lectures cover more information, and with more sophistication, than high school lectures. College textbooks are harder to read; they bristle with dozens of new terms and present difficult theories and concepts. College tests are tougher, and they are graded according to higher standards. Only a firm grasp of study skills will enable you to survive, and succeed, in this setting. If you feel that your study skills are weak, get help immediately. Most colleges have study-skills workshops or courses, so take advantage of them. Campus learning or tutoring centres often have guides to college study skills free for the asking. And campus bookstores carry many books that can help you learn and practise essential study and reading skills.

Learn to Concentrate

A final key to college success is learning the art of concentration. This ability seems to get more difficult every year; television rarely challenges its viewers to watch anything that requires concentration or to give a subject more than ten minutes' worth of attention at a time. And much of the reading we do in daily life requires less concentration than ever: newspapers specialize in brief stories with limited vocabularies and many colour pictures; books on the best-seller list are filled with cartoons, jokes, and diagrams of exercise techniques. Switching from this kind of mental fluff to the intense concentration needed to study college material is indeed a challenge.

You can take several steps to improve your concentration. If your ability to concentrate is "flabby," these moves will get you into shape. First, have a positive attitude toward studying. No matter how unattractive your task seems, think of it as a means to a goal that is important to you—getting a college degree. Next, keep yourself in good physical shape. Exhaustion or illness effectively shuts down your ability to concentrate. Also, create a good study environment. Have a place in your dorm room, apartment, or house where you keep all your class-related materials and where you have the basics for a productive study session: a good light, paper, pens, your computer, a calculator, and so on. You will save yourself time if your setting is well-equipped, and your concentration will not be interrupted because you have to find a note pad. Before you begin to study, jot down a brief list of goals for the study session. For example, you might write: "(1) Read Chapter 10 in soc., (2) Memorize definitions for chemistry, (3) Rough draft of English essay." Having specific, doable goals can make the session less intimidating. Finally, keep control of your ability to concentrate by *noticing* when your mind wanders and the conscious effort needed to pull it back. This can be done as simply as making a check mark with a pencil whenever you find your mind losing concentration. The deliberate effort to begin concentrating again should strengthen your ability and make concentration for longer periods possible.

Knowing how to take control of your time, making a strong start at the beginning of each semester, practising study skills, and concentrating effectively are the four keys to success in school. If you make the effort to use these keys, you will open the door to the kind of life you want.

■ **12   Writing a Paragraph Summary: II**

Obtain a copy of *Maclean's* or *Time* that is no more than three months old. Write a summary of a cover story in either magazine. Follow the guidelines given in the previous assignment. Attach a copy of the article to the summary before turning it in to your instructor.

Writing the Essay

You will probably be asked in college to write papers of several paragraphs that support a single point. The central idea or point developed in a several-paragraph essay is called a *thesis statement*, rather than, as in a paragraph, a *topic sentence*. The thesis statement appears in the introductory paragraph, and specific support for the thesis statement appears in the paragraphs that follow.

Read through the clearly organized student essay that follows, and then look at the comments on pages 451–452.

BUYING A HOUSE TODAY

Introductory paragraph

      In Canada in the late 1990s, it is easier than ever for singles and couples to buy their first home. This is a delightful discovery my partner and I made when we decided we wanted to stop paying rent, build up some equity, and establish a more settled life for ourselves. After visiting the bank we had been dealing with for two years, we learned three facts that helped us become home-owners: interest rates on mortgages were at an all-time low, that first-time buyers were offered appealing incentives, and that we could even make tax savings with a registered home-owners' savings plan.

First supporting paragraph

      The first fact that "hit home" for us was that all those news items we had been hearing on the news and reading in the papers about the reviving federal and provincial economies had more bearing on us than we had realized. Interest rates on mortgages and lines of credit were the lowest they'd been in years. For us, this meant that, even with the very low down-payment we could muster, the monthly payments on a $100,000 mortgage stretched over twenty years, would not be much more than the rent we were paying. For us, after working hard, and continuing to work while in college, the feeling that we could be building our future was very important.

Second supporting paragraph

      The next discovery we made occurred when we saw what builders were offering at some of the housing developments that we had driven by. We'd read their billboards, but never realized we could take advantage of the incentives and deals these builders were offering. Down-payments required on some town-houses were so low that, with what we'd saved, and a few thousand from the line of credit the bank offered us as first-time buyers, we were able to put down almost twenty per cent of the total cost of our "dream home." Other surprises that came with our purchase were items we'd thought of as luxuries we would have to wait for. Our town-house came equipped with carpeting, kitchen appliances, and a fire-place. We could live more comfortably than we had ever dreamed.

Third supporting paragraph

      Our last, and least expected surprise came in the form of income tax breaks. Our province has a plan for people wanting to buy a first home, designed so that they can keep their savings in a special registered account, whose contents can be deducted from their taxable income. For us, this was a real advantage, since, as full-time students working at part-time jobs, we would be getting a larger tax return, which would add to our temporarily slim cash-flow next spring. In the past, with both of us working, we had not been able to take advantage of any tax deductions available to us, and ended up trying to save money and having to pay extra income tax at the same time. Now, while we spent nearly a year looking for that "perfect home," we really made our savings work for us. For once, we *could* believe what we read in the papers, and take advantage of the improvements in the Canadian economy.

Concluding paragraph

      We had always thought, like our parents, that we would have to wait, finish college, and get firm footings in our careers before we could ever think of buying a house. Hoping that eventually we could stop pouring rent-money "out the window," we had tried to keep putting money aside, but we hadn't thought we could make our dreams a reality by paying attention to the news, changes in banks' offerings, and tax laws, and seeing their relevance to us. In a few months, we will be living in our "dream home," and building our own futures.

Comments: The essay begins with an *introductory paragraph* that attracts the reader's interest. The thesis statement is clear: "This is a delightful discovery that my partner and I made when we decided we wanted to stop paying rent, build up some equity, and establish a more settled life for ourselves." The final sentence of the paragraph outlines a plan of development, a preview of the major points that will support and explain the thesis and opening statement: "... we learned three things that helped us become home-owners: interest rates on mortgages were at an all-time low, that first-time buyers were offered appealing incentives, and that we could even make tax savings ..."

The *second paragraph* presents the first supporting point, or topic sentence ("The first fact. ... was that all those news items ... about the reviving federal and provincial economies had more bearing on us than we realized."), and specific details of the couple's experiences that give evidence for that point.

The *third paragraph* presents the second supporting point ("The next discovery we made occurred when we saw what builders were offering at some of the housing developments ...") and specific evidence for the writer's second point.

The *fourth paragraph* offers the third supporting point ("Our last, and least expected surprise came in the form of income tax breaks.") and backs up this point with specific information explaining and supporting this point.

The *concluding paragraph* restates, in its final two sentences, the main point of the paper, and offers a parting thought in its first sentence.

■ 13   Providing Reasons or Examples

Write an essay in which you provide reasons or examples to support a thesis statement. Listed below are several thesis statements, any one of which you might develop into an essay. Choose one of the statements and fill in three reasons or examples you can use to support it. Then check your work by answering the questions that follow.

There are several reasons why I have decided to come to school.

There are several reasons why the _____ won (*or* lost) their league championship.

There are three ways my town or city could be made a safer place in which to live.

Students who work at the same time they are going to school face special difficulties in their lives.

Several people in my life have helped me appreciate the meaning of courage.

Your thesis: _____

_____

Support 1: _____

Support 2: _____

Support 3: _____

Take your time with the outline. Check its logic by seeing if you can answer *yes* to the following questions:

a Does each of my three reasons or examples truly support the thesis statement?

b Can I back up each of my three reasons or examples with good supporting details?

Be prepared to do some plain hard thinking to come up with a strong outline. The outline is probably the most important single step you can take in writing an effective paper.

Now write your paper, taking it through the three or four drafts that may be necessary to complete it satisfactorily. Use the checklist on the inside back cover of this book to proofread the paper for sentence-skills mistakes, including spelling.

■ 14 Self-Analysis

Many people use New Year's Day as the occasion for declaring to themselves changes they would like to make in their lives. Probably at any time of the year, most of us could think of three qualities or habits that we would be better off without. Write an essay in which you describe three things you would like to change in yourself. One student who did such a paper used as his thesis the following statement: "There are three flaws in my character—laziness, jealousy, and impatience—that have created some difficult times in my life in the past few months."

Use the five-part structure of introduction, three supporting paragraphs, and a conclusion. And refer to the checklist of sentence skills on the inside back cover when proofreading your paper for sentence-skills mistakes.

■ 15 A Letter of Praise or Criticism

Most of us watch at least some television, and we can all name certain shows we find especially enjoyable or offensive. Write a letter to one of the major television networks in which you compliment or criticize a particular show. Don't just say you like or dislike the show. Instead, give two or three detailed reasons that support your feelings either way.

Your letter should have the essay form already discussed—an introduction, a paragraph for each supporting reason, and a conclusion. It should use a standard address format and should begin with the salutation *Dear Sir or Madam*. Use the checklist on the inside back cover to proofread your letter carefully for sentence-skills mistakes.

The networks are sensitive to thoughtful letters from viewers. Your letter, if carefully constructed and neatly written, is almost sure to get a reply.

Here's where to send your letter:

Canadian Broadcasting Corporation, Box 500, Station A, Toronto, ON M5W 1E6

CTV Television Network Ltd., 250 Yonge Street, Toronto, ON M5B 2N8

CanWest Global System, 81 Barber Greene Road, Toronto, ON M3C 2A2

Capital Cities/ABC, 24 East 51st Street, New York, NY 10022

CBS, 51 West 52d Street, New York, NY 10019

NBC, 30 Rockefeller Plaza, New York, NY 10020

PBS, 475 L'Enfant Plaza West, S.W., Washington, D.C. 20024

APPENDIXES

INTRODUCTION

Three appendixes follow. Appendix A consists of diagnostic and achievement tests that measure many of the skills in this book. Appendix B supplies answers to the introductory projects and the practice exercises in Part One. The answers, which should be referred to only after you have worked carefully through each exercise, give you responsibility for testing yourself. (To ensure that the answer key is used as a learning tool only, answers are *not* given for the review tests in Part One or for the reinforcement tests in Part Two. These answers appear only in the Instructor's Manual, where they can be copied and handed out at the discretion of your teacher.) Finally, Appendix C contains a series of handy progress charts that you can use to track your performance on all the tests in the book and the writing assignments as well.

DIAGNOSTIC AND ACHIEVEMENT TESTS

SENTENCE-SKILLS DIAGNOSTIC TEST

Part 1

This test will help check your knowledge of a number of sentence skills. In each item below, certain words are underlined. Place an *X* in the answer space if you think a mistake appears at the underlined part. Place a *C* in the answer space if you think the underlined part is correct.

A series of headings ("Sentence Fragments," "Run-Ons," and so on) will give you clues to the mistakes to look for. However, you do not have to understand the heading to find a mistake. What you are checking is your own sense of effective written English.

Sentence Fragments

_____ 1. After I had done fifty push-ups. I felt like a worn-out rubber band. I wasn't planning to move until the middle of next week.

_____ 2. My little brother loves to go out at night, especially when the moon is full. My sister is convinced he's a werewolf.

_____ 3. Cecile stood on tiptoe and craned her neck. Trying to see over the heads of the people in front of her. Finally she decided to go watch the parade on television.

_____ 4. Lisa was excited about the job interview. She decided to have her hair cut. And bought a new briefcase so she would look like an executive.

Run-Ons

_____   5. The teacher assigned two chapters of the <u>book, he</u> also handed out a library research project.

_____   6. Something was obviously bothering <u>Maria a</u> small muscle in her temple was throbbing.

_____   7. The tires on my Chevy are <u>worn, but</u> the car itself is in good condition.

_____   8. I could afford the monthly car <u>payments, I</u> did not have enough money to pay for insurance as well.

Standard English Verbs

_____   9. Aunt Joan <u>sees</u> much better when she puts on her bifocals.

_____   10. The game was lost when the other team <u>score</u> a fourth-quarter touchdown.

_____   11. At the end of the hike, we <u>was</u> covered with mosquito bites.

_____   12. Donna <u>have</u> only three more courses to take to earn her diploma.

Irregular Verbs

_____   13. That show must be a rerun; I <u>seen</u> it at least twice.

_____   14. If I had <u>taken</u> more notes in that class, I would have done better on the exam.

_____   15. I accidentally <u>throwed</u> away the parking ticket when I cleaned out the glove compartment of my car.

_____   16. At the end of the practice session, all the players <u>drank</u> Gatorade.

Subject-Verb Agreement

_____   17. The major story on all the news programs <u>concerns</u> the proposed tax hike.

_____   18. There <u>was</u> only two handkerchiefs left in the drawer.

_____   19. My sister and her husband <u>take</u> my father bowling every Thursday night.

_____   20. Each of my little boys <u>need</u> a warmer jacket for the winter.

Consistent Verb Tense

_____   21. After I checked my bank balance, I <u>realized</u> I did not have enough money for a new stereo.

_____   22. Upon finding a seat on the bus, Randy unfolded his newspaper, <u>turns</u> to the sports section, and began to read.

Pronoun Reference, Agreement, and Point of View

_____ 23. All students should try <u>their</u> best to get good grades.

_____ 24. My first year in college I stayed in a residence, where <u>they</u> chose a room-mate for me.

_____ 25. Our company never gives bonuses to its employees, no matter how hard <u>you</u> work.

Pronoun Types

_____ 26. Paula writes much better than <u>me</u>.

_____ 27. My sister and <u>I</u> have both gotten part-time jobs.

Adjectives and Adverbs

_____ 28. The children smiled so <u>sweet</u> that I knew they were up to something.

_____ 29. The professor spoke <u>honestly</u> to me about my writing strengths and problems.

_____ 30. Weighing 160 kilos, Max the Mauler was the <u>most heaviest</u> of the four wrestlers in the ring.

_____ 31. Soap operas are <u>more enjoyable</u> to Maria than game shows.

Misplaced Modifiers

_____ 32. At the new video store, we bought a VCR <u>that has a stop-action feature</u>.

_____ 33. I returned the toy to the store <u>that was broken</u>.

Dangling Modifiers

_____ 34. <u>While playing cards</u>, two pizzas were eaten.

_____ 35. <u>Glancing out the window</u>, Melissa saw a strange car pull into the driveway.

Faulty Parallelism

_____ 36. Before I can settle down to studying, I must take out the garbage, dry the dishes, and <u>the leftovers have to be put away</u>.

_____ 37. Three ways of treating a cold are bed rest, chicken soup, and <u>taking vitamin C tablets</u>.

Capital Letters

_____ 38. Daylight saving time usually ends on the last <u>sunday</u> in October.

_____ 39. Last summer I worked as a stock person at <u>Eaton's</u>.

_____ 40. Most of the people who live in that neighbourhood are <u>doctors</u>.

_____ 41. Vince yelled, "<u>hurry</u> up, the show's starting in ten minutes."

Numbers and Abbreviations

_____ 42. So far <u>7</u> students have dropped out of my math course.

_____ 43. The assignment starts on page <u>132</u> of the math book.

_____ 44. André's insurance <u>co.</u> increased his rates after he was involved in a car accident.

End Marks

_____ 45. Are you going to the church service tomorrow<u>.</u>

_____ 46. I wondered if I should give Terry a call<u>.</u>

Apostrophes

_____ 47. <u>Lucys</u> goal is to become the head nurse at the same hospital where her mother once worked.

_____ 48. I <u>wasnt</u> able to sleep at all the night after my wisdom teeth were pulled.

_____ 49. I did some careful thinking before I rejected my <u>lawyer's</u> advice in the matter.

_____ 50. Several storm <u>windows'</u> in the house are badly cracked.

Quotation Marks

_____ 51. <u>Margaret Atwood wrote, "Fear has a smell, as love does."</u>

_____ 52. <u>I'll be with you in just a moment, the harried salesperson said."</u>

_____ 53. <u>If that's your opinion," said Lisa, "you're more narrow-minded than I thought."</u>

_____ 54. <u>Time is money, the manager said, and I don't have much."</u>

Commas

_____ 55. The dessert consisted of homemade ice cream and a choice of fresh <u>straw-berries blueberries or peaches.</u>

_____ 56. My <u>brother, who lifts weights, rarely</u> loses an argument.

_____ 57. When I opened the door to my <u>apartment I</u> quickly sensed that something was wrong.

_____ 58. It was supposed to rain heavily all <u>day, but</u> we only got a light drizzle in the morning.

Spelling

_____ 59. If I had <u>controlled</u> my time better this semester, I would have been a successful student.

_____ 60. Maureen has <u>alot</u> of definitions to study for her biology test.

_____ 61. My room-mate wants to hold <u>partys</u> in our apartment every weekend.

_____ 62. The house we just bought has two baths and a sunken <u>liveing</u> room.

Omitted Words and Letters

_____ 63. <u>As a child, I always cut the crusts my bread.</u>

_____ 64. <u>All three music stores in the mall have sales on CDs and tapes.</u>

_____ 65. <u>All the outside doors in our house have dead-bolt lock.</u>

Commonly Confused Words

_____ 66. I'm very sorry to hear that <u>your</u> not feeling well.

_____ 67. You can't judge a book by <u>it's</u> cover.

_____ 68. The car was going much <u>to</u> fast to stop at the light.

_____ 69. The tenants decided to take <u>their</u> property manager to court.

Effective Word Choice

_____ 70. Our car was <u>totalled</u> in the accident; we're lucky to be alive.

_____ 71. Without financial aid, my children are going to have a lot of trouble trying <u>to make ends meet</u>.

_____ 72. Ernest <u>was promoted</u> more quickly than other employees in the company.

_____ 73. My <u>expectancy</u> is to become a doctor someday.

_____ 74. <u>In my personal opinion</u>, I think that a tax hike is ridiculous.

_____ 75. <u>Because of the fact</u> that Jennifer missed the final exam, she failed the course.

PART 2 (OPTIONAL)

Do the following at your instructor's request. This second part of the test will provide more detailed information about skills you need to know. On separate sheets of paper, number and correct all the items you have marked with an _X_. For example, suppose you had marked the word groups below with an _X_. (Note that these examples were not taken from the actual test.)

4. When I picked up the tire. Something in my back snapped. I could not stand up straight as a result.

7. The phone started ringing, then the doorbell sounded as well.

15. Marks goal is to save enough money to get married next year.

29. Without checking the rear-view mirror the driver pulled out into the passing lane.

Here is how you should write your corrections on a separate sheet of paper:

4. When I picked up the tire, something in my back snapped.

7. The phone started ringing, and then the doorbell sounded as well.

15. Mark's

29. mirror, the driver

There are over forty corrections to make in all.

SENTENCE-SKILLS ACHIEVEMENT TEST

Part 1

This test will help check your knowledge of a number of sentence skills. In each item below, certain words are underlined. Place an *X* in the answer space if you think a mistake appears at the underlined part. Place a *C* in the answer space if you think the underlined part is correct.

A series of headings ("Sentence Fragments," "Run-Ons," and so on) will give you clues to the mistakes to look for. However, you do not have to understand the heading to find a mistake. What you are checking is your own sense of effective written English.

Sentence Fragments

1. After I finished my morning classes. I had a quick lunch in the cafeteria. Then I hurried off to my job as a supermarket cashier.

2. My family loves outdoor sports, especially street hockey. We often play outside until it's dark.

3. Simone waved her hand back and forth. Trying to catch the teacher's attention. She wanted to ask a question and make a comment about the lecture.

4. The teacher handed back my term paper. She told me to rewrite the conclusion. And reformat the citations so that the form was correct.

Run-Ons

_____ 5. Melissa was angry at <u>herself, she</u> had forgotten to pick up some potatoes on the way home.

_____ 6. My husband often sings in the <u>morning our</u> cat hides under the bed.

_____ 7. Ed is an absent-minded <u>person, so</u> he writes notes to help remember things.

_____ 8. I kept drinking cups of <u>coffee, I</u> had a lot of studying to do that night.

Standard English Verbs

_____ 9. My husband <u>thinks</u> more clearly in the morning than at night.

_____ 10. When the pile of rags caught on fire, Dave <u>reach</u> for the hose.

_____ 11. At Saturday's football game, we <u>was</u> the only couple that brought an umbrella.

_____ 12. I don't think that Roger <u>have</u> thought enough about his future.

Irregular Verbs

_____ 13. My boyfriend and I <u>seen</u> the new Jackie Chan movie at the Cineplex last night.

_____ 14. We should not have <u>taken</u> the children shopping with us today.

_____ 15. The second baseman fielded the grounder, stepped on the bag, and then <u>throwed</u> to first for a double play.

_____ 16. My cotton sweater <u>shrank</u> so much in the wash that I gave it to my daughter.

Subject-Verb Agreement

_____ 17. The price of the theatre tickets <u>seems</u> much too high.

_____ 18. There <u>was</u> only three pieces of wood left in the pile.

_____ 19. The new tenant and her little boy <u>make</u> a lot of noise.

_____ 20. Each of the support staff <u>work</u> from 9 to 5.

Consistent Verb Tense

_____ 21. My father interrupted me as I studied my accounting and <u>asked</u> me to balance his chequebook.

_____ 22. When they got back from the party, Ann lost her temper, <u>screams</u> at her husband, and then refused to talk about the cause.

Pronoun Reference, Agreement, and Point of View

_____   23. All registered voters should do their duty at the polls.

_____   24. Carol joined the women's group because they have the same interests that she does.

_____   25. I'm going to move out of the city because you never feel safe there.

Pronoun Types

_____   26. Larry had a lot more to eat than me.

_____   27. My brother and I are getting married in the same month.

Adjectives and Adverbs

_____   28. The dress was made beautiful, with a full silk lining and covered buttons.

_____   29. The boy walked timidly up to the baseball player and asked for his autograph.

_____   30. Which would you say is the more harder exercise—swimming or jogging?

_____   31. General Psychology is the most interesting course I am taking this semester.

Misplaced Modifiers

_____   32. At the campus bookstore, I just bought a diary that has a genuine leather cover.

_____   33. Most people do not go on summer vacations that are poor.

Dangling Modifiers

_____   34. While carrying the packages out of the store, my ankle was sprained.

_____   35. Jogging down the street, Phil was almost hit by a car.

Faulty Parallelism

_____   36. This weekend, Steve has to mow the lawn, take the dog to the vet, and the family station wagon needs to be washed.

_____   37. Barbara was frightened, upset, and a nervous wreck; she had three exams in the next two days.

Capital Letters

_____   38. The sale ends this coming tuesday.

_____   39. I just got a call from zurich that my insurance is being dropped.

_____ 40. Frank's goal is to become a successful <u>accountant</u> someday.

_____ 41. Linda asked, "<u>who</u> wants to go out and get some more ice?"

Numbers and Abbreviations

_____ 42. Before the game was over, <u>four</u> players had been ejected.

_____ 43. Your doctor's appointment has been scheduled for <u>8:15</u> tomorrow evening.

_____ 44. I spent almost ten <u>hrs.</u> studying for the exam.

End Marks

_____ 45. Do you know where Bob is tonight<u>?</u>

_____ 46. Rita wondered how long the sprain would take to heal<u>.</u>

Apostrophes

_____ 47. <u>Sams</u> proudest moment came when he got his first A on a paper.

_____ 48. <u>Doesnt</u> your bank stay open late on Fridays?

_____ 49. The <u>doctor's</u> advice contradicted that of the other doctor I had seen.

_____ 50. The little girl at the front door explained that she has some <u>puppies'</u> for sale.

Quotation Marks

_____ 51. <u>Mae West once said, "I generally avoid temptation unless I can't resist it."</u>

_____ 52. <u>"I'd rather make a fast nickel than a slow dollar, the store owner said."</u>

_____ 53. <u>"Don't come back after lunch," the boss said, "because you're fired."</u>

_____ 54. <u>"After you finish writing the essay," said the teacher, be sure to proofread it carefully."</u>

Commas

_____ 55. Stella just learned that she is allergic to <u>shrimp crabmeat and salmon</u>.

_____ 56. My Uncle <u>Al, who is very forgetful, always</u> asks me my name.

_____ 57. As the vampire was about to bite his <u>victim he</u> saw that the sun was shining.

_____ 58. Last summer I worked in a <u>factory, but</u> this summer I'll have a job in a resort hotel.

Spelling

_____ 59. Through someone's mistake, my name was <u>dropped</u> from the list of graduating students.

_____ 60. It's <u>alright</u> with me if you skip breakfast.

_____ 61. There are three unidentified <u>bodys</u> in the police morgue.

_____ 62. The counsellor asked how many courses I planned on <u>takeing</u> next semester.

Omitted Words and Letters

_____ 63. <u>The kids in street played ball with cut-off broom handles.</u>

_____ 64. <u>Sharp splinters jutted out of the wooden pilings on the pier.</u>

_____ 65. <u>I need at least a thousand dollar to pay off my debts.</u>

Commonly Confused Words

_____ 66. If <u>your</u> in the mood for some shopping, so am I.

_____ 67. The supplement helps my body get <u>it's</u> daily dose of potassium.

_____ 68. Caroline is <u>to</u> self-centred to be a good friend.

_____ 69. The players will forfeit <u>their</u> salaries if they go on strike.

Effective Word Choice

_____ 70. Someone broke into my car and <u>ripped off</u> my CD player.

_____ 71. I need a new coat; my old corduroy one has <u>seen better days</u>.

_____ 72. The employee layoff was <u>handled in a sensitive way</u> by the company.

_____ 73. My parents are <u>desirous of my earning</u> a college degree.

_____ 74. <u>Owing to the fact that</u> we don't play cards, we weren't invited to the party.

_____ 75. <u>Personally, my own belief</u> is that every home will have a computer someday.

Part 2 (Optional)

Do the following at your instructor's request. This second part of the test will provide more detailed information about skills you need to know. On separate sheets of paper, number and correct all the items you have marked with an _X_. For example, suppose you had marked the word groups below with an _X_. (Note that these examples were not taken from the actual test.)

4. <u>When I picked up the tire.</u> Something in my back snapped. I could not stand up straight as a result.

7. The phone started <u>ringing, then</u> the doorbell sounded as well.

15. <u>Marks</u> goal is to save enough money to get married next year.

29. Without checking the rear-view <u>mirror the</u> driver pulled out into the passing lane.

Here is how you should write your corrections on a separate sheet of paper:

4. When I picked up the tire, something in my back snapped.

7. The phone started ringing, and then the doorbell sounded as well.

15. Mark's

29. mirror, the driver

There are over forty corrections to make in all.

ANSWERS TO INTRODUCTORY PROJECTS AND PRACTICE EXERCISES

This answer key can help you teach yourself. Use it to find out why you got some answers wrong—you want to uncover any weak spot in your understanding of a given skill. By using the answer key in an honest and thoughtful way, you will master each skill and prepare yourself for the many tests in this book that have no answer key.

SUBJECTS AND VERBS

Introductory Project (9)

Answers will vary.

Practice 1 (pages 11–12)

1. I ate
2. Water snakes swim
3. Sally failed
4. movie ended
5. Kerry borrowed
6. children stared
7. newspaper tumbled
8. Crystal starts
9. job limits
10. windstorm blew

Practice 2 (12)

1. <u>sister</u> <u>is</u>
2. <u>chips</u> <u>are</u>
3. <u>defendant</u> <u>appeared</u>
4. <u>Art</u> <u>became</u>
5. <u>ride</u> . . . <u>seems</u>
6. <u>building</u> <u>was</u>
7. <u>weeks</u> . . . <u>were</u>
8. <u>banana split</u> and . . . <u>cake</u> . . . <u>look</u>
9. <u>Jane</u> . . . <u>feels</u>
10. <u>Rooms</u> . . . <u>appear</u>

Practice 3 (12)

1. <u>clock</u> <u>runs</u>
2. <u>player</u> . . . <u>is</u>
3. <u>shoppers</u> <u>filled</u>
4. <u>trucks</u> <u>rumbled</u>
5. <u>children</u> <u>drew</u>
6. <u>picture</u> <u>fell</u>
7. <u>Chipmunks</u> <u>live</u>
8. <u>uncle</u> <u>monopolized</u>
9. <u>tomatoes</u> <u>were</u>
10. <u>company</u> <u>cancelled</u>

Practice (13–14)

1. ~~For that course,~~ <u>you</u> <u>need</u> three different books.
2. The <u>key</u> ~~to the front door~~ <u>slipped</u> ~~from my hand into a puddle.~~
3. The check-out <u>lines</u> ~~at the supermarket~~ <u>moved</u> very slowly.
4. ~~With his son,~~ <u>Frank</u> <u>walked</u> ~~to the playground.~~
5. No <u>quarrel</u> ~~between good friends~~ <u>lasts</u> ~~for a very long time.~~
6. ~~In one weekend,~~ <u>Maria</u> <u>planted</u> a large vegetable garden ~~in her backyard.~~
7. <u>Either</u> ~~of my brothers~~ <u>is</u> a reliable worker.
8. The <u>drawer</u> ~~of the bureau~~ <u>sticks</u> ~~on rainy days.~~
9. ~~During the movie,~~ several <u>people</u> <u>walked</u> out ~~in protest.~~
10. ~~At a single sitting,~~ my <u>brother</u> <u>reads</u> five or more comic books.

Practice (15)

1. He <u>has</u> <u>been</u> <u>sleeping</u>
2. <u>foundations</u> <u>were</u> <u>attacked</u>
3. <u>I</u> have not <u>washed</u>
4. <u>teacher</u> had not <u>warned</u>
5. <u>bus</u> <u>will</u> <u>be</u> <u>leaving</u>
6. <u>You</u> <u>should</u> not <u>try</u>
7. <u>They</u> <u>have</u> just <u>been</u> <u>married</u>
8. <u>He</u> <u>could</u> <u>make</u>
9. <u>Carol</u> <u>has</u> <u>decided</u>
10. <u>company</u> <u>should</u> <u>have</u> <u>purchased</u>

Practice (16)

1. <u>hypnotist</u> <u>locked</u> and <u>sawed</u>
2. <u>Connie</u> <u>began</u> and <u>finished</u>
3. <u>Nissans</u>, <u>Toyotas</u>, and <u>Hondas</u> <u>glittered</u>
4. <u>Tony</u> <u>added</u> and <u>got</u>
5. <u>car</u> <u>sputtered</u>, <u>stalled</u>, and <u>started</u>
6. <u>Whiteflies</u>, <u>mites</u>, and <u>aphids</u> <u>infected</u>
7. <u>Lori</u> <u>shot</u> and <u>stuffed</u>
8. <u>We</u> <u>walked</u> and <u>bought</u>
9. <u>Tony</u> and <u>Crystal</u> <u>looked</u> and <u>bought</u>
10. <u>aunt</u> and <u>uncle</u> <u>married</u>, <u>divorced</u>, and <u>remarried</u>

SENTENCE FRAGMENTS

Introductory Project (18)

1. verb
2. subject
3. subject . . . verb
4. express a complete thought

Practice 2 (22–23)

Note: The underlined part shows the fragment (or that part of the original fragment not changed during correction).

1. <u>Although the air-conditioner was working,</u> I still felt warm in the room.

2. <u>When Tony got into his car this morning</u>, he discovered that he had left the car windows open. The seats and rug were soaked <u>since it had rained overnight</u>.
3. <u>After cutting fish at the restaurant all day</u>, Jenny smelled like a cat-food factory.
4. Frank raked out the soggy leaves <u>that were at the bottom of the concrete fish pond</u>. <u>When two bullfrogs jumped out at him</u>, he dropped the rake and ran.
5. <u>Because he had eaten and drunk too much</u>, he had to leave the party early. His stomach was like a volcano <u>that was ready to erupt</u>.

Practice 1 (25)

1. Bill lay in bed after the alarm rang, <u>wishing that he had $100,000</u>.
2. <u>Investigating the strange, mournful cries in his neighbour's yard</u>, George found a ferret tangled in its leash.
3. <u>As a result</u>, I was <u>late for class</u>.

Practice 2 (26)

1. <u>Glistening with dew</u>, the gigantic web hung between the branches of the tree.
2. Maria is pleased with the carpet of Astroturf in her kitchen, <u>claiming that crumbs settle in the grass so she never sees them</u>.
   Or: Maria is pleased with the carpet of Astroturf in her kitchen. She claims <u>that crumbs settle in the grass so she never sees them</u>.
3. Ron picked through the box of chocolates, <u>removing the kinds he didn't like</u>.
   Or: He removed <u>the kinds he didn't like</u>.
4. The grass I was walking on suddenly became squishy <u>because I had hiked into a marsh of some kind</u>.
   Or: The reason was <u>that I had hiked into a marsh of some kind</u>.
5. Steve drove quickly to the bank <u>to cash his paycheque</u>.
   Or: He had <u>to cash his paycheque</u>.

Practice 1 (28)

1. For example, he managed <u>to cut his hand while crumbling a bar of shredded wheat</u>.
2. All day, people complained <u>about missing parts, rude salespeople, and errors on bills</u>.
3. For example, she suggests <u>using club soda on stains</u>.

Practice 2 (28–29)

1. My little boy is constantly into mischief, such as <u>tearing the labels off all the cans in the cupboard</u>.
2. For example, it had <u>a hand-carved mantel and a mahogany banister</u>.

3. For instance, he chewed <u>with his mouth open</u>.
4. A half hour later, there were several explosions, <u>with potatoes splattering all over the walls of the oven</u>.
   Or: Potatoes splattered <u>all over the walls of the oven</u>.
5. Janet looked forward to seeing former class-mates at the high-school reunion, <u>including the football player she had had a wild crush on</u>.

Practice (30)

1. Fred went to the refrigerator to get milk for his breakfast cereal <u>and discovered about one tablespoon of milk left in the carton</u>.
   Or: He <u>discovered about one tablespoon of milk left in the carton</u>.
2. <u>Then I noticed the "Out of order" sign taped over the coin slot</u>.
3. Our neighbourhood's most eligible bachelor got married this weekend <u>but did not invite us to the wedding</u>.
   Or: But he <u>did not invite us to the wedding</u>.
4. Also, he <u>was constantly criticizing his choice of friends</u>.
5. Wendy stared at the blank page in desperation and <u>decided that the first sentence of a paper is always the hardest to write</u>.
   Or: And she <u>decided that the first sentence of a paper is always the hardest to write</u>.

RUN-ONS

Introductory Project (36)

1. period
2. but
3. semi-colon
4. although

Practice 1 (39)

1. down. He
2. station. A
3. panicked. The
4. exam. The
5. wood. One
6. hand. Guests
7. earth. Earthworms
8. party. A
9. time. His
10. stacks. The

Practice 2 (39–40)

1. class. His
2. increasing. Every
3. properly. We
4. it. Half
5. places. Our
6. water. This
7. speeding. He
8. times. Nobody
9. names. For
10. floor. His

Practice 1 (42)

1. , and
2. , for
3. , but
4. , for
5. , for

6. , but
7. , and
8. , so
9. , but
10. , so

Practice (43–44)

1. out; nobody
2. rerun; the
3. cool; everyone

4. year; an
5. stop; he

Practice 1 (44–45)

1. insecticide; otherwise, the
2. props; also, I (*or* in addition *or* moreover *or* furthermore)
3. basement; instead, he
4. week; consequently, I (*or* as a result *or* thus *or* therefore)
5. semester; in addition, she (*or* also *or* moreover *or* furthermore)

Practice 2 (45)

1. seat; however,
2. match; as a result,
3. headache; furthermore,
4. razors; consequently,
5. hair; nevertheless,

Practice 1 (46–47)

1. because
2. When
3. While *or* When

4. After *or* When
5. before

Practice 2 (47)

1. Because (*or* Since) Sharon didn't understand the teacher's point, she asked him to repeat it.
2. Although (*or* Even though) Fred remembered to get the hamburger, he forgot to get the hamburger rolls.
3. After Michael gulped two cups of strong coffee, his heart started to flutter.
4. When a car sped around the corner, it sprayed slush all over the pedestrians.
5. Although (*or* Even though) Crystal loved the rose cashmere sweater, she had nothing to wear with it.

STANDARD ENGLISH VERBS

Introductory Project (52)

played . . . plays
hoped . . . hopes
juggled . . . juggles

1. past time . . . . -*d* or -*ed*
2. present time . . . . -*s*

Practice 1 (54)

1. hates
2. messes
3. feels
4. covers
5. smells

6. C
7. blurs
8. thinks
9. pretends
10. seems

Practice 2 (54–55)

Angela reacts badly when she gets caught in a traffic jam. She opens the dash-board compartment and pulls out an old pack of Juicy Fruit gum that she keeps for such occasions. She unwraps a dried-up stick of gum and chomps down viciously, trying to revive its flavour. She gets out of the car and looks down the highway, trying to see where the delay is. Back in the car, she drums her fingers on the steering wheel. If the jam lasts long enough, she starts talking to herself and angrily kicks off her shoes.

Practice 1 (55–56)

1. raced
2. glowed
3. walked
4. sighted
5. stared

6. decided
7. C
8. needed
9. scattered
10. decided

Practice 2 (56)

Bill's boss shouted at Bill. Feeling bad, Bill went home and cursed his wife. Then his wife screamed at their son. Angry himself, the son went out and cruelly teased a little girl who lived next door until she wailed. Bad feelings were passed on as one person wounded the next with ugly words. No one managed to break the vicious cycle.

Practice 1 (58)

1. has
2. does
3. is
4. are
5. was . . . had

6. was
7. did . . . was
8. were
9. had
10. am

Practice 2 (59)

1. ~~be~~ is
2. ~~is~~ are
3. ~~has~~ have
4. ~~don't~~ doesn't
5. ~~is~~ are

6. ~~have~~ had
7. ~~done~~ did
8. ~~have~~ had
9. ~~has~~ had
10. ~~was~~ were

Practice 3 (59)

My mother sings alto in our community choir. She <u>has</u> to go to choir practice every Friday night and <u>is</u> expected to know all the music. If she <u>does</u> not know her part, the other choir members <u>do</u> things like glare at her and <u>are</u> likely to make nasty comments, she says. Last weekend, my mother <u>had</u> houseguests and <u>did</u> not have time to learn all the notes. The music <u>was</u> very difficult, and she thought the other people <u>were</u> going to make fun of her. But they <u>were</u> very understanding when she told them that she <u>had</u> laryngitis and couldn't make a sound.

IRREGULAR VERBS

Introductory Project (61)

1. screamed . . . screamed
2. wrote . . . written
3. stole . . . stolen
4. asked . . . asked
5. kissed . . . kissed

6. chose . . . chosen
7. rode . . . ridden
8. chewed . . . chewed
9. thought . . . thought
10. danced . . . danced

Practice 1 (65)

1. ~~chose~~ chosen
2. ~~done~~ did (*or* had done)
3. ~~were~~ worn
4. ~~wrote~~ written
5. ~~gived~~ gave

6. ~~be~~ was
7. ~~broke~~ broken
8. ~~lended~~ lent
9. ~~seen~~ saw
10. ~~knewed~~ knew

Practice 2 (65–67)

1. (a) sees
   (b) saw
   (c) seen
2. (a) chooses
   (b) chose
   (c) chosen
3. (a) takes
   (b) took
   (c) taken
4. (a) speaks
   (b) spoke
   (c) spoken
5. (a) swims
   (b) swam
   (c) swum

6. (a) drives
   (b) drove
   (c) driven
7. (a) wears
   (b) wore
   (c) worn
8. (a) blows
   (b) blew
   (c) blown
9. (a) begins
   (b) began
   (c) begun
10. (a) goes
    (b) went
    (c) gone

Practice (68)

1. lays
2. lay
3. Lying

4. laid
5. lay

Practice (69)

1. sit
2. setting
3. set

4. sat
5. set

Practice (70)

1. rise
2. raise
3. risen

4. raised
5. rises

SUBJECT-VERB AGREEMENT

Introductory Project (72)

Correct: There <u>were</u> many applicants for the position.
Correct: The pictures in that magazine <u>are</u> very controversial.
Correct: Everybody usually <u>watches</u> the lighted numbers while riding in the elevator.

1. applicants . . . pictures
2. singular . . . singular

Practice (74)

1. stain ~~on the sheets~~ comes
2. jacket, ~~along with two pairs of pants,~~ sells
3. roots ~~of the apple tree~~ are
4. sisters, ~~who wanted to be at his surprise party,~~ were
5. albums ~~in the attic~~ belong
6. cost ~~of personal calls made on office telephones~~ is
7. cups ~~of coffee in the morning~~ do
8. moon ~~as well some stars~~ is
9. wiring ~~in the apartment~~ is . . . needs
10. Chapter 4 ~~of the psychology book, along with six weeks of class notes,~~ is

Practice (75)

1. <u>are</u> <u>lines</u>
2. <u>were</u> <u>dogs</u>
3. <u>were</u> <u>dozens</u>
4. <u>are</u> <u>pretzels</u>
5. <u>were</u> <u>Janet</u> and <u>Maureen</u>
6. <u>are</u> <u>rats</u>
7. <u>were</u> <u>boys</u>
8. <u>is</u> <u>house</u>
9. <u>were</u> <u>fans</u>
10. <u>lies</u> <u>pile</u>

Practice (76)

1. ignores
2. dances
3. deserves
4. were
5. appears
6. offers
7. owns
8. has
9. thinks
10. has

Practice (76–77)

1. match
2. have
3. are
4. plan
5. are

Practice (77)

1. were
2. stumble
3. blares
4. give
5. appears

CONSISTENT VERB TENSE

Introductory Project (80)

Mistakes in verb tense: Alex <u>discovers</u> . . . <u>calls</u> a . . . present . . . past

Practice (81–82)

1. causes
2. decided
3. picked
4. hopes
5. informs
6. sprinkled
7. discovered
8. asked
9. overcharges
10. swallowed

ADDITIONAL INFORMATION ABOUT VERBS

Practice (Tense: 86–87)

1. had walked
2. was feeling
3. had placed
4. was trying
5. is growing
6. had looked
7. has studied
8. has seen
9. was watching
10. had thrown

Practice (Verbals: 88)

1. *P*
2. *G*
3. *G*
4. *I*
5. *I*
6. *P*
7. *P*
8. *I*
9. *P*
10. *G*

Practice (Active and Passive Voices: 89–90)

1. Angela organized the surprise party.
2. The comedian offended many people.
3. The neighbours pay for the old woman's groceries.
4. The boys knocked the horse chestnuts off the trees.
5. The exorcist drove the devil out of Regan.
6. Four perspiring workers loaded the huge moving van.
7. The inexperienced server dropped a tray of glasses.
8. My forgetful Aunt Agatha is always losing umbrellas.
9. Wayne Gretzky finally broke Gordie Howe's NHL scoring record.
10. The airport security staff found a bomb in the suitcase.

PRONOUN REFERENCE, AGREEMENT, AND POINT OF VIEW

Introductory Project (91)

1. b   2. b   3. b

Practice (93–94)

Note: The practice sentences could be rewritten to have other meanings than the ones indicated below.

1. Mario insisted that it was Harry's turn to drive.
   Or: Mario insisted to Harry, "It is my turn to drive."
2. I failed two of my courses last semester because the instructors graded unfairly.
3. Don's parents were very much pleased with the accounting job Don was offered.
   Or: The accounting job Don was offered pleased his parents very much.
4. Tony became very upset when he questioned the mechanic.
   Or: The mechanic became very upset when Tony questioned him.
5. I was very nervous about the unexpected biology exam.
6. Paul told his younger brother, "The dog chewed your new running shoes."
7. My cousin is an astrologer, but I don't believe in astrology.
8. When Liz was promoted, she told Elaine.
   Or: Liz told Elaine, "You have been promoted."
9. Whenever I start enjoying a new television show, the network takes it off the air.
10. When the centre fielder heard the crack of the bat, he raced toward the fence but was unable to catch the ball.

Practice (95)

1 they . . . their	4. it
2. it	5. they
3. them	

Practice (97)

1. his	6. his
2. his or her	7. her
3. his	8. she
4. his	9. its
5. her	10. his

Practice (98–99)

1. I always feel hungry
2. they have finished
3. they work
4. we can never be sure
5. she should register
6. he (or she) should check
   Or: If people plan . . . they should check
7. I do not get paid for all the holidays I should.
   Or: One does not get paid . . . one should.

8. you should take action
9. we had
10. we want it

PRONOUN TYPES

Introductory Project (102)

Correct sentences:

Andy and I enrolled in a computer course.
The police officer pointed to my sister and me.
Crystal prefers men who take pride in their bodies.
The players are confident that the league championship is theirs.
Those concert tickets are too expensive.
Our parents should spend some money on themselves for a change.

Practice 1 (105–106)

2. I (*S*)
3. they (*did* is understood) (*S*)
4. her (*O*)
5. she (*S*)
6. he (*S*)

7. She (*S*)
8. We (*S*)
9. I (*am* is understood) (*S*)
10. She and I (*S*)

Practice 2 (106)

2. me *or* him
3. me *or* her *or* him *or* them
4. me *or* her *or* him *or* them
5. me *or* her *or* him
6. I *or* he *or* she

7. I *or* he *or* she
8. them
9. him *or* her *or* them
10. us

Practice 1 (108)

1. who
2. which
3. who

4. whom
5. who

Practice (109)

1. ~~its'~~ its
2. ~~him~~ his
3. ~~mines~~ mine

4. ~~they~~ their
5. ~~ours'~~ ours

Practice 1 (110)

1. That dog
2. This fingernail
3. Those girls
4. those shopping bags
5. that corner house

Practice (112)

1. himself
2. themselves
3. yourselves (*or* yourself)
4. themselves
5. ourselves

ADJECTIVES AND ADVERBS

Introductory Project (114)

Answers will vary for 1–4.
adjective . . . adverb . . . ly . . . er . . . est

Practice 1 (116)

kinder . . . kindest
more ambitious . . . most ambitious
more generous . . . most generous
finer . . . finest
more likeable . . . most likeable

Practice 2 (117)

1. most comfortable
2. most difficult
3. easiest
4. less
5. best
6. longest
7. most memorable
8. more experienced . . . most experienced
9. worse . . . worst
10. better

Practice (118)

1. violently
2. quickly
3. angrily

4. considerable
5. gently
6. really
7. regularly . . . regular
8. quietly . . . angrily
9. carefully . . . exact
10. Slowly . . . surely

Practice (119)

1. well
2. good
3. well

4. well
5. well

MISPLACED MODIFIERS

Introductory Project (121)

1. Intended: The farmers were wearing masks.
   Unintended: The apple trees were wearing masks.
2. Intended: The woman had a terminal disease.
   Unintended: The faith healer had a terminal disease.

Practice 1 (122–123)

Note: In each of the corrections below, the underlined part shows what was a misplaced modifier.

1. Driving around in their car, they finally found a laundromat.
2. In the library, I read that Marc Garneau was a Canadian pilot who became an astronaut.
   Or: I read in the library that Marc Garneau was a Canadian pilot who became an astronaut.
3. Taking the elevator, Trisha was thinking about her lost chemistry book.
4. Crystal selected a doughnut filled with banana cream from the bakery.
   Or: From the bakery, Crystal selected a doughnut filled with banana cream.
5. Simon worked almost twenty hours overtime to pay some overdue bills.
6. Tickets have gone on sale in the college bookstore for next week's championship game.
   Or: In the college bookstore, tickets have gone on sale for next week's championship game.
7. I returned the orange socks that my uncle gave me to the department store.
8. Looking through the binoculars, the camper saw the black bear.
9. I earned nearly two hundred dollars last week.
10. In the refrigerator, mushrooms should be stored enclosed in a paper bag.

Practice 2 (124)

1. In our science class, we agreed to go out to dinner tonight.
   Or: We agreed in our science class to go out to dinner tonight.
2. On a rainy day in June, Bob and I decided to get married.
   Or: Bob and I, on a rainy day in June, decided to get married.
3. Weighed down with heavy packages, Cecile decided to hail a taxi.
   Or: Cecile, weighed down with heavy packages, decided to hail a taxi.
4. Without success, I've looked everywhere for an instruction book on how to play the guitar.
   Or: I've looked everywhere without success for an instruction book on how to play the guitar.
5. Over the phone, Mother told me to wash the car.
   Or: Mother told me over the phone to wash the car.

DANGLING MODIFIERS

Introductory Project (127)

1. Intended: The giraffe was munching leaves from a tall tree.
   Unintended: The children were munching leaves.
2. Intended: Michael was arriving home after ten months in Bosnia.
   Unintended: The neighbours were arriving home after ten months in Bosnia.

Practice 1 (129–130)

1. Since it was folded into a tiny square, I could not read the message.
   Or: I could not read the message, which was folded into a tiny square.
2. As I waded into the lake, tadpoles swirled around my ankles.
3. C
4. Hanging on the wall was a photograph of my mother.
5. Settling comfortably into the chair, I let the television capture my attention for the next hour.
   Or: After I settled comfortably into the chair, the television captured my attention for the next hour.
6. As I was driving home after a tiring day at work, the white line became bleary.
   Or: Driving home after a tiring day at work, I saw the white line become bleary.
7. The batter hit the first home run of his career, which soared high over the left-field fence.
8. Since the rug was threadbare and dirty, Maria decided to replace it.
   Or: Maria knew it was time to replace the rug, which was threadbare and dirty.
9. After we spent most of the night outdoors in a tent, the sun rose and we went into the house.
   Or: After spending most of the night outdoors in a tent, we went into the house when the sun rose.

10. While they were hot and sizzling, we bit into the apple tarts.
    Or: We bit into the apple tarts, which were hot and sizzling.

FAULTY PARALLELISM

Introductory Project (133)

Correct sentences:

I use my TV remote control to change channels, to adjust the volume, and to turn the set on and off.
One option the employees had was to take a cut in pay; the other was to work longer hours.
The refrigerator has a cracked vegetable drawer, a missing shelf, and a strange freezer smell.

Practice 1 (135)

1. aching arms
2. freshly made soups
3. bad-tempered
4. replacing weather stripping
5. her green eyes
6. hear him sing *or* hear his songs
7. praying
8. attended
9. complaining about her strict parents
10. chased by bill collectors

PAPER FORMAT

Introductory Project (139)

In "*A*," the title is capitalized and centred and has no quotation marks around it; there is a blank line between the title and the body of the paper; there are left and right margins around the body of the paper; no words are incorrectly hyphenated.

Practice 1 (141)

2. No quotation marks around the title.
3. Capitalize the major words in the title ("The Generation Gap in Our House").
4. Skip a line between the title and first line of the paper.
5. Indent the first line of the paper.
6. Keep margins on either side of the paper.

Practice 2 (141–142)

Here are some possible titles:

1. Selfishness in Young Children
2. The Values of Daily Exercise *or* The Health Benefits of Daily Exercise
3. My Stubborn Son *or* My Stubborn Teenage Son
4. Essential College Study Skills
5. Drawbacks and Values of Single Life

Practice 3 (142–143)

1. The worst day of my life began when my supervisor at work gave me a message to call home.
2. Catholic church services have undergone many changes in the last few years.
3. An embarrassing incident happened to me when I was working as a server at the Royal York Hotel.
4. Correct
5. Many television commercials that I watch are degrading to human dignity.

CAPITAL LETTERS

Introductory Project (144)

1–13: Answers will vary, but all should be capitalized.
14–16: On . . . "Let's . . . I

Practice (146–147)

1. Halloween . . . Thanksgiving
2. If . . . I'm
3. Ford . . . Quebec . . . Florida . . . Goodyear
4. *Star Weekly* . . . World War
5. Northside Improvement Association . . . Third
6. Soundworks . . . Laurier Boulevard . . . Panasonic
7. Camp Borden . . . Germany
8. Thursday . . . Weight Watchers'
9. February . . . *Return of Dracula* . . . *Alien*
10. Club Monaco . . . Burlington Mall

Practice (149–150)

1. Aunt Esther
2. Spanish . . . Aerobic Exercise
3. Dr. Purdy's
4. French Canadian . . . Gaspé
5. Intermediate Math

Practice (150)

1. summer . . . sunbathe . . . magazines
2. week . . . tune . . . melody
3. high school . . . provinces . . . college
4. title . . . paper . . . teacher . . . grade
5. friend . . . college . . . degree . . . life

NUMBERS AND ABBREVIATIONS

Introductory Project (153)

Correct choices:

First sentence: 8:55 . . . 65 per cent
Second sentence: Nine . . . forty-five
Second sentence: brothers . . . mountain
Second sentence: hours . . . English

Practice (154–155)

1. five . . . three
2. Two
3. 8:30
4. nine o'clock
5. $282
6. 23
7. May 31, 1956
8. 2 . . . 5
9. 50 per cent
10. five . . . twelve

Practice (155–156)

1. cousin . . . apartment
2. television
3. account . . . month
4. moving . . . president . . . company
5. kilograms . . . weeks
6. favourite . . . especially
7. secretary . . . temporary . . . minute
8. brother . . . high school
9. litre . . . streets
10. hospital . . . room

END MARKS

Introductory Project (158)

1. depressed.
2. paper?
3. parked.
4. control!

Practice (160)

1. continue?
2. road!
3. arthritis.
4. visit?
5. wallet.

6. cars.
7. sunglasses!
8. *Rings.*
9. mess!"
10. wig?"

APOSTROPHES

Introductory Project (161)

1. The apostrophes indicate omitted letters: *You are, he is, does not.*
2. In each case, the apostrophe indicates possession or ownership.
3. In the first sentence in each pair, the *s* in *books* and *cars* indicates plural number; in the second sentence in each pair, the *'s* indicates possession.

Apostrophes in Contractions

Practice 1 (162)

aren't	wouldn't	who's
you're	we're	doesn't
they've	hasn't	where's

Practice 2 (163)

1. I'll . . . you'll
2. It's . . . wouldn't
3. shouldn't . . . you're

4. isn't . . . weren't
5. I'd . . . who's . . . it's

Practice (164)

1. They're . . . their
2. You're . . . your
3. Who's . . . whose

4. It's . . . it's
5. you're . . . their . . . it's

Apostrophes to Show Ownership or Possession

Practice 1 (165–166)

1. Crystal's sneakers
2. Melanie's lipstick
3. His brother's house
4. The car's tires
5. Jan's bicycle

6. the blue jay's nest
7. my paper's title
8. My mother's arthritis
9. My sister's boyfriend
10. anybody's game

Practice 2 (166)

2. Georgia's
3. friend's
4. teacher's
5. girlfriend's
6. Albert's
7. daughter's
8. boss's
9. night's
10. son's

Practice (166–167)

Answers will vary, but the following possessors should be used:

2. neighbour's
3. car's
4. sister's
5. doctor's

Practice (167–169)

1. onions: simple plural meaning more than one onion
   Rons: Ron's, meaning "eyes of Ron"
   eyes: simple plural meaning more than one eye
2. mothers: mother's, meaning "recipe of my mother"
   relatives: simple plural meaning more than one relative
   friends: simple plural meaning more than one friend
3. Sailors: simple plural meaning more than one sailor
   stations: simple plural meaning more than one station
   ships: ship's, meaning "alarm of the ship"
4. kites: kite's, meaning "string of the kite"
   branches: simple plural meaning more than one branch
5. girls: simple plural meaning more than one girl
   colleges: college's, meaning "football game of my college"
   movies: simple plural meaning more than one movie
6. cuffs: simple plural meaning more than one cuff
   mens: men's, meaning "pants of men"
   pants: simple plural meaning more than one pant leg
   ashes: simple plural meaning more than one ash
7. tubes: simple plural meaning more than one inner tube
   rivers: river's, meaning "rushing currents of the river"
   currents: simple plural meaning more than one current
8. directors: director's, meaning "specialty of the director"
   films: simple plural meaning more than one film
   vampires: simple plural meaning more than one vampire
9. copies: simple plural meaning more than one copy
   companys: company's, meaning "tax returns of the company
   returns: simple plural meaning more than one return
   years: simple plural meaning more than one year

10. Scientists: simple plural meaning more than one scientist
    Africas: Africa's, meaning "Congo region of Africa"
    relatives: simple plural meaning more than one relative
    dinosaurs: simple plural meaning more than one dinosaur

Practice (169–170)

1. fighters'
2. drivers'
3. friends'
4. grandparents'
5. soldiers'

QUOTATION MARKS

Introductory Project (172)

1. Quotation marks set off the exact words of a speaker.
2. Commas and periods following quotations go inside quotation marks.

Practice 1 (174)

1. "Have more trust in me," Crystal said to her mother.
2. The teacher asked Sharon, "Why are your eyes closed?"
3. Christ said, "I come that you may have life, and have it more abundantly."
4. "I refuse to wear those itchy wool pants!" Jesse shouted at his parents.
5. His father replied, "We should give all the clothes you never wear to the Salvation Army."
6. The nervous boy whispered hoarsely over the telephone, "Is Linda home?"
7. "When I was ten," Crystal said, "I spent my entire summer playing Monopoly."
8. Tony said, "When I was ten, I spent my whole summer playing basketball."
9. The critic wrote about the actor, "She runs the gamut of emotions from A to B."
10. "The best way to tell if a mushroom is poisonous," the doctor solemnly explained, "is if you find it in the stomach of a dead person."

Practice 2 (174)

1. Fred said, "I'm going with you."
2. "Everyone passed the test," the teacher informed them.
3. My parents asked, "Where were you?"
4. "If you don't leave soon," he warned, "you'll be late for work."

Practice 1 (176)

2. Lisa replied, "I thought you were going to write them this year."
3. Nick said, "Writing invitations is a woman's job."
4. Lisa exclaimed, "You're crazy!"
5. Nick replied, "You have much better handwriting than I do."

Practice 2 (176–177)

1. He said that as the plane went higher, his heart sank lower.
2. The designer said that shag rugs were back in style.
3. The supervisor asked Jake if he had ever operated a lift truck.
4. My nosy neighbour asked if Cosmo and Ellen were fighting.
5. Maria complained that she married a man who eats Tweeties cereal for breakfast.

Practice (177–178)

1. The young couple opened their brand-new copy of <u>Cooking Made Easy</u> to the chapter titled "Meat Loaf Magic."
2. Annabella borrowed Hawthorne's novel <u>The Scarlet Letter</u> from the library because she thought it was about Demi Moore.
3. Did you know that the musical <u>West Side Story</u> is actually a modern version of Shakespeare's tragedy <u>Romeo and Juliet</u>?
4. I used to think that Richard Connell's short story "The Most Dangerous Game" was the scariest piece of suspense fiction in existence—until I began reading Bram Stoker's classic novel <u>Dracula</u>.
5. Every year at Easter we watch a movie like <u>The Robe</u> on television.
6. During the past year, <u>Canadian Geographic</u> featured an article about mosquitoes titled "Biting Flies: Plagues with a Purpose."
7. My father still remembers the way that Julie Andrews sang "I Could Have Danced All Night" in an early Toronto production of <u>My Fair Lady</u>.
8. As I stand in the supermarket check-out line, I always look at a feature titled "Life in Canada Today" in <u>Maclean's</u>.
9. My favourite Nylons song is "Under the Boardwalk," which can be found in their album <u>Illustrious</u>.
10. Absent-mindedly munching a Dorito, Donna opened the latest issue of <u>Toronto Life</u> to its cover story, "Where to Get Stuff Cheap."

COMMAS

Introductory Project (181)

1. a. news, a movie, a *Forever Knight* rerun,
   b. cheque, write your account number on the back,
   (commas between items in a series)
2. a. indoors,
   b. car,
   (commas after introductory words)
3. a. opossum, an animal much like the kangaroo,
   b. Derek, who was recently arrested,
   (commas around interrupters)

4. a. pre-registration, but
    b. intersection, and
        (commas between complete thoughts)
5. a. said, "Why
    b. interview," said David, "I
        (commas with direct quotations)
6. a. 1,000,000
    b. Boulevard, Pierrefonds, Quebec, October 12, 1994,
        (commas with everyday material)

Practice 1 (183)

1. a red flag, white snow, and green maple leaves
2. laundry, helped clean the apartment, waxed the car, and watched
3. patties, special sauce, lettuce, cheese, pickles, and onions

Practice 2 (183)

1. Cold eggs, burnt bacon, and watery orange juice are the reasons I've never returned to that diner for breakfast.
2. Bill relaxes by reading Donald Duck, Archie, and Bugs Bunny comic books.
3. Tonight I've got to work at the restaurant for three hours, finish writing a paper, and study for an exam.

Practice 1 (184)

1. When I didn't get my paycheque at work, . . . According to the office computer,
2. After seeing the accident, . . . Even so,
3. Once there, . . . Also,

Practice 2 (184)

1. Even though Tina had an upset stomach, she went bowling with her husband.
2. Looking back over the last ten years, I can see several decisions I made that really changed my life.
3. Instead of going with my family to the mall, I decided to relax at home and to call up some friends.

Practice 1 (185–186)

1. deadline, the absolute final deadline,
2. cow, a weird creature, . . . dish, who must also have been strange,
3. Tod, voted the most likely to succeed in our high-school graduating class, . . . Cruisers, a local motorcycle gang,

Practice 2 (186)

1. My sister's cat, which she got from the animal shelter, woke her when her apartment caught on fire.
2. A bulging biology textbook, its pages stuffed with notes and handouts, lay on the path to the college parking lot.
3. A baked potato, with its crispy skin and soft insides, rates as one of my all-time favourite foods.

Practice (187)

1. no comma needed
2. mountain, and
3. eating, but
4. speech, and
5. no comma needed
6. car, but
7. no comma needed
8. hairdressers, but
9. no comma needed
10. math, for

Practice 1 (188)

1. fries," said Crystal. . . . She asked, "What
2. Coke," responded Tony.
3. grief," said Crystal. . . . In fact," she continued, "how much

Practice 2 (188)

1. "You better hurry," Lucy's mother warned, "or you're going to miss the last bus of the morning."
2. "It really worries me," said Dwayne, "that you haven't seen a doctor about that strange swelling under your arm."
3. The student sighed in frustration and then raised his hand. "My computer has crashed again," he called out to the teacher.

Practice (189)

1. sorry, sir,
2. 6, 1954,
3. June 30, 1996,
4. Cat Heaven, 3257 Dunmore Road S.E., Medicine Hat, Alberta.
5. Leo, turn

Practice (190)

1. Jerome said to me that
2. must be added to
3. cat fur and dust,
4. on the corner asked,
5. tractor rumbled
6. and Toronto are
7. young man who
8. money and
9. reads a lot
10. invite her to

OTHER PUNCTUATION MARKS

Introductory Project (194)

1. Artist:
2. life-size
3. (1856–1939)
4. track;
5. breathing—but alive.

Practice (195)

1. work:
2. The Bay:
3. Hazlitt:

Practice (196)

1. death; in . . . death; and
2. ridiculous; for example,
3. Bank; Jay . . . Bank; and

Practice (197)

1. condition—except
2. minutes—in fact,
3. work—these

Practice (198)

1. sixty-five dollars . . . sixty-five cents
2. ten-year-old . . . self-confident
3. split-level . . . un-able

Practice (198)

1. charts (pages 16–20) in
2. prepare (1) a daily list of things to do and (2) a weekly study schedule.
3. drinkers (five or more cups a day) suffer

DICTIONARY USE

Introductory Project (200)

1. fortutious (fortuitous)
2. hi/er/o/glyph/ics
3. be

4. oc/to/ge/nar′/i/an
5. (1) an identifying mark on the ear of a domestic animal
   (2) an identifying feature or characteristic

Answers to the activities are in your dictionary. Check with your instructor if you have any problems.

SPELLING IMPROVEMENT

Introductory Project (209)

Misspellings:

akward . . . exercize . . . buisness . . . worryed. . . shamful . . . begining . . . partys . . . sandwichs . . . heros

Practice (212)

1. studied
2. advising
3. carries
4. stopping
5. terrified
6. compelled
7. retiring
8. hungrily
9. expelling
10. judges

Practice (214)

1. groceries
2. towns
3. supplies
4. bodies
5. lotteries
6. passes
7. tragedies
8. watches
9. suits
10. bosses

OMITTED WORDS AND LETTERS

Introductory Project (218)

bottles . . . in the supermarket . . . like a wind-up toy . . .
his arms . . . an alert shopper . . . with the crying

Practice (219–220)

1. When I began eating the box of chicken I bought at the fast-food restaurant, I found several pieces that consisted of a lot of crust covering nothing but chicken bones.
2. Sally had a teacher who tried to light a piece of chalk, thinking it was a cigarette.
3. In his dream, Harry committed the perfect crime: he killed his enemy with an icicle, so the murder weapon was never found.

4. Dr. Yutzer told me not <u>to</u> worry about <u>the</u> sore on my foot, but I decided to get <u>a</u> second opinion.
5. As <u>the</u> little girl ate <u>the</u> vanilla sugar cone, ice cream dripped out <u>of a</u> hole at the bottom onto her pants.
6. When thick black clouds began <u>to</u> form and we felt several drops <u>of</u> rain, we knew <u>the</u> picnic would be cancelled.
7. After spending most <u>of</u> her salary on new clothes, Susan looks like something out of <u>a</u> fashion magazine.
8. As wasps buzzed around <u>the</u> room, I ran for <u>a</u> can of Raid.
9. Sam put <u>the</u> pair <u>of</u> wet socks in <u>the</u> oven, for <u>he</u> wanted <u>to</u> dry them out quickly.
10. Because <u>the</u> weather got hot and stayed hot for weeks, my flower garden started <u>to</u> look like <u>a</u> dried flower arrangement.

Practice 1 (220–221)

1. boyfriends . . . blows
2. curses
3. paragraphs . . . events
4. windshields . . . cars
5. houses . . . highways
6. days . . . times
7. billboards
8. chairs . . . pillows
9. watchtowers . . . provinces
10. motorists . . . trucks

COMMONLY CONFUSED WORDS

Introductory Project (223)

1. Incorrect: your   Correct: you're
2. Incorrect: who's   Correct: whose
3. Incorrect: there   Correct: their
4. Incorrect: to   Correct: too
5. Incorrect: Its   Correct: It's

Homonyms (223–231)

all ready . . . already
brake . . . break
coarse . . . course
here . . . hear
hole . . . whole
It's . . . its
knew . . . new
no . . . know
pear . . . pair
past . . . passed
piece . . . peace

plain . . . plane
principal . . . principle
write . . . right
then . . . than
there . . . their . . . they're
through . . . threw
To . . . two . . . too . . . too
wear . . . where
weather . . . whether
whose . . . who's
you're . . . your

Other Words Frequently Confused (231–237)

an . . . a	dessert . . . desert
Except . . . accept	Does . . . dose
advise . . . advice	fewer . . . less
affect . . . effect	former . . . latter
Among . . . between	loose . . . lose
besides . . . beside	quite . . . quiet
can . . . may	Though . . . thought
cloths . . . clothes	

Incorrect Word Forms

being that (237)

1. Since (*or* Because) she's a year older
2. since (*or* because) the bus drivers
3. Since (*or* Because) I didn't

can't hardly/couldn't hardly (237–238)

1. I can hardly
2. You can hardly
3. You could hardly

could of/must of/should of/would of (238)

1. Anita must have
2. I should have
3. they would have
4. she could have

irregardless (238)

1. regardless of the price
2. regardless of their age
3. Regardless of the risk

EFFECTIVE WORD CHOICE

Introductory Project (241)

Correct sentences:

1. After the softball game, we ate hamburgers and drank beer.
2. Someone told me you're getting married next month.

3. Psychological tests will be given on Wednesday.
4. I think the referee made the right decision.

1 . . . 2 . . . 3 . . . 4

Practice (242–243)

1. If you don't start working regularly in this course, you're going to fail the midterm exam.
2. Living with a room-mate is troublesome, but the extra money helps when the rent is due.
3. We were badly beaten in the football game.
4. If people keep saying bad things about Gene, soon no one will be friends with him.
5. I got so anxious when the teacher called on me that my mind went blank.

Practice 1 (244)

1. Substitute reveal the reason for shed any light on.
2. Substitute was relieved for heaved a sigh of relief.
3. Substitute became a best seller for began selling like hotcakes.
4. Substitute did not care for could not have cared less.
5. Substitute sick for feeling under the weather.

Note: The above answers are examples of how the clichés could be corrected. Other answers are possible.

Practice (245)

1. My television is broken.
2. We went to the mall to see the new fall clothes.
3. Vince said he didn't like fish.
4. The fans booed when the pitcher played badly.
5. How long have you lived in that city?

Practice (247)

1. Because it was raining, I didn't go shopping.
2. I do not feel that prostitution should be legalized.
3. Please call me to arrange an interview.
4. While I was sick I missed three math tests.
5. Only well-trained people get high-paying jobs.

PROGRESS CHARTS

PROGRESS CHART FOR MASTERY TESTS

Enter Your Score for Each Test in the Space Provided

Individual Tests	1 Mastery	2 Mastery	3 Mastery	4 Mastery	5 Ditto	6 Ditto	7 I's M	8 I's M
Subjects and Verbs								
Sentence Fragments								
Run-Ons								
Standard English Verbs								
Irregular Verbs								
Subject-Verb Agreement								
Consistent Verb Tense								
Added Information about Verbs								
Pronoun Reference, Agreement, and Point of View								
Pronoun Types								
Adjectives and Adverbs								
Misplaced Modifiers								
Dangling Modifiers								
Faulty Parallelism								

(Continues on next page)

Note to Instructors: Mastery tests are on perforated pages in this book. Ditto master tests, ready to run, are available free with *Sentence Skills*. Tests in the Instructor's Manual are full-sized and can be reproduced on a copying machine.

PROGRESS CHART FOR MASTERY TESTS (CONTINUED)

Individual Tests (continued)	1 Mastery	2 Mastery	3 Mastery	4 Mastery	5 Ditto	6 Ditto	7 I's M	8 I's M
Capital Letters								
Numbers and Abbreviations								
End Marks								
Apostrophes								
Quotation Marks								
Commas								
Other Punctuation Marks								
Dictionary Use								
Spelling Improvement								
Omitted Words and Letters								
Commonly Confused Words								
Effective Word Choice								

Combined Tests	1 Mastery	2 Mastery	3 Mastery	4 Mastery	5 Ditto	6 Ditto	7 I's M	8 I's M
Sentence Fragments and Run-Ons								
Verbs								
Pronouns								
Faulty Modifiers and Parallelism								
Capital Letters and Punctuation								
Word Use								

PROGRESS CHART FOR EDITING AND PROOFREADING TESTS

Date	Step	Comments	To Do Next	Instructor's Initials
9/27	1a	Missed -ing frag; 3 copying mistakes	1b	JL
9/27	1b	No mistakes—Good job!	2a	JL

(Continues on next page)

PROGRESS CHART FOR EDITING AND PROOFREADING TESTS (CONTINUED)

Date	Step	Comments	To Do Next	Instructor's Initials

PROGRESS CHART FOR COMBINED EDITING TESTS

Enter Your Score for Each Test in the Space Provided

Editing Test 1		Editing Test 7	
Editing Test 2		Editing Test 8	
Editing Test 3		Editing Test 9	
Editing Test 4		Editing Test 10	
Editing Test 5		Editing Test 11	
Editing Test 6		Editing Test 12	

PROGRESS CHART FOR WRITING ASSIGNMENTS

Date	Paper	Comments	To Do Next
10/15	Worst job	Promising but needs more support. Also, 2 frags and 2 run-ons.	Rewrite

Date	Paper	Comments	To Do Next

INDEX